Toward a Social History
of American English

Contributions to the Sociology of Language

39

Editor
Joshua A. Fishman

MOUTON PUBLISHERS · BERLIN · NEW YORK · AMSTERDAM

Toward a Social History of American English

by
J.L. Dillard

with a chapter on Appalachian English
by Linda L. Blanton

MOUTON PUBLISHERS · BERLIN · NEW YORK · AMSTERDAM

CIP-Kurztitelaufnahme der Deutschen Bibliothek

Dillard, Joey L.:
Toward a social history of American English / by J. L. Dillard.
With a chapter on Appalachian English by Linda L. Blanton. –
Berlin ; New York ; Amsterdam : Mouton, 1985.
(Contributions to the sociology of language ; 39)
ISBN 3-11-010587-X Pb.;
ISBN 3-11-010584-5 geb.
NE: GT

Library of Congress Cataloging in Publication Data

Dillard, J. L. (Joey Lee), 1924-
Toward a social history of American English.
(Contributions to the sociology of language; v. 39) Biblio-
graphy: p.
1. English language – United States – History. 2. English
language – United States – Social aspects. 3. English lan-
guage – Dialects – Appalacian Region.
I. Title. II. Series.
PE2809.D544   1984   420'.973   84-20644
ISBN 0-89925-046-7
ISBN 0-89925-047-5 (pbk.)

Printed on acid free paper

Typesetting: Asian Research Service, Hong Kong. – Printing: Druckerei Hildebrand,
Berlin. – Binding: Lüderitz & Bauer Buchgewerbe GmbH, Berlin.
Printed in Germany.

Contents

Acknowledgements

My debts to creolists like William A. Stewart, Ian F. Hancock, Douglas Taylor, Jan Voorhoeve, and others are too great and too all-pervasive to be adequately acknowledged. To my great regret, it has been even harder to make direct references to the work of my greatest influences in language contact, Henry and Renée Kahane.

Others have been almost equally helpful. Emanuel Drechsel and Hiram F. Gregory have provided much valuable information about Louisiana and the Southeast. Even James Sledd, while professing bitter enmity to my position, has provided a useful attestation of American Indian Pidgin English in Georgia.

Random House, Inc., was kind enough to release materials previously used in *All-American English* (1975) and *American Talk* (1976). Linda Blanton almost providentially appeared to provide a chapter on Appalachian English. Donald Hatley, by failing to deliver his promised chapter on the language of the railroads, forced me to consider the matter more carefully myself and to make that chapter a more integral part of the book.

Many professional friends have contributed either data or encouragement when I was on the verge of giving up in pessimism or disgust. Besides those mentioned, Marshall Berger, R.M.R. Hall, Mary Rita Miller, and Kelsie B. Harder are noteworthy. None of these is, however, in any way responsible for any of the failings of this book.

Preface

In one of a series of articles opposed to the "creolist" theory of the origin of Black American English, a theory which is central to this work, Schneider (1983: 57) writes

> . . . it can be demonstrated that this [preverbal auxiliary] *done* has been in regular use with white speakers in America and Britain since the Middle Ages.

At first, one is inclined to brush aside the faulty modification structure. No one, surely, is so naive historically as to believe that English has been spoken in America "since the Middle Ages."

On the other hand — to borrow Schneider's transition above deleted — the subconscious assumption that English has "always" been spoken in America, whether by users of preverbal *done* or not, may be a significant part of the belief system of those whose orientation Schneider shares. The traditional picture of the history of American English (i.e., that sponsored by the Linguistic Atlas of the United States and Canada) has greatly underestimated social factors in migration as well as almost everything else except raw demography. Insofar as the Atlas has dealt with population movements, it has worked on the tacit model of the hypothetical Anglo-Saxon migration to England or of the even more hypothetical Indo-European migration rather than taking into account the multiethnic and multilingual migration which brought the United States and the North American continent its present population.

In that tradition, it has been permitted, even required, to ignore language contact patterns. The Angles, Saxons, and Jutes presumably began as speakers of related Germanic dialects and remained speakers of those dialects when they had settled in England; the Proto-Indo-Europeans are virtually required to have started and ended as (essentially monolingual) speakers of dialects of Proto-Indo-European. The latter position has come in for some criticism recently (C.-J. Bailey 1982). The former seems ripe for attack, although I do not know of any concerted attack on it. But one does not need to challenge these familiar theses to doubt that they are adequate models for the origin and development of American English.

The most obvious alternative, the use of special contact varieties like pidgins, meets with a kind of instinctive opposition. Pidginization, creolization, and decreolization — any or all stages of which may need to be reconsidered and expanded in the light of recent studies in the pidgin/creole field — are quite new insofar as their impact on the traditional European languages, including English, is concerned. It may be necessary to resist giving them either too little or too much importance — the latter especially in the case of Middle English.

As presented herein, the primary users of auxiliary contact languages — which might as well be called "pidgins" until a complete revision of the terminology has been effected — are groups which have not been speaking English at all "since the Middle Ages" — primarily Blacks and American Indians. The latter joined the basic migratory pattern in formation of the current American population by being moved against their will and thrown into new cultural and linguistic relationships; one part of those relationships was American Indian Pidgin English. These days that variety and its modern results are represented more and more as "interlanguage," but Beverly Flanagan Olson (personal communication) has completed a dissertation on AIPE and its relationship to the maritime lingua franca tradition.

The speech of American Blacks, although hardly more symptomatic of the general process, has attracted a great deal more attention. The creole origins theory (B. Bailey 1964, Stewart 1964, Dillard 1965 — to leave aside an earlier formulation by Schuchardt of which Glenn Gilbert [personal communication] tells me) can hardly be overlooked any longer; indeed, there is a lively group of younger scholars developing the theory (Mufwene 1984, De Bose ms.). Attempts like Schneider's to eliminate the creole origin and thus to return Black speech to the province of spreading British regional dialects (and thereby to Germanic philology) were to be expected from Germany. It would really seem, however, that better historical material could be used than the quite late ex-slave narratives. (Stewart and I both used them, but only after the historical thesis had been formulated on other materials, and primarily for convenience and accessibility.) The narratives, being as they are interviews with old people, have obvious connections to the methodology of European dialect geography — including the frequently cited defects of that approach. Even where the WPA ex-slave narratives are concerned, there is a crying need for a sociology of knowledge approach to the way in which the (sometimes Black) fieldworkers were edited by the (usually white) project supervisors like Lyle Saxon and Robert Tallant. (These were, obviously, in Louisiana; my observations are based upon firsthand study — supplemented by those of Donald Hatley — of WPA papers in Watson Library of Northwestern State University in Natchitoches, Louisiana.)

Like Stewart and B. Bailey, I assume that creole origins of Black English would involve transmission and not some factor like a "bioprogram." Bickerton (1982) has attracted an immense amount of attention with the latter theory. He holds that transmission is an impossible explanation of the widespread T[ense] M[odal] A[spect] pattern. Bickerton's method of ruling out transmission in Hawaiian English, which is basic to his presentation, involves elicitation from older informants to the exclusion of historical records: Those elderly informants have had a lifetime to change their language through age-grading and other factors. Even if "substratum" influences are ruled out — as they may well be in any theory which demands explanatory accuracy — there is still the matter of the many parallels in vocabulary and in collocations ("idioms"), pointing to some kind of transmission at least among the "Atlantic" creoles. Holm and Shilling (1982) make an excellent case for "pan-Creole" forms.

Another stricture is that the TMA formula is simply too limited. There are other auxiliaries to be considered. Spears (1982) makes a good case for a quasi-auxiliary *come* in Black English, and in an unpublished NYU proposal he makes an even better case for additional semi-auxiliaries like *fèk* in Haitian Creole. Baugh (1984) makes an at least equally convincing case for Black English *steady* in a creole-type grammar. Dillard (1971) made a comparison of such "quasi-modals" as Haitian Creole *fèk*, West African Pidgin English and Black English *done* (postverbal in some "Atlantic" varieties), Creole Portuguese *kaba*, Hawaiian *pau*, etc., in which *steady* and *come* might well have figured.

Variationists present an alternative which is more apparent than real. Black English and other historical creoles typically show a lot of variation, especially when they are in direct contact with the standard variety of the language. The rather innocuous term *code-switching* has been in disrepute for the past few years, and it may well be that *variation* describes the process better.

Both Joan Fayer (personal communication) and Wolfram (1984) stress the variation between presence and absence of past tense markers in Pidgin English. Wolfram, especially, makes too much of this; that is why attention should be directed rather to the studies of Mufwene and Spears. Positive identification of factors like aspect is far more important than "absence" of something like tense marking — or than variation between presence and absence of tense markers.

Fayer's abstract cites the diary and letters written by eighteenth-century Efik trader Antera Duke. She asserts that "there is no evidence . . . that aspect markers developed before tense markers." Here, however, the writing traditions of ordinary English, in which tense marking has always been more clearly recognized than that of aspect, must surely have had a lot of influence.

There seems to be every reason to believe that inherent variation, although not by any means limited to contact between a pidgin/creole/decreolized variety and a standard dialect, is far more noteworthy in such a situation than elsewhere. It is no accident that Labov's version of variable rules grew out of the overt and deleted copula rules of the Black English Vernacular. Is it going too far to assert that the more intimate the contact is, the more there is variability? As I see it, variable factors are an important adjunct to other sources of data on language history, but by no means a substitute for them.

Some readers may notice a less polemic tone in this book than in some of my earlier writings. Perhaps this is the mellowing of age. This is not to say that attacks are missing — or that those that are to be found are intended personally. One can, it is to be hoped, attack a linguistic theory without disliking or disrespecting the author of it. Surely one can admire James Sledd — to take possibly the preeminent case in the study of American English — greatly and still deprecate the tendency to treat his speech as though it were the central issue in American dialectology. Closer to home, what reads like an attack on Emanuel Drechsel (p. 9) was not intended that way; Drechsel is a friend and valued colleague from whom I have learned a lot and upon whom I depended for Mobilian Jargon.

Chapter I

English Goes International: the Prehistory of American English

One who reads through the history of British world exploration hoping to find exact information on how the early explorers, immigrants, and colonists solved the many communication problems which must have arisen is doomed to a certain amount of frustration. Sifting through, for example, the myriad accounts of John Smith's experiences in Virginia, one reads only – and, because of the tangled bibliography of those accounts, has a hard time discovering the same passage again – of Smith's surely exaggerated competence in acquiring a new language. One can find accounts of interpreters – and, if he looks hard enough, of chains of interpreters. The problem is not in finding out how a chain of Indian-language interpreters managed to provide translations for Europeans from any one language group; it is rather how the European link first made contact with the Amerindian chain. If it can be explained how an Englishman – or a Frenchman, Dutchman, etc. – first learned to speak to the first Indian interpreter, then it probably can be understood how the Indian interpreter found other bi- and multilingual translators to put the Europeans into communication with various Indian groups. The same would be true, presumably, of West African, Australian, or China Coast multilingual problems.

John Smith may not be a bad place to start. If he provided no clear explanation of what success he had – he may not have actually known himself – he is fairly well representative of others who found themselves with that problem. Smith, whatever else may be said of him, was no stay-at-home. Before coming to the New World, he had traveled in France, Italy, and Transylvania; he had been captured by the Turks and sent to southern Russia, later going through Russia, Poland, and Transylvania again – and even to Africa.

It is all too easy for the twentieth-century speaker of English to see the solution to the linguistic problems of Smith's day in terms of today's expectation that "almost everyone speaks a little English." English was, obviously, not a world language during the period of the geographic explorations. The use of Latin for those in international contact, going well back into the Old

English period, is well known. It is also a commonplace of language history that England had long been under the domination of foreigners; for five centuries, with only sporadic relief, English had been subjugated to Norse or to Norman French. English was not, until the fifteenth century if then, socially a vehicle for use abroad.

The "defense and illustration" (in the Early Modern English sense of those terms) is well known; a good account can be read in almost any textbook of the history of the English language. It is noteworthy that Italian and French, and perhaps Spanish, were a century or so ahead of English in this respect. The sailor involved in exploration would hardly have the same attitude that Elyot and Ascham had to the adequacy of English as a language; like them, however, he would have had to look to other languages and language practices as a part of his total communicative behavior.

John Smith, like the more ordinary English travelers of the exploration and colonization period, must have been thoroughly familiar with the need for a language of wider communication. The spectacle of an English speaker calling out, like the American professor in the 1960 movie *Never on Sunday*, "Doesn't anyone here speak English?", could hardly have been seen in the early seventeenth century. (The televised science fiction series, *Dr. Who*, extends the notion that English – and generally British English at that – is spoken everywhere on an intergalactic scale.) Smith and the others who came to the eastern coast of North America must have utilized at least some of the devices for communication with foreigners which had been available to Englishmen, as to Europeans in general, for some centuries and which had just recently been brought into much wider use and put to stronger tests by language contacts of an extensiveness hardly dreamed of in previous centuries. It seems idle to speculate about what strategies were tried, found wanting, and then discarded. It is problem enough to determine just which ones may have worked. In this context, it may be well to review, superficially enough, the past history of such communication strategies.[1]

The use of Latin as the general European lingua franca of the High Middle Ages and Renaissance is well known – perhaps even too well known. Sumption (1975: 193) makes the point that "few medieval men, however cultivated they were, understood more than a few words of any language but their own or Latin." His statement refers, however, to the language problems specifically of pilgrims, not to those of sailors and traders. It seems rather strikingly significant that the spread of Sabir, a kind of Romance-based lingua franca, began at roughly the same time. Of course, it was used by sailors and merchants and would not come to the attention of someone interested in pilgrims (and literary men).

Sumption does specify that Italian was one of the more usable languages of the Holy Land; the speculation is not entirely closed to the possibility that

"Italian" was the Italianate Lingua Franca (Schuchardt 1909). Bertrandon de la Brocquiere, for example, arranged through a polyglot Turk to find a Jew there who spoke "a little Italian and some Turkish" (Sumption 1975: 194). As travelers' reports go, this may be as close as anyone could generally come to characterizing the Lingua Franca. Crouch (1704: 60) reported that a Moor whom he had known addressed him in the "Frank Tongue," but French is not entirely ruled out by that expression. (Neither, of course, is the "French-colored" Lingua Franca.) Still, the thrust of Sumption's report concerns the large sums of money spent on interpreters and phrase books in the absence of such a language of wider communication.

In the absence of detailed information on those merchants and sailors, it may be necessary to fall back on historical truisms and common sense in order to make statements about their language. In the case of the English seafarers, common sense would seem to decree that language practices were not so far different from those of their European counterparts whose use of Lingua Franca is attested. And it seems perhaps banal, but necessary, to add that English seagoing men would have learned and absorbed more of the ways of continental populations than those Englishmen who never left the island. While in the area of the offensively obvious, it might be well to include the facts that sailors and sea travelers ran into many more languages than stay-at-homes, and that the foreign languages most influential upon English (Latin, Norse, Norman French) actually arrived by sea.

Although it is quite well known that the Norse invasion of England was a maritime operation and a part of a much larger Scandinavian nautical expansion, it has not been the general practice to draw attention to that fact in connection with language history. It is, then, somewhat unusual to read a statement like that of Geipel (1971: 108):

> Many Scandinavian expressions – particularly Norse having to do with navigation and shipbuilding – found their way into Norman French where a number of them remain to this day.

It is not the business of this work to deal with the possibility that secondhand Norse words came in, at least temporarily, from Norman French to English, but it does seem that the general historians of English have missed a point there.

Sandahl (1951: 21) stresses the comparative lack of Old English sea terms and the variety and richness of the equivalent Middle English vocabulary, with the intermediate Norse and Norman French contacts as the most likely explanation. He comments that the most striking feature of the latter period as compared to the former is the great percentage of loan words, and further observes that the majority are "Old Norse and Low German (Low Dutch)." Maritime contact between Scandinavia and Britain did not stop with the Norman invasion; in fact, according to Sandahl (1951: 22):

. . . up to the sixteenth century the mercantile contact at sea between England and the continent was close, and the sailors of the two races [sic] met and mingled not only in the sea ports of Holland but also at other ports at which they both trades.

From this protracted contact there results that many "primary" sea terms are Old Norse in origin: *bitt, carling, halse (hawse), keel, kelson, scarf, stern.* Aside from these, which still exist in English, there are others that disappeared after the Early Modern English period and some found only in East Anglian and North Country accounts, dealing with ships that were very similar to Viking long ships: *brand, clove, crafte, halsing, helm-wale, kelgrys, stam, stam-lock, underlout.*

It was the invading Normans who brought the language in which some speakers of Old English or early Middle English must have communicated when they found their dialects mutually unintelligible. The frequently-cited text by Caxton, although based only on the lexical confusion of *egges* and *eyren,* illustrates that some such problems existed until around 1500. And no one misses that the "good wyf" in the "hows" first thought that the "marchaunt" was speaking French to her.

With the decline of French, the need for standardization of the language of a now-unified country became strong. It is no surprise that most of our historical research has sought out the diversities rather than the uniformities; the methods of traditional philology are designed to make that kind of triumph possible. Nevertheless, once the diversification and the relative success of dialect identification became commonplace, the question of subsequent standardization seems to be becoming prominent again.

Some of this latter research has been almost apologetic on tone. Samuels (1963) is excessively careful to apply his finding only to the written language:

We are concerned with the spoken language only in so far as any written standard must be ultimately based on it; but the evolution and spread of standard English in the fifteenth and sixteenth centuries was primarily through the agency of writing, not speech, and depended on the quantity written.

One almost wonders how Samuels knows these things, if so little can be found out from written texts. One is reminded of how structuralists, smarting from a beating by Chomsky and the transformational-generativists, gathered in isolated conferences to proclaim that Chomsky's rules "applied only to written English."[2]

But at least the problem of a standard English for the period of the fifteenth and sixteenth centuries has been tackled, and it is no longer tied in an embarrassing manner to a literary great, like Chaucer, whose English the historian of language read as an undergraduate in a literature course.

Samuels (1963: 88) deals with a "Chancery Standard" consisting of "that flood of government documents that starts in the years following 1430." Samuels (1963: 89) tabulates some differences from Chaucer: *gaf* instead of *yaf, not* instead of *nat, thes*(e) instead of *thise, but* instead of *bot, thorough* or *borowe* instead of *thurgh, such(e)* instead of *switch(e),* and *shulde* instead of *sholde*. Samuels traces the influence on Chancery Standard not without some hesitation to Central Midlands, rejecting the hitherto popular theory of East Midland (and particularly East Anglian) influence.

The tendency to insist upon regional factors, area dialects combining in some strange way to form the standard, is markedly present in the work of Samuels (1963: 93). He hypothesizes that the standard language

> evolved later, from a combination of spoken London English and certain Central Midland elements, which themselves would be transmitted via the spoken, not the written language

although again it is not clear on just what grounds the two (written and spoken English) can be so confidently differentiated.

In spite of the tradition in which he worked, Samuels noted a contrary tendency (1963: 93):

> . . . it was more common for reasonably educated men to write some form of their own regional dialect, gradually purging it of its grosser provincialisms, than to make a direct attempt to imitate Chancery Standard.

This procedure does not seem to be much different from that practiced by a lot of Americans — for example, from the attempt to eliminate *you all* and *might could* from academic papers (at the freshman level, mainly) written in the southern United States, and *hadn't ought* and *you(se) guys* from those done further north. Another way of putting it would be that there was a tendency toward standardization, primarily on the part of men whose contacts extended beyond their region of residence. It is not certain which is most important, this supra-regional sphere of interest or "education"; in practice, the two probably overlapped a great deal.

Another influence on the spreading is identified by Samuels and by Warner (1982): the Wycliffites. Once one looks beyond the "Wycliffe" Bible, interesting as it is from the viewpoint of biblical translation, to Wycliffe's sermons, the suggestion that here is something closer to the mainstream of English (the language, without regard to the history of literature) immediately occurs to him. Samuels (1963: 85) stresses the importance of the Lollards in "spreading" this "standard literary language":

> The Lollards, naturally, although they cannot be said to have invented it, were a powerful influence in spreading it, in their bibles, sermons and tracts; once they had adopted it, they copied it faithfully, probably fanatically so.

Whether they were any more "fanatic" in insisting upon standards than Simon (1980) or Newman (1974) is not a decision that can be made *a priori*.

Unfortunately, the importance of this "Lollard standard" came to my attention, if forcefully, too late for any real attention in this book. Given the importance of a dissenter-type religion in the American colonies and the contemporary attestations of the "uniformity" and "purity" of the colonies'

English (see pp. 59 -- 61), this particular development may be of the first importance. Warner (1982: 10) reinforces Samuels's statements about the Wycliffite or Lollard standard as "the first major literary standard to emerge in ME."

It is interesting and probably significant that, while this marked tendency toward standardization was being manifested, English was beginning to "go international." Perhaps the first major influences of the English language were on the Celtic-speaking survivors in the British Isles. Russ (1982: 31) reports the official establishment of English in Wales through the Acts of Union of 1536 and 1542. Given the overwhelming importance of the language on the same island by an economically more advantaged people, it would hardly be possible that unofficial spread of the language did not somewhat precede official provision for that spread.

Evidence from a source like Shakespeare's *Henry V*, although hardly to be considered free from anachronism, shows English becoming a medium for a kind of British unity under the leadership of Henry V. Captain Fluellen, a Welshman, Captain Jamy, a Scotsman, and the Irish Captain Macmorris discuss the strategy of the Battle of Agincourt:

> *Irish.*　. . . tish ill done! The worke ish giue ouer, the Trompet sound the Retreat.
> *Welch.*　Captain *Macmorrice,* I beseech you now, will you voutsafe me, looke you, a few disputations with you, as partly touching or concerning the disciplines of warre . . .
> *Scot.*　It sall be vary gud, gud feith, gud Captens bath, and I sall quit you with gud leue, as I may pick occasion, that sall I mary.

The Scotsman's *sall* for *shall* and the graphic indications of vowel differences were commonplace indications of what was going on in the dialect history of English; the Irishman's *tish* for *tis* and *ish* for *is* scarcely less so. Fluellen, a highly competent military man who seems to have replaced Falstaff in the confidence of the now grown-up Prince Hal, is not in any way the object of ridicule for his English. Once, when he attempts to discourse of Alexander the Great and produces "Alexander the Pig" (Act IV, Scene 7), there is some fun with his accent. But Shakespeare seems to link language and politics, as the "quips and quiddities" of Falstaff's verbal brilliance give way to the military practicalities of Fluellen's stylistically more limited but work-oriented Welsh dialect.

Russ (1982: 33) points out that Shakespeare's linguistic observation is not especially praiseworthy here, that it is "the substitution of [p] for [b] — a misunderstanding by an outsider of consonant mutation in Welsh." Is it possible that Shakespeare was following a dramatic convention of Welsh dialect, or at least a stereotype well known among Englishmen, rather than reporting his own observations of Welshmen? The weak joke is extremely farfetched; there is necessary an unexplained change from *great* to *big*. One can imagine Shakespeare's dashing the line off in a great hurry, rather than doing any kind of careful investigation. But what would be expected on other grounds, the use of Welsh-accented English by bilingual Welshmen, is confirmed.

It is noteworthy that the Acts of Union and *Henry V* come fairly close to framing, chronologically, a series of events far more significant for the worldwide spread of English, the participation of Englishmen in the early geographic explorations. The consequences of the Acts of Union have been studied hardly at all with reference to their importance for the history of the language; Shakespeare's plays, perhaps to excess. It is not surprising that literary scholars have preferred to study *The Tempest* rather than to read the reports of some of the travelers to the New World; it is unfortunate that, linguistically and otherwise, there is hardly an account less grounded in reality. It is absurd to argue that histories of literature should give more weight to Defoe than to Shakespeare, but it is regrettable that histories of the language do not give at least as much. More of the latter would then incorporate materials from a writer who at least talked to genuine travelers. Many of our prominent dialectologists began as English literature majors, and the kinds of great authors read in their formative years undoubtedly had something to do with the inward-looking rather than outward-looking approach to the language of a very "outgoing" age.

It has frequently been pointed out (e.g., by Marckwardt 1958, 1980) that the earliest American colonists spoke "Elizabethan English" among themselves. Insofar as the term designates a historical period, it has a minimal amount of accuracy. The insight provided by such a term is, however, slight indeed. There were more varieties of English than one before the language was brought to the New World, and it does not appear that there were much more than chance affinities between the English of the earliest colonists and that of leading Elizabethan literary figures like Shakespeare, Lyly, Marlowe, Lodge and Green (the list is that of Marckwardt 1958: 11). With the rise, especially, of maritime varieties, the question becomes not whether American English began as seventeenth-century British English but what kind of English it came from and became.

Indications that there were special features in sailors' English were noted as early as Matthews (1935, 1937). Comparisons of the sailors' pronunciations to the Krio of Sierra Leone have been made by Hancock (1972, 1976). Observations of maritime elements in the English of Central American Miskito Coast Creole have been made by Holm (1983); nautical usages in the Bahamas have been treated by Holm and Shilling (1982). It will be argued extensively below that varieties like Krio, Bahamian English, and Miskito Coast Creole are especially significant for comparison purposes because they represent the kind of multilingual contact which was characteristic of the New World and must have utilized, in the early period especially, some version of the institutionalized solution to the problems which arose from that contact.

The focus on Shakespeare by some language historians trained first in literature has been unfortunate. Except for treatments of the English of foreigners like Fluellen, Shakespeare's plays have little that is of any importance for New World English. For example, impersonal constructions like *it dislikes me, it yearns me,* and *methinks* are simply not characteristic of early American English. The other great monument of Renaissance English literature, the King James translation of the Bible, is almost equally irrelevant, although it is a fairly safe guess that the colonists read the Bible more than Shakespeare.

In the European colonial expansion of which the settlement of America was a part, the language situation was greatly different from anything the Europeans had known at home. The most similar situation was in the Mediterranean, where the Lingua Franca had been used at least as early as the Crusades and probably a great deal earlier. Certain reflexes of that lingua franca are observable today in loan words (Kahane, Kahane, and Tietze 1958). According to Schuchardt (1909) the earliest form of the Lingua Franca was probably Italian-"colored," reflecting the dominance of the Italian city states at one period of Mediterranean history. Hotten (1887; reprinted 1972: 2) had reported: "The vulgar dialect of Malta and the Scala towns of the Levant — imported into this country and incorporated with English cant [see Hancock 1973] — is known as the Lingua Franca, or bastard Italian." Hotten's list of over fifty Lingua Franca forms in British English has been corroborated by Hancock (1973). Later versions of the language were French- and especially Portuguese-"colored." (Alleyne 1980 insists upon "Iberian" rather than "Portuguese," and his point seems well taken. For one thing, it eliminates the problem of deciding whether Palenquero of Colombia is Portuguese or Spanish in provenience.)

This Iberian trade pidgin had an amazing worldwide distribution by the seventeenth century. DeCamp (1971) reports the use of an "old Portuguese pidgin" from India to Indonesia and up to Japan. Reports like those of Barbot (1732) also tend to show its use along the West African coast. The Caribbean creoles, deriving in some way from pidgins used there (Whinnom 1965, Taylor 1956) would extend the influence to the New World.

Whether by "relexification" or otherwise, Pidgin English developed along the lines of the Lingua Franca and the Iberian reconnaissance language. Christophersen (1959) shows how *fetissero* (translated *Predicant* by a seventeenth-century Dutchman and in turn *Priest* by Samuel Purchas) was taken by English traders to be an "African" word. Even more interesting is *dash,* which has Romance cogeners in French *dache,* Spanish *dacio,* and Italian *dazio.* Christophersen would also derive *juju* from a reduplicated [d₃ u], from *joss* which in turn comes from Portuguese *deos.* (For *joss* in Pidgin English, see Chapter II.) The very widespread Pidgin English extended, whether directly or indirectly, the scope of this Lingua Franca tradition.

A great deal of resistance to the recognition of the pidgin influence has developed, especially from the reconstructive tradition, whose representatives largely overlooked the pidgin-creole factors, especially in North American varieties. Even Drechsel and Makuakane (1982: 460), in the process of showing how

> . . . some sailors, traders, and whalers — whether Hawaiians or Europeans — visited both the Northwest Coast [for influence on Chinook Jargon] and the Bering and Arctic Seas [for influence on Eskimo Jargon]

and how

> . . . the visitors could have established an indirect historical link between the two pidgins

still insist that such influences may be reported

> . . . without presuming the existence of a world-circling pidgin/creole.

The chief problem here seems to be with the term *world-circling.* If it is virtually synonymous with *world-encompassing,* Drechsel and Makuakane are probably right. Not even the most ardent proponents of the relexification or monogenetic theory (Taylor 1960, Voorhoeve 1973) would give such an attribute to the undoubtedly existing pidgin/creole. If, however, *world-circling* means only 'found at points around the globe', the term is more accurate than Drechsel and Makuakane seem to allow.[3] Their conclusion of

> . . . a loose sociolinguistic network that interconnected, at least at the lexical level, various Pacific (contact) languages

again demands interpretation. That the network was *sociolinguistic* rather than linguistic presumably reflects the polyglot background of pidgins; otherwise, why would one say that the linguistic situation of the Germanic *Völkerwanderung* was linguistic and not sociolinguistic? (That is, would one assert that there were no social relationships along with the linguistic ones, and no specifically sociolinguistic factors like stratification?) The other obvious question is, "How loose is loose?" That pidgin/creole use was "looser" than that of Germanic among the migrating tribes can be readily assumed. That it was so "loose" that pidgin was a rare and exotic variety to sailors (as it was to the Pilgrims in Massachusetts) seems to be beyond credibility.

Within what is apparently developing as a central tradition, it is generally pointed out that a native Iberian (or Portuguese) "reconnaissance language" (Naro 1978) was used in contact with groups like the West Africans. Hancock (1972) shows how beached Portuguese sailors (*lançados*) helped in the spread of the contact variety in Africa. Others, like Ferraz (1976) have stressed the African language influence on the European-based contact language. It does not really matter, for these purposes, whether the basic structure came from Iberian, from African and other indigenous languages, or from a kind of spontaneous outcropping of language universals (Bickerton 1982). Historically, it is quite evident that the Iberian contact vernacular spread over the sea routes. In Africa and on the China Coast — and probably elsewhere — the formation of an English-"colored" lingua franca (herein considered to be virtually identical to Pidgin English) was preceded by the use of the Iberian variety by English travelers. Like Francis Moore, whose *Travels in the Inward Parts of Africa* was published in 1738, the travelers themselves often called the variety Portuguese, even (in the case of Moore) "Creole Portuguese."

Even at these dates, the general contact circumstances were not new to Englishmen. The "Frank Tongue," which according to Kahane and Kahane (1976) may have been called after Charlemagne's Franks as more or less types of Westerners, was encountered by travelers like the Englishman in Rhodes at the end of the sixteenth century (Kahane and Kahane 1976: 35) who had this linguistic adventure:

> As we weare a drinkinge, thare came unto us tow stout Turkes, and sayd: Parlye
> *Francho*, sinyore? which is, Can you speake Itallian, sinyor? Soe cothe Mr. Maye
> . . . leavinge Mr. Maye and the under butler talkinge with the Turkes, for they tow
> could speake Italian a little, and so could none of us.

The "Frank Tongue" could be Italian-colored, Spanish-colored (Kahane and Kahane 1976: 36), or of an indeterminate Romance cast. A 1606 report of "The Voyage of Monsieur de Montis into New France, written by Marke Lescarbot" (Hakluyt 1850: 18: 277) gives a typical statement about communication with a foreign group, in this case the "savages" in a part of Canada:

> Whereof the Savages being astonied, did say in words borrowed from the Basques,
> Endia Chave Normandia — that is to say, that the Normans know many things.

Since the Basques are not known to have been prominent in such travels, the name may have been only a way of designating 'foreigners'. Far from the Mediterranean, the New World "savages" would not be likely to "think Italian." *Normans* may be a little closer to its literal meaning; it was frequently used of seagoing Frenchmen (Hall 1953, Faine 1939). *Chave* is almost certainly *savvy,* a pidgin vocabulary item (see p. 49). By default, *endia* must mean 'many things'.

An extreme version of the "monogenesis" theory (Voorhoeve 1973) has an original Iberian Trade Pidgin relexified with English and French words to form pidgins for those languages, with later creolization. Others (Hancock 1972) have stressed the domestic elements in the pidgins, and it is rather obvious that the monogenesis theory cannot handle pidgins and creoles based on non-Indo-European languages. A common-sense approach would seem to be that, when the "reconnaissance language" was a kind of ship's jargon, re-lexification was a relatively active phenomenon. As a shore jargon, used by non-European populations, the contact language was subject to a great deal of influence from native languages of the area where it was used. Use, both serious and jocular, by essentially monolingual English-speaking ships crews (seriously with other populations, jocularly among themselves — both uses are well documented) would permit the inclusion of some British dialect forms (Holm and Shilling 1982).

It is rather obvious that the Iberian Trade Pidgin influenced Pidgin English in many areas. Portuguese terms, relatively few in number but significant in function and distributed over wide geographic area, remained in English sailor talk of the eighteenth, nineteenth, and even twentieth centuries. *Pikin* 'small' and the related *picaninny, savvy, palaver, mas que* (which became *maskie* 'never mind') and dozens of derivatives like Saramaccan *fa* (from *falar*), used to embed a noun clause (Alleyne 1980: 94) like *say* in more completely English-based varieties, became widely distributed in pidgins where the lexicon was basically non-Iberian. English pidgins picked up words like *bob* and *bobbery* 'noise, disturbance' from somewhere and carried them virtually around the world.

The pidginist view of, particularly, Black American English and the Caribbean Creoles holds that West Africans who fell victim to the slave trade, wrenched from their own tribes, cultures, and languages, picked up the pidgin auxiliary languages out of harsh necessity as they waited on the west coast of Africa to be transported to the New World, as they sweltered in the holds of slave ships with little to remind them of their human status except the attempt to establish communication with neighbors who came from different tribes and cultures, or as they found themselves on the plantations of the Caribbean islands or in North or South America. Since the slaves used pidgin languages primarily to establish communication with other slaves, there being evidence (Hancock 1969) that some West Africans were taught more or less standard English as early as 1594, they mixed in West African language forms rather freely. Words like *nyam* 'eat', *poto poto* 'mud', *obeah*, and *troki* 'tortoise' were widespread in the Afro-American varieties of the New World.

Slave traders like William Smith, John Atkins, and Hugh Crow recorded Pidgin English utterances in passing, and often in the context of relating something done by an African that they regarded as funny. A British sea captain not in the slave trade, William Fitzwilliam Owen, and his Lieutenant Boteler recorded long conversations in that variety in the nineteenth century. Fictional representations of Pidgin English appear in the works of Daniel Defoe, the one British literary figure who, as historian of trade and of the pirates, was likely to have some command of the seaborne varieties. (Surely no reader will think that I mean Friday's speech on "Tabago" in *Robinson Crusoe* to be an early attestation of the dialect of Tobago!) Such American writers as Cotton Mather (1721) and Benjamin Franklin recorded the use of Pidgin English by Blacks or "Africans" by the end of the eighteenth century.

Any problem of the credibility of these sources seems to be resolved by their very number and by the amount of agreement between disparate sources. These men were not, however, comparable to trained linguists; details of their transcriptions are of course open to question. Their graphic conventions are, in most cases, familiar ones, however. The Dutch conventions used by Herlein (p. 13) are transparently different from the English ones of the other attestations cited below. The apparent two extra syllables in *backarara* for *buckra* as rendered by Horsmanden (p. 17); compare Benjamin Franklin's *boccarorra*) very likely represent a phonological quality which has been called "drawl."

The sailors of slave ships and the slave traders and masters did not bother to report on the unity or diversity of their practices; they were too busy making everything from a hard living to fabulous fortunes in the buying and selling of human cargo. But some of them, like John Atkins, William Smith, and Hugh Crow, did eventually write memoirs of their experiences. And early explorers and travelers like John Barbot, not tainted with the slave trade, provided elaborate descriptions of at least those phenomena which caught their attention. From these sources, it is possible to piece together a great deal of the language chronicle of the slave trade. What is lacking, especially phonological indications, from their transcriptions can be partly balanced by the random nature of their observations. At least they did not administer questionnaires formulated in accordance with some linguistic theory.

Some indications of what those observers recorded (not what they thought, since they theorized little or not at all about language processes) can be gained from the quotations that follow. I have chosen a few representative ports, primarily for their importance in the slave trade, in West Africa and the Americas for the attestations of Pidgin and Creole English there. A few islands and a few additional areas are represented in the hope of indicating the spread of the contact language. The list is far from exhaustive, and the examples chosen may well represent some unconscious selective processes on my part.

Sierra Leone
(1791-2-3)

Oh! he be fine man, rich too much, he got too much woman.
(Falconbridge 1794: 77)
God amity sen me dat peginine, true, suppose he no black like me, nutting for dat, my woman drinkee red water, and suppose peginine no for me, he dead.
(Falconbridge 1794: 82)

Bonny
(c. 1790)

What he dat ditto? Can I eat 'em — or drink 'em — or wear 'em? I think he be some thief man and big rogue that make that thing ditto.
(Crow 1791: 93-4)

No fear — it be Capt. Crow palaver!

(Crow 1971: 96)

Crow! What debble man send this hard and sauce mouth fellow to Bonny?

(Crow 1791: 96)

Ya, ya, what me do to me god! — puncheon of brandy! go away! I no want you at all!

(Crow 1791: 86)

Poor boy, you can't havey king.

(Crow 1791: 87)

You no play man no more, you devilly man, Crow, you have quite spoil the king!

(Crow 1791: 95)

(African from Bonny on Crow's ship in Montego Bay, Jamaica)

Massa Crow, something bite me too much, and me no can see 'im; and me want you for give me some was mouth and two mouth tacken.

(King Peppel — or "Grandy King George" — of Bonny, a letter of protest to King George IV of England)

Brudder George . . . send warship look um what water bar hab got, dat good . . . E no send warship, for cappen no peakee me, no lookee me face. No, no, no; me tell you, No. Suppose you come all you mout full palaver, give e reason why e do it, me tell you, you peakee lie, you peakee lie, you peakee d—m lie. Suppose my fader, or my fader fader, come up from ground and peakee me why English man do dat, I no sabby tell um why.

(Owen 1833: 41)

Why you make many things stand for table one time? dat makee me sick, appetite no come up.

(Owen 1833: II: 205)

Old Calbar
(Duke Ephraim to new consul, Mr. T. J. Hutchinson, 1856)

I beg you to do something to stop white men from going into the house of Calabar men and knocking them. You white men have fashion to bind men to keep the peace, so I beg you to do this, and no let palaver come up again.

(Dike [1956]: 17)

Surinam
(1718)

My belle well.
You wantie sie don pinkinine?
Jo wantje gaeu wakke lange mie?

(Herlein 1718: 121-23)

Demarara and Essequibo Rivers
(1830)

"Me no care, suppose lost," replied Quaco, "Massa schooner, massa nigger — all massa's loss."

(Alexander [1833]: 34)

Jamaica

(Kingston)

God bless massa! how poor massa do? Long live massa, for 'im da fight ebery voyage.

(Crow [1791] : 120)

(Inland plantation)

Marly, being ignorant of the negro corrupted dialect, or the talkee talkee language, did not understand the expression [grandy nyam].

(*Marly, or Life in Jamaica* [1818] : 13)

Dey good nyamn for him neger, massa! Him, Sir Charles Price, good nyamn for him neger, massa! Him good as hims hens pickeniny, massa!

(Ibid., p. 52)

(A slave named "Tom Paine" who preaches a sermon more or less in imitation of a missionary)

Him Adam and him Ebe, hab lib upon an estate, and it called Paradise. It hab be a greedy big estate, much grandy better dan Paradise to leeward; and dere was dere, ebery ting good for nyam, and all de fruit on it, him Adam and him Ebe, could nyamn but de forbidden fruit.

(More of the same preacher)

Dere hab be him oder man, and him called Soloman. Him hab be king of de folks called Jews, de same folks as de Jews on de Bay, but not him Jew Soloman who hab de store. Him savey grandy much more dan all de oder folks, and him de grandy much savey man in de world.

(Ibid., p. 135)

(A speaker of standard English)

"Him no savey, massa." She caught herself in a moment . . . Her island education had shown itself too broadly in this.

(Ibid., p. 210)

British Guiana

(1830)

"No can work, massa." . . . "Very seek, massa."
"Snake bite um foot, massa — no can walk, massa.

(Alexander [1833] : 129)

Barbados

(1772-1785)

Massa buy me he won't killa me
Oh Massa buy me he won't killa me
Oh Massa buy me he won't killa me
Oh 'for he kill me he ship me regular.
  'For I live with a bad man
oh la 'for I live with a bad man o budda-bo
  'For I live with a bad man
oh la 'for I would go to the Riverside Regular.
Ante Nanny, Open da door, Pater want da
sour-sop soup, Ante Nanny, open da door,
Pa-ter want da sour-sop soup, Run Mr. Cunningham,
run for you life, run Mr. Cunningham
run for you life. Pater da come wid a o-pen knife.

(Handler and Frisbie 1972: II)

Tobago
(Seventeenth century — ascription to this island probably arbitrary)

"Me make they no eat you, me make they much love you."

(Defoe, *Robinson Crusoe*, p. 270)

"Take, kill Friday, no send Friday away."

. . .

"No, they no kill me, they willing love learn."

(Ibid., p. 272)

(1830)

"Ax de bottle what he da want, Massa full him, Massa full him."

(Alexander 1833: 192)

Grenada
(1830)

"No, massa, shark neber eat him negger here." . . . "No, massa, neber touch negro Grenada; two tree day gone, two negger capsize in canoe with plenty fish; two shark come eat up all de fish, negger quite safe."

(Alexander 1833: 241)

Barbados, Grenada, and Antigua
(1825)

"What for me isn't free? We have good massa, good country, plenty to eat, and when me sick, massa's doctor plenty to eat, and when me sick, massa's doctor physic me; me no want free, no not at all."

Antigua
(1825)

"Me no longer young, sir, and have a daughter to maintain."

(Coleridge 1826)

Miskito Coast, Central America
(1847)

[A Carib Indian] "Now me glad — good buckra come. *Gracias á Dios.*"

(Cited in Holm 1983: 99)

Charleston, South Carolina
(c. 1790)

One dollar more for 'em da: I have 'em, negro buy buckra now! Three bit more for 'em da: I have 'em, negra buy buckra now.

(Crow 1791: 9)

(c. 1856)

All berry like you, massa. What a many family you hab, massa.

(Ferguson 1856: 129)

(c. 1923)

Yo' see, Boss, dat deer been a punish wid de miskeeter bite um, coz him bin a lib een de swamp and das weh de skeeter lib and breed.

(Jane Screven Hayward, *Brown Jackets*, pp. 53-4)

Edisto Island

(c. 1949)

Me master show me all kind of thing. I think it been a Friday, in July. He show me hell; he show me heaven; he show me how to get religion. And when he get through, he open a big Bible; and then he bless my soul. Then he tell me – he say, "Go in peace and sin no more. Your soul is set free." And after while I come out, and all various thing I see. The most I see been a young mans, and a girl, and children, and my father and people – all up in a bundle.

(Turner 1949: 271, transliterated and regularized by Turner)

Philadelphia

(1799-1802)

"God help us," cried the poor creature, "very bad news. Buckra die in heaps. Bye and bye nobody live to buy pepper-pot, and old Black woman die too.

(Davis, 1909: 48)

(1850)

"I'm in the cheap line, massa," said the other, – "No 'nop'ly's my word."
"Cheap! – neber mind him, Sa; he's only a nigga from Baltimore, just come to Philadelphy . . . I'se born here, Sa, and know de town like a book. Dat ere nigga not seen good society yet – knows nuffin – habn't got de polish on. – Git out nigga and clean you self."

(Mackay 1850: 133)

Halifax, Nova Scotia

(c. 1791)

No Work, No Yam.

(Winks 1971: 84)

(1791)

No, Massa, me no hear no no mind. Me work like slave can not do worse Massa in any part of the world, therefore me determined to go with you, Massa, if you please,

(Clarkson MS, Howard University Library)

(1791)

Top lilly bit; you say me just forsake my wife. Only one of them. Which that one, Jesus Christ say so? No, no, massa; Gar amighty good; he tell somebody he must forsake him wife and children. Somebody no wicked for forsake him wife. No, massa, dis here talk no do for me.

(Campbell 1872: 201)

("old Negro proverb")

When buckra tief, he tief plantation; when nigger tief, he tief piece of cane.

(Greaves 1930: 71)

(Nova Scotia Indians)

"Suppose me killum? – scalpum?"

(Payzant 1935: 163)

"Pictou man no shootum dead goose."

(Payzant 1935: 176)

"Mattie, my wife: He gone long way off. He no come back. He dead twelve moons gone."

(Rayzant 1935: 116)

New York City

(1741)

His master live in tall house Broadway. Ben ride de fat horse.

(Horsmanden 1744: 128)

Backarara . . . 'Negro language, signifies white people'.

(Horsmanden 1744: 331)

the house . . . This in the Negroes dialect signifies houses, i.e., the town

(Horsmanden 1744: 209)

Prince William County, Virginia

(c. 1800)

Please God Almighty! how sweet that mocking bird sing. He never tire.

(Davis 1909: 312-3)

Connecticut

(1821)

"Not often, misse; sometimes I get so hungry for it, I begin feel wicked; then think how Jesus hungry in the desert. But when Satan tempt him to sin, to get food, he would not. So I say, Sarah won't sin to get victuals. I no steal, no eat stole food, though be hungry ever so long.

(*The Religious Intelligencer*)

This is only a chance sampling, but such attestions are actually quite easy to find. The writers who record this variety of English come from many different backgrounds. Emanuel Drechsel (personal communication) has objected that they do have one common and therefore possibly biasing characteristic — they all speak (some variety of) English! There are native speakers of other languages (Grade 1892), but it is inescapable that all observers must have some competence in one form of English — Pidgin!

Bickerton (1977) objects to the artificiality of, especially, attestations from *The Religious Intelligencer*. It is true that a pidgin language is used in special contexts, virtually by the definition of *Pidgin*. Thus, if the kind of communication situation which has been characteristic of, for example, the Linguistic Atlas tradition is sought, little Pidgin will be found. Nevertheless, the stretches of Pidgin English speech recorded by American missionary David Brainerd and the use of Cameroonian Pidgin English in Catechisms surely are not in themselves indications that the language is the result of some kind of fraud. It would be a strange operational requirement to reject all records kept by missionaries. For Pidgin English attestations, it is equally unrealistic to demand that some "normal" speech act — say, a grandfather telling traditional tales to his grandchildren — be recorded. The domain of pidgins is precisely in other kinds of speech act. Nor would it seem to be a necessary condition that all the renditions be perfectly accurate. In almost any other philological circumstance, it would be assumed that an outside recorder would alter an unfamiliar variety in the direction of his own native variety, rather than introducing "bizarre" forms out of his own imagination.

The tradition (Krapp 1925) has considered that the attestations by authors like James Fenimore Cooper and by some of those cited above belong to a literary convention, with the fictional aim of establishing ethnic authenticity. If this is true, it was one of the most widespread traditions in world literature – practiced by men who often were not very bookish and who would on the face of it be deemed very unlikely to know each other's work. A factor common to stereotyping for literary representation, the repetition of a few key features as a convenient way of indicating what variety is in use, is undoubtedly operative in these attestations. Caricature of Pidgin English is frequent, especially in nineteenth- and twentieth-century texts. But surely caricaturists work best with something that is known to have a real existence.

Although a fair number of observers recorded Pidgin English, few of them indeed gave any consideration to it as a serious language variety. As acute an observer as Owen (1833) could write:

> Along the West Coast of Africa, tnose natives who speak English are in the habit of using a number of words and phrases often so strangely misapplied as to create amusement. To enumerate them all would fill a volume; but among the most remarkable are, "bob" for, noise or threats; as "Suppose I teif [sic] dat man wife, bob come my side." – "lib" or "live" for remain, or to express locality; – as "Ship lib here two moons;" "rock lib here:" – "chop" for eating; as "Suppose go long way among Bullaman, he chop you."

A phrase like *strangely misapplied* has long since given way to "new modes of extending the vocabulary" (Mühlhäusler [1983]: 55), even though the "volume" has hardly been filled yet.

Professional linguists have, of course, never shared Owen's notions about "misapplied" words and phrases. On the other hand, few were interested enough in pidgins to make any attempt to correct such misconceptions. As long as a pidgin construction can be interpreted in terms of Standard English, almost everyone has been willing to accept its near-identity with Standard English. Thus, when Smith (1744) quoted an African as saying *this fit wife for you*, most would not bother to consider *fit* as anything except an adjective and *wife* as anything except a noun. Considered as pidgin, however, *fit* is most likely an auxiliary verb, *wife* a main verb, and *for* an object marker.

American Indians, who used Pidgin English with West African slaves if they did not necessarily learn it from them, also became users of the variety. There are differences between West African Pidgin English (WAPE) and American Indian Pidgin English (AIPE) and many similarities. The complex language contact situation into which American imperialism, disguised as "Manifest Destiny," forced them as they were pushed farther and farther west made Pidgin English as much of a communicative advantage for the Indians as it was for the African-derived slaves or for Australian aboriginees when they were displaced by Englishmen.

Having worked with local developments for most of their careers, and being thoroughly indoctrinated in dialect geography, historical linguists who worked with pidgins were predisposed to see them as "springing up" anew in each different area. Once these predispositions are discarded, however, it is not hard to see how Pidgin English could have spread quickly along the trade routes. It is also rather easy to understand how linguists who looked at primarily inland developed missed the whole pidgin/creole complex.

As early as 1784, New Englanders from Massachusetts were hearing Pidgin English in the China trade. Morrison (1961: 65) reports how a Chinese said to a Bostonian trader:

> You and I olo flen; you belong honest man only no get chance . . . Just now have settee counter. All finishee; you go, you please.

Morrison also reports (1961: 78) another, in the same year, saying

> Too muchee strong gale; sea all same high mast head – no can see sky.

Dulles (1930: 20) gives no examples but specifically reports the American use of pidgin in the China trade:

> During this period [again, about 1784] the sole medium of communication between the Chinese and their visitors was that queer jargon known as Pidgin English.

Dulles's footnote is revealing;

> The dialect largely made up of English words with some Portuguese and Chinese embellishments.

Neither the transcription in Morrison's source nor the historical sequence reported in Dulles need be considered infallible. A speaker who used the enclitic vowel in *settee* would probably also do so in *get*; one who used it in *muchee* would probably also do so in *mast*. If anything, English Pidgin was an "embellishment" on the Portuguese, insofar as history is concerned. The important thing is that two responsible historians found Pidgin English in the documents of the Chinese trade and did not hestitate to use them.

Specifically Chinese Pidgin English began to be documented for the American West Coast slightly after 1849 (Dillard 1972: Chapter IV) and remained in use almost constantly thereafter. Leland (1900) and Meredith (1929) are among the many who reported it, although their methods of reporting differed. Asbury (1933) relates how a Chinese named Lem Duck was able to warn his friend George McMahon, "Georgie Man! Georgie Man! Highbinder stealum whistle." Let no Chinese onomastician question the name Lem Duck; it is well known that American English speakers (or British English speakers, for that matter) do not do well with Chinese names.

The relatively small number of terms from Chinese Pidgin English now in use does not really tell the story about historical influence. There seem to have been others in use at one time which have now become almost totally unfamiliar. Among the words and expressions indicated by Colcord (1945) to have been "brought home by sailors" are

Changee for changee 'The other way around' or 'Let's exchange'.
Chow 'Food'.
Joss-pidgin 'Church forms and ceremonies'.
Makee look-see 'To reconnoiter, search for'.
Maskee 'All right, no matter'.
Samshoo 'Ardent spirits of any kind'.
So-fashion 'Thus'.
Three piecee bamboo 'A three-masted vessel'.
Topside 'Up'.

Colcord reports specifically that *maskee* was "not in common use," with the implication that the others were — at least in coastal areas. She calls *so-fashion* "in general use alongshore."

Maritime varieties of English (or of the other European languages) have not received anything like their due in the investigation of the histories of those languages. One reason may be that the monolingual model which linguists have found so comfortable will hardly work at sea; neither, in fact, will models of stable bilingualism or even of stable multilingualism. For some time, it has been obvious that "trade," "contact," or "marginal" languages were employed by the European sailors who did the actual work, as against the reporting of that work and the taking of the honors, of geographical exploration.

It has generally been held that these language varieties were evanescent, that they had no appreciable influence on any variety spoken on land. Thus, statements like those by Mathews (1935, 1937) about the very special qualities of sailors' language could either be discounted as overstatements, referred to the category of a kind of "sailors' slang" which disappeared once the sailors came ashore, or considered as "archaism." The chief example cited in support of the last position is, of course, the referring to a ship as *she*. Perhaps there were a few archaisms in the speech of British seafarers. On the other hand, they were in constant contact with speakers of other languages, the easiest situation for innovations to take place. Did those innovations perish without consequence? Did they go the way of the learning of *bulkhead* for *wall* and *deck* for *floor* by the inductee into the United States Navy in World War II, to be dropped as soon as readjustment to civilian life became a reality?

There is no really good record of the early spread of the European-based pidgins, and it is notorious that scholars of the period were little concerned with contact varieties, either ignoring them or consigning them to the company of deprecated varieties like "slang," "cant," or "jargon." It is, then, very likely that the varieties were in existence well before they were recorded. This is surely no heresy in historical linguistics; no one assumes that, for example, Proto-Germanic did not exist before one of the "daughter" languages was recorded. Much of what can be said about the early spread of the pidgins is, then, frankly speculative. It could hardly be said to be more speculative, however, than statements about the importation of British regional dialects, which are never attested in the Americas. At least Pidgin English, when attested, is clearly recognizable.[3]

Attestations of Pidgin English in the United States can be found from seventeenth-century sources, although they do not become abundant until the eighteenth (Dillard 1972 and below). There seems to be good reason to believe that some variety of WAPE had developed earlier (Dalby 1972, Hancock (forthcoming) writes of the separation of Afro-Seminole Creole (now of Bracketville, Texas) and Sea Island Creole (Gullah) between 1670 and 1760, and the abundance of attestations in various parts of the Americas by 1720 or so makes it seem rather likely that at least the ship's jargon stage was well established in the continental colonies by the earlier date. A generation, at least twenty years, is required for creolization, in the standard view.

If, as Holm and Shilling (1982: V) hypothesize, "pockets of eighteenth century American Creole survived in the Bahamas," there surely must have been some form of Pidgin English used by Blacks in the colonies at at least a slightly earlier time. Literary evidence favors the late seventeenth century (Dillard 1972).

The hypothesis of Holm (1983: 95) for the Central American ("Miskito") Coast, ignored until recently, would place the coming of the pidgin still earlier. Holm asserts that "M[iskito] C[oast] C[reole] grew out of a simplified variety of contact English brought to Central America by the British in the 1630's." The date seems a fairly good guess for the coming of Pidgin English to North America. Both Hall (1966) and Goddard (1977, 1978) point out that American Indians of the New England area are represented in the earliest attestations, but recent developments in the field of pidgin studies suggest strongly that a maritime pidgin must have been transmitted to them. That pidgin may have arrived as early as the first decade of the seventeenth century. Holm assumes nearly 80 years between the arrival of pidgin on the Miskito Coast and the first reference to "broken English," around 150 between that and the first attestation. Greater literacy in New England may explain the smaller time gap there, but there almost certainly was such a gap.

One of the earliest conveniences of creole language study was the dichotomy into the pidgin and creole stages, with the latter being conceived as the nativization of the former. In a rough sense, such processes can be seen to be going on in places like the West Cameroon and presumably in the Pacific. A great many quibbles have been raised about this general picture, including objections to the idea that the creolizing pidgin became the "only" language of the speech community. Particularly where African languages were concerned, there was a kind of emotional support for reversal of the older opinion that the languages had died out almost immediately. While in an absolute sense this view did not confuse the picture as much as the earlier notion that everything had disappeared to clear the way for European regional dialects, it did not promote any great clarity in the field.

Emotional and political considerations were not often absent. Early works on the "creole" of a given West Indian island (e.g., Cassidy 1961) became a kind of rallying point for insular pride, even for the spirit of independence. It was popular to consider each island — or at least each political unit— separately, so that the ludicrous picture of separate arrival of Pidgin English on each island, "disappearance" of the African languages, and creolization as a completely separate development became the unwanted foster child of those who used the theory.

Another broad generalization which was convenient but which attracted an incredible amount of quibbling was the "monogenesis" theory (Whinnom 1965, Voorhoeve 1973). Probably every linguist who ever wrote about it assumed a gradualism which the opponents of the theory were almost never willing to take into account. It then became as though the monogenticists had assumed a virtually overnight replacement of (e.g.) Portuguese Pidgin pre-verbal particles with (e.g.) English: *kaba* with *done*. And, again, it was occasionally assumed that every island to which a distinctive name could be given to the creole (even so simple a one as Antiguan Creole) must have seen the same process. Grave searching for early Portuguese populations took place in some studies which are best forgotten.

It soon became apparent that the terms *pidgin* and *creole* were being used to apply to a number of rather different situations. It could be shown that both stages could exist within one speech community; Tsuzaki (1971) found Hawaiian Pidgin English, Hawaiian Creole, and (partly decreolized) Hawaiian Island Dialect on those islands. The absolute requirement that the native language have vanished completely, in such cases as the West African languages of the West Cameroon, could obviously not be met.

Studies had early assumed (Stefansson 1909) that different stages of the pidgins could be observed. The "ship's jargon" observed among the Eskimos seems to match what Naro (1978) calls a reconnaissance language. Insistent, even truculent studies (Gilman 1979) accord primary emphasis to (e.g.) West African language influence; Hancock (1976) saw the influence of an unattested Pan-Guinean Pidgin behind West African Pidgin English and saw the language practice of *lançados* on the West African coast as extremely important even in the development of the Portuguese pidgin.

Again, the two views do not seem to be irreconcilably in conflict. The "ship's jargon" stage would have represented the European contribution, based in some way on Sabir, the Mediterranean lingua franca. The "shore jargon" stage would involve a very large accretion of influences from the native languages of West Africa or other relevant areas. If a pidgin is looked upon as being essentially the shore jargon stage, perhaps only the "function words" and an indeterminate number of lexical items of a rather basic nature would survive the ship's jargon stage. A small inventory of such items, although not in any way conceived as basic to language in any psychological sense, were very useful for tracking the pidgin language over the seas and around the world. The practice is not much different from that of tracing language influences in any other context, for example the observation of *rubber binder* for *rubber band* in the United States.

Perhaps the most bitterly-resisted idea of them all was "relexification," another term of convenience. Very early creole studies had commented upon the predominance of (e.g.) *sabi* in some dialects and of a reflex of *know* in another, or on the variability between the two in some locales. This would, of course, entail no such picture as a group of sailors being drilled to replace their lingua franca Portuguese forms with French or English forms before jumping ashore in an area where one of the latter languages predominated. Very early stages of creole languages seem to show some such replacement; later stages take on loanwords with the kind of specialized distribution that is commonplace in the history of borrowing. The situation was not helped by the fact that an early, very influential treatment of the process was disseminated by word of mouth and was reduced to writing only in very fragmentary form (Stewart 1962a).

The "classical" paradigm of "relexification" to form ship's jargons based on individual European languages, "expansion" to shore jargons in places where the native languages were extremely influential, and later creolization where the native languages did not serve as the main vehicles of communication must surely belong to the early stage of European colonial expansion. Very rapid movement, resulting in a kind of cataclysmic contact, was characteristic of this stage, and multilingualism rather than bilingualism of the conventionally studied type was the norm for such contact situations. Something of this type probably began as early as the sixteenth century and was almost certainly in full swing in the seventeenth and eighteenth centuries. The spread of pidgin varieties in the twentieth century (Woolford and Washabaugh 1983) may duplicate some but probably not all of those characteristics.

Looking at the Atlantic creoles especially, it soon becomes obvious that virtually no single case still embodies that early historical situation. Hancock (forthcoming) writes that "practically all of the languages have been subject to abrupt modification and cross influence, this last sometimes from three or four other creoles." It is a factor strongly in favor of Holm and Shilling (1982) that they do not even try to explain Bahamian English in terms of a purely native creole tradition.[4]

Hancock and Holm and Shilling have also given more serious attention to British dialect parallels than did some of the earlier relexificationists. This should be a good counteractant to the notion that creolists have espoused "Africanized" versions of English (or French, etc.) exclusively. But the older notion of tracking a migrating population back to its homeland by its language forms can hardly be served thereby. If one found, for example, even a large number of Yorkshire dialect forms on St. Kitts, one would hardly be justified in concluding that St. Kitts was originally settled by a predominantly Yorkshire population. On the other hand, there is no *a priori* reason why Yorkshire or any other British dialect should not have contributed some forms to the prototypical ship's jargon. The only reservation would be that such forms were probably to be heard from speakers who came from Devonshire soon after the different groups came together in ship's companies. That one or another historically prominent figure known for his exploits in the New World should have spoken a regionally recognizable dialect to the end of his days is hardly relevant. Superordinated figures are precisely those who would not need to modify their language use.

It was when these linguistic developments were at or approaching their height that Englishmen settled the islands and coasts of the Americas. The Pilgrim fathers settled on Cape Cod because, according to Paine (1919: 2), they

> expected to wrest a livelihood mostly from salt water. Both pious and amphibious were these pioneers whom the wilderness and the red Indians confined to the water's edge.

The Puritans who came to Massachusetts Bay in 1629 were "even more energetic in taking profit from the sea" (ibid.). An important part of the population when the Revolution of 1776 broke out was whalers, merchantmen, and sailors.[5]

At about the time of or slightly after the Revolution, Black speakers of the already creolized pidgin were taking their language variety to the Bahamas (Holm and Shilling 1982: V), and waves of language influence hardly noticed until recently were at full tide by the end of the eighteenth century.

Probably much more than in any parts of England except the ports themselves, the actual sailors of ships were at home with and close to the Americans ashore. They were closely involved in whaling, slaving, and the rum trade when those three types of trading were basic to the colonies. When the wagon trains and the cattle drivers set out across the continent, they took a lot − including some language − from the sailors. And when the great economic development of 1848-9, the gold rush, took place in the West, fleets of ships came from the shipyards of New York and Boston and from the ports of Medford, Newburyport, Portland, and others to the California coast. Many of the sailors jumped ship and went on the gold rush (Paine 1919: 164-6). The influence of maritime language never really ceased.

The internationalization of English was not a simple matter, and it cannot be simply represented. Two major currents seem, however, to be a necessary part of the presentation: the production of a common dialect to eliminate the greatest divergences within English itself and the adoption of a mechanism to cope with the multilingual problems arising from a rather new kind of contact with populations which used a great number of largely unfamiliar languages. It is not the suggestion of this work that either process was perfectly complete. Leveling can hardly have been perfect, and not everyone who traveled to pidgin-speaking territory became proficient in pidgin. Especially where there was long-term contact with relatively settled, agrarian populations, the more well-known consequences of stable bilingualism were produced. English competed with Dutch, German, French, and Spanish in different parts of North America at different times. In some areas of the United States, the competition continues today. With the possible exception of German,[6] each of the competing languages developed special contact varieties. The evidence for these historical factors is abundant, and it can be considered in some detail.

NOTES

1. It is necessary to resist the temptation to belabor a point here, but the lack of investigation of such matters in the tradition is striking. For example, a seriously intended textbook of Middle English (C. Jones 1972) contains the following passage:

    In addition to speakers of Norman French [in William the Conqueror's army], there were almost certainly many whose *only* [emphasis added] language was either Breton (spoken in the extreme northwest of France and related to the Celtic spoken in Wales and Ireland) or Flemish, a language still spoken today in Belgium.

    In other words, there were groups of soldiers in William's army who could speak to no other group in the invading force! The next sentence in the same work calls William's armies "rather small in number." A few hundred Breton or Flemish speakers in an army of "a mere 10,000-15,000 (or less)" (Jones 1972: 17) who could not speak to the other groups would not, one would think, be much of a military asset. Jones's intention is clear, however; he, like many before and after him, wants to minimize the effect of Norman French on Middle English.

2. C. Jones (1972: 50) accepts this distinction between written and spoken standards. His book is probably typical enough of the rather automatic reaction of historical linguists whose interests in the period do not focus on this problem. No special criticism of Jones is intended; his statements about the matter were merely sought out in a chance (in the absence of time for a random) sample of what textbooks have done with these questions.

3. Hall (1983: 669) writes of a "Muscovite Pidgin English which may have been used in the English Muscovy trade in the 16th-17th centuries, and which may have left undocumented traces in later dealings of Russians with foreigners." Hall almost expressly refrains from connecting this hypothetical pidgin with more "traditional" contact varieties; nevertheless, this seemingly well-grounded speculation concerns a pidgin variety of English which fits into the pattern of the "going international" of English at just about the 16th-17th century period.

4. Now Holm (1983: 1) finds that "Both Gullah and Bahamian appear to have an immediate ancestor in the eighteenth-century creole English spoken on plantations in the American South."

5. It is probable that Pidgin English came to the maritime provinces of Canada, although there is no research directly related to this matter. Paddock (1966, cited by McDavid and McDavid in Wolfram and Clarke 1971) finds some of the "stigmata" of Black English in the English of those provinces. Maritime Pidgin English is the likely common ancestor for the forms in the Canadian dialects and Black English.

6. But see the materials provided by Beadle (1878) and the discussion on pp. 99-100.

Chapter II

Pidgin and Maritime Influence on Other Varieties

That special maritime varieties were in use at sea and in ports almost everywhere the European colonial expansion reached is apparent. It can still be argued, of course, that such varieties had little effect on the more landlubberly population. For a long time it has been assumed, and written into general treatments of American English (Pyles 1964: 220), that a trip across an ocean has no influence on a language, therefore [!] that English did not change between England and the overseas colonies. With the articles of Mathews (1935, 1937), it seems obvious, on the other hand, that something made a difference in the speech of sailors. The conventional approach has been to assert that the influence never reached inland, that the important early relationships of the American continental colonies to the West Indian islands and their dependence upon maritime contacts with the rest of the world simply had no linguistic consequences.

Workers outside the linguistic mainstream (Chase 1942, Colcord 1945) have pointed out the effects of sea terms on the language of mobile groups ashore. The trail herds driven by the cowboys and the wagon trains of the pioneers had some nautical influence (pp. 141-142). The railroads, which in a sense replaced those two methods of transportation, also took over a great deal from the sea (see Chapter VIII). Even the automobile took over terms like *fenders* from shipping.

If it is easy to forget the multilingual situation in early America when the language of the inland United States is being considered, it is hardly possible to do so when considering the maritime trade. Some words conventionally traced with great confidence to one language can only be explained in terms of two or three (see the material on *filibuster*, p. 101 on *yankee* pp. 99, 150.) The Lingua Franca solution to the polyglot complexity was widespread in the Mediterranean and elsewhere (Kahane, Kahane, and Tietze 1958, Whinnom 1965), and it is not beyond possibility that Sabir itself reached the shores of the United States.

That was precisely the suggestion of Farmer and Henly (1891) for *cavort*, which they traced to the Lingua Franca *cavolta* 'prancing on horseback'. The branch dictionaries (OEDS, DA, Webster's Third) indulge in weak suggestion of "alteration of *curvet*." The word may, however, join other examples of the Romance etymon for 'horse' in providing contact language vocabulary in the United States; see Delaware Jargon *kabay* and Gulf Corridor and Southwestern *cavvyard* (pp. 138-142). Farmer and Henley compare Spanish *cavar* 'the pawing of a spirited horse' and (in a somewhat puzzling manner) French *bourbetter.*

There is, in the early attestations, an interesting variation with *cavault.* The alternation /r/~/l/ /_C is commonplace in the contact language situation, although admittedly it is not unknown elsewhere. OEDS and Webster's Third, while not accepting the historical association with 'horse', include a notably large number of examples which involve horses and cattle. Partridge (1950, 1970) has no such trouble; he simply traces both *cavort* and *cavault* to a Romance etymon for 'horse', and one has the strong feeling that Partridge has simply avoided becoming mired in the excessive subtlety which seems to be fostered in the branch dictionaries by what is almost an outright unwillingness to acknowledge the Lingua Franca tradition.

Moving outside the narrow circle of "Americanisms," one finds other forms — surely *used* in American English — which are even clearer cut. Such a word is *lingo,* which OED hypothesizes to be a "corrupt" form of "LINGUA (franca)"; it cites, somewhat more objectively, "Pg. *lingoa.*" Webster's Third, on the basis of no visible evidence, says "probably fr[om] Prov[encal] *lengo, lingo.*" Colcord (1945) is nontechnical but surely correct when she writes, "It was brought home from the Mediterranean where 'lingua franca', a mixture of many tongues, is generally used." The OEDS designation as "a contemptuous designation for foreign speech or language; language which is strange or unintelligible to the person who so designates it, language peculiar to some special subject, or employed (whether properly or affectedly) by some particular class of persons" is not strange in view of what customarily happens to contact language forms where prestige is concerned. See Hotten (1887) Hancock (1973) for the connection between contact languages and "cant."

Association between the Lingua Franca and pidgins goes at least as far back as Hesseling (Markey 1983). Fairly systematic investigation of pidgins and creoles goes back to Schuchardt, and sporadic observation — including attestations of their occurrence in what is now the United States — goes back virtually to the beginning of the Europeans in the New World. The "looseness" of the distribution of Pidgin English, as discussed by Drechsel and Makuakane (1982), may well have been only a looseness of observation rather than a genuine characteristic of the language spread.[1] The people who left the records were simply not prepared, by their education or by any tradition, to encounter such language varieties. When they did, they tended to describe them with amusement or even with contempt. They were not trained to give adequate descriptions once the varieties were more or less forced upon their attention. One need only consider the early fantasies about the relationship between the Amerindian languages and Hebrew to realize what the observers were prepared to find.

Pidgin English influence, if "loose," was extremely widespread. American and British sailors were exposed to it at sea and in port. According to Granville (1962), the influence on "those officers and men who have served in the China trade" with the Royal Navy remained appreciable even as late as World War II. It extended into the period when relatively standard varieties of English came into widespread use as the world's lingua franca. What that influence must have been in the eighteenth and nineteenth centuries can be appreciated to some extent by looking at the wide variety of sources in which Pidgin English is reported. The evidence suggests that its influence on seagoing populations was very great indeed. If, as the evidence from American Indian Pidgin English seems to suggest, the pidgin was widespread even in the seventeenth century, influence on American English in the colonial period may have been extensive.

Many of the sources reflect apparent pidginisms like *too much* where Standard English might have *very much*. Admittedly, the distinction is difficult for many foreign learners in a simple bilingual situation, but it is also impressive how widely diffused the term is in Pidgin English around the world. (See the Falconbridge [1794] citation below and this chapter *passim*.) Holm and Shilling (1982) call it "Atlantic"; attestations from Pidgin English in the Pacific are, however, abundant (e.g., Mühlhäusler 1983: 65). They are struck, as so many researchers have been, by the relationship to other languages used in the European maritime expansion, citing Portuguese Creole *dimaás* 'very much' versus Portuguese *demais* 'too much'.[2] Granville himself recognized Portuguese connections with vocabulary like *maskee*:

'It doesn't matter; it is of no account'.
. . . Skeat derives the word from Portuguese *mas que.*

Even those whose familiarity with such language is limited to the reading of Richard McKenna's 1963 novel of China-side American sailors *The Sand Pebbles* will find the word not unfamiliar.

Like other investigators, however, Granville took some possibly Portuguese (or general Iberian) forms for Spanish. He regarded, for example, *loco da poco* as a fanciful elaboration of Spanish *loco*. Corominas (*Breve Diccionario Etimológico de la Lengua Castellana*) labels *loco* "*palabra propria* del *cast[ellano] y el port[ugués]*, citing *louco* from the latter. As we shall see later, especially in dealing with the language of the early cattle trade, varieties which appear to be Iberian or even Romance without being identical to any of the officially recognized languages or "patois" have a far-reaching influence. The phrase cited by Granville appears to have been in jocular use; precisely that use has been made of forms from the maritime trade languages for centuries. But the terms themselves often have a wide extension in serious use; Krio of Sierra Leone has *loko* 'crazy', but no other specifically Spanish vocabulary. It may be necessary to indulge in this kind of quibbling rather often, since the issue of borrowing from a special contact language or from a "standard" language like Spanish (or Portuguese) is an important one.

Overemphasis on Spanish seems virtually endemic to studies of contacts with American English. Colcord (1945) traces *savey* to Spanish *sabe*, in spite of the obvious possibilities of derivation from general Iberian or from Portuguese. (Cf. the presence of the form or a closely related form on the China Coast.) She further traces *No bono* "An emphatic 'no good'" to Spanish, although she places it among phrases "brought home by sailors" and cites Spanish *bueno*. Colcord says nothing about the stressed vowel nucleus. More formal linguistis have, however, been a little careless with vowels of these varieties. (See pp. 140-146).

Where *joss* and its compounds are concerned, Granville seems on firmer ground:

> The word is Pidgin-English for the Portuguese *deos* (Latin *deus*), a god, hence *joss house*, a temple or church. *Joss* means luck or good fortune.

Granville lists these derivatives of *joss*:

> *Joss-house man.* Parson.
> *Jossman.* Measure of Plymouth rum with picture of monk on bottle.
> *Josspiece.* Talisman or mascot of any kind. Popularly supposed to bring luck to its wearer.
> *Chinchin joss.* Church service ashore in China.

Some of the same words, combinations, and meanings were common in those parts of the American frontier where Chinese speakers were present. Beadle (1873: 180) reports how the Chinese call the greatest of gods "Topside Josh." *Joss* is a fairly frequent variant for slang *josh* (usually a verb, rarely a noun) and it may well be that the origin is a meaning like 'treat (mockingly) like a god'. This is as likely as the accepted derivation from *Joshua*. In the same section (1871: 173-182) Beadle provides abundant evidence of the use of Chinese Pidgin English in the West.

Granville, who does associate *chinchin joss* with Chinese Pidgin English, does not trace *chin food* 'gossip or meaningless boring conversation' to the same source. It seems obvious, however, that there is a connection to *chinchin*. Later American *chin music* very likely has some connection. Although not all of the compounds with *joss* are attested on the frontier, it is quite likely that the Chinese there at the time the gold rush was in full swing used more of them than anyone recorded. Of course, one can still see *Joss House* on the Chinatown tour in any city large enough to have such a section.

Other elements in Granville's vocabulary fit into the picture of a widely influential Pidgin English of the maritime trade. There is, for example, the compounding element *-side,* as in *China-side*:

The China station. In Pidgin English side = place.
Cf. TOP-SIDE, SHORE-SIDE, etc.

Granville specifically comments that *shore-side* 'the beach' is Pidgin English "used by old 'China birds'." *Topside* is perhaps overly familiar from "Topside Galah," the Pidgin English translation of Longfellow's "Excelsior" (Meredith 1929). But such use of *side* also suggests Cameroonian Pidgin English *husay* 'where?' and Krio *usai* in the same meaning. In both of these Creole languages, the second element is usually thought of as derived from *side*; Anglicizing orthographies in the Cameroun spelled the word *whose side.* Krio has, additionally, *us-pat,* rationalizable as 'whose part?' and *we-pat* 'what part?' Holm and Shilling (1982) call *side* in this use Caribbean, cite Haitian Creole *bò côté* '*endroit*', and postulate a loan-translation from Twi and/or Yoruba. Even Papia Kristang (Hancock) has an analogous formation, *turu-banda* (literally *all band*) 'everywhere'.

Among the pidgin-like forms which Granville cites are *makee-learn* and *decky learner.* Granville specifies that the latter is the equivalent of the former for the fishing fleets. The former is defined as

1. Naval novice, a beginner in any branch of the service.
2. A merchant Navy cadet or 'apprentice'.

Both of these have the apparent enclitic vowel, although only Granville's perhaps intuitive identification links them. Jocular use on a pidgin pattern, observable in many cases, is a definite possibility.

Whatever its ultimate source, the Chinese Pidgin English term *chop chop* 'at once, immediately, on the run' is also British sailor talk. Granville identifies it only as "China-side," but other sources like Leland (1900) stamp it pidgin. Granville does give a definite "Chinese pidgin" label to

Look-see. Check up or general look around; a cursory inspection.

and in

Look-stick. A long glass or telescope; a 'bring-em-near'

even the gloss is transparently pidgin.

American colloquial usage just about everywhere uses *look-see,* an interesting example of general pidgin and creole serial verb construction. Adams (1968) took it for

A cow-man's term for an inspection tour or an investigation of some sort; the word *look* is rarely used by itself.

Use of Pidgin English in the west has long been noted (Rollins 1936) but not taken into account in linguistic treatments.

In Granville's list, it is also likely that

Merry-merry. Slightly intoxicating drink sold in Gibraltar. Ingredients dubious

and the famous *Johnny-come-lately* are Pidgin. The last, according to Adams

(1968), was one of many pidgin expressions taken over by the American cowboy. It became an integral part of American popular culture, as did "Sorry 'bout that," which apparently comes from Pidgin English in Vietnam.

Generally unknown to Americans is Granville's *cookem fry*, where the second syllable of the first word (as printed) is obviously the transitivizer, the suffix which marks a transitive verb in many varieties of Pidgin English. (Cf. *bring-em-near.*) This "odd expression"

> is a survival of those lawless times when sailors had reputations so bad that they never expected to be candidates for heaven, and were, therefore, reconciled to 'cookem fry' in Hades.

Indirectly, also, the expression testifies, as do many others (like *chin chin joss*) to the intimate association of missionary activity and pidgin English in many places. In many cases, the best and even the only early evidence comes from the writings of missionaries.

Although Granville does not so identify it, *no wantchee* 'I don't want it' is Pidgin English which recurs in many places, including the American frontier. (Cf. the quotation from Herlein above, p. 13). Granville does provide the very useful information that the expression is "Wardroom" or officer talk (in contrast to "Lower Decks," language of the enlisted men) and that it is from China-side.

With the existence of a Pidgin English in the China service well established, it seems likely that pidgin rather than widespread or even occasional bilingualism was responsible for the transmission of words like *chai* 'tea'. The same can probably be said for *chow*, which Granville calls short for *chow chow*, "pidgin English – probably from Chinese for 'a mixture'."

Another interesting term from Granville is *fly* 'artful', which could point to a Maritime Pidgin English origin for some once very popular Black ethnic slang (cf. the movie *Superfly*); Matsell (1859) lists it as "rogues'" or traveling underworld figures' slang in the nineteenth century:

fly – knowing; up to him
"The bloke was fly." The man was aware of what I wanted.

There is no reason why a maritime term should not have found its way into "rogues' " slang; Weseen (1934) records *no likee* 'poorly received, unsuccessful' in theatre slang and as *do(es) not like* in general slang; he also has *no go* 'lack of agreement' as general slang.

Ash cat or *bunker cat* 'R.N. stoker serving a coal-burning vessel, fireman in a merchantship' is interesting for the reason that Dalby (1972) has shown "cat" in such words as *hepcat* to have a reasonable West African origin (Wolof *hipikat*). Mixing of maritime and African vocabulary and features is one of the problems which must be taken into account in dealing with the history of the maritime contact varieties. Forms in the Black English Vernacular (like *higo* 'here is', possibly from *here go*, and *dago*, 'there is', possibly from *there go*) have parallels in varieties like that of Pitcairn Island, which had many sailors but few if any Africans among its sailors (Ross and Moverley 1964).

The reason why some creolists see striking resemblances between the China-coast language contact situation and that of the Americas is demonstrated by the entry

> *Talkee-talkee.* Conference or mass meeting. A 'matter party'. Wardroom via China-side.

Talkee Talkee (Taki Taki) is a widely used designation, in places like Surinam and Sierra Leone, for Pidgin English or for a variety ultimately developed from a pidgin. Semantically parallel names for languages are seen in Papiamentu (Old Portuguese *papiar* 'to chat') and in Papia Kristang.

There may be some doubt about whether *chinky*

> A rating who is always talking about his adventures on China-side and using Pidgin English. The lower deck's version of CHINA-BIRI.

is "true" pidgin or a Royal Navy innovation on the analogy of pidgin forms. Fictionally and actually, English speakers who have come in contact with pidgin like to improvise with the devices of the variety, like the Honolulu used car dealer who advertized *Geev-um Low, Low Prices* in 1967. Whatever the exact details of its origin, *chinky* has the enclitic vowel as in *piecee*:

> *olo piecee* 'China-side for Old piece'

and

> *piecee one* 'first class; anything that has priority'

Holm and Shilling (1982) compare "Caribbean" *piece* as a quantifier to the Chinese Pidgin English form, which is often more of a quantifier than in these examples.

The enclitic vowel and other factors in the compounding leave no doubt about

> Outside walkee, 'Paddle steamer whose paddles "walk" outside the hull'

or its opposite, *inside walkee.*

As Granville points out, *no can do* is definitely pidgin. It was the title of a 1945 popular song with lyrics by Charles Tobias and music by Nat Simon that achieved Tin Pan Alley popularity and thus became one of the most widely known pidgin phrases among Americans in general. Granville (1950) also lists *No-can-go-ists* 'Naval nonconformists', which never seems to have achieved any currency outside the R.N.

Distribution according to different styles or registers also appears to emerge from the pidgin examples, or from imaginative innovations on them, which Granville gives. An example is

> *M.R.U. Much Regret Unable.* The formal signal made by officers unable to accept .... The informal is *N.C.D. (no can do).*

Elsewhere, pidgin phrases are shown to be appropriate to less formal levels of communication only:

> *Maskee.* 'It doesn't matter; it is of no account . Pidgin English used on informal

occasions for the more serious-[1950 service-] sounding "belay." "You can *maskee* that, Bosun, we shall not want it after all."

One of the consequences of contact with a pidgin is influence on the "slang" or technical "jargon" of some particular group, like R.N. sailors or the woodsmen of the Northwest (cf. 150-152). The same maritime contact factors that the British sailors encountered were basic to the early American experience. Unfortunately, however, we have no work for American naval slang comparable to Granville's dictionary of Royal Navy expressions. We do, however, have dictionaries for special occupational groups (McCulloch 1958, Adams 1968) which make inferences possible. Conclusions must perhaps be conjectural, but some of them seem to be virtually unavoidable.

Although I know of no documentation in American usage of the *foo* words which Cranville discusses, there are analogous developments in American sailor talk. These are, according to Granville, lower deck rather than wardroom terms — as extensive use of terms for faeces was characteristic of enlisted sailors rather than of naval officers in World War II. We are told

Foo foo is the Chinese for faeces and is also used as a pejorative adjective

and it hardly takes extensive research to tell a World War II veteran that *shit* and *shitty* had the same function. Granville also attests the compounds *foo foo barge* 'sewage barge in the Yangtse River', *foo foo band* 'squeegee band', and *foo foo valve*

Like WIFFLO GADGET, this is any piece of mechanism to which the non-technical cannot give a name.

The use of *shit* to express the inexpressible was certainly characteristic of the talk of the armed services during World War II, and it seems to have spread soon thereafter to the general population.

The word itself, one of the more strangely tabooed of the fabled "four-letter words," has a more generalized, less indecent function in Pidgin English. In Cameroonian Pidgin English, *shit fo' fire* means only 'ashes'; in Melanesian Pidgin English *shit bilong fire* has the same meaning. There are many comparable phrases involving *shit* in the various pidgins. Among American sailors, some of whom played around with pidgin, the contemptuous *shit on shingle* for creamed beef on toast may have meant no more than general disapproval. But the American sailors would have been more sensitive to the indecent possibilities than the Chinese or the Melanesians, to whom it was only part of an auxiliary language. And of course the true shock value could only be appreciated by "innocent" civilians who had never been exposed either to Pacific pidgins or service talk.

Many words that are taboo in ordinary English are innocuous in pidgins, although that does not mean that no hearer will find them "indecent." An example is the developments from *arse,* which, according to Cassidy (1977: 182) "was certainly borrowed early into pidgins and continued in creoles." The word had metathesis in Jamaican *raas*, Krio *rasol* 'rectum' and *rasklot* 'sanitary napkin', and lambdacism (change of /r-/ to /l-/) in Cameroonian and Sranan *lasi* 'arse'. Cassidy also cites Chinese Pidgin English *as* 'buttocks', but the word frequently came to mean 'foundation' or even 'origin' in pidgin varieties. In Melanesian Pidgin English *as bilong haws* is 'foundation of a house', *as bilong diwai* is 'foot of a tree', and *as bilong musket* is 'gun butt'. Granville (1950) lists *arse of the ship* 'the stern' and adds, "This phrase, like the *arse of a block* 'pulley', is used almost as a technicality in the Royal Navy."

Uses in this sense are commonplace in the Atlantic varieties as well. Holm and Shilling (1982) call it "Caribbean" and cite Creole French and Trinidadian Spanish parallels, as well as similar uses in Yoruba and Ibo and a similar usage in the Black English Vernacular. Hancock (1977) also reports Krio forms like *ah go buss you wais* 'I'll deal with you' and *heice you wais* 'get up'. Parallel developments are far from unknown in Pacific varieties; Samarin (1980: 221) cites *astingtin* (*arse* + *think* + *thing*) 'reason' and *asples* (*arse* + *place*) 'place of birth, origin'.

That this "taboo" usage was also spread by servicemen returning from World War II, who had become familiar with it in some cases in the relatively innocuous pidgin context, is at least a tenable hypothesis. A famous use by a speaker known not at all for indecent language was Jimmy Carter's proclamation that, if Teddy Kennedy became a rival for the presidency, "I'll whip his ass."

The Chinese were not the only linguistically complex group that early American sailors had to deal with. New England-based ships began engaging in the slave trade as early as 1643, when an American ship coming from the Canary Islands stopped off at Barbados and bought tobacco "in exchange for Africoes, which she carried from the Isle of Maio" (Bailyn 1955: 84). Thus Americans entered the infamous "triangular slave voyage" pattern, engaged in by Hugh Crow and others.

If the situation at sea was the same that obtains today in West Africa and elsewhere, Englishmen and Americans who use Pidgin English are not automatically authorities on it. If they want to use the variety, they must learn to do so from the Africans, Indians, Chinese, and others who are expert (if, by definition, not native) speakers. Usually, the native speakers of English are quite clumsy in their attempts to use pidgin; they are often objects of mockery by more proficient users. Jones (1962) reports that African speakers of Krio often simplify that creolized variety in order to make themselves understood by Europeans.

Although it is likely that at the very beginning the impetus for Pidgin English came from British sailors, "ownership" soon passed to other hands. We have little record of the reaction of sailors to the use of Pidgin English by other populations, although more pretentious observers often confuse the issue by calling both it and foreign-accented talk *broken English*. At any rate, pidgin came to be used rather quickly by Africans, Asians, and Polynesian islanders. Missionaries (who, by profession, may be somewhat more likely to seek explanations for phenomena) were often puzzled, like those who wrote of the African "repatriation" settlement at Regents Town in Sierra Leone in the interestingly entitled periodical *The Religious Intelligencer*:

> Natives of twenty-two different nations were here collected together; and a considerable number of them had been but recently liberated from the holds of slave vessels; they were greatly prejudiced against one another, and in a state of common hostility with no common medium of intercourse but a little broken English.

A simplistically liberal view of history would like to see an invention in both the hostility and the "broken" English; however, hostility between newly enslaved Africans of different tribal backgrounds and the use of "broken" language varieties are reported in various parts of the Americas; see, for example, Genovese (1974).

The emergency type of language contact in which a pidgin is a happy solution afflicted no other group so much as the African slaves; no other group was so completely uprooted and so definitively turned away from its cultural heritage. (This is by no means to say that there were no cultural survivals among the slaves, but all of them found a new context. On this point see especially Price 1972.) The European intervention in Africa not taking the form of enslavement alone, many of those who remained saw cataclysmic changes. By mid-nineteenth century Pidgin English had established itself along the West African coast (Christophersen 1953, 1959; Dalby 1969).

In 1824, "Grandy King George" of Old Calabar wrote letters to the British crown in Pidgin English, and texts have survived (Owen 1833: II). A New Testament translated into "Blackman's English" was reported by English traveler Sir Richard Francis Burton (1863: I: 215). So important was West African Pidgin English (WAPE) and its Caribbean and continental American derivatives to Christian evangelism that German missionaries in Bautzen prepared a *Kurzgefaste Negerenglische Grammatik* (1854).

The records of the missionaries show that Africans were by no means the only non-European users of Pidgin English. Especially in insular and coastal areas, people all around the now-encircled globe were beginning to be exposed to multicultural and multilingual contexts. Between African attestations in *The Religious Intelligencer* for 1821, there are letters dictated by Hawaiian King Tamoree of Atooi, who had "for many years been able to speak broken English," and his queen, who signed herself (by proxy) Charlotte Tapolee. The queen's letter is quoted below:

Atooi, July 28, 1820

Dear Friend,

I am glad your daughter came here. I shall be her mother now, and she be my daughter. I be good to her; give her tappa; give her mat; give her plenty to eat. By and by your daughter speak Owhyee: then she learn me how to read, and write, and sew; and talk of that great Akooah, which the good people of America love. I begin spell little: read come very hard, like stone. You very good send your daughter great way to teach the heathen. I am very glad I can write you a short letter, and tell you that I be good to your daughter. I send you my *aloha* and tell you that I am

Your friend
CHARLOTTE TAPOOLEE
Queen of Atooi

The hand of the transcriber is evident, especially in the letter format. Regularizations like *by and bye* (*bimeby*) are commonplace in Europeanizing representations.

This 1821 attestation from *The Religious Intelligencer* does not by itself — or with others in the same magazine — indicate the beginning of full-scale utilization of Pidgin English. In the Hawaiian Islands, extensive use seems to have come later. The persons quoted above are royalty, interested in international communication. The workers who used Pidgin English on the plantations came later (Relnecke 1969). But missionary William Ellis, who traveled in the islands in 1822 and 1823, found that "the natives"

use *kaukau* (a word of Chinese origin) instead of the native word for eat, and *pikaninny*, for small, supposing that they are thereby better understood.[3]

Since these two words are among the most widespread pidginisms in the Pacific at least, it would appear that Hawaiians could use at least some Pidgin English "to make themselves understood" — an almost perfect commonsense statement of the communicative function of a pidgin — as early as the 1820s. (This influence from the outside on HPE, while not outright contradicted, is played down in Bickerton 1982.)

The early missionaries made earnest attempts to preach to, and others to deal with, the Hawaiians in their own language; Hawaiians struggled to use English with the minority of native speakers of that language. The "lower end of this spectrum" was called "Hapa Haole" ('half white') (Bickerton 1981: 7). As long as the language contact situation was a relatively simple bilingualism, Hapa Haole (like "Spanglish" in Puerto Rico) was adequate. Later, when Chinese, Japanese, and even Puerto Ricans joined Hawaiians and Americans, Pidgin English spread (or "developed" according to Bickerton) rapidly, becoming an important variety by about 1880. (Bickerton 1981: 7 identifies a "pidgin based on Hawaiian and known as *olelo pa'i'ai* 'taro language' contemporary with Hawaiian Pidgin English.") Use of Pidgin English was even promoted by a kind of textbook, *Me Speak English*. Today, not only pidgin but a creolized version and a slightly decreolized variety (called Island Dialect by Reinecke) coexist with Standard English, and a few linguistically talented islanders can manage all three, in addition to an "ethnic" home language like Chinese, Japanese, or Hawaiian.

American seamen like Richard Henry Dana, who wrote *Two Years Before the Mast*, came into close and extensive contact with Pidgin English. Dana (1911: 179) observed:

> A considerable trade has been carried on for several years between California and the Sandwich Islands, and most of the vessels are manned with Islanders, who, as they for the most part sign no articles, leave whenever they choose, and let themselves out to cure hides at San Diego, and to supply the places of the men left ashore from the American vessels while on the coast. In this way a little colony of them had become settled at San Diego, as their head-quarters.

Reporters like Dana do not, of course, use the term *Pidgin English*; but there is little else to be made from these quotations of "Kanakas" (Hawaiians), in Dana's 1835 observations:

> Aole! Aole make make ika hana. Now, got plenty money; no good, work. Mamule, money *pau* – all gone. Ah! very good, work! – maikai, hana hana mi.
> (p. 175)
> Aye! Me know that. By-'em'by money *pau* – gone; then Kanaka work plenty.
> (p. 175)

Not even *picaninny* has a wider pidgin distribution than *bimeby*, although the former is quoted by Dana:

> Me no eatee Cap'nee Cook! Me pickaninny – small – so high – no more! My fader see Cap'nee Cook! me – no.
> (p. 181)

Pidgin English is mixed with what Dana and others called "the Sandwich Island language," which at this date could easily be a carry-over from Hapa Haole. In addition to the first quotation above, there are other mixed attestations:

> New Zealand Kanaka eatee white man; Sandwich Island Kanaka – no. Sandwich Island Kanaka *ua like pu na haole* – all 'e same a' you.
> (p. 181)

John Reinecke (personal communication) questioned the accuracy of Dana's reports. But Dana himself claims

> During the four months I lived here [San Diego] I got well acquainted with all of them, and took the greatest pains to become familiar with their language, habits, and characters.
> (p. 179)

Furthermore, Dana's use of nautical terminology like *knocked off* (p. 202), *clapped a stopper* (p. 405), and *sleep in* (p. 14) seems authentic. Most likely, Dana knew what he was doing when he transcribed pidginisms like *alle same, spose* 'if', and the other items cited:

> No! we no all 'e same a' you! – Suppose one got money, all got money. You, – suppose one got money – lock him up in chest. No good!
> (p. 182)

Hawaiian Pidgin English is quite commonly observed toward the middle of the nineteenth century. Clark (1847) tells of an 1840 Hawaiian who "could speak a little English tolerably well"; among his sayings was

fall into some of the holes and kill his neck.

Collocations like *kill* and *neck* above are the kind which are apparently quite frequent in pidgin/creole varieties (see pp. 151-2). In other respects, the Hawaiian forms are not so unlike Pidgin English elsewhere. The phrase *jam up* 'disrupt' (bought on a humorous decal in Honolulu in 1977) resemble Bahamian usages like *jam* 'foil a person's plans' and *jam up* 'to fight'.

One must accept some strange notions if he is to believe that even pidginisms in popular humor "spring up" spontaneously. A phrase like *broke-um-up* 'demolish' could seemingly not occur "accidentally" in both K. Bowman (n.d.) and Camerounian Pidgin English. Arguments for the international nature of the variety were given as early as Sayer (1939) and are present, although in a more reserved format, in Hall (1966). Other arguments for this maritime and international character of Pidgin English are given on p. 49.

Despite persistent efforts to localize Pidgin English, anyone who examines the records must be struck by the extreme mobility of the variety. The earliest reported speaker of "Hawiian" Pidgin English could be said to be Henry Obookiah, whose reported speeches took place in Connecticut. An early convert to Christianity, Obookiah, who died in Connecticut in 1818, is extensively quoted by his biographers Beecher and Harvey (Reinecke 1969: 198), who explicitly indicate their intention to represent, as closely as possible, his exact words. They wrote that he said

Owyhee gods! They *wood,* burn; Me go home, put 'em in a fire, burn 'em up. — They no *see,* no *hear,* no *anything* . . . We make them — Our God . . .*He make us.*

But the reader of Beecher and Harvey (1818) soon learns that Obookiah had traveled at sea extensively before coming to Connecticut and being converted. It was at sea that he must have learned Pidgin English, which was maritime and in no real sense any more "Hawaiian" than it was "Connecticut." When territorial claims like those sometimes made for "Hawaiian" forms are made dogmatically, they often seem so oppressive as to explain, if not to justify, diatribes against the placing of "bench marks" by a tradition which had not taken adequate account of the contact varieties (Dillard 1980: 2).

If Pidgin English is in truth linked to the Maritime Lingua Franca tradition it must have begun by at least the early seventeenth century. The first attestations, admittedly, are from non-maritime American Indians (Goddard 1977, 1978). Transmission to them by West African slaves is, however, entirely possible (Dillard 1972a). The striking similarities between the Pidgin English varieties make it difficult to avoid some speculation about transmission. The records suggest an impressively, but not impossibly, broad spread —

unless, of course, one regards the spread of British — and European — influence at the same time as "impossible".

There are enough records to indicate that Pidgin English spread all over the maritime routes at a very early period. It must have come to Australia and New Guinea almost as soon as the British reached those shores. Ramson (1966) cites evidence for a well-known, although not universal, Pidgin English by 1832 in a journal by E.T. Mitchell:

> The string of low slang words which the natives nearer the colony suppose to be our language, while our stockmen believe they speak theirs, was of no use here. In vain did Dawkins address them thus: *What for you jerran budgerry white-fellow? Whitefellow brother belongit to blackfellow.*

Although it is very difficult to see how a multilingual situation could spawn a Pidgin English (or even "generate" language forms, including some lexical items), it is obvious that extremely complicated situations favor its spread. Baker (1966: 310) estimates that about five hundred "aboriginal" languages were spoken in Australia in the early period of contact with Englishmen.

Except that it is hardly necessary to limit the spread to the Pacific, there is little reason to doubt the formulation by Turner (1966: 203):

> New Guinea Pidgin, or Neo-Melanesian, is a regional variety of a large group of pidgin languages spread by traders through the Pacific.

Even a cursory acquaintance with Atlantic varieties of English, however, makes one want to discount Turner's further statement:

> Some of its vocabulary, e.g., *pikinini* 'small', *save* 'know', reminds us of its origin in regions where Portuguese and Spanish Pidgin languages were already formed.

That Portuguese (or, as Alleyne [1980] insists, Iberian) Pidgin preceded Pidgin English and was significantly related to it seems hardly beyond question. That such shipboard varieties have to be formed in "regions," however, seems to be excessively restricting. It would not seem to be necessary to assert any radically different principles of genesis for the pidgin languages, but it would seem to be necessary to keep in mind how much faster the sailors of the sixteenth to nineteenth centuries moved around than did the Europeans of the centuries when the Romance languages were taking shape.

There is little denying the astonishingly wide spread of certain Portuguese vocabulary. Ramson (1966: 109) reports a record "by Threlkeld in 1834 [which] includes three non-Australian words, *gammon, piccaninny,* and *strike-a-light.*" Although Ramson finds it "less convincing, he cites Dawson's 1831 *Present State of Australia*:

> "I tumble down pickaninny here . . . Belonging to me all about, massa; pose you tit down here, I gib it to you . . ."

It hardly seems to be necessary to argue for the ubiquitous spread of *pickny/pickaninny*; some American linguists may be inhibited by their memory of the latter form in the American racist vocabulary, but Stewart (1970) has dealt in what should be final fashion with such scruples.

There is now general recognition that the languages with which Pidgin English came into contact added positive features to it; the "simplification" beloved of theorists applies rather to a few superficial features, like personal endings of verbs and the "loss" of concord. Especially when the contact language passes the "reconnaissance language" (Naro 1978) or "ship's jargon" (Stefánsson 1909— stage, it may take on structural features which hardly seem to be part of that irreducible minimum of morphology which one would attribute to "language universals." Turner (1966: 203) describes a well-known case:

> The use of a general numeral and adjective suffix seems to have its origin in the Chinese classifiers or 'itemizers'. Chinese Pidgin used to distinguish animates, e.g., *wan fela man* from inanimates, e.g., *wan pisi tebal*, but in later Chinese Pidgin and in Neo-Melanesian *-fela* or *-pela* alone is used.

The Chinese, who seem likely to have had the Pidgin well before the Australians, could have been a great influence in spreading it. Only slightly later than they came to the California gold rush in North America, Chinese gold seekers went to Australia in large numbers in 1860. Pidgin English spreads rather easily from one national or ethnic group to another; since it is not a national language, no one thinks of its origin as he presumably would if using French or Portuguese, or even Standard English, for lingua franca purposes. That kind of neutrality makes it an especially useful language of wider communication in a place like New Guinea, where there is "a multiplicity of peoples, divided by language, belief, and custom" (Read 1965: 7).

The spread by "traders" in the Pacific poses no great emotional problem for historians of Pidgin English, even though it is rather well known that "native" populations were often exploited. Objective treatment of Atlantic contact varieties is made somewhat more difficult by the inescapable fact that the *slave* trade was involved there. But many of the circumstances of contact were strikingly similar. Early relations between the Africans and the Europeans were largely confined to coastal areas; the word *inland* in the title of Francis Moore's 1738 book *Travels in the Inland Parts of Africa* is completely accurate only because the Gambia goes a long way inland. Sailors who operated there brought the cultural and linguistic adaptations of the maritime trade to West Africa just as surely as they carried them to the China coast and to New Guinea. And the Africans just as surely exerted their own subtle influence on the international contact language as did the Chinese and the Melanesians.

"Local" variation is undeniable, but the basic unity of the "European" pidgins seems only slightly less certain. The Europeans' lack of perception in lumping together West Africans from tribes of great diversity in culture and language is to be deprecated as a moral issue, but surely the history of the language(s) is not to be rewritten so that the whole process will seem more virtuous. These vastly different African tribes — some of them bitter enemies in their home continent and even in some cases in the New World – were welded together in the process, giving a cultural and linguistic homogeneity among Black citizens of the United States, in spite of great diversity of tribal origin, and a basically similar cultural pattern which has fascinated anthropologists ever since Herskovits. The West Indianist has to smile a little at the belated discovery of a "creole speech community" by Labov (1980).

The earliest observers seem to have assumed that the "peculiarities" and "misapplied 'phrases" of the Pidgin English they heard were characteristic of their own area alone. The very bizarreness, to the ears of one who spoke ordinary English, seemed to argue for limited spread. The "bizarre" forms were, however, quite widespread in the pidgins. For example *bob* (p. 18) seems to be related to *bobbery,* defined as 'every kind of noise, disorder, quarrel, disagreement, fuss, and trouble' in Leland (1900). Apparently widespread in eighteenth-century Pidgin English, it exists but is comparatively rare in Krio today. *Tief* 'steal' is attested even in the Black English of Canadian Negroes, and a West Indian proverb appears in many forms similar to

Tief tief tief, God laugh 'If a thief robs a thief, God laughs'

Holm and Shilling (1982) call this use of *tief* Atlantic.

As many pidginists (especially Woolford and Washabaugh 1983) are now showing, such usages are not "misapplied phrases" but examples of what Hancock (1973) called lexical creativity in a pidgin situation. Among such adaptations attested by Owen (1833) are *two mouth tacken* 'stockings with two mouths' for what Owen called *drawers* and most Americans today would call *underwear* or *shorts.*

Since it is still necessary for pidgins – now almost alone of languages – to be "defended" in terms of communicative adequacy, it is not surprising that their possible importance and even any minimal contributions in long-familiar language situations, like the early American colonies, should be underestimated or even denied completely. But studies of the processes of language contact even in those situations are not impressive for their thoroughness. In fact, very little has been said about them at all – unless one counts the familiar lists of loanwords (Marckwardt 1958). Along the way, a lot of other important material has been left out of consideration.

The sea and the frontier were possibly the two most important factors in the early history of the Europeans on the "new" continent. Neither has been given adequate attention in our language histories, and what they have in common has hardly been calculated. The early colonists consistently underestimated the distance between the two oceans, often taking large rivers as the beginning of the Pacific. They felt themselves to be – and were – in a maritime environment. Attitudes and strategies associated with the sea, even some of the words and phrases, were kept as the language of the sea became that of the frontier. A few observers like Washington Irving (1895 I: 54) have made statements showing perceptions about the relationship; he called the Canadian *voyageurs* "the lords of our internal seas, and the great navigators of the wilderness."

Maritime Pidgin English appears to have had an independent existence. An African-flavored version was used in the slave trade and early established itself on many parts of the West African coast. Gilman (1979) makes a strong case for African influence as the base of the pidgin, but it seems impossible, given all the similarities in the Pacific varieties, that the influence of West African languages was the exclusive factor. The widespread nature of the pidgin on the Atlantic coasts of the Americas seems to be reflected in the development of English creoles which established themselves more or less well from Nova Scotia to Surinam. In the former Dutch Guiana, the most extreme varieties of English Creole extant, with a very heavy degree of African influence and a great deal from Portuguese, became the languages of the "bush Negro" tribes and a medium of exchange with the Indians of the interior (de Goeje 1908). Runaway slaves transmitted their own variety of English to the Seminoles in Florida and probably to Indian tribes elsewhere in the United States; the Plains Indians were making extensive use of Pidgin English by the end of the eighteenth century.

As in other areas of European expansion, the natives of North America were forced to learn some form of lingua franca, depending upon which European groups they happened to need to cope with. (For pre-European Indian lingua francas, see 126-127.) Eyewitness accounts exist, although in characteristic fashion they do not examine the Indians' pidgin-learning practices very carefully, apparently thinking they took place by a kind of magic. Bradford (1896) gives possibly the first account of the language variety used by Indians in contact with the English:

> . . . about the 16th of March [1621], a certain Indian came boldly among them and spoke to them in broken English, which they could well understand but marveled at it.

The circumstances of pidgin acquisition can be inferred rather easily:

> At length they understood by discourse with him, that he was not of these parts, but belonged to the eastern parts where some English ships came to fish, with whom he was acquainted and . . amongst whom he had got his language.

It further turned out that Samoset (the best the Pilgrims were able to make of his name) knew another Indian named Squanto (otherwise Tisquantum), "who had been in England and could speak better English than himself."[4] This Squanto had learned his English after having been carried away by "one Hunt, a mr. of a ship, who thought to sell them for slaves in Spain." He had managed to return to Massachusetts in 1618, possessed of a knowledge of some variety of English.

In this case, it is very important that a widespread Maritime English would have been available to at least a few Indians like Squanto, no matter how unfavorable the conditions under which they acquired it. The circumstantial evidence is reinforced by the almost immediate occurrence of documented use of American Indian Pidgin English.

The use of West African Pidgin English by slaves who were brought to the same areas seems highly probable (Dillard 1972a, 1972b). To some extent, the records tend to indicate that American Indian Pidgin English was even earlier (Goddard 1977, 1978); that is, earlier attestations exist for AIPE than for WAPE. It is surely giving too much weight to the accidents of transcription, however, to assume that WAPE was not around for some time before being written down. Again, the casual attitudes of the Europeans, who kept the records, are crucial and complicating factors.

In Massachusetts in the 1640s, where African slaves were already present along with Indians and Europeans, Pidgin English was also clearly present. Religious historian Winslow (1968) described the streets of Roxbury, Massachusetts, in the following terms:

> something to sell, something to buy, brief exchange in half-understood Pidgin English or Pidgin Algonquian phrases, not quite friendship, not quite conscious fear on either side: mere acceptance.

Vocabulary items like *netop* 'friend' have not survived, but they were widely current in the AIPE of Massachusetts and passed into eighteenth-century American English. An item like *strawmere/stomany* may give twentieth-century linguists more problems than it gave seventeenth-century colonists. The word occurs in attestation from Massachusetts around 1675 (quoted in Kittredge 1912: 354):

> "Umh, umh, me no stawmere fight Engis mon, Engis mon got two hed, Engis mon got two hed, if me cut off one hed, he got noder, a put on beder as dis."

Leechman and Hall (1955) suggested weakly that the word might be from *stomach,* but Drechsel (1976) makes clear that it belongs with *stomany* 'understand'.

Other words, like *squaw* and *papoose,* were picked up in the same area and carried across the continent by frontiersmen. Along with the Indian language forms went pidginisms like *no-see-'em* 'a minute biting fly or midge of the family Chrionomidea', attested from Maine in 1848 (Thoreau) to the Pacific in 1949.

The study of English borrowings from Amerindian languages has apparently been predicated on an Indian language-English bilingualism which hardly existed in any large population of the British immigrants. Pidgin English, however, provides a much better attested vehicle for transmisson.

Vocabulary borrowings from Indian languages have been treated over and over again, and further examination seems unproductive. Counting only individual vocabulary contributions from the Indian languages, there was a "relatively minor" impact on American English. Krapp (1925: I: 106) counted "all of the words of Indian origin, exclusive of personal, place, and other proper names . . . that had at some time or another greater or less currency as English words" and came up with more than 230. More recent treatments tend to reduce that number, and therefore the consequences of the contact with Indian languages.

A surprising exception is that of Marckwardt (1958: 32). He quoted an unidentified "estimate" by which "functional changes, compounds, and derivatives" made "less than fifty loan words" into "some 1700 words" in present-day English. Functional changes make *tomahawk* and *skunk* not only nouns but verbs; compounding makes *poke* into *pokeweed* and *pokeberry* and *hickory* into *hickory leaf borer, hickory horned devil,* and *hickory gall aphid.* Derivation adds *caucusable, caucusdom,* and *caucusified* – used, one would think, only by speakers with an overwhelming interest in politics – to *caucus.* The word *opossum* is an insignificant enough addition to English (except for fans of *Pogo*), but it can expand into a phrase like *playing 'possum* 'pretending to be dead or [in certain sports] out of the competition'. The name of the marsupial also figures in *possum haw* (Viburnum prunifolium), *opossum mouse* (a pigmy species of the marsupial), *opossum rug* (the skin of an Australian species), and *opossum shrimp,* a special type of crustacean. More terms and institutionalized phrases than now survive were probably current in the nineteenth century. Mackay (1846-7) reports Philadelphia Blacks touting travelers to hotels for which they work with words like:

... Barnum's – only house in town – rest all sham– skin but no 'possum ...

Perhaps even more important than such uses of Indian words, however, were phrasal compounds in English which would not have developed apart from Indian influence. Two obvious examples are *take up the hatchet* and *bury the hatchet.* In July, 1775, the Continental Congress wrote "A Speech to the Six Confederate Nations" with terms borrowed from Indian English (Ward 1952: 143):

This is a family quarrel between us and Old England. You Indians are not concerned in it. We don't want you to take up the hatchet against the King's troops. We desire you to remain at home and not join on either side, but keep the hatchet buried deep.

The use of *great* or of some approximate synonym, as in such terms as *great water* 'ocean' and *great canoe* 'ship', is another feature of Indian-influenced American English which is no less authentic for having figured in innumerable fictional treatments. Bishop (1971: 74) reports how earlier, when four Indian chiefs had been sent to an audience with Queen Anne in London, Peter Schuyler, the mayor of Albany and the protector of the Mohawk, had provided them with an address in Standard English interspersed with translation phrases from their own language. The chiefs accompanied the presentation of belts of wampum to Anne with the words:

As a token of our friendship we hung on the kettle and took up the hatchet. . . .
Messengers crossed the Great Water in great canoes.

Etymons for 'big' or 'great' are very much a part of the entire pidgin-
creole syndrome. *Grandy,* a Pidgin English adaptation of Iberian, figures early
in WAPE and in "Negro" Pidgin in the United States (Dillard 1972: 146) and
heap (somehow related to Papiamentu *hopi,* it would seem) soon replaced it
in AIPE. The Pidgin English attestations of the Seminoles frequently show
ojus in the same function.[5] Holm and Shilling (1982) call derivational compounds with *big* Pan-Creole, a position partly adumbrated by Dalby (1972).
Owen (1833: 184) quotes the people of Cape Lopez:

Toby Philpot! . . . You no sabby him; got big mouth, big eye, and big belly; all de
same as big cappen of frigate me tell you of.

Every *big* in the speech of these "natives" may refer simply to size, but *big eye*
in West African English and varieties influenced by it can mean 'greed' (Dalby
1972) and West African English *big day* is 'holiday'.

Melville's *Typee* (1846) represents Polynesians using Pidgin English,
including *big canoe* 'ship'. (This is, in fact, the second such entry in the
Dictionary of Americanisms.) The same novel represents the Polynesians
using *big hog* 'horse' (also in their own language *puarkee nuee*). It is, of
course, possible that Melville learned the terms in the United States and then
projected them into Polynesia. It is also possible that American sailors carried
a term characteristic of Indian English into the maritime trade. The Dictionary of Americanisms cites *big* "Indian talk or with reference to Indian usage
as *big canoe.*" But there is a strong third possibility: the maritime term "came
ashore" in various land areas, especially in the speech of now-displaced
ethnic and language groups who were compelled to use some contact variety
in order to meet the new communicative needs as their own societies col-
lapsed. The first listing of *big canoe* in the *Dictionary of Americanisms* seems
rather clearly Indian, but it is only thirty-three years before Melville's use.

The practices of the historical dictionaries, closely tied to the phonological
shape of words or to their graphic rendition, tends to obscure semantic
relationships. Like Shakespeare's Fluellen, whose Welsh accent could make
(Alexander) the Great into "the Pig," users of the contact varieties were
obviously able to make use of more than one of the words indicating great
size. A characteristic variant of *big canoe* occurs in Washington Irving's
frontier novel *Astoria.* An Indian had beheld in great dismay the coming of
a "big war canoe" under British colors. He reported

King George . . . has sent his great canoe to destroy the fort.

As a virtually automatic substitute for *big, great* occurs in the significantly
stereotypical *great white father* as early as 1808 (OED Supplement).

This particular interchange was no peculiarity of any geographic area.
Wullschlägel (1856), in a work which appropriately for my purpose does not

distinguish the Creole varieties of Surinam, shows many compounds with both *bigi* (i.e., plus enclitic vowel) and *gran* (where, according to Alleyne's [1980] optional nasalization rule, the final /-N/ does not break the canonical syllable pattern). With what seems to be a secure feeling for the language, Wullschlägel placed hyphens in examples like

etwas Bedeutendes, wan bigi-sani
Feierlichkeit, wan gran-sani
Begehrlichkeit, bigi hai-fasi

as an indication of their institutionalized compound quality. It would be hard for one familiar with Black ethnic slang in the United States not to compare *wan bigi-sani* to (*It ain't no*) *big thang*; the initial consonant difference and the enclitic vowel in *sani* seem rather obvious matters of regular phonological change.

Wullschlägel has a number of such phrasal compounds in *bigi* or *gran*. Great numbers of them occur in American English, whether attributed to "Indian" usage or not. Wentworth and Flexner (1975) list 63 *big* compounds. Farmer gives *big* "used not only as regarded quantity, but quality also" and asserts that "what in England would be called fine old whiskey and brandy would, in America, be designated *big whiskey,* etc." He further lists (omitting attributive uses) *big bugs, big dog* (*of the tanyard* and *with the brass collar*), *big drink* 'the Mississippi', *big figure* (to *go the big figure* is to "go the whole hog"), *big meeting* 'protracted religious meeting', *big money* 'a large sum', *big trees* 'Sequoia gigantea'.

In its "Indian talk" examples, the *Dictionary of Americanisms* cites *big canoe, big chief* (cf. Surinam *granman*), *big hearts, big lodge, big medicine, big river, big talk, big village, big water.*

Place names in *big, great,* and *grand* are very numerous in the United States, and an Indian etymon like Choctaw *četo* is found, especially as the second unit in compounds, very frequently. Harder (1976), who considers the element "descriptive of size," lists at least 69 place names beginning with *Big* (not counting repetitions), 49 with *Grande* or *Grand* as the first element (thus eliminating obvious examples like *Rió Grande*), and 25 beginning with *Great.* Harder also (personal communication) cites the spread of such names across the United States and comments upon the lack of similar names in England. Whether a "natural," spontaneous development or something transmitted, an almost dummy element homophonous with a word meaning 'large, of great size' has figured strongly in American English.

Clearly, the picture of language contact in the formation of American English cannot be adequately handled in terms of a relatively small number of borrowings only. The Indians had a profound effect on the lives of the early European settlers, and the Indians and associated groups had an equally profound effect on at least certain aspects of the language. Neither has generally been acknowledged, perhaps due to the white man's chauvinism (Forbes 1962).

Strangely, early commentators — perhaps not burdened with the "scientific" apparatus of word counts — felt that Indian influence on colonial English was great. The American periodical modeled on the British *Lounger, The Port Folio* "By Oliver Oldschool, Esq." for August 1, 1801, objects that a certain Americanism "can be found in no *English* author. It is undoubtedly the growth of the wigwam, and is a vicious scoundrel and true American word." It does not really matter whether the word in question, *lengthy*, is technically an Americanism by the somewhat artificial procedures of the branch dictionaries or not. The point is that early observers thought of some American usages as "wigwam words" and enjoined Englishmen not to use them.

As the maritime varieties spread to the West, they frequently came into contact with Spanish and with French — as well as occasionally with a trade language like Mobilian Jargon — and borrowed from them and competed with them as a lingua franca (R. Bowman n.d.)[6] A typical incident in the West is that reported by Adams (1931), in which some cowboys have tried to communicate with Indians in a version of Spanish only to have one of the latter say, "in fair English, 'Me buck.'"

These were the language varieties of mobility, in a country in which, with rare exceptions, mobility has been the rule. They were used by unsettled, non-prestigious people who in most cases had neither property nore respectability. Their records are not so detailed as those of the landowners and more respectable citizens. In fact, it is amazing that they left any records at all. But the very circumstances of their movement seem to argue for a greater importance for them than the records would indicate. They provided the extreme variations from a coastal regularity which was extremely noteworthy in the beginning (see Chapter III). In popular parlance, the "bad" English of the frontier came from the innovations and contacts of these mobile representatives of maritime practices put ashore.

NOTES

1.   Workers on Pacific English pidgins apparently do not have the trouble that Drechsel and Makuakani, or researchers trained in the reconstructive tradition, seem to have. Clark (1983: 14) writes:
    A number of grammatical and lexical features occur in examples of South Seas Jargon from a sufficiently wide range of sources to justify the belief that the language was not simply a series of local ad hoc systems but that it possessed a continuity of tradition throughout the region and the period.
    The only problems which this statement would pose for those who have looked at the worldwide unity of the "Sabir" pidgins are the identity of "the region" and

"the period." If we extend the Pacific to the Atlantic and the Indian oceans, and the period from just before the beginning of the nineteenth century to perhaps as early as the beginning of the seventeenth, we have a picture of just what Drechsel and Makuakani find so threatening. The features listed by Clark are *all same* 'like', the future time adverbial *by and by*, *plenty* 'much, many, a lot', *suppose* 'if', *too much* 'very, very much', and the contrasting pair *very good* 'good' and *no good* 'bad'. Except perhaps for the last pair, all of these can be found in Africa, North America (American Indian Pidgin English), and the China Seas (Chinese Pidgin English). In most places, preverbal *bin* as an anterior marker can be added. The transitivizer *-um* or *-im* has, equally, an almost worldwide distribution, as do some vocabulary items like *savvy, palaver,* and *pickny* or *pickaninny*. Many of these features occur over and over again in citations throughout this work, *passim.*

2. Elsewhere, however, Alleyne (1980: 110) reports, "The first layer of European vocabulary replacing African vocabulary apparently came from Portuguese . . . in many instances Saramaccan displays a Portuguese word where Njuka and Sranan have an English or Dutch word." That the pidgin itself should have been Iberian (apparently Alleyne's conclusion), and later influence have come from more ordinary Portuguese, is by no means improbable.

3. 1917 reprint of the 1827 edition. As in many cases in this book, I owe this citation to William A. Stewart.

4. Smith (1953: 188) identifies this Squanto further:

    In 1605 George Weymouth . . . explored the Penobscot and Maine coast, returning to England with five captive Indians, one of whom was to achieve fame as Squanto, the savior of Plymouth.

    Smith also reports (1953: 189) that Squanto was a passenger on a ship with John Smith, who had promised to return him to his people on Cape Cod.
    The apparent discrepancy between "one Hunt" and Weymouth could probably be resolved in a number of ways, the most likely being that Hunt was a member of the Weymouth expedition.

5. Rebecca Bateman (n.d.) gives attestations of *plenty* in the same function.

6. Cf. the mixture of Creole English and Spanish in Central America (Holm 1983, esp. 101-111).

Chapter III

On Leveling and Diversity in the Early Period

The traditional position, stated by Kurath (1972: 65) concerning the derivation of American regionalisms from British regional dialects, is supported by very little evidence, and such evidence as is presented is limited to the domains of the farm and the home. Atwood (1953) expressed reservations about arguing that a certain form had been brought to an American colony from a particular area of England, and Francis (1961) also voiced reservations. Kurath's data would not impress very many linguists if the presentation came from a linguist of lesser reputation: *cade* or *cade lamb* 'pet lamb', *hap* 'quilt', and *whicker, nicker,* and *whinny* — the last three words for the noise made by a horse and all but the last regionally restricted in both England and the United States. Kurath himself (1972: 67) asserts that only with "precaution" can these "hand-picked" examples function as "tracers" of population movements or migration routes. Phonetically, Kurath finds that "all varieties of American English largely conform to the phonemic pattern of Standard British English" but that American English has a trend toward "eliminating structural differences and tolerating substructural regional features" (1972: 69). It is not really necessary to quibble about the apparent equation of "structural" and "phonemic." The failure to find any clear-cut correlations between even "sub-structural" features of American English and British dialects means that the region-to-region framework of the history of American English can hardly be supported by phonological considerations. The alternative which has apparently been resisted at all costs may be the one that must be selected: give up on the notion that British regional dialects hold the key to the history of American English.

All of the British immigrants to the Americas encountered a linguistically complicated situation — although, obviously, not the same kind of complexity faced by non-British immigrants — but the *Mayflower* passengers, who are often chosen as the illustrative example (Marckwardt 1958), provide especially obvious exceptions to the alleged principle that unmodified British dialects came to the Americas.

Regionally, the Pilgrims may have been more homogeneous than others of the generally heterogeneous British emigrating groups. The seat of that little congregation which eventually led the way across the sea to New England was in Scrobby in Nottinghamshire. A majority of the members came from that general geographic area. Thus the Pilgrim group may at one time have actually represented the closest thing among the American immigrants to a regional British group with its dialect. A great deal of complication occurred, however, even before the group set sail for the Americas. And language contact, even on the other side of the Atlantic, was a major part of that complication.

What is commonplace to historians but apparently forgotten in general works on American English is that the Pilgrim group went from England not directly to the Americas but to Holland. Leaving secretly to escape religious persecution, they came to Amsterdam in 1607 and 1608. Dissatisfied with Amsterdam, they moved on to Leyden in 1609. Although their early descriptions of the latter city are glowingly enthusiastic, they soon found reason to feel that they should leave. The specific reasons are rather interesting for language history; according to Andrews (1919: VI, 6):

> They were breaking under the great labor and hard fare; they feared to lose their language . . .

Although the fears of "losing their language" may have been exaggerated, it is difficult to believe that some linguistic change was not present to motivate such a feeling.

The fear of losing the language may well have been a real one. Plooij (1952: 91) points out how much assimilation the Pilgrims underwent, in a comparatively short time, in Holland:

> It is curious to notice how these English people became absorbed in the Dutch, so that not only their names have acquired a Dutch form but even their signatures have the Dutch form.

Assimilation to Dutch ways also increased the associations with the sea that all American immigrants had to have to one degree or another. Coleman (1881: 44) describes the situation in the following terms:

> Their children were marrying off among the Dutch, and were seeking their fortunes in the four quarters of the globe, wherever Dutch ships sailed. They were making no converts. Their sect was too obscure to attract notice, and it was rapidly losing its identity.

Thus when the *Mayflower* went to the New World Carrying 202 passengers, representing two-thirds of the entire Pilgrim population, it carried passengers who could hardly have represented the regional dialects of England at all — much less in pure form.

What happened to the Puritans, linguistically, in Amsterdam and Leyden cannot be determined with any precision on the basis of the documents. For the rather large number who went to sea with the Dutch, some learning of one of the maritime contact varieties was certainly possible — although, again, not presently demonstrable. At the very least, the group had been exposed to a great deal of language contact before it ever sailed for the New World.

The limited records we have from the Pilgrim fathers reflect neither much Dutch influence nor appreciable British "regional" dialect survival. According to Fisher (1919: 192)

> The diaries and letters of colonial native Jerseymen, the pamphlets of the time, and John Woolman's *Journal* all show a good average education and an excellent use of the English language.

Excellent use of the English language is the kind of phrase that recurs over and over again in the records of observation of the speech of North American colonists, including the Pilgrim fathers. *Excellent* in this case cannot mean 'like a native', since every observer knew that all of them were native speakers of English. A closer examination of the actual attestions from the colonial period may help to explicate this term *excellent*.

Although the Plymouth Rock pilgrims were neither an especially large nor an especially significant group except for their symbolic value, the Massachusetts Bay colony which they founded was the most flourishing of the North American colonies. Gipson (1960: 4) calls it "the heart of old New England in 1750, as in 1650." Boston was the greatest commercial and shipping center outside the British Isles themselves. Trade was carried on with the West Indies and Honduras Bay, the Madeiras and Canary Islands, and with other areas. Rum made from molasses from the French sugar-producing islands in the West Indies was the basis of trade with the southern colonies, the Indians (furs), Newfoundland (fish), and the "Guinea Coast" of Africa (slaves and gold). The contacts of Massachusetts merchantmen with Chinese and Chinese Pidgin English have been indicated in an earlier chapter (p. 19). Massachusetts Bay men were engaged in fishing for mackerel in the beds to he south of the Strait of Canso and in whaling in the subarctic regions. Although it is not usually publicized, slavery was no stranger to Massachusetts in the eighteenth century (Green 1942), and the pidgin or early creole stage of the Black English Vernacular has some of its first attestations from that area (Dillard 1972b).

Like the Massachusetts Bay group, the generality of that part of the new "American" population that came directly from England was diverse and heterogeneous. Far from being an isolated group preserving a regional culture, they were subject to great numbers of influences from elsewhere. The two factors that brought them together could be called the desire for religious freedom and the seeking of economic opportunity – what could less respectfully be called the desire to get rich quick. As William Eddis wrote on June 8, 1770 (quoted in Read 1933: 323):

> The colonists are composed of adventurers not only from every district of Great Britain and Ireland but from almost every other European government.

For many of them, particularly for the New Englanders, the maritime trade remained, for a long time, the principal enconomic element in which they would operate. They were, thus, never really beyond maritime influences on their language.

Kurath himself (1972: 70) points out how

> Later changes . . . are confined to coastal areas: eastern New England, South Carolina, and the states along the Gulf of Mexico.

The "states along the Gulf of Mexico" would presumably include Louisiana, and New Orleans – of which more shortly. Kurath asserts (1972: 70) that

> The most important of these changes is the development of an additional free vowel owing to the loss of postvocalic /r/ as such in the latter part of the eighteenth century.

One aspect of this important change is the change /ə r/→/ə y/ in words like *bird, shirt*, etc. Berger (1980) takes up this change and shows its spread to be intimately connected with the cotton trade between New Orleans and New York City. The same coastal change has been reported for Liberia, Watling Island in the Bahamas (cf. Holm and Shilling 1982: viii-ix), and Charlotte Amalie, St. Thomas, in the U.S. Virgin Islands.

In the early colonies, there were not only strong associations between ports like New Orleans and New York but close connections between the colonies and the West Indies. Holm (1983: 95-7) recounts how

> . . . later English Puritans maintained a colony on nearby Providence Island . . . until 1641, when they were routed by the Spanish. The Puritans had established trade with the Indians on the Miskito Coast (probably Sumu of Chibchan stock), presumably using a simplified form of English.

To some degree, the relationship of an individual continental colony to the islands may have been stronger than its relationship to another colony. Bailyn (1955: 84) reminds us:

> The colonization of the American mainland had been part of the same movement of European expansion that led to the peopling of the West Indies, and New England grew up, as it were, in the company of these island dependencies. The Pilgrims at one point had considered settling on the Caribbean Coast of South America.

Nor were the early New Englanders guiltless in the slave trade for which the West Indies and the Southern states are generally if unfairly remembered; Bailyn (1955: 84) provides another reminder:

> And it was in that year [1643] that the first triangular slave voyage in New England history was made by one of the vessels trading in the Canaries, for she returned via Barbados where she bought tobacco "in exchange for Africoes, which she carried from the Isle of Maiao." This voyage introduced New England to the trade in Negroes; but more important was the fact that its success stressed to the merchants the rich possibilities of commerce with the West Indies.

There is hardly any denial that pidgin and other maritime varieties were in use in the West Indies during this period. The New Englanders would certainly have been exposed to such influences in that trade.

It has been traditional to consider the British-derived colonists somewhat artificially, as though they had been – unlike other known immigrant groups – a self-contained unit, apart from any other influences. This was, in fact, the very opposite of the true situation. Even if such isolated groups did exist, however, it is not unreasonable to suppose that they would undergo some linguistic change. The most obvious type of change is leveling, in the sense of C.–J. Bailey (1973). Outside of the Americas, dialect leveling is a fairly well-studied process, as in the case of *koiné* Greek or the Israeli Hebrew *koiné* (Blanc 1968). To cite this groups as evidence that the process is a linguistically natural one is not, however, to claim any great similarity insofar as the leveled dialect of American English is concerned.

The evidence of contemporary attestations seems to show that the leveling of dialects must have reached its fullest extent in the middle of the eighteenth century. Dialect leveling tendencies must have been present, however, from the very first period of American immigration. Şen (1974) pointed out that the English of the early American colonists contained a lot of (apparently intra-personal) variation with little regional distribution or social stratification.

Insofar as the dialect history of the United States has dealt with purely regional (British and American) and not social factors, it has been motivated by lofty and even noble ideals, Kurath (1936: 19) wrote that

Folk speech and cultivated speech are very close together in recently settled and democratically organized America.

It is virtually impossible to avoid noticing that *recently settled* leaves out the American Indians and that a dialectology founded on such high innocence would not given an adequate account of the English of the descendants of West African slaves. To deal with social dialects in American English has been almost unavoidably to involve oneself in controversial political issues. See especially Stewart (1970).

It has been widely asserted that the great majority of American immigrants came from the southeast of England, that – perhaps by sheer bulk of numbers – they dominated the speakers of any other dialects present. Kurath traces the idea through early writers like Whitney (1868), Sheldon (1892), and Krapp (1925). These writers came at a time when the very legitimacy of American English was in question, when it was necessary to combat the notion that Americans had "corrupted" the English of the British Isles. In combatting those notions, the work of Kurath, Sheldon, Whitney, Krapp, and others was of course praiseworthy. The trouble is that the corollary derivation from British "regional" dialects tended to replace the older idea of American English as "bad" English – and to become dogma in the same way.

This claim that speakers of British regional dialects brought a great amount of dialect diversity to the Americas, enough to form the basis of all subsequent dialect diversity in the latter, was made by Kurath (1928) and reiterated in Kurath (1965). One of the consequences was that it was necessary to recognize in the speech of American Blacks an incredibly elaborate amalgam of dialect features from areas of England like East Anglia; McDavid (1967) made a rather strong claim to that effect, supported by little evidence and rebutted by Dillard (1968). It would apparently be necessary to trace Black (and some Southern white) "injective" or "implosive" consonants to British dialects where there is no other record of them, since according to Kurath:

> Features of pronunication now more widely current in rural areas than in the great population centers derive either from British folk speech or from earlier stages of S[tandard] B[ritish] E[nglish].

These suppositions are made, however, on far from conclusive demographic data. Fiske (1889: 63) provides a confident statement which has often been cited:

> While every one of the forty counties of England was represented in the great Puritan exodus, the East Anglian counties contributed to it far more than all the rest. Perhaps it would not be out of the way to say that two-thirds of the American people who can trace their ancestry to New England might follow it back to the East Anglian shires of the mother country . . .

An early critique by Orbeck (1927: 141-2) voices a number of caveats against such conclusions. He objects:

> If he [Fiske] meant to include in his "Eastern Anglian counties" Essex, Middlesex, and London as well as Norfolk, Suffolk, Cambridgeshire, Northamptonshire, Bedfordshire, Hertfordshire, it appears that his statement of the origins is more than borne out, for in the above distribution slightly over 71.52 percent of those who can be traced are represented as coming from those counties. If Essex, Middlesex, and London, however, are not included in the term, the number that came from "the Eastern Anglian counties" was 47.44 percent.

The clause *who can be traced* is important here, since only a relatively insignificant portion of the original emigrant group can be traced with any confidence to their places of origin in England. Orbeck concluded:

> On the whole the above tabulation shows a slightly more scattered distribution than Fiske's statement indicates. The center of the exodus was certainly Suffolk, and omitting London the two adjoining counties, Norfolk to the north and Essex to the South, came next.

Phonological evidence, according to Orbeck (1927: 141-2), tended to be even less clear than demographic. Consider these statements from his *Early New England Pronunciation*:

> The only piece of evidence about which there can be little doubt is the characteristically Kentish, southern, and southwestern past participial form. On the other hand, there are no examples of the southern development of OE *ie* . . ., no forms indicating the characteristic southern voicing of final *f* and *s*, no clear examples of western *u*, and the few forms that can be explained as reflecting Kentish e (from OE y) can also be otherwise explained.

or

> Some few features may possibly be of dialectal origin, but they are at present so widely current that it is altogether impossible to determine which dialect is to be credited with them. There are isolated forms here and there which may be explained on the basis of the northern dialects. On the other hand it should be pointed out that there are no examples in the records of the northern plural. Nor

is there much evidence for the typical Scotch scribal habit of representing vowel length by orthographic *i*.

One of the most explicit of Orbeck's demonstrations concerning the dialectal origins of the English of towns in Massachusetts comes not from the town records but from Bradford's oft-cited *History of Plimouth*:

> The northern *sall* occurs in Bradford's *History of Plimouth*; Bradford himself, however, came from Southern Yorkshire within the provenience of the midland dialect.

Overall, Orbeck seemed to be stumbling toward the reluctant conclusion that an immigrant to the colonies did not necessarily bring the dialect forms of his birthplace with him; for a theoretical presentation concerning this same matter, see Leopold (1959).

Despite the uncertainty of the demographic data, Orbeck continued with what would have been expected in the reconstructive tradition of his time; he asserted that "we are to look for the roots of eastern Massachusetts speech in the eastern dialects of England" (1927: 145). But he also reported (1927: 143) that he had not found the expected distributions, even for the limited area of three seventeenth-century towns in Massachusetts:

> Altogether it does seem strange that the records, written by men from various parts of England, should reflect a form of speech so uniform in character and so near the standard speech of England.

His conclusion (1927: 142) is rather hesitant:

> On the other hand early New England speech may reflect the east midland and, to a lesser extent, the southern and southeastern dialects, the main features of which had in the early modern period blended to form the basis of standard London speech.

Dialect uniformity and dialect blending are matters that Orbeck was almost reluctant even to discuss, but they may be the considerations upon which a more modern description can be based. The main addition needed, one would think, would be some consideration of class dialects; Orbeck even provides some speculation on that matter:

> Nor is it impossible to think that some of the divergencies ennumerated above may reflect not regional but class dialects, some features of which may have passed into regional dialects not too remote from London.

Unlike Kurath (1965), Orbeck did not discuss any evidence for "r-lessness" in the town records and diaries. He did record (1927: 9) some cases where "[r] is confused with [l]." One should avoid the temptation to discuss extreme possibilities here. It could even be concluded that the speech of the earlier Puritans had been influenced by some foreign language, like Chinese, one or another of the American Indian languages, or some West African language. Alleyne (1980) considers "l ~ r alternation" a "major [phonological] process identifiable as [a] West African continuity," although of course he would insist upon a context in which, on other grounds, Afro-Creole varieties may have existed. Proponents of "natural" (i.e. apparently, biologically conditioned) change are quick to point out that [l] has only one feature not found in [r] . It would obviously be absurd to suggest that a familiar relationship like Mary~Molly provides evidence for one of these extreme theories. It is, however, apparent that some not wholly justified conclusions have been based upon documents like the New England town records.

Although the emigrant groups from England came chiefly from relatively low social strata, they did not transplant the British class/caste relationship. Integral groups (the lord of a manor, say, and his peasants) did not migrate together. The old social order was broken up — as a matter of rather clearly articulated policy on the part of the emigrants. Although those who seek to leave a certain social group and way of life characteristically take with them more than they think in subconscious behavior patterns, social conditions from England were not reconstituted in any precise way in the colonies. Except for professions, one's status in which might be preserved, and other special relationships like membership in the underworld, the social dialects of England probably had as little *direct* reflection in North America as did the "regional" dialects.

These are matters of basic importance to the history of American English. In the conventional formulations, geographic and social factors, whether synchronic or diachronic, are always stated as the most important in dialect distribution — with a primacy given to geography perhaps because of its seniority in the field rather than for its greater explanatory power. Until works like Blanc (1954), Gumperz (1958a and b), and Labov (1966, 1972a and b, 1973) began to emphasize factors like ethnic group loyalties, relationships within a peer group, social stratification, and even religious factors, it was perhaps essential that the language historian using dialect data should think primarily in terms of regional distribution. It has often been the case that the regional dialect distributions of about 1900 in England (approximately the data of Wright's *England Dialect Dictionary*) have been taken for the ca. 1600 distributions that would have affected the colonies (assuming that regional distributions in the mother country do affect those distributions in the colony, which can be called in question). One caveat was entered, almost without notice, by Francis (1961), who hypothesized that the Atlantic seaboard regions had probably been "dialectal melting pots." Even the most prominent dialect geographers themselves (McDavid and McDavid, 1951) have criticized the unevenness of training and the lack of systematic procedure of earlier scholars like Wright, whose geographic statements have however been accepted almost without question.

Occupational and religious affiliations were the most likely ones to be maintained in the colonies and to exert influence on colonial behavior patterns, including language. Since religious freedom was often the slogan that united a group of immigrants, and since formerly separated and persecuted groups came together in the name of religious tolerance, the linguistic influence from religious groups could have been of paramount importance.

The most obvious example was the Quakers, whose *thee* and *thou* addressed to all persons was only one of their offenses, which included refusing to remove their hats in public (Fisher 1919: 3). Religious terminology was indeed much used in some parts of the colonies. In 1744, Scottish physician Alexander Hamilton was struck by the talk of *justification, adoption, regeneration, free grace, reprobation, original sin* and "a thousand other such chimerical knick knacks, as if they had done nothing but studied divinity all their leif-time" Hamilton felt that the equivalent would be like speaking "Greek, Hebrew, or Arabick" in England. Nevertheless, there is little evidence that either the Quaker pronouns or the religious terminology had a major effect on American English.

With such farfetched attempts to isolate striking differences, it can almost be concluded on negative evidence alone that the primary characteristic of the period was leveling. A number of British commentators made statements that can be given that interpretation; the examples are from Dillard (1975), with an obvious debt to Read (1933).

William Eddis, who had naively expected the contrary from such a heterogeneously derived group, wrote on June 8, 1770:

> The language of the immediate descendants of such a promiscuous ancestry is perfectly uniform, and unadulterated; nor has it borrowed any provincial, or national accent, from its British or foreign parentage.

Eddis found another characteristic of American English striking enough to be worthy of note:

> This uniformity of language prevails not only on the coast, where Europeans form a considerable mass of the people, but likewise in the interior parts, where the population has made but slow advances; and where opportunities seldom occur to derive any great advantages from an intercourse with intelligent strangers.

One may question the sophistication of Eddis's observations, but it is striking that almost identical reports came from other observers, like the Reverend Jonathan Boucher seven years later:

> It is still more extraordinary that, in North America, there prevails not only, I believe, the purest pronunciation of the English tongue that is anywhere to be met with, but a perfect uniformity.

In the same year, Nicholas Creswell wrote:

> [the inhabitants of the American colonies] in general speak better English than the English do. No Country or colonial dialect is to be distinguished here, except it be the New Englanders, who have a sort of whining cadence that I cannot describe.

Because we know that certain other population groups, like the West African slaves (Stewart 1967, 1968; Dillard 1972) and the North American Indians (Leechman and Hall 1955; Miller 1967) were speaking such divergent varieties as pidgin English, such statements may at first seem puzzling. But it soon becomes clear that Boucher, Creswell, Eddis, and the others who made similar statements were reporting on the only Americans about whom they knew anything — the white descendants of Englishmen and those few other whites who had completed the process of assimilating to the norms established by those Englishmen without difficulty. The more complicated general picture begins to emerge when the observations of a few more wide-ranging commentators are considered.

The Reverend James Adams wrote a linguistically sophisticated work for his own time (1799). It embodied a kind of perception about the relationship between spelling and the spoken word that was unknown among even professional linguists before the late 1950's; he saw, for example, the derivational relationship between *bile* and *bilious*. (One need hardly credit Adams with any influence on Chomsky and Halle [1968] to appreciate his insight, especially if one remembers some of the things that were being written about English spelling by phonological specialists of the early 1950s.) Adams reported not only the leveling among the British immigrants but something of the condition of the West African-derived slaves:

> The Anglo-Americans speak English with great classical purity. Dialect in general is there less prevalent, except among the poor slaves.

Others, with no such structural insights as Adams, saw the same things:

> It is a curious fact, that there is perhaps no one portion of the British empire, in which two or three millions of persons are to be found, who speak their mother-tongue with greater purity, or a truer pronunciation, than the white inhabitants of the United States.

Not only did this commentator, the London editor of *Ramsay's History of the American Revolution* (1782), show some awareness of the differences in the "colored" population, but he went on to offer an explanation for the "curious" uniformity among the whites (Read 1933: 324-25):

> This was attributed by a penetrating observer [identified by Read as perhaps John Witherspoon, whose weekly papers called "The Druid" had appeared in Philadelphia in 1781] to the number of British subjects assembled in America from various quarters, who, in consequence of their intercourse and inter-marriages, soon dropped the peculiarities of their several provincial idioms, retaining only what was fundamental and common to them all; a process which the frequency of or rather the universality of school-learning in North America, must naturally have assisted.

Like many others, this "penetrating observer" attributed to parents and to teachers what children were largely responsible for; but this is so universal a fault that we can hardly have expected anything better from him. Even modern linguists have been much too inclined to look to the home and the schoolroom rather than the playground for language influence.

These early reporters, whatever their limitations as sociolinguists might have been, were not limited in their geographic experience of the colonies.

They characteristically tried to get the overall picture – perhaps because many of them hoped to write a book about the upstart nation-in-the-making when they got back to England. John Harriot, a military man who came to America in 1793, asserted that American English was

> better spoken by the whole mass of people, from Georgia to Quebec, (an extent of country more than 1200 miles), than by the bulk of people in the different countries of England.

The reliability of such observers is of course open to question; no credence could perhaps be given to any one of the above in isolation, and even a larger group could be questioned if the situation they report were not perfectly feasible historically and supported by other data. Historical linguists, who have to depend somewhat upon texts no matter how powerful they believe their reconstructive formulae to be, have typically avoided such explicit statements, preferring to use only those commentators who can be labeled "orthoepists" or to depend upon such controversially reliable indicators as the identity or near-identity of rhyme. The rather well-known tendency to strain after differences might be invoked in favor of the reliability of these statements of similarity. Exaggeration may well be present, but it seems likely that there *was* a striking uniformity which provided the material for popular overstatement.

The major early observations of extreme variation are made in terms of ethnic, not geographic, groups. Some, like Adams and the anonymous London editor, commented overtly on the "dialect" of the West African-derived slaves. Others, like John Davis (1809), C.W. Janson (1807), and J.F.D. Smyth (1784), reported relatively long stretches of slave speech. A quite large number of others quoted American Indians who were very obviously using Pidgin English. The Reverend Jonathan Boucher also saw some influence from European languages in "some scanty remains of the croaking idioms of the Dutch, still observable near New York" (Boucher, quoted in Read 1933).

But aside from the slaves, whom the caste rules may have prohibited from using the leveled dialect even if they had any real opportunity to learn it, and some still-unassimilated white ethnic groups, the speakers of English in the North American colonies had achieved the kind of unity that astonished European visitors. In the light of studies like Gumperz (1958), it is not at all surprising that victims of a caste system like the slaves and the generally ostracized Indians should not have participated in the major dialect development of the first three-quarters of the eighteenth century. Somewhat different factors need to be invoked to account for ethnic and cultural dialect maintenance among the Pennsylvania "Dutch", the Cajuns of Louisiana and the Chicanos of the Southwest.

The use of phrases like "good English" and "English of great classical purity" by eighteenth-century observers has tended to confuse the issue in language history. If the standards of the twentieth-century classroom are projected onto the earlier century and the very different situation, "good English" will be interpreted as involving the "proper" choice in such shibboleth situations as *ain't/aren't/isn't* and *The game was called due to rain* versus *The game was called because of rain.* Very many of those who see fit to deal at all historically with American English (e.g., Daniels 1983) are concerned with refuting allegations that Americanism is somehow going to be the "death" of English (Newman 1966, 1974; Simon 1980). Usually these last think of the "imprecise" or "illogical" nature of written expression by such people as college students and sportswriters, especially as contrasted with English literary greats of the past.

To make such considerations the issue would seem to be to attribute some kind of special colonial affinity for the literary dialect of British English. Actually, the American colonists had relatively little access to books and little opportunity to master the kind of literary dialect used in the London coffeehouses and by the magazines of the time. Colonial America was certainly not any such case as medieval Iceland, where there was a flowering of literary creation in an overseas colony. *Good* obviously means, when applied to the colonial context, something quite different, and it must be interpreted in a different frame of reference.

In fact, the statements quoted tend to show a recognition of colonial American English as without recognizable, stereotypable social or geographic features. To Americans, such statements — especially about region — have constituted virtual heresy. To even fairly popular and utilitarian British writers on language (Schur 1973), however, it has not been strange to observe a "universal" form of English, "not tied to any particular region of country."

For those immigrants to North America who enjoyed the advantages of such liberty as was provided in the new environment and were not tied to other languages, access to the leveled dialect was possible within one generation. (This is not quite the same as a statement that the leveling process was complete one generation after the first group of English-speaking immigrants arrived.)

At this point, it is necessary to part company with on-the-spot observers, especially insofar as their explanations are concerned. It is easy to credit the accomplishment of leveling — and it was so regarded — to the schools, school-teachers, and to other adults, but it is pretty clear that the dynamics of peer-group interaction among children had a great deal more to do with it. Their greater influence is generally recognized, although not without some cavils (Kazazis 1970). Stressing "the range of data that the child copes with," C.-J. Bailey (1973: 24) makes a general statement that surely applies to the eighteenth-century colonies: "The result is that what the child produces gets more and more restricted to the exemplar of his peers (unless he is isolated from them) . . ." Attribution of such influence to peers is a fairly new thing in linguistics, and it was largely absent from the work of the Linguistic Atlas of the United States and Canada (Underwood: 1974). Significantly if amusingly, an early statement about linguistic assimilation in the United States (Hills 1928) is placed in a school context:

> The explanation is of course the public schools, where the American children americanize the immigrant children in a rough and ready fashion, making life miserable for them if they ever use a foreign world.

In this dialect-mixing situation, what colonial American children did was to "make life miserable" for any other child who used not just a word but even a pronunciation or a syntactic feature that could be observed to be peculiar, individual (in terms of the group norm) or unusual. Whatever dialects their parents may have retained when they came to the Americas, the colonial children leveled their dialects for the best of reasons – if they did not, they would have to bear the ridicule of their peers.[1]

Such processes are by no means peculiarities of the colonial situation or of the United States as "melting pot." Leveling processes, although not traditionally given much emphasis in historical linguistics, are observable almost everywhere there are dialects in contact. Meillet (quoted in Hills 1928: 432) wrote of how "Parisian" as a dialect of French was disappearing, "drowned" in what he called a *koiné* because of the influence of "provincials" and "foreigners." It is likely that certain class/caste factors may inhibit the leveling process. But those factors were absent from the British immigrants to the thirteen colonies to at least the degree that an extreme case of leveling took place.

The American colonies were not alone in this process insofar as the British emigrants were concerned. We find evidence of the same process in Australia. As is well known, the British who emigrated to that continent came from many parts of Britain. The preponderance of convicts among the early settlers is familiar and no doubt exaggerated; responsible historians have pointed out that the "convicts" were often people guilty of no greater crime than being poor and in debt. But the Australian immigrants, like the American, were not upper class; they came, like the Americans, from all parts of the mother country. According to Eagleson (1982: 432), "the full range from broken and pidgin English to a complete mastery of standard English" is found in Australia.

There are reports about the language of the early population of the continent "down under" that parallel those of the thirteen American colonies. James (1892: 336) wrote that the English of the Australians was

> free from any distinguishing accent or provincialisms to a marvellous extent

and there are other such statements quoted in Bernard (1969).

Leveling in Australia did not, obviously, produce a result identical to that of America. It was the pattern that was analogous, the merging of items rather than the items merged. The resultant dialect is quite unlike American English; attempts have been made, not very convincingly, to trace it to Cockney (Hammarstrom 1979).

Such dialect differences as are described in Australia are of Broad, General, and Educated Australian (Mitchell 1946, quoted in Baker 1966) rather than of regional differences. (In the usage of some, *lectal* rather than *dialectal* would be used for this kind of variation.) Bernard (1969) describes the failure to find regional differences, apparently despite some rather elaborate attempts. Eagleson (1982: 425) comments, "That studies so far have not uncovered regional varieties in Australia is to some degree surprising, given the isolation of early settlements." (Turner 1966: 15) asserted rather, "The nomadic life of the rural workers helps to explain the uniformity of Australian speech and idiom." Clearly, "isolation" and a "nomadic life" are only apparent contraries; just as clearly, neither condition has as its necessary result either uniformity or diversity.[2] As will be argued later (especially Chater VI), the most "nomadic" groups of Americans were deeply involved in the basic change from uniformity to diversity in the English of the United States.[3]

It is true that Witherspoon (1791), writing fairly late in the period at which the leveling is postulated to have taken place, reported that "being much more unsettled and moving frequently from place to place, they [Americans] are not so liable to local peculiarities either in accent or phraseology." It is important here not to assume, as is in fact regularly done, that "local peculiarities" and "diversity" are synonymous.

Very possibly, if it had not been for the many immigrating European ethnic groups, the Spanish, French, and other colonizing groups, and certain of the language contact factors to be discussed in the following chapters, American English would have attained and maintained a geographic uniformity of dialect distribution equal to that of Australia. As it was, however, there were a great many social, economic, and political differences, some of which, like the changing attitudes toward slavery, eventually correlated with region.[4]

A later immigrating British group came to the Appalachian Mountains in the eighteenth century – considerably later than the main group discussed here. They may well constitute a kind of exception to the processes under discussion here. See the chapter by Blanton for a more complete treatment.

Characteristics of the leveled dialect are, of course, not recoverable from statements about "good English," "striking uniformity," and the like. Contemporary observers are much more likely to record oddities – or what they perceive as oddities – than they are to describe what they mean by "regularity." It is also to be cautioned that *approval* is not to be identified with *perception of regularity*. (The case of Australian provides an interesting corroboration of this point.) When, roughly, nineteenth-century disapprovers of American English began to point out its flaws, they were often quite specific as to the forms to which they objected. It would be natural to assume that those "objectionable" forms were something different from those which motivated observations of "astonishing regularity." Taken from a broad viewpoint (say, from the termini of 1725 and 1825), such an equivalence is probably valid. Some care should be observed, however, in evaluating individual statements about specific forms.

After the period of British-visitor approval was over, great changes occurred in the comments. It is as dangerous, to attribute this perception of "bad English" to any one factor as it is to do so with statements about "good English." However, indications of something afoot begin to appear in reports like that of John Davis of Salisbury, Wiltshire, who published his volume of American travels in 1803. This viewpoint is attributed to a Mr. George, an Irishman living in the States:

> The English language is not written with purity in America. The structure of Mr. Jefferson's sentences is, I think, French; and he uses words unintelligible to an Englishman.

Two basic causes of this lack of intelligibility suggest themselves: retention of archaisms (even of *koiné* forms from the leveled dialect) and new developments in America. For the latter, the frontier may have special importance.

Among the structures pointed out by other disapproving visitors, the combination of a verb with a preposition (*build up, look out, see to, think about*) is rather prominent. Such combinations were not unknown even in Old English, but they become more commonplace in British English in the eighteenth century than ever before. Shortly thereafter, however, the construction lost favor in British English, which has relatively few examples compared to American English today. British philologists have usually considered expressions like *lose out* to be Americanisms, and even the OEDS is not very clear on some of these compounds. We find *brew up* traced to 1916 but glossed 'make tea'! The OEDS lists *lose out* as "orig. U.S.", with its first attestation in 1858, but has nothing on *lose out on*. The nounal *hurry-up* is called "orig. U.S.", but there is nothing on verbal *hurry up*, which strikes me intuitively as primary. We still have nothing authoritative on *start up, write out,* and *visit with*.

Considered in the context of change from uniformity to diversity, other words often adduced provide no such conclusive evidence as they have been considered to do when regarded as archaic survivals in American English. Davis (1803) cited three of the most frequently discussed words: *lengthy, belittle,* and *illy*. These, along with *banter, boatable, budge, calculate* ('suppose'), *carry on* ('raise a pother'), *chaperon, cleared, coax, collide, creek* (one meaning of), *derange* (verb), *enterprise* (verb), *expect* ('think, suppose'), *extinguishment* ('extinction'), *fall* (time of year), *feaze* (verb), *fellow country-men* ('countrymen'), *fib, fop, fun, gap, guess* ('suppose, opine'), *influential, immigration, loan* (verb), *lynch, memorialize, notify* ('inform'), *portage, progress* (verb), *reckon* ('suppose, opine'), *row* ('a disturbance'), *spur, square* ('a small city park'), *statehouse, stingy, suppose, swap, swimmingly, talented, touchy, upland,* and *wobble* were among words once condemned as Americanisms but to be found in earlier citations from British authors. (One is hardly allowed to speculate that they might have been re-innovated in the United States.) In the latter part of the eighteenth century, Hume disapproved of Franklin's use of *pejorate, colonize* and *unshakeable* — all of which are apparently "Briticisms" in the narrow sense, it making little difference to this approach that the first is hardly in modern usage whereas the other two are so familiar that it is hard to imagine how anyone could object to them. *Bamboozle* practically screams out to be called an Americanism, but it does not qualify — in the narrow sense, anyway.

Not surprisingly, some of the specific objections of the nineteenth-century British traveler were without philological foundation. There is no doubt, however, that he identified what he heard as something other than "classical purity." Hamilton (1833: 127) wrote:

> Though the schoolmaster has long exercised his vocation in these states, the fruit of his labours is but little apparent in the language of his pupils. The amount of bad grammar in circulation is very great; that of barbarisms enormous. Of course, I do not speak now of the operative class, whose massacre of their mother tongue, however inhuman, could excite no astonishment; but I allude to the great body of lawyers and traders; the men who crowd the exchanges and the hotels, who are to be heard speaking in the courts, and are selected by their fellow-officials to fill high and responsible offices . . .

Charles Dickens, perhaps the most famous literary man of all these observers, evidences the same kind of attitude. In Chapter II of *American Notes,* Dickens reports that he did not understand what a waiter meant when he asked if Dickens wanted his dinner *right* away. In Chapter XXVII of *Martin Chuzzlewit,* Martin does not understand the American Mrs. Hominy when she asks "where do you hail from?" Not only "tobacco spitting sailor[s]" but "drunken Texan[s]" and "frontier badmen" were quoted as examples of the "go ahead Yankee" in *Household Words* (Lohrli 1961: 84). DeQuincy also made frequent unfavorable comments about Americanisms. According to Hollinger (1948: 204) his

> . . . use of ridiculous speech is often directed to some satiric end in keeping with his Tory patriotism; his attitude toward the United States and its speech is part of that early nineteenth century derogation of American culture.

A host of other early nineteenth century writers joined in that derogation. John Witherspoon, a transplanted Briton who was president of Princeton and author of "The Druid," a column in the *Pennsylvania Journal and Weekly*

Advertiser (Philadelphia), sounded the alarm as early as 1781, although many of his criticisms of current American usage were pedantic. Humphreys' 1815 play *A Yankee in England* contains a "Glossary of words used in a peculiar sense . . . by the inhabitants of the United States; including new-coined American, obsolete English, and low words in general."

Somewhat like DeQuincy, whose pseudo-Latin word for *in American* seems to have been *Kentuckice,* the Americans themselves regarded the frontier as the special locus of "bad" English. We have statements like that from (not yet General) Ethan Allen Hitchcock about the "prominent defects [in language] among our border people, West and South" (1833: 127). Hamilton asserted, however, that even by the educated and respectable class, the commonest words are often so transmogrified as to be placed beyond the recognition of an Englishman." Hitchcock himself, who knew the frontier, related incidents in which Blacks and Indians used Pidgin or Creole English. He also recorded the case of a Mr. Foreman, a Cherokee, who was engaged in translating the Bible into English. This gentleman is not further discussed, but his "pure English . . . free from border defects," must have been one of the rare successes among the generally inefficient attempts to teach the Indians English (Hitchcock 1930: 51).

Like Hitchcock, Albert D. Richardson (1865) heard "bad" English in the less thickly populated areas "beyond the Mississippi." He wrote:

> In Kansas [about 1858] one heard the slang and provincialisms of every sector of the country, beside some indigenous to the soil.

Like Hitchcock, Richardson reports frequent conversations in Pidgin English and in creolized or partly decreolized varieties. Bourke (1892: 89) described the English of Arizona when that state was characteristically frontier:

> While the language of conversation [at a dance] was entirely Spanish, the figures were called off in English, or what passed for English in those days in Arizona.

The lingusitic experiences of the frontier promoted anything but uniformity and classical purity. Perhaps the first relatively large group to be exposed to polyglot influences away from the civilized coastal areas were the fur trappers or "mountain men" (see   -   ). The trappers of British extraction were often in contact with French Canadians, who Washington Irving in *Astoria* said "with difficulty could reconcile themselves to the service of the new-comers, so different in habits, manners, and language from their former employers" (I: 51). Irving asserted (I: 52):

> Their language is of the same piebald character [as their dress], being a French patiois embroidered with Indian and English words and phrases.

Comments from all sections of the frontier tend to agree about the language. Better-known fiction writers who dealt with the West, like Bret Harte and Mark Twain, attest the strangeness of the speech of the frontier. There is wonderful evidence of the mastery of the latter in the short story "Buck

Fanshaw's Funeral." But, like most literary artists, Twain concentrated upon suggesting the flavor of frontier language rather than reporting it exactly.

More prosaic sources give tantalizing, if not fully adequate, glimpses of what the language was like. Marcy (1866: 383) wrote of the Southwest:

> The people inhabiting the rural districts of the Southwestern states have . . . adopted many words and phrases which are not found in Webster's Dictionary or sanctioned by any of our grammarians. They have also taken the liberty of changing the pronunciation of many words in such a manner, and applying them in such novel ways, that it is almost impossible for one not familiar with these peculiarities to comprehend their meaning in ordinary conversation.

Like a lot of other amateur observers, Col. Marcy was better at recording his impressions than at detailing what made up "these peculiarities." He quoted a Texas hostess, from the dense forest region of the northwestern part of the state:

> "Well, now, stranger, my ole man he ar out on a bar track, but I sort-o-reckon maybe you mought get to stay . . . that there war narry shaw of vittles in the house barrin some sweet taters and a small chance of corn."
> "What my name mought be," "she knowed a heap of Massys (Marcy) in ole Massasip . . . me an him allers 'lowed that them thar Massys was considdible on bar and other varmits."

In addition to *bar*, Marcy gave *do* for *door, char* for *chair, star* for *stair,* and *crap* for *crop.* Perhaps more significantly, he quoted Indians like Black Beaver, a Delaware interpreter who had moved from the Northwest, in American Indian Pidgin English. One Negro woman spoke a partly decreolized version of Plantation Creole (1866: 377). According to Marcy's evidence, the dialect of the frontier whites was not identical to either of those varieties, although it is quite possible that there had been some influence.

During the same period, similar reports were coming from other parts. World traveler Sir Richard Francis Burton (1860: 207) was astonished at what he heard in Salt Lake City:

> . . . every word was apparently English, but so perverted, misused, and mangled, that the home reader would hardly have distinguished it from high Dutch; e.g., "I'm intire made as a meat axe; now du don't, I tell ye; say *you,* shut up in a winkin, or I'll be chawed."

Jargon is the term most usually applied to such "bad" language, so that the worker on contact languages is resigned, even a little gleefully on occasion, to using popular descriptions like *Chinook Jargon* (or *patois*) which the populace has hung on the varieties he works with. My position (Dillard 1975, 1976) is that the intuition of such observers may well have had a certain validity, in that they tended to apply the same (imprecise) term to comparable linguistic varieties. Nothing is to be gained, at least, by assuming that they were always wrong.

As Hamilton indicated, although hardly with the prospects of success that he granted them, the schools and allied agencies struggled valiantly against this "deterioration" of the English language. It is unlikely that they had any consciously formulated standard, although there may have been some remnants of the impossible dream of talking like upper class Englishmen. In retrospect, given the nature of the enemies they were struggling against, it is impressive that the forces of linguistic "respectability" succeeded even as well as they did.

By the end of the eighteenth century, statements about the diversity of American English were as commonplace as observations of its uniformity had been a few decades earlier. But recognition of diversity was not approval — quite the opposite, in fact. Attempts to eliminate variation and restore uniformity, whether or not motivated by eighteenth-century grammatical theory, tended to center around the church, the early media, and the schools. The last are the focus of most such attempts; almost everywhere is found "the usual assumption (still pervasive) that New England correctness could (and should) by education eradicate Western crudeness" (Fraser 1982).

Very likely the complex repertories of the speakers themselves, coupled with a feeling of respect for "educated" speech, explain why the relatively uniform dialect was not completely forgotten. One of the models for "culti-vated" English was provided by the Lyceum, which "spread . . . along the line of westward emigration from New England as far as the Mississippi" (Perry 1918: 175). Its successor in this endeavor was the Chatauqua (Slosson 1921: 281). The third, and perhaps even the strongest, was the church. It has been observed that "well into the nineteenth century, traveling preachers continued to be astonished at lack of concern for religion in the backwoods" (Phares 1964: 3). In addition, in many cases the preachers spoke the same dialects as their congregations (Phares 1964: 10-19). But there was some pressure for them to be cultivated and educated — with schools like Harvard and Princeton founded first as institutions for the training of clergymen — and the association of the preacher with his congregation was likely to be more intimate and lasting than that of the lecturer with his audience.

Soon, widely circulated books and magazines presented written models of the uniform dialect. By the time radio became a national medium, it was commonplace that announcers must speak "good" English and only comedians could use dialect — often a stereotyped version presented for comic purposes. After the famous test case of Dizzy Dean in St. Louis in the 1940's, sportscasters were given essentially the same dispensation as comedians. It is almost incredible, however, how much worry went into the consideration of the effect that Dean's "He slud into second base" might have on youthful listeners, and how much debate went on as to whether he would "ruin" the children's English.

The self-image of the speaker of American English, although not precisely accurate, probably has a great deal to do with the preservation of the leveled dialect. It is easy to set up an informal experiment in which American speakers judge themselves to be rather close to the "network" or "standard" dialect they are asked to characterize — or, rather, to describe that dialect as having many of the features of their own speech. Even dialect geographers have been forced to admit this tendency; Atwood (1963: 11) observes somewhat ruefully that "in the United States . . . no one wants to admit that he speaks a dialect."

Network television, despite its well-known inability to transmit Standard English to ghetto children, provides perhaps the greatest reinforcement of these leveling tendencies. Network Standard (Tucker and Lambert 1969) is, of course, not the creation of the television networks but the dialect which the administrators (concerned about having "good" English) demand of regular, full-time working speakers. C. — J. Bailey (1974), like some other students of variation, has raised the objection that nonstandard forms are used on television by "senators and clergy," but this seems a trivial objection. Politicians (Lyndon Johnson is perhaps the most striking example) are superordinated figures not subject to many of the pressures, including pressure toward using the standard dialect, that many less fortunate Americans feel. For a discussion of some members of the "clergy," see p. 226. Rather than Johnson, John F. Kennedy, and Billy Graham, Walter Cronkite, Roger Mudd, Dan Rather, and others like them are the "informants" to be considered. (Perhaps a graduate assistant in the English Department at the University of Texas, Austin, would be more truly relevant than James Sledd.) One would have thought, from listening to the merciless satire of "Baba Wawa" by *Saturday Night Live's* Gilda Radner, that Barbara Walters had no /r/ at all. Listening to her telecast speech, one hears an almost imperceptible weakening of the sound.

In summary, it appears — especially from the documented reactions of on-the-spot observers — that American English underwent a general leveling process, beginning as early as the first quarter of the eighteenth century and continuing well into the last quarter. In the last years of that century, and in the nineteenth, contact with frontier varieties — contact varieties of English and of other languages, and foreign languages spoken by immigrants from other countries — brought such comparatively rapid change as almost to reverse the judgments of contemporary observers.

These tendencies have been noticed before. Read (1933) noted the leveling tendency and its "naturalness" in colonial situations, although he made little of it. Marckwardt (1958: 131-2) noticed the diversity and fitted it into his conception of *regional* diversity. He noted that Mrs. Ann Royall called attention to Southernisms in the second quarter of the nineteenth century, that Dr. Robley Dunglison identified many Americanisms by 1829, that Dickens recognized regional differences in American English, and that William Howard Russell

. . . reporting on Abraham Lincoln's first state banquet, at which he was a guest, mentions his astonishment at finding "a diversity of accent almost as great as if a number of foreigners had been speaking English."

Strangely, it never became the fashion to combine these two observations. Nor was any particular account taken of their chronology. That the observations of leveling tended to be clustered in the second and third quarters of the eighteenth century and the wondering at diversity in the nineteenth (note that none of Marckwardt's examples is before 1829) was surely easy to see, but its significance was apparently overlooked. That the great tides of immigration by speakers of foreign languages and the great movement out onto the frontier were both well under way at the time the changes came to be noted seems both unavoidable and of potentially overwhelming significance.

Leveling tendencies seem to have become less pronounced during or soon after the third quarter of the eighteenth century, for reasons which probably have to do with individual population groups. One of the notable groups which came from the British Isles after that date was the population of the Appalachian mountains, which might then be expected to exhibit somewhat different tendencies.[5]

NOTES

1. Recently, Dulay, Burt, and Krashen (1982: 30-31) have stressed the linguistic influence of peers, above that of teachers and parents.
2. Sharpe and Sandefur (mimeo) report a contact vernacular used by Aborigines resident at Ngukurr (Roper River) and Bamyili (near Katherine) which is referred to as "Pidgin English" but has become creolized. Similar creoles, they state, may be spoken in cattle station areas of the Northern territory. Some speakers, fluent in English, keep English and creole separate; others, less fluent in English, speak a mixture to non-Aborigines, the mixture varying with the speakers' familiarity with English. It is approximately this situation which I would postulate for the American frontier, although apparently the Australian mixture is restricted in scope whereas that of the American frontier would have been general.
3. Eagleson (1982) reports, like other observers, three varieties: broad, general, and cultivated.
4. Greenway (1950: 163-9) points out the similarity between the cattle trade of the United States and that of Australia:
   Working methods are much the same, though the stockman prefers the long stockwhip to the lasso as a general working implement, and likes to leave most of the driving work to this preternaturally intelligent cattle dog.
   In the light of Jordan (1981), the pre-Southwestern American cattle trade may not have had even these differences from that of Australia. Linguistically, the two cattle businesses show a similarity in *waddy* (compare also *puncher*), *squatter*, and *station* (American *ranch* but *station wagon*). Allen (1959: 23) stresses the greater social strength of the American Indian, which made them "better fitted for the ordeal by civilization than the original inhabitants of Australia." He excludes, of course, tribes like the Digger Indians. He also emphasizes (1959: 24) the things which the Amerindians, unlike the Australian aborigines, were able to teach the newcomer. Allen (1959: 26) asserts that "in both Australia and the United States, as well as

in Canada and New Zealand, the whole impact of the frontier upon the original inhabitants conformed remarkably to the same pattern." Like Turner (1906), Allen looked primarily at the *geographic* impact of the frontier. If, as he suggests, the geographic impact in most aspects of life was strikingly similar in the two frontier environments − and if the leveled dialects of English ran quite different courses in the two places − factors other than geography would seem to be needed for explanation. Those factors would surely be social. Allen (1959: 16-26) finds dissimilarities, especially among the non-white settlers. The first non-white group in the United States which he deals with, the Negroes, "furnish the most startling contrast with the composition of the Australian population" (1959: 17). Thus, there seems to be some agreement between Allen's view of the basic demographic influences and my feeling that, although groups like the Spanish, French, Dutch, Amerindians, Germans, Jews, etc., contributed heavily to the different situation in the United States, the great single difference is introduced by the Black population.

Allen (1959: 19) explicitly finds similarities between American Black slavery and penal servitude in Australia. It would seem, then, that the difference is not to be explained by an oppression model (as much as oppression is to be deplored in either country) but by cultural factors − maybe even African cultural survivals and specifically Afro-American adaptation processes.

5.   Lomax and Lomax (1934) report a lecture at Bryn Mawr by a professor of music from Oxford, in which it was claimed that "Since America has no peasant class, there are, of course, no American folk songs." Lomax and Lomax proceed to refute that claim, citing twenty-five types of American folk songs − of which only five have any special regional character.

Early dialectologists seem to have made pretty much the same mistake that the Oxford professor of music made. He had assumed that only "peasants" could have folk songs, and they had apparently assumed that "peasants" would be present where there were dialects. They then proceeded to ignore, largely, the mobility of the American population in general (Pickford 1956).

The Appalachian mountains are prominent in thinking about regional dialects as about a settled, peasant-like group. (See Blanton's chapter, this book.) It is interesting that they are also prominent in the American folk song picture. But surely no one would call them more innovative than the Blacks in their folk blues. Appalachian songs are, rather, known to be full of British retentions, although certain alterations have been made.

Chapter IV

Southern Appalachia: Social Considerations of Speech

The settlement history of Breathitt County in southeastern Kentucky mirrors that of all Southern Appalachia, usually spoken of as an area covering the eastern portions of Kentucky and Tennessee, the western portions of North Carolina and Virginia, and the mid and southern region of West Virginia. The first settlers came to Breathitt County in November 1780[1] and the descendants of those early pioneers still remain – among them the Neaces and Nobles, the Littles and Jetts, the Spicers and Turners, the Heralds and Coombses. A glance at the current telephone directory will attest to that. In fact, names are commonly used by area residents to discriminate between those who are local and those who are strangers to the area, like outsiders.

Jack Weller (1965: 10) cites the discovery of the Cumberland Gap in 1750 as the event that triggered the stream of settlers to and through the Appalachian Mountains, the mountains no longer blocking the move westward. In addition to coming into the area through the Cumberland Gap from southwest Virginia and western North Carolina, settlers came down the Ohio from the Pittsburgh area and across the Big Sandy from West Virginia (McDavid 1980: 97, 98).

The Neeces and Nobles and other families who stayed were, according to Weller, in search of freedom from the restraint of law, order, and a differing culture. They were people who had been "embittered by civilized life in England and Scotland and had come to the mountains in rebellion against the very kind of society which they found already entrenched on the eastern shore" (Weller 1965: 10). Horace Kephart (1913) places their origins as a people in Ireland, more precisely in the six counties of Ulster, where they were transplanted – from England and Scotland – by James I in 1607 to occupy the estates confiscated from the native Irish. There they lived for a century, amid hostile Hibernians who hated them as usurpers, until they too came into conflict with the Crown as their leases on the land began to expire. Persecuted and then evicted, these Scotch-Irish, as Kephart calls them, left Ulster in large numbers "for a land where there was no legal robbery and where those who sowed seeds could reap the harvest" (1913: 361).

Kephart characterizes those who sought out and settled in the Southern Appalachians as "quick witted as well as quick tempered, rather visionary, imperious, and aggressive" (1913: 362), and he attributes these characteristics to their history in Ireland. Their Irish history also explains, according to Kephart, their push into the mountains in the late 1700s, their violent independence, and their distrust of authority; the underpopulated and relatively isolated mountains provided them the refuge that they were looking for. With a common history to begin with, these Scotch-Irish families created what J.L. Dillard calls a "stable American peasantry,"[2] their presence together perpetuating a single racial, ethnic, and linguistic stock.

This cultural homogeneity is further perpetuated by community attitudes which militate against people being "different" from others in the same community. More precisely, people can actually be different in that they can have newer cars, or nicer houses, or more education, but they cannot act as if they think they are different. In other words, within the collective opinion of the community, they cannot put themselves "above" others. Security comes from group approval, thereby signaling group inclusion. I have commonly heard it expressed about someone in the Jackson community that he or she is not at all "uppity" or that someone "talks just like everyone else." The insider/outsider distinction is a manifestation of this group orientation and a source of misunderstanding on the part of strangers to the area who may either try "too hard" to be insiders, becoming patronizing as they try, or who may stand outside in disapproval, approaching real people as if they were Snuffy Smiths or Li'l Abners.

In dealing with Southern Appalachia today, it is often difficult to separate the myth from the reality. The mountain area may appear to outsiders as a world apart. Traveling southeast from Lexington, Kentucky, toward Breathitt County — where the Mountain Parkway ends and curvy, twisting country roads begin — even the place names have a unique ring: Shoulderblade, Mousie, Brightshade, Dwarf, Turkey, Kingdom Come. The highway often follows a creekbed or cuts through a mountain pass. Where the natural terrain provides no space for a road, tons of earth are chopped out to make room. Few houses are visible from the highway, but trails and dirt roads marked by mailboxes lead up narrow valleys, called hollers, where those who own the mailboxes live. Occasionally the kind of house that appears on a humorous postcard, labeled "Home Sweet Home," nestles beside the road, a refrigerator on the front porch, two or three broken-down cars scattered about the yard, chickens pecking the packed earth, a hound dog sleeping by the door, and smoke curling out of the stovepipe chimney. And then again, a mile down the road, a modern brick ranch-style house with manicured lawn reminds the passers-through that this is not a land totally separated in time or space.

The language and culture of Southern Appalachia are often stereotyped by outsiders. Comic-strip mountain characters in the Sunday newspapers wear patched overalls and stovepipe hats, defend their independence from the law with a shotgun, and fuss and fume in nonstandard English. Ghosts and spirits are frequent sources of humor, precisely because they are taken seriously by the hillbilly characters. The myth of the hillbilly, the mountain rube, pervades American humor. The Snuffy Smiths and Li'l Abners are illiterate and ignorant, oblivious to their poverty and isolation. They are figures of gentle and not-so-gentle ridicule.

The language of comic strips captures the attention of readers with dialect spellings of authentic-sounding phrases such as "daider'n a door knob," "a leetle tetched in the haid," and "shif'less skonks" (Inge 1977: 123). The spelling goes on, however, to depict as mountain speech even those pronunciations that in their reading are General American English: "wz" for *was,* "iz" for *is,* "sez" for *says,* "wun" for *one.*[3] These practices perpetuate the aura of separateness and backwardness of the characters, their language, and their culture.

The stereotyping loses whatever humor it may have — when limited to mere comic strips — as real people are hurt by it. L. Davis (1971: 36, 37), studying the educational problems of Southern Appalachian families who move to Chicago, finds that even educated mountain speech "sounds" nonstandard to most northerners, causing native Chicagoans to ridicule the speech of Appalachians. Davis concludes that the pronunciation of mountain speech triggers a stereotyped impression of mountain people as lazy and not to be taken seriously. Employers do not hire them, and, even more tragically, children are stifled in their attempts to learn to read by teachers who misconstrue a child's received pronunciation as "misreading" what is printed on the page.

For learning the language and culture of their own region, Appalachian children are often further penalized on standard tests given by the schools (Wolfram 1977a).[4] Low scores which result from these children interpreting tasks and answering questions according to the rules of their own speech community are interpreted to mean that the children are "linguistically disabled" or "linguistically impoverished" and are thus in need of remedial language training.

Families who go from the Southern Appalachian Mountains to metropolitan centers like Chicago, Detroit, and Cincinnati in search of work assimilate only in part, if at all. In Chicago, for instance, they band together in a narrow, rundown stretch, called Uptown, along the lake and north of the central business district. There they exist packed in small apartments, many of them on welfare. Some return to the mountains beaten by the struggle to keep a job and to feel accepted. Others return out of homesickness. However long they are away, the mountains remain home, the security of kin and culture acting as a formidable magnet.

Those who stay in the mountains also fight a losing economic battle, as evidenced by the plight of Breathitt County residents. Most families in Breathitt County are rural, some living clustered four or five together in tiny communities and others living in homes barely within walking distance of another house. Jackson, with a population of 2,651,[5] is the largest town in Breathitt County and the county seat. The population of the entire county is only 17,004, spread over 483 square miles. It is important to keep in mind the mountainous terrain with its ridges and narrow valleys in order to understand the sparseness of population, the impossibility of farming as a viable source of income, and the visual and often psychological isolation of families from each other. Although rural families in Breathitt County still garden and preserve some of their own food, the number of actual farms has declined dramatically in this century: between 1950 and 1970 alone, the number of farms dropped from 2,738 to 554. Many families who tried to farm for a living couldn't "make a go of it"; the farms "played out" and people gave up trying. Even for those who still try to make a living at farming, it is on a subsistence level. The current annual market value of all agricultural products sold from county farms is $1,322 per farm, compared to a Kentucky state average of $6,155 per farm. Farming on the hilly, rocky slopes and in small patches cleared of timber is simply not economically viable. While many families have stayed put, sociological labels for the Southern Appalachian Mountains have shifted—from that of an agrarian society to a non-agrarian one, from a society of poor farmers to rural poor.

Some county residents whose farms played out looked for work in the coal mines, earning pay higher than they had ever known. What they got in return, however, was a life of physical danger from hazardous mine conditions. Those who escaped mining accidents sometimes contracted black lung disease from years of breathing coal dust. Some also became indebted to coal companies by borrowing against earnings to the point where they entered a life of economic servitude, always earning less than they had come to owe. Anyone who is interested in the damage done by coal companies to the psyche of the people and to the land itself should read Harry Caudill's *My Land Is Dying*, a heart-wrenching account of the rape of Southern Appalachia by coal companies owned and controlled by business interests outside the region.

In spite of some mining jobs, some few who still farm, some government and educational jobs in Breathitt County, most people have no work. Of the 11,832 in the labor force, only 4,102 are employed, a fourth of these as machine operators, helpers and laborers and another fourth in managerial and professional positions. There is a middle class in Breathitt County, as attested to by the 909 employed in managerial or professional positions, but the facts remain that a quarter of all Breathitt County families have an annual income of less than $5,000, half of all adults have no more than an eighth-grade education, and a fifth of all houses have no indoor toilets and/or bathtubs or showers. While the statistics on education, housing, and income lend fuel to the creation of comic-strip caricatures, there is no humor in being poor and ill-educated. Nor are lack of money and education synonymous with lack of intelligence or concern. In Southern Appalachia there live real people with difficult social and economic problems.

In taking an overview of Appalachian language study, one should perhaps begin by pointing out that the language of the southern portion of the Appalachian range has been studied by many students of language and folklore over the last hundred years, although our understanding of it is far from complete. The early linguistic studies, as Wolfram (1977b) documents in an overview of Appalachian studies, focused on the conservation of an earlier form of English. Wolfram quotes Combs (1916: 283) who says:

> The Southern mountaineers are the conservators of Old, Early, and Elizabethan English in the New World. These four million mountaineers of the South from West Virginia to northern Alabama form the body of what is perhaps the purest Old English blood to be found among English-speaking peoples. Isolated from the outside world, and shut in by natural barriers, they have for more than two centuries preserved much of the language of Elizabethan English.

Twenty years later, on much the same note, Beth Alice Owens (1936: 89) wrote:

> Folk Speech in the Cumberlands [a plateau in Kentucky and Tennessee: part of the Appalachians] has a Shakespearean flavor. Like the family names, customs, characteristics, and ballads of this region, it takes us back to good Queen Bess.

In response to Owens' assessment, Davis (1971: 2) points out that the vast majority of those who settled in the southern mountains came from the British Isles in the eighteenth century long after 1604, the year in which Queen Elizabeth died.

Although an occasional linguist still resorts to a romanticized characterization of the speech of the southern mountains as Elizabethan or Shakespearean English, most current linguists show the picture to be much more complex with both linguistic retentions and innovations, as pointed out by Wolfram (1977b). On categorizing a variety of English on the basis of linguistic retentions, Marckwardt (1980: 70) retorts:

> . . . . . acutally it is quite wrong to suppose that any form of American English has preserved the language of the fourteenth or the sixteenth century without any change whatever.

Marckwardt (1980: 87) says further:

> We have found evidence [in American English] of [the retention of relic forms] in the vocabulary, in pronunciation, in inflectional forms, and in syntax. Nor is English the only language in which a colonial offshoot shows a tendency toward archaism. Canadian French reflects features of continental French antedating the revolution.

In other words, all varieties of American English retain features of the earlier language. By picking out archaisms and thereby evaluating the speech of Southern Appalachia as an archaic form of English, even while singing its charming praises, relic-oriented linguists assigned to it a socially stigmatized status which it has never lost. The people and their culture were stereotyped as backward by outsiders to the region, and so was their speech.

The dialect geographers who began work on the Linguistic Atlas of the United States and Canada in 1928 rejected the simplistic categorizations implicit in the work of the relic-oriented linguists. Approaching all varieties of English as equal and valid, the linguists working on the Atlas set out to trace the settlement history of the United States as seen in the patterning of existing dialects.

Appalachian English is not designated a *dialect* in the Atlas work, but the geographical area of the Southern Appalachian Mountains is included in the South Midland dialect area, which is itself subdivided into three dialect areas: 1) the Upper Potomac and Shenandoah, 2) southern West Virginia and eastern Kentucky, and 3) western Carolina and eastern Tennessee. The latter two areas are more central to Southern Appalachia and the second, which includes Breathitt County, is the focus of recent, more comprehensive studies (Hackenberg 1972; Blanton 1974; Wolfram and Christian 1976; Christian 1978), studies which will be referred to later in this chapter. It is important here to reiterate then that not all current linguists agree that there is an Appalachian dialect, distinct from other regional dialects of English. Wolfram (1977b: 95) notes a negative response from dialect geographers to the designation of *Appalachian Speech* as the title of his 1976 study conducted with Donna Christian in Monroe and Mercer Counties, West Virginia.

It is, however, the question of standardness or nonstandardness of Appalachian and other such dialects that has most often drawn attention to such studies. It seems appropriate, at this point, to pull together several of the threads being woven through this chapter: 1) the stereotyping of the language and culture of Southern Appalachia by the public at large, and 2) the simplistic categorization of the regional language by early linguists, and a few later ones as well, looking to confirm notions of Elizabethan or Shakespearean speech. Whether such linguistic studies reinforced public opinion, or whether general stereotyping influenced those interested in language study, is impossible to ascertain; no doubt they are inseparable. To tie up these threads, an attempt must be made to answer the following questions:

Are obvious socially stigmatized features, perhaps some of them relics, unique enough to the speech of Southern Appalachians to set them off from English speakers of other regions—from, let's say, Midwestern farmers or New England fishermen?

And if there can be said to be an Appalachian speech, can it be called a *nonstandard dialect* of American English?

The term *socially stigmatized* and *nonstandard* need to be defined here before going on. Labov (1964: 102) says that a listener reacts to features of a speaker's language which indicate to the listener the social status of the speaker. Labov terms these features *socially significant* and classifies them into three types:

1) social indicators, linguistic items that vary socially, but which have little effect on the listener's judgment of the speaker's status;
2) social markers, items that vary socially and stylsitically among different people and that affect the listener's judgment of the speaker's social status;
3) social stereotypes, items that are overtly commented on by listeners or speakers and which may or may not correspond to actual linguistic behavior.

To illustrate, the speech of hillbilly comic strip characters contains socially stereotyped items such as *ain't* and *plumb* (as in "Yore plumb right"). Features like *he don't* and *they don't do nothin'*, heard everywhere, are social markers. Social indicators in some regions include features like *aunt* /ant/, as opposed to *aunt* /ðɐ̃nt/, and *either* /ayðɔ̃/, as opposed to *either* /iyðɔ̃/. Socially stereotyped items tend to be lexical. Social markers are often syntactic; social indicators tend toward the phonological. The classification of any linguistic item as any of the three types may shift over time. For example, the use in speech of *who,* instead of *whom,* as a relative object pronoun (as in *John is the boy who we saw in the park*) was once a social marker; now, it is at best a social indicator. And most modern grammar books direct students of the language to make the distinction only in formal writing.

Socially stigmatized features, then, are those linguistic items that negatively affect the listener's judgment of the speaker's social status. In Labov's scheme, these are the features classified as social makers or social stereotypes, not those classified as social indicators. Nonstandard speech, then, is speech containing socially stigmatized linguistic features.

To return to the first question—whether many of the same socially stigmatized linguistic features are part of the speech of other regions in the United States or are unique to Southern Appalachia—a geographical comparison of linguistic features classified primarily as social markers can provide an answer. The features chosen are all syntactic ones that would be judged by most speakers of standard American English to make a sentence "ungrammatical" or nonstandard. The features to be compared are first listed below and can be heard in the speech of native-born residents of Breathitt County, Kentucky. The sample utterances come from Blanton (1974) and the numbers in parentheses indicate the informant number in the corpus of that study.

A listing of socially stigmatized linguistic features found in the speech of some Southern Appalachians to be later compared across geographic areas:

1. a 3rd person singular subject with an unmarked verb (no -*s* ending)
   example: *I like a teacher that explain things* (02)

2. a plural subject followed by a verb with an -*s* ending
    example: . . .*me 'n some more boys does* (08)
3. past tense *was* with a plural subject, to be called invariable *was*)
    example: . . . .*before you girls was born* (11)
4. present tense negative *don't* with a 3rd person singular subject, to be
    called invariable *don't*
    example: *He don't like for me to go to ball games* (01)
5. the expletive *there,* contracted to form *there's* and often pronounced
    /ðeyz/, followed by a noun plural subject
    example: *They's big families on both sides* (19)
6. multiple negatives within a clause and across clauses
    example: *I never had nowheres to sleep* (14)
    > *I don't know any of 'em hardly personally I wouldn't
    > think* (13)
7. *ain't* as a generalized negative replacing *hasn't, haven't, aren't, isn't,* or
    am not
    example: *I ain't lyin' to ya son* (15)
    > . . .*but he ain't never heard from it since* (05)
8. *liketa* [liked to] followed by a past tense verb, a form meaning
    "almost"
    example: *I liketa fell over* (03)
    > *We liketa died* (19)
9. the prefix *a-* /ə/ before -ing verbs
    example: . . *if the school ain't a-gonna go on* (21)
    > . .*me 'n my baby boy's out a-hoein' in the garden* (15)
10. a nonstandard use of a past tense verb form, to be called a nonstandard
    preterit
    example: *Lo' no honey. . .I don't know what she ever done with it*
    (19)
    > . . .*'n he come home 'n made chairs* (07)
11. a nonstandard use of a past participle verb form
    example: *she said her parents had gave 'em what they started out on*
    (03)
    > *I had wrote out a little ol' time news* (20)

The following chart, adapted from Feagin (1979: 259), takes each of the eleven features listed above and indicates with an *X* the occurrence of the same feature in the South (among Whites), in New England, the Middle Atlantic states, or the Upper Midwest. The chart shows that all eleven features are found as part of the working class speech of at least two other geographical areas of the United States.

Figure 1. Qualitative comparison of features of speech of Southern Appalachia to the White Southern speech of Northern Alabama, to areas to New England, the Middle Atlantic, and the Upper Midwest. [Sources: Atwood 1953; Labov et al. 1968; Blanton 1974; Allen 1975; Feagin 1979.] Figure adapted from Feagin (1979: 259).

	So. Appalachia (Blanton)	White Southern (Feagin)	New Engl. (Atwood)	Mid. Atlan. (Labov)	Upper Midwest (Allen)
3rd sing. + ∅	X	X	?	X	0
Pl. + -s	X	X	X	X	?
Invariable *was*	X	X	X	X	X
Invariable *don't*	X	X	X	X	X
There's + NP pl.	X	X	X	X	X
Multiple neg.	X	X	?	X	X
ain't	X	X	X	X	X
liketa + preterit	X	X	?	X	?
a- + verb-*ing*	X	X	X	X	X
Nonstand. preterit	X	X	X	X	X
Nonstand. past part.	X	X	X	X	X

X = examples found in source
? = no mention found in source
0 = contrary evidence or circumstantial evidence aginst occurrence

Although quantitative differences in frequencies in the use of socially stigmatized forms may also influence a listener's perception of a speaker's social status, the chart at least shows that there are no qualitative differences in the items chosen for comparison between the speech of Southern Appalachia and that of some other areas of the country. In other words, these eleven linguistic items are not unique to Southern Appalachian speech. (I have termed all eleven items *socially stigmatized;* it should be pointed out, however, that *there's* + *NP plural* is losing its stigma and is probably well on its way to becoming a social indicator and not a social marker.)

Of the eleven items charted above, five are shown by Feagin (1979: 260) in her study of Northern Alabama speech to be older forms that also still exist in Regional British English: *liketa, a-* + verb- *ing,* multiple negatives, nonstandard preterits, and nonstandard past participles. These five archaic forms, which also still exist in Breathitt County, are documented as relics by Feagin thorugh the OED, Visser (1963-73), Wright (1905), and Grant and Murison (1931).

To consolidate an answer to the first question then, the following points should be delineated. First, socially stigmatized features can be found in the speech of Southern Appalachians. Of eleven such features compared, all eleven can also be found in the speech of White Southerners and of residents of New England, the Middle Atlantic states, and/or the Upper Midwest. In other words, nonstandard features of speech, and in fact most of the same ones, can be found throughout American English. Next, relics of older forms of English can be found in the speech of Southern Appalachians. Of five relic forms included in the comparison, all can also be found in a number of other geographical regions. In other words, relic forms are not unique to the speech of the southern mountains. The point to be made is this: focusing on the linguistic differences between regional groups, or between any one group and an idealized standard language to the exclusion of similarities, can lead to unjustified conclusions. The data simply do not support the characterization of the linguistically backward or linguistically different mountaineer.

The second question raised earlier in this chapter—whether the speech of Southern Appalachians can be labeled a nonstandard dialect of English— is much more difficult to answer primarily because of the complexities of what constitutes a dialect. As stated earlier, the dialect geographers working on the Linguistic Atlas place eastern Kentucky and southern West Virginia in one of the three subdialect areas of the South Midland dialect. More recent studies (Hackenberg 1972; Wolfram and Christian 1976; Christian 1978) talk about *Appalachian speech* and *Appalachian English* with more certainty than I as to its existence as an entity. Hackenberg simply assumes that it exists; Wolfram and Christian, and particularly Wolfram (1977b), are more tentative.

First, there needs to be some discussion of what a dialect is before considering whether the speech of Southern Appalachians can be spoken of as *nonstandard*. According to Ferguson and Gumperz (1960: 3), a variety of a language is:

> . . . .any body of human speech patterns which is sufficiently homogeneous to be analyzed by available techniques of synchronic description and which has a sufficiently large repertory of elements and their arrangements or processes with broad enough semantic scope to function in all normal contexts of communication.

A dialect then is:

> . . . .any set of one or more varieties of a language which share at least one feature or combination of features setting them apart from other varieties of the language, and which may be treated as a unit on linguistic or nonlinguistic grounds. (Ferguson and Gumperz 1960: 7)

In short, varieties constitute a dialect and dialects constitute a language. Feagin (1979: 244, 245) uses Ferguson and Gumperz's definitions in her study to argue for Southern White English as a geographical and social dialect, consisting of both a standard and a nonstandard variety.

Judging by the eleven nonstandard features compared earlier across geographical areas, the speech of Southern Appalachians could not constitute a dialect in Ferguson and Gumperz's terms. Not any of the features compared sets it apart. This, of course, does not eliminate the possibility that other features or patternings of features will be found to sufficiently define a Southern Appalachian dialect. The comparison here has been limited to syntactic features; future study might discover phonological patterns that set the speech of the region apart.

There is one other part of the Ferguson and Gumperz definition of a dialect that should be looked at more closely before going on and that is the consideration that varieties of a dialect may be treated as a unit on non-linguistic grounds. This gets to the heart of social dialects where the attitude of group solidarity is an important feature. Ferguson and Gumperz (1960: 7) state that

. . any group of speakers of language X which regards itself as a close social unit will tend to express its group solidarity by favoring those linguistic innovations which set it apart from other speakers of X who are not part of the group.

It is offered here as a conjecture that when more comparative studies are completed across geographical regions and features are perhaps found which do set the speech of the southern mountains apart, it will be on social grounds that we term it a dialect, the cultural boundaries superseding the geographical ones. It may have once been the mountains which set the people apart to develop their culture and speak the language in relative isolation; but it is, in my opinion, cultural solidarity reinforced by economic and educational factors that keeps the language community in the southern mountains intact. The power of group inclusion and the strong distinctions between outsiders and insiders, referred to earlier, are important features of this cultural solidarity.

A further conjecture is that when linguistic and ethnolinguistic studies are completed in the Ozark Mountains of northern Arkansas and southern Missouri, it will be on nonlinguistic grounds —on social grounds—as well as on linguistic grounds that Ozark English will eventually be found to form a set with Southern Appalachian English. Wolfram and Christian are now beginning a linguistic study in Newton County, Arkansas, which will yield data from which such conclusions can perhaps begin to be drawn.

Though there is no proof to establish Appalachian speech as a separate linguistic entity, it is possible to answer with more certainty the question of whether the speech of Southern Appalachians is accurately labeled nonstandard. To attempt an answer, reference will be made here to the speech of a socioeconomic cross section of native-born Breathitt County residents, samples of which were given earlier in this chapter, recorded as part of an oral history project and studied by Blanton (1974) for its linguistic variation in the use of verb forms. The study, carried out within a sociolinguistic framework, analyzed spontaneous speech in order to quantify the frequencies with which certain verb-related features occurred within the speech of any one speaker and within the speech of the language community as a whole. An important assumption within this framework is that a speaker may opt to "apply" a linguistic rule part of the time but not all of the time and that the frequency with which variable rules are applied may be affected by sociological factors such as education and economic class well beyond a speaker's conscious knowledge or control.

To show how often nonstandard features occur in the speech of those in the Breathitt County language community, nine of the eleven features compared earlier are quantified below. The percentages represent the average frequencies of occurrence in the speech of all twenty-two speakers recorded. Two features from the earlier list (*liketa* + preterit and *a* + verb- *ing*) are not included because they were noted but not counted in the original research. The first item in Figure 1 has been refined here into 3rd person singular + ∅ (no -*s* agreement) of verbs other than *be* and 3rd person singular present *is*, used with plural subjects (here called invariable *is*).

Figure 2. Incidence of nonstandard verb-related features in the speech of 22 Breathitt County, Kentucky, residents. The percentage if the average frequency of occurrence of nonstandard forms. The numbers in parentheses are the number of nonstandard realizations of any one form over the total number of times the form occurred—both standard and nonstandard.

	Frequency of nonstand. occurrences
3rd singular + ∅ (not *don't*, not *be*)	9% (47/552)
Invariable *is*	20% (43/215)
Plural subject + -*s*	14% (81/587)
Invariable *was*	58% (106/184)
Invariable *don't*	65% (33/51)
There's + NP plural	82% (146/177)
Multiple negatives	13% (147/1134)
ain't	7% (46/690)
Nonstandard preterit	14% (436/3186)
Nonstandard past participle	13% (117/931)

As shown in Figure 2, only three of the ten nonstandard forms— invariable *was* with 3rd plural subjects, invariable *don't* with 3rd singular subjects, and *there's* + NP plural—predominate over standard English *were, doesn't* and *there are/were*. As mentioned earlier, *there's* + *NP plural* is questionably nonstandard, with more and more speakers who would unquestionably be considered standard English speakers no longer making *is/are* distinctions, although they continue to distinguish between *was* and *were* and avoid contractions with these forms as well. In regard to *there's* + *NP plural*, then, the speech of Southern Appalachians is farther along the continuum of language change; in other words, *there's* + *NP plural* as a predominant form can be termed a linguistic innovation.

Several details not reflected in Figure 2 are worth pointing out here. First, of the 9% third singular subjects with uninflected verbs, almost a third (14/47) are with the verb *seem* in the verb phrase *seem like* and not necessarily with the verb *seem* in other lexical contexts, such as *She seems tall for her age.* I agree with Christian (1978: 170, 171) that *seem like* may simply be a frozen phrase and not actually a productive case of subject-verb agreement difference. The occurrence of *seem like* more often without the subject *it* lends support to this supposition; it is almost as if there is no subject to the verb. Second, of the 20% third plural subjects with *is*, almost a fifth (9/43) are with the collective plural *people,* a correspondence observed also by Christian (1978: 164, 165) in Monroe and Mercer Counties, West Virginia. Since some collective nouns, such as *faculty* and *police,* fluctuate in American English as singulars and plurals without social stigma, the use of *people* among Breathitt County speakers may reflect an extension of the option to use a third singular verb with that collective noun as well. Finally, of the 14% nonstandard preterits, a third (145/436) of the most frequently occurring are *come, done, give, run,* and *seen,* the same ones found by Wolfram and Christian (1976) and Hackenberg (1972) among their West Virginia informants and also found by Feagin (1979) among urban working class speakers in northern Alabama. The fact that so many of the nonstandard preterits occurring in any one person's speech are the very same ones again and again indicates that the formational rule for preterits is relatively static.

While Figure 2 quantifies the incidence of nonstandard verb-related features in the speech of 22 Breathitt County informants as a single entity—a speech community—it is important for the purposes of this discussion to show that there are divisions within the community along educational and economic lines. Given the powerful sociocultural pressures toward group inclusion discussed earlier, these divisions are often subtle and more blurred than in communities without such strong cultural bonds.

Figure 3 below charts these subtle divisions. *There's + NP plural* included in Figure 2 is left out here because it did not correlate to socioeconomic status (including education) in the original study; it is predominantly non-standard for everyone, if in fact it is still valid to call it nonstandard. Invariable *is* and *was* are combined, for the purpose of simplicity, into a category called *nonstandard subject-verb agreement: be.* Invariable *don't,* 3rd singular + ∅ (affirmative), and *plural subject + -s* are combined into *nonstandard subject-verb agreement: non-be.* The latter two categories have also been broadened to include first plural and second person distinctions, which also showed some variation in subject-verb agreement in the original study. This broadening of two categories gives less detailed information about specifics of the language, but it does not change the patterning along educational lines, which it is the purpose of Figure 3 to demonstrate.

Figure 3. Incidence of nonstandard verb-related features in the speech of 22 Breathitt County, Kentucky, residents grouped according to the speaker's education. Percentages are the average occurrence of nonstandard forms within the speech of those in different educational groups.

	low education	medium education	high education
Nonstandard s-v agreement: *be*	12%	8%	10%
Nonstandard s-v agreement: non-*be*	15%	10%	9%
Multiple negatives	16%	11%	8%
ain't	14%	2%	2%
Nonstandard preterit	18%	10%	11%
Nonstandard past participle	20%	13%	12%

Low = 8th grade education only or below
Medium = some high school education only
High = high school graduation only or some college (including college graduation)

In Figure 3, a line is drawn between the column labeled "low education" and the other two in order to highlight the linguistic patterning evident along educational lines. It is interpreted as important that there are no consistent differences in the frequencies of occurrence of nonstandard forms between those speakers with some high school education (medium education) and those who have graduated from high school and have perhaps gone on to college (high education). (In the original study, there were no significant linguistic differences between high school graduates and college graduates or those with some college education; for that reason, those speakers are grouped here.) The patterning evident in Figure 3 I take to be a sociolinguistic division within the community along educational lines. In other words, speakers with more than an eighth-grade education consistently use nonstandard forms less frequently than do those with an eighth-grade education or lower. The most powerful social marker is *ain't*.

Poverty and lack of education are linked in Breathitt County, just as they are everywhere. The poor families in the county are often rural and are often large with six or more children, a combination not unusual either. When the 22 informants whose speech is the subject of discussion here were grouped in the original study according to their locale (rural/living in the town of Jackson), the speech of rural residents showed almost twice as many nonstandard occurrences within the six categories outlined in Figure 3, except for nonstandard preterits and past participles; regarding these two features, the speech of rural residents was slightly more standard (by 2%: 12% nonstandard preterits for rural and 14% nonstandard for Jackson, 14% nonstandard past participle for rural and 16% for Jackson). When grouped by sex, the speech of females was more standard than that of males in four of the six categories; females used more multiple negatives (15% vs. 10% for males) and there was no difference between males and females in their use of subject-verb agreement (both 10%). When grouped by age, there was no consistent linguistic patterning evident among the residents.

A consistently strong patterning does emerge, however, when informants are grouped according to the condition of their housing, a sure but subtle economic indicator in Breathitt County. While a lot of homes may look more or less the same because those with more money do not want to appear conspicuous, what is important is whether a family owns or rents, and whether the house has indoor plumbing. Everyone in the community seems to know these facts about every other family, although social rules prohibit people from knowing each other's income.

When informants are grouped according to housing criteria as they are in Figure 4 below, a clear linguistic pattern emerges. Those who are poor—i.e. live in a house with no indoor plumbing and/or rent the house—are consistently more nonstandard in their speech than those who are less poor—i.e. have indoor plumbing *and* own their homes.

Figure 4. Incidence of nonstandard verb-related features in the speech of 22 Breathitt County, Kentucky, residents grouped according to housing status. Status is determined by presence or absence of indoor plumbing and/or ownership.

	No indoor plumbing and/or rent	Indoor plumbing and own home
Nonstandard s-v agreement: *be*	11%	10%
Nonstandard s-v agreement: non-*be*	19%	9%
Multiple negatives	15%	12%
ain't	14%	3%
Nonstandard preterit	14%	13%
Nonstandard past participle	17%	14%

Although the frequencies shown in Figure 4 are negligible for subject-verb agreement with *be* and nonstandard preterits, the consistency of the patterning across all six categories is strong enough to support the conclusion of a sociolinguistic division along economic lines. *Ain't* and nonstandard subject-verb agreement with non-*be* verbs (as in *he don't know* and *the boys goes*) are the two features most socially stigmatized by those who are not of the lower economic class. *Ain't* is also the one feature of the six most avoided by those with more than an eighth grade education (as seen in Figure 3). *Ain't* can then be called, in Labov's terms discussed earlier, the strongest social indicator among speakers of Breathitt County English.

The data support the conclusion offered here that there are two varieties of English in Southern Appalachia, as generalized from the speech of Breathitt County residents: the speech of the poor and the poorly educated, and the speech of those who are better off both economically and educationally. Each variety is sufficiently homogeneous to be analyzed, in keeping with the Ferguson and Gumperz definition of a variety discussed earlier, and the varieties are discernible only when analyzed against each other. If we define standard English as the variety perceived and upheld by most speakers of the language of a culture to be superior to all other varieties or that variety used by the educated and ruling classes (Fries 1940: 11-13; Francis 1958: 46-49; Wolfram and Fasold 1974: 17-23; Feagin 1979: 3), then we can conclude that there exists a standard Southern Appalachian English spoken by the educated class and a nonstandard Southern Appalachian English spoken by the working class, with the nonstandard exhibiting a higher frequency of certain socially sitgmatized linguistic forms than the standard. It is of no immediate consequence, for the purposes of our definitions here, that standard Southern Appalachian English exhibits within certain frequencies forms that are considered nonstandard when it is matched against the literary standard or the standard of other English-speaking cultures. In other words, it does not change the validity of our definition if a real or imagined standard English speaker in Boston or Carbondale, Illinois, never uses *ain't* and a standard Southern Appalachian English speaker uses it 2% of the time. Standards in speech as well as in behavior are determined by the culture in which they operate.

Conclusions to Dialect Considerations

To conclude and summarize now a long answer to the question of whether the speech of Southern Appalachia constitutes a dialect and, if so, whether it is nonstandard, it is argued here, although it is unproven, that there is a dialect that can tentatively be called Southern Appalachian English. On the basis of cultural solidarity, the boundaries of this dialect are more social, more cultural, than geographical—a consideration which may allow for the inclusion of Ozark English within the dialect boundary when future studies are complete. We will perhaps discover that there exists a southern mountain dialect encompassing the two.

With stronger supporting data, it is also argued here that Southern Appalachian speech is composed of two varieties—a standard and a non-standard. Both varieties contain linguistic features that are socially stigmatized by speakers of some other dialects of American English. Therefore, from outside the southern mountain culture, and when matched against the literary standard of mainstream Americans, both varieties of Southern Appalachian speech can be labeled nonstandard.

One final point of discussion remains and that is to point out why some of the conclusions drawn here are at variance with those in other recent linguistic studies. Wolfram and Christian (1976), using the same data that Christian (1978) later used, set out to study linguistic forms which were considered most divergent from standard English. They consequently chose informants who were socioeconomically of the lower class. Although their studies offer well-documented and highly detailed information on linguistic features found in their corpus, their findings show what they call Appalachian speech to be more nonstandard when compared to the idealized standard than the findings presented in this chapter show it to be. This is obviously because the speakers whose speech more closely approximates the idealized standard were left out. Nor do their studies discern two varieties of Southern Appalachian speech, for the same reason.

Hackenberg (1972) came closer to social distinctions among speakers' use of socially stigmatized forms in his West Virginia study when he concluded that there was a strong relationship between education and linguistic variables related to subject-verb agreement. His study was hampered, however, by his socioeconomic classification of informants according to the education of head of household rather than by the education of the informants themselves. His interest in differences between the speech of his informants and the idealized standard also led him to transcribe only instances of nonstandard occurrence of the various features he studied, except for verb concord and relative pronoun deletion.

Acknowledging the limitations of these studies, Wolfram himself (1977b: 98) says later that

> The study of Appalachian English is also in need of investigation with respect to social class differences. Most of the current definitions are limited to a description of the nonmainstream variety spoken by the lower social classes of the area. . . . Certainly not all the people residing in the region speak what has been described in various studies as Appalachian English. . . . Furthermore, variables such as rural and urban locales need to be integrated into a comprehensive study of social class and language differences in the region.

The hope is also expressed here that those researchers will bring their considerable talents to bear in analyzing the speech of all southern mountain speakers, so that the conjectures and assertions presented here can be supported or disproved.

NOTES

1. The history of Breathitt County was written up in 1941 by the Writer's Program of the WPA and published by Bacon, Percy, and Daggett, Newport, N.Y., under the title *In the Land of Breathitt*.
2. Dillard (personal communication). Dillard's concerns have been primarily with the absence of such a population from the United States in general. See comments on this matter in later chapters.

3. Brought to my attention by Donna Christian.
4. Michael Montgomery brought this article, as well as others, to my attention.
5. All statistics pertaining to population, education, income, farming, housing, and labor are from the publications of the U.S. Department of Commerce, Bureau of the Census, for Kentucky (1970 and 1980).

Chapter V

Immigrants — Some of Them Involuntary

No one doubts that the United States and the Americas in general are populated primarily by the descendants of immigrants. The entire question of American English depends to an extraordinary degree on the question of what happens to languages in migration. Most of the principles for studying those languages, and for (re)constructing their history, were formulated on the relatively static populations of Europe. Those principles caused the historical linguistics still at the base, especially, of our dialect studies, to be founded on the principle of "language as an organism that undergoes transformation by its own internal rules" (Alleyne 1980: 20). Increasingly, however, change is coming to be viewed as "generated by social factors falling outside of the formal structure of language" (ibid.). The latter viewpoint finds some of its strongest support in the examination of immigrant influence upon American English — a viewpoint which was formulated on the basis of a lot of data if little linguistic sophistication by Mencken (1919) and then almost lost sight of in succeeding editions and Supplements to *The American Language.*

As is well known, the European dialectologists from whom the Americans took their models worked best with rural speech. They avoided the cities in general, and until Labov (1966) there was little attention to the cities — where the most notable groups of immigrants have tended to gather — in American dialectology. Even when studying a city, traditional dialectologists (Shuy et al., 1967) have felt more comfortable in Detroit than in a seaport.

Ports are, however, of basic significance for the history of the United States — including its language. Berger (1980) shows the significance of New Orleans, and the even earlier and more basic importance of New York hardly needs to be shown. It was always one of the most complex parts of the colonies, linguistically. Dutch was the official language up to 1664, when the stronger British "traded" Surinam to Holland for New York. (It is one of the glaring ghost issues of creole studies how English managed to "influence" the slaves' speech so much that Saramaccan, Ndjouka, and Sranan Tongo were formed between 1651 and 1664. Even creolists can hardly believe that some varieties developed internally to the African slave-derived population.)

Dutch remained the language – or at least the first language – of many New York for a long time thereafter, as anyone can find out by reading the novels of James Fenimore Cooper. But the linguistic complexity of Holland itself was reflected in the use of Flemish and Walloons in the American colony. Palatine Germans early settled along the Hudson. The British – including Irish, Scots, and Welsh – moved in even before the trade was made. Jewish traders were present from early times and even had a Hebrew school. Italians and Portuguese were also included in the early commerce of New York. All of these competed with Swedish settlers in Delaware, and there were Danes in New York itself. Even if we leave out – as it has become traditional to do – the American Indians and the Black slaves who were numerous on Manhattan island in the eighteenth century, we still find a picture of extreme linguistic complexity in New York City and in other ports from the very beginning.

In the nineteenth century, migration of foreign language speaking groups was an important feature of the life of the United States and a major influence on the language. Borrowings from those immigrant languages have been examined often, and it has frequently been pointed out that ethnic slur words resulted from the occasional friction between the different groups and formed an interesting if not notably large element in the American English vocabulary. Four examples of the latter in early nineteenth century American English – if not "Americanisms" in the narrow sense of that term – were *gyp, jew, welsh,* and *nigger,* the first three basically verbs and the last ordinarily a noun. The use of the first three was suggested in an article by William Safire in the New York *Times;* as usual, when Safire and I use the same materials our treatments differ. All of the these terms are moderately problematic in their development; all are interesting international in some sense.

Coming most probably from *Gypsy* (from *Egyptian*), the very name of the Romani, the verb *gyp* which probably describes the activities of traveling traders relatively few of whom were actual Gypsies – is listed as "orig. U.S." in OEDS although not claimed by either the DA or the DAE. In this case, the conservative attitude of the older dictionaries has a great deal to recommend it. The term belongs rather to the international trading vocabulary than to England or to America. The ordinary American may well use the term innocently of any intent to slur an ethnic group, although criminal argot (according to Alderson 1953) uses it to mean 'a Gypsy'. A *Mutt and Jeff* comic strip of perhaps forty years ago had a contrived Egyptian swindling Jeff, to Mutt's punning "E-gypt-ya?" The point of the (rather weak) joke would have been lost completely if readers had made any connection between the words *gyp, Gypsy, and Egyptian* – although the middle one is irrelevant to the comic strip.

It is not surprising that the verb *jew* should be equally international, since

Jewish traders were very widely known before the discovery of America. Both the DAE (from 1834) and the DA (1825) claim the verb as an Americanism. OEDS cites an earlier attestation which illustrates the inadequacy of the "Anglicism" — "Americanism" dichotomy. American painter C. Harding, who was in England when he made the relevant diary entry, is now the first recorded user. Given the international character of the usage, assignment to one side of the Atlantic or another is unrevealing and hardly necessary. Middle America may have become more familiar with with *jew down* 'induce a seller to accept a lower price' from 1870 than with *jew*. OED mentions *Jew peddler* but not *Jew store,* although the latter was more familiar in the Southwest by the 1930s. Weseen's *Dictionary of American Slang* lists *jew flag* 'a dollar bill; any paper money' from hoboes and tramps.

Whatever variation, social or regional, there may have been, the direction of the supposed ethnic reference (it really seems unnecessary to say "ethnic slur") is consistent. Very sensitive Jewish persons may object, but others can discuss the terms and even joke about them. Certainly these forms do not have the offensive connotation of *kike.*

Welsh 'to fail to pay off a bet', although listed in Weingarten's *Dictionary of American Slang,* has hardly been claimed as an Americanism in the narrow sense. In fact, the ethnic-slur characteristics of the word itself are doubtful here; several (rather weak) theories have been advanced for another etymology. If, however, *to welsh on a bet* is an ethnic slur in origin, the average American user of the expression is even less aware of the etymology than he is when he uses *to gyp.* As Adams (1944) points out, only in "more settled communities" does *gypped* mean 'cheated'. To cowboys, it referred to the unfortunate results of drinking water with a high gypsum content.

Although other groups, like the Dutch and the Scots, are targets of some ethnic abuse and slur words, there has been no word which has provoked so much emotion, bitterness, and outright violence as *nigger.* Furthermore, no other slur word gets so little of its effect from purely linguistic factors; the social influence is everything where this one is concerned. The average American user has as little idea of the etymology of *nigger* as of *Dutch treat,* about which Slater (1951) has written:

> Although the phrase *Dutch treat* is in general and consistent American use and has produced a sturdy offspring *to go Dutch,* there seems to be no knowledge of its origin.

Intuitively, one would not expect to be embarrassed if he said, "Let's go Dutch" to a friend whose ancestors came from The Netherlands, but to "jew down" a Jewish person would be extremely crude, and in the presence of a black American even *Negro* or the very word *black* itself almost certainly generates tension.

The precise origin of *nigger,* although probably innocuous, is not beyond doubt. It is well not to be so dogmatic as Major (1970) in deriving it from French, or even as Mencken in tracing it to Spanish and Portuguese. Spears (1981) seems more on target when he derives the word from Latin *niger* "via the Romance languages in various spellings since the later 1500s." Major, however, captures quite well the curious social constraints:

> . . . when used by a white person in addressing a black person it is offensive and disparaging; used by black people among themselves, it is a racial term with undertones of warmth and good-will – reflecting, aside from the irony, a tragi-comic sensibility that is aware of black history.

The opprobrious sense is not the original one. In Haitian Creole, *nèg* simply means 'person'. *Li gro nèg* means 'He/she is an important person', not 'He/she is a big nigger'. (Holm and Shilling report the same meaning of *nigger* in the Bahamas.) Under the right circumstances, a white person can be called *nèg* in Haiti. In Puerto Rican Spanish, *negro* and *negra*, especially as nouns of address, are intimate-style terms betokening solidarity and even affection, often without color connotations (Álvarez Nazario 1974: 344). Álvarez Nazario also points out (1974: 359) that the phrase *trabajar como un negro* developed on the sugar cane plantations and in the sugar mills and soon came to be applied, like its American English equivalent, to arduous labor performed by any person. There is no date for the Puerto Rican Spanish expression; DA, DAE, and OEDS show 1836 as the first attestation.

The speech of the mountain men reflects the innocuous use. *This nigger* was used as a jocular but inoffensive way of referring to the first person. *This coon* was also so used. According to Mencken (1945: 632), *coon* was first applied to Negroes in the 1880s and the song "All Coons Look Alike to Me" was first sung in 1896, popularizing the expression as applied to a black person. Ernest Hogan, himself black, was the composer; he was astonished at the racial conflict which came to center around the words, the title, and even the very tune of his song. The offensive connotation, once established, seems permanent: One of the most vitriolic examples of "black" (i.e., malicious, as distinct from Black) humor of the late 1950s and 1960s was to refer to an important leader and national figure as Martin Luther Coon.

In spite of improvement over the last three decades, America's greatest social problem remains the division between black and white, and the language reflects that fact. The widespread use of perjorative compounds like *nigger work* 'lowly paid drudgery' and *nigger lip* (verb 'to cover too much of a shared cigarette with one's lips') both reflected and sustained the racial unpleasantness in the South for a long time.

In Louisiana, where racial betterment of the Acadians is hardly less recent, an athletic team can call itself the Ragin' Cajuns; one can hardly imagine a team calling itself the Niggers or even the Negroes, with or without attributive. Louisiana Frenchmen have even learned to make pseudo-indecent *coonass* (sometimes in the hypocoristic form *coonie*) a label self-applied with some pride. A German-American informant with the partly Anglicized name Stinebaugh (from Steinbach) has told me of having been hurt by the term *kraut* during World War I; shortly after World War II he could joke about it. Perhaps closest to the reaction of Afro-Americans are those of Spanish-American ancestry, who can accept *Chicano* but find it hard not to show anger at *greaser*. Italians do somewhat better with *wop*, although perhaps not with *Guinea*. A cursory survey of the documents of slavery shows that *blacks*, *darkies*, *Negroes*, *coloreds*, and various other forms have faded in and out of fashion without a single one managing to make itself completely inopprobrious.

Early American writers in general were as conscious of the dialect patterns of these population groups as Chaucer was of Northerners or Shakespeare of low-life characters in the London of his day or of Welshmen. Some attempt to represent the special characteristics of their English is a special feature of colonial literature. Except perhaps for the Indians, no group had its English more thoroughly documented or more imbued with special characteristics than the African-derived slaves. After an early assumption that the extensive representation was itself evidence of the complete inaccuracy of the dialect documentation (Krapp 1925), the point was well made (Stewart 1967, 1968) that such a diverse group of recorders could hardly have invented the same speech forms, which by an extension of the coincidence had a strange similarity to Afro-Creole English forms still observable, independently.

The West Africans who came over as slaves at least as early as 1619 have a claim to be among the earliest of American "immigrants" – if the term can be used of a people who came so completely against their own volition. Their dialect is, also, strikingly the most distinctive among American English speakers, especially when one considers that it has a very wide geographic distribution and that its history does not show any special localization at any time in the past.

Traditional dialectology might have preferred to deal first, among ethnic groups, with the Irish, "the first great ethnic 'minority' in American cities" (Sowell 1981: 17). This predisposition may even be reflected in the prevalent dialect euphemism of the 1960s, when studies of Black dialect were referred to in terms of "urban" dialect. But very little of any distinctive nature survives in second- and third-generation Irish speech. Some rather extreme claims are now being made as to the Irish provenience of certain Black English and Creole English forms (see below, p. 118) but, rather strangely, it has never been claimed that any of them are present in the speech of the Irish population which purportedly transmitted them.

Barry (1982) lists a few characteristic syntactic structures of Southern Hiberno-English, only one of which (indirect questions preceded by *whether* or *if* being represented by a direct question) has any special relevance to American English nonstandard dialects. That structure is rather strikingly like the Black English Vernacular:

I don't know is that right or not
'I don't know whether or not that is right'.

This particular subordination structure, which is related to lack of *do*-support in BEV basilect and different conditions of question inversion, is, however, a better candidate for a "language universal" explanation than many other features of the dialect.

It is very strange that, with all the effort to find Irish sources of BEV, the one strikingly Irish variety in the United States has been fobbed off on Gypsies (or Rom – to keep things straight). Irish Travelers in the United States Hancock (1980) who emigrated at the time of the potato famine (1845-52) brought Cant, based on earlier Shelta. Rather than a language variety as such, it seems now to consist of about 150 "secret" words. According to Hancock, Shelta (with 1,000-2,000 Irish-derived words and an appreciable amount of Irish-derived idiom) is not known to the Travelers, who tend to lose Cant in settled communities, although there are places in North America where it survives.

In addition to those Germans who came among the Dutch, there were others, like the Mennonites who came to Germantown, Pennsylvania, in 1683. In those places where they settled in relatively great numbers, the Germans appear to have been more influential, linguistically, than the Irish. Benjamin Franklin, who in 1753 expressed the fear that Pennsylvania would not be able to preserve the English language, typifies the alarm of some of the colonists at the force of the 45,000 or so Germans who were in the thirteen colonies by 1745. During World War II, Americans worried about possible sabotage by citizens of German ancestry. Besides the German newspapers in Philadelphia part of the cause for Franklin's alarm, there were others out in the hinterlands; Jordan (1966: 203) reports on Texas:

The last German-language newspaper ceased publication [in Texas] in the 1950's, but in the streets and stores of towns like Fredericksburg, spoken German can still be heard though it has long since been infiltrated by English words and expressions. In a few churches, German services are still held.

For subgroups like the Amish, who isolated themselves from outsiders, English was a language to use only with relative strangers – as it remains to some degree today. Less-extreme sects like the Mennonites have assimilated to a much greater degree. Mennonite workers may be found in unexpected places, like among the partly detribalized (or perhaps never historically tribal) "Choctaws" of Clifton, Louisiana. In such a function they are partly the agents of assimilation, although they seem always to have a healthy respect for the cultures of the groups with whom they are working.

Today, in perhaps the closest approximation that exists in American

English to a simple substratum relationship (compare, however, the Louisiana "Cajuns"), the Pennsylvania Dutch speak a heavily German-influenced English, although many of them know little or no German. Some of their patterns, like the identification or confusion of *let* and *leave*, both of which are *lassen* in German, are well known; Archie, the "manager" of the tavern in the old radio and television program *Duffy's Tavern*, which had an only incidentally German atmosphere, brought a feature of the dialect to the public in the title of a mock-romantic ballad "Leave Us Face It," which traded on the allegedly malapropistic nature of a nonstandard dialect ("In a little French chapeau we was mated"). The use of *all* to mean 'finished' was spotlighted in the Broadway comedy title *Papa Is All* (1942). Schach (1954: 49) even suggests that the designation of George Washington as *the father of his country* is "an apparent translation of *Des Landes Vater.*"

Other characteristics of Pennsylvania German-English include the use of *make* in senses which other American English-speaking groups do not find idiomatic (Snader 1965):

Make the window shut
It make down (rain) soon
The bell don't make. Bump.

The verb form in a conditional clause, long a bugaboo for American school-children of many ethnic groups, has a special twist in Pennsylvania German English:

You better wouldn't do that
If he would be here, you wouldn't say that

Anyone with some experience of this variety who is asked to give examples will almost immediately cite *spritzen the lawn* and *outen the light.* Even the old saws like

Throw your father down the stairs his hat
Throw the cow over the fence some hay

have a kind of representative validity, like most stereotypes. Tourist publications in the Reading, Pennsylvania area make a lot of the designation *ferhoodled* 'crazy' for the variety of English. They are, of course, more interested in collections of oddities than in seriously collected data, but there is a certain accuracy to the forms they do record.

Although there are the usual predictions that Pennsylvania German English will "soon" disappear, the variety not only may have more vitality than has been suspected but may also prove to have had a more extensive historical influence than it has been accorded in conventional treatments. As a variety used for bilingual, or perhaps even multilingual, contact situations, it participated in a great many kinds of language relationships where a lingua franca would be used. Beadle (1878: 119) reported on a "Hoosier dialect" which he called

the result of union between the rude translations of "Pennsylvania Dutch", the Negroisms of Kentucky and Virginia, and certain phrases native to the Ohio valley.

This Hoosier "language" which Beadle describes appears to be basically a variety of English. He is naively struck by its "abundance of negatives," which he believes to be uncharacteristic of "English and Latin." The commonplace Americanism *I reckon* strikes him as being on the same level with other "grammatical" factors; he apparently regards it as a Hoosierism, "offset" by *I guess*, which he regards as specifically Yankee. In view of such commonplace observations, Beadle's "ordinary conjugation" for this "language" is astonishing; after a "present tense, regular, as in English," he offers

> Imperfect tense.–I done it, you done it, he done it. Plural–We'uns done it, you 'uns done it, they 'uns done it.
> Perfect tense.–I gone done it, you gone done it, he gone done it. Plural – We 'uns gone done it, you 'uns gone done it, they 'uns gone done it.
> Pluperfect – I bin gone done it, you bin gone done it, etc.
> First Future – I gwine to do it, you gwine to do it, etc.
> Second Future – I gwine to gone done it, etc.

The intriguing thing here is the use of *bin* in the "pluperfect" – an analysis not far from that given for Black English preverbal *been*, although the specific sequences reported here do not match any known variety. The prevalence of *done*, although hardly in the forms cited, also suggests the Black English Vernacular. If Beadle was an accurate observer of language, then something was going on the frontier which has hardly been suspected. In the absence of fuller information, I can only conclude that he heard something like the forms he put down, noticed the presence of Blacks and perhaps of some Pennsylvania Germans, and make up an impressionistic paradigm reporting, according to the best of his memory, the language forms they used. Of course, there may really have been an unusual contact variety where he says it was.

Because of the racial implications, very few other writers have linked Pennsylvania German-influenced English and Plantation Creole, or any other stage of the Black English Vernacular. In at least one feature, however, they are strangely similar. Both use a form resembling English *ain't* for echo questions: Pennsylvania German *ain't* (Snader 1965: 18)

> Mom, ven it comes a little red box, why then the train's all, ain't?

and Gullah (considered as the survival of a stage very similar to Plantation Creole) from Gonzales (1964: 163)

> You mus' be t'ink dem duh hoe, enty?

As Beadle's perhaps unfortunate use of the popular name of the Pennsylvania Germans indicates, Americans have not always distinguished between citizens of that ancestry and those whose forefathers came from Holland. The latter undoubtedly had a greater influence on American English in general, partly because they once formed a polity within the continental colony area English and Dutch were, moreover, closely associated in the minds of many who were engaged in international commerce in the seventeenth century. In *Purchase His Pilgrimes* we can read:

We may reckon those Englishmen in diverse of those Dutch voyages around the globe, Timothy Shotten, Thomas Spring, John Caldwell, and others. Yea, the name of Englishman were [sic] so famous in the East, that the Hollanders in their first trade thither, varnished their obscurities with English luster and gave out themselves English.

In the maritime trade, which was so vitally important to early American English, a Dutch sailor was sometimes known as Janke, 'Little John'. Although there are many complications in the etymology, either that Dutch form or Mencken's favored Jan Kees (a kind of Dutch John Doe, with *Kee* as a back formation) contributed to the noun *yankee*. (For the reinforcing influences which almost certainly were at work, see p. 150.)

Complications arise almost as soon as the Dutch contribution is considered. The doublets *freebooter* and *filibuster*, historically related to Dutch *vrijbuiter* 'one who goes in search of plunder, a pirate' but not related to each other in any simple way, provide an interesting example. The former entered English because of the importance of Dutch shipping and was also apparently transmitted to the maritime vocabularies of other nations. The latter is supposed to come from Spanish, then to have been borrowed by English and specialized to refer almost exclusively to the action of a congressman in talking to death a bill he opposes. Originally, the legislator seems to have been accused of "pirating" the nation's time. (In this domain of borrowing, it is joined by *poppycock,* from Dutch *papekak* 'soft dung', first recorded in an 1865 attestion alluding to a congressman's speech.)

The first part of the explanation has, however, some serious deficiencies. The /fr-/ cluster has been broken, apparently in Spanish, by a vowel, a characteristic of many borrowing situations but hardly explicable in terms of Spanish, which has /fr-/ in a large number of words (*franco, fregar, friar, frontera, fruta,* etc.) Since /l/ and /r/ neutralize in Spanish, even in dialects like Puerto Rican, only in non-prevocalic position, the change of the liquid is hardly to be referred to Spanish. Corominas suggests a Dutch form in /fl-/, but the same objection holds insofar as the intrusive vowel is concerned, Spanish having *flauta, flexible, flictena, flojo, fluir,* etc. Even Valkhoff (1931: 138-9), in his discussion of French *flibustier,* cites the English form without attempting to explain the intrusive vowel.

Other discussions, as in the OED, bring little light to this development. The canonical syllable form /CVCV/ is, however, well known for contact languages, especially pidgins. Alleyne (1980) traces this tendency in Afro-American creoles to African language patterns, but it obviously functions in other situations and is a development from some other process here. If a Pidgin Dutch preceded the attested Dutch Creole or *Negerhollands* of the Virgin Islands (Hesseling [1905], de Josselin de Jong [1924]) and perhaps even of New Jersey (Prince [1910]), there may have been a process like Camerounian Pidgin English *sikin* for English *skin.*

Another interesting maritime Dutch form which came into American English is *boom,* which was at least found in the Mediterranean Lingua Franca (Kahane, Kahane, and Tietze 1958) and which also entered Portuguese (*bome*) and Italian (*boma*). Valkhoff (1931: 66) traces French *bome* to Dutch *boom* '*toute vergue servant a haler une voile*'. In nautical usage, a ship with its sails "boomed out" would be really "booming along." In the American West, the verb *boom* was used, around 1831, of a river to mean 'rush strongly.' By 1884, *booming* meant 'splendid, grand'. The noun *boom* 'a period of great economic activity' came about the same time. The attestation of *boomer* 'enthusiastic supporter or adovcate' in 1880 and of *booming* 'prospering or increasing greatly' in 1891 shows that the whole complex of economic uses of the term was developing around the end of the nineteenth century. *Boomer* 'squatter, nester, homesteader' is also attested for 1884.

Basically maritime Dutch words, although not "Americanisms" in the narrow sense, were also abundant. Colcord (1945) cites *stow* from Dutch *stoewen* 'to cram, press' and *scoot* from *schuyt* 'sail fast'.

Without invoking *dollar* (from Dutch and Low German *daler* but pegged to the value of the Spanish peso, with smaller units made on the analogy of the peseta, according to a pattern widespread in the New World including the West Indies), we can see that the Dutch influence on American English functioned in a multilingual context. Dutch-owned slaves like Sojourner Truth are attested in language strikingly similar to the creole-related Black English Vernacular (Stanton, Anthony, and Gage 1889: 165-6), and Dr. Alexander Hamilton's earlier servant Dromo, whose English is also BEV (Needler 1967), was reported in some amusing contacts with the Dutch language in 1744.

Van Loon (1938: 39) comments, with little linguistic sophistication, on a "jargon of mispronounced American with a hybrid syntax and no more than a fair sprinkling of words of a real Dutch origin" spoken in New York, giving as an example, "*Weet you dat joe was where je gheen business had?*" as an example. This evidence is no more significant than Veltman's (1940: 81) from Holland, Michigan,

I am frontsigner at ———'s church.
Sometimes I'm a little off the wise, but that doesn't stick so narrow.

translatable as

I am songleader at ———'s church.
Sometimes I'm a little off tune, but that doesn't disturb anyone very much.

Other evidence, however, shows that the situation in New Jersey was of a different order.

In a classic article, Prince (1910) had provided better data on the Dutch of the New York-New Jersey area:

Up to thirty years ago this was the common idiom of many rural districts in northern New Jersey, employed alike by Dutch, English, German, and French settlers. It has, during the past three decades, been driven from its former territory by the public schools, and now survives only in the memories of some two hundred old persons, nearly all of whom are over seventy years old. Prince's article is "classic" in terms of the information provided, not the interpretation. Not unlike other amateur observers of language, he tends both to overestimate the influence of the schools and to miss the implications of a contact variety. Nevertheless, he seems to have taken care to indicate the language groups who used it.

Unless Prince had been Hugo Schuchardt, he could hardly have understood the significance of a Black man named William DeFreece among his informants. Part Minsi Indian, DeFreece was described by Prince as "an excellent authority on the negro variant of the dialect." Prince found that other informants "characterized many of his [DeFreece's] words as distinctly 'nigger'." Prince further observed (1910: 464):

> There is a small colony of old Negroes living on the mountain back of Suffern, N.Y., who still use their own dialect of Jersey Dutch, but they are very difficult of access, owing to their shyness of strangers.

Other observers, like Vanderbilt (1881) and Van Loon (1938), had observed the "bad English and worse Dutch" of Negroes in the area.

Prince's treatment, linguistically more complex at least than the others referred to, provides evidence that the "Negro" dialect of Jersey Dutch was a variety of Dutch Creole, perhaps somewhat like that spoken until very recent times in the Virgin Islands. (There may be a speaker or two alive still.) The elderly informant used a "present tense" form of a verb in a "past tense" context; that is, in the terms of Alleyne (1980) his grammar had zero for a perfective. (Alleyne's description pertains to Afro-American English varieties, but there are marked similarities in creole languages in general — especially the West Indian creoles.) Prince stated, in fact, that DeFreece "knew no past tense at all" — the kind of remark often made by an investigator unwittingly dealing with a creole language. The old man also used the English *when* for the Dutch subordinate time conjunction *waner* and indulged in "the most curious negroism" in the form of *plôt* 'foot' rather than the Standard Dutch *pôt*. The insertion of /l/ may have been hypercorrection; speakers of Afro-Creole varieties (including BEV) often "leave out" (or vocalize) /l/ and /r/ after consonants; in hypercorrection, on the model of the standard language a liquid is often inserted between an obstruant and a vowel: hypercorrections like *phrase* for *faze* are not especially rare in BEV, for example.

Van Loon (1938: 46) provides an example of how historians have occasionally recognized contact, if not creole, varieties where dialectologists have ignored them:

> Both the Mohawk-Hudson Dutch and the Jersey dialect sounds were an evolutionary process starting with the earliest colonists who were a Dutch citizenry composed of Hollanders, Frisians, Germans, Irish, English, French, Negroes, and of course the omnipresent Indian.

In this contact situation, it seems quite probable that a word like *boss,* from *baas,* was acquired. (This suggestion derives ultimately from a lecture by the late E. Bagby Atwood. There are, however, nineteenth-century statements about the Negro's substitution of *boss* for *master.*)[1] In the South, Blacks, and some whites influenced by them, have *bossman* 'master, foreman'. The word has a wider range of meanings in BEV than in ordinary English. Black speakers use it to mean 'excellent, superior' (Boss Bat, the name of a Washington, D.C. car belonging to a Black in 1967; Boss Hoss, to a Natchitoches, Louisiana Black in 1983. See Dillard 1976b.) Surinam Creole *basi* has a very similar semantic range. (This is not to present the facile statement that BEV took the form from any creole of Surinam, or *vice versa*; an underlying CVCV form apparently dropped the enclitic vowel in BEV whereas it was retained in Surinam.)

The three immigrant groups so far treated represent clear cases of major language contact influence, although in the case of the Irish such developments were rather far in the past and probably not a part of the American English situation. German and Dutch have some rather clear cases of special contact varieties within the continental United States; it is perhaps significant that borrowings from those languages (including phrasal compounds like *pot cheese, horse thief, hot cake,* and *how come*? from Dutch) are much more extensive than from Anglo-Irish or any Celtic language. There is no attempt made here to detail those borrowings; conventional lists can be found in Marckwardt-Dillard (1981).

A group even more obviously polyglot than the Dutch brought a tremendous amount of influence from Yiddish and even a little from Hebrew into the United States. While I want to avoid any controversy over the origins of Yiddish, it is spectacularly obvious that this and other (e.g., Ladino) Jewish varieties are the results of the incomparably complex language contact of a proverbially wandering people. Further, no participant in this controversy (Hebrew adapted for the contact situation in German, creole, German dialect with a lot of Hebrew borrowings, etc.) could ignore that there is some relationship between Yiddish and the more conventional Germanic languages. In fact it is not at all certain whether locutions like *"Why not?"* (to a question like "Why do you do X?"), (*I don't have*) *what to eat, already* in final position, and inverted word order in some sentences (*Throw mama from the train a kiss*) derive from Pennsylvania German or from Yiddish influence (Feinsilver 1970).

Steinmetz (1981) surveyed the "Jewish English" of approximately one million Orthodox Jews. He found that there are Orthodox Jews in all major cities across the country but that the center of American Orthodoxy is, as it always has been, New York City and its environs. Because they maintain intimate contact with Yiddish, Orthodox Jews have a distinctive form of

English. There has been much acculturation – most of the million are probably English-dominant – but they have influenced the language and culture of the United States as well.

The German (Ashkenazic) Jews who had the greatest influence on the language of the United States were the second such group to arrive. Sephardic Jews came in the seventeenth century and had a synagogue in New York by 1695. Ashkenazic Jews, largely from Germany, came later – the first only a short time after the Sephardic. Larger groups of the former came in the nineteenth century, so that the 3,000 Jews estimated to be in the colonies in 1776 had become four or five times as many by 1820 and ten times as many by 1850, with another tenfold increase to over half a million by 1880. They came mainly to the cities, but many rural areas knew Jewish peddlers whom one could try to "jew down."

The preponderance of urban Jews in the communications media brought an incredible flood of "Yinglish" phrases, Yiddish borrowings, and "rhetorical devices" (Ornstein 1983). Julius (1983: 124) states that "at least 80%" of American comedians are Jews. Beginning with radio, Jewish communicative strategies at levels from the word to the discourse came to a bewildered hinterlands population which laughed at groups like the Marx Brothers without realizing how much the joke was on the laughers. (In this respect, the most nearly comparable minority group language activities are the early spirituals and the blues lyrics of the Blacks, wherein disguised meanings are superabundant.) Vaguely aware of the meaning of *schmuck,* Americans either accepted that word innocently or leered broadly when they heard *schlemiel.* Even a gentile who has lived in New York may have been exposed to the information that a little schmuck is a *schmekl.* "Mink, schmink, so long as it keeps you warm" and other prominent examples of a characteristic initial consonant variation drew laughter on the Jewish-dominated radio comedy broadcasts primarily because of the accents of the speakers, often broadly exaggerated and stereotyped by their perceptive users. Studio audiences, before the time of canned laughter, reacted to the Bar Mitzvah implications of "Today I yam a man," and innocent *goyim* in the provinces thought the funny thing must the phonetics of the glide /y-/.

Feinsilver (1970) gives an extensive if nontechnical exposition of the influence of Yiddish in fields like advertising. Like Ornstein, she points out how discourse patterns and rhetorical devices are influential – perhaps the most influential factor – . on American English in general. Among the translations from Yiddish which she has noted as spreading are *Wear it in good health* (*trug es gezunterheyd*) and *I need it like a hole in the head* (*Ich darf es vi a loch in kop*). Ornstein (1983: 139) writes of a "supra-sentence pattern distinguished by a series of simple sentences punctuated by buzz-words and phrases expressing exaggerated emotion, surprise, dejection, elation, and others." Ornstein adds "maledictions of old world *shtetl* type," including

You should drop dead.

Variations on this malediction, including such gems as

Fall fatal five times, fella

were popular on American college campuses in the late 1940s.

Words like *borscht, gefilte fish, dokus* or *tochus, schmo, schmaltz* and *schmaltzy, schnozzle,* and *phooey* (which could also be from German) came into the general American English vocabulary. Much more is current in large eastern cities. There, an occasional brave protestant will attempt *mazel tov.* Ornstein calls *kibitzer* "completely well-known in colloquial styles of English" and *maven* 'guide' or 'expert' "known mostly by [members] of the intellectual establishment."

The Yiddish influence on the English of, especially, New York City, is virtually incalculable, although it is not so simple as to be explained by a "substratum" principle. Labov (1972: 298) shows how the raising of the vowel of *cab, hack, ask, dance,* with "short a" raised to [ɛ], began as a kind of Yiddish "interference" on the phonology, although the complete explanation cannot be made from this alone. Later Italian immigrants, whose interference patterns would tend rather to lower the vowel to [a], "reach[ed] for native status by removing themselves as far as possible from the low-prestige pattern of their parents." Thus, second and later generations of Italian immigrants carried the vowel even higher. As Labov clearly shows, ethnicity became a stronger factor than interference in such cases.

Beginning around 1820, small groups of Northern Italian immigrants came to New York and California. In the last quarter of the nineteenth century and the early twentieth, much larger numbers arrived from southern Italy. These, however, often indulged in "return migration." Bilingual problems plagued them, and there was considerable retention of Italian. Puerto Ricans as late as the 1950s reported having associated first with the Italians in New York City because of the similarity of some Italian words to their equivalents in Spanish. An Italian accent, for some menial occupation like fruit peddler, was easily parodied by a Jewish comedian like Chico Marx. A rather small number of opera buffs have long used Italian words like *allegro, diva, aria, cavatina, tutti, da capo,* and *buffo.* The populace in general knows *"Bravo!";* to call *"Brava!"* after the performance of a female singer would probably be considered "one-upmanship." Food names like *spaghetti, macaroni,* and *ravioli* have been in use even in the hinterlands since World War I; *pizza* spread from the east coast after World War II. The food itself has become so widely diffused that the late Al Capp, in *Li'l Abner,* once had a character saying it had replaced pork and beans as the national food. The small town of Natchitoches, Louisiana, once had four fast-food pizza "palaces," two on each side of the street across from each other with only an ice cream parlor breaking up the continuity on one side. Away from centers of Italian population, however, *pizzeria* is suspect; many Americans suspect that it is the Italian version of *pissoir*. In the early 1960s, an Italian restaurant in Waco, Texas — probably one of the first in that small city — advertised itself as a *Pizza-ria*.

All of these groups assimilated reasonably well, except where religious or cultural loyalties caused them to be intentionally separate. The religious associations of Hebrew, the international usefulness of Yiddish, and general loyalty factors have been adequate to preserve a recognizable Jewish dialect of American English stereotypable as "Yinglish," although of course there are many Jewish speakers who use only standard English — or who are bidialectal. In striking contrast, the Irish dialect of English, so strong and so successful a group identifier that any real need for Celtic languages in Ireland has been obviated, has had only a negligible survival in the United States, despite the great numbers of Irish immigrants. Italian immigrants, also, have apparently leveled out to the dialect of surrounding Caucasians — or, in the case of New York, to a generalized dialect which they helped form — in most parts of the United States. Strange things do happen, however; a student of mine (in Natchitoches, Louisiana) named Sharbino just recently entitled a composition on final tests (in an otherwise all-English context) *Examine*. When only these groups are considered, the melting-pot metaphor for the population and for the English of the United States seems generally valid in spite of a few obvious objections.

More difficulty comes, however, from the non-Caucasian groups. Chinese who were likely to speak no English except for pidgin (Meredith 1929, Leland 1900) began coming to California, especially, in 1849; there were 25,000 by 1851. They were employed in the hard physical labor of building the railroads and often driven away from the lucrative mines of the gold rush. Like the early Irish on the East Coast, they were repulsed from attractive jobs. ("No Irish Need Apply" was apparently known as far away as the West of Mark Twain's "Buck Fanshaw's Funeral.") The Chinese were expected to labor under the worst conditions, but they were not incapable or protest. Nee and Nee (1972: 41) report:

Eight hours a day good for white man, all the same good for Chinaman.

Expression like *can do, no can do,* also widely used in maritime speech may have been at least partly diffused by these Chinese immigrants. *Chow* and *chow chow* spread even to the hinterlands — the latter known as a "homey" condiment in East Texas in the 1930s or earlier. In the bigger cities, Chinese opened restaurants which gave a lot of food terms (*won ton, chow mein, chop suey, chopsticks, egg foo young,* and many others — the inventory for connoisseurs is probably unlimited). They also opened laundries, many of which are still plainly visible in the large cities, although some who have not been able to come to grips with stereotyping want to attribute them to the movies and comic strips. The stereotyped line "Notickee, no laundee; alle samee to me" is perhaps too trite to be even a serious insult to a Chinese person today; but McLeod (1948) reports it in the form, "No sabbie. No tickee, no washee." *Sabbie* (or *savvy*, etc.) is well attested as a general pidginism; for *alle samee*, or some variant, see the citation from Nee and Nee (1972). As far as ethnic slurs are concerned, *chink* would probably be about like *nigger* to a Chinese person today, with *Chinaman* not far behind; but see the Nee and Nee citation. *China-John*, widely used in the nineteenth century, seems to be extinct. There was actually a Tin Pan Alley song entitled "China Boy" in 1922. Early attestations of the Westernism *you bet* are often in a Chinese Pidgin context although the phrase could easily have arisen independently in pidgin and in ordinary English.

As with the Chinese, Japanese migration to the United States was intimately involved with their coming to Hawaii. Thus, Pidgin English has played an important role in the language contact of the Japanese, but the tradition of pidgin usage is not nearly so old among them as among the Chinese. The first really large body came to the continent in the 1880s, thus well after the gold rush; Japanese may have been as important in the economic life of this country, but specifically Japanese linguistic contributions are much harder to find. *Nisei* and *Sansei* — the first nativized generation and the third generation of Japanese Americans — are terms well known in academic contexts and familiar to the general populace on the West Coast. *Issei* is much more restricted, perhaps known primarily in works on immigration. Food terms like *sukiyaki* and *teriyaki* have been known for a long time in the larger cities and have recently spread inland. *Skosh* 'a little' (especially in the phrase *just a skosh*) and *moose* 'a native concubine' had a certain currency during the Korean War and with its veterans for a short time thereafter.

The emigrants from Nova Scotia whose story was popularized in Longfellow's *Evangeline* have been the subject of a major legend and more than a little romanticism. In particular, it may have tended to obscure the historical situation, in which French speakers from varying backgrounds, many of them maritime, drifted into southern Louisiana. There they were neighbors to, and often mixed with, Black speakers of a historically different French-based variety, "Gumbo" Creole (called "patois" in popular works). The controversy over Louisiana French Creole is as live an issue as that over any other creole language, but there was almost certainly involved a maritime trade version of French with a heavy overlay of West African language influence (Hull 1979).

The "Cajun," when he wanted to give an account of crossing the prairies, used the verb *naviguer*. He even "set sail" (*méttait la voile*) on land. Several sources tell us how a Cajun's daughter all dressed up to be married was described in the terms, *"N'est-ce pas que'elle une goelétte bien gréée?"* 'Isn't she a well-rigged schooner?'

Among the marginally native users of English, and perhaps representative of them in being the target of generally good-humored traditions which see their English as humorous arid full of malapropisms, "Cajun" speakers are easily identified by their carryovers from their variety (nonstandard, and still without a really good description) of French. An obvious example is the pronoun repeated, at the end of the sentence, for emphasis:

> I don't like that, me

and by such characteristic idioms as

> It looks to you 'It's your responsibility'
>
> (French *Ça te regard*)

Humorist Justin Wilson is well known for his presentations, some of them recorded, in "Cajun dialect"; collections of supposed malapropisms and allegedly humorous usage like Sothern (1977) sell well in Louisiana. Some of Sothern's examples (*very close* for *varicose* and *four michael* for *formica*) seem to belong to the general folklore of humorous misusage. Others like *fay dodo* 'a dance' (*fais dodo*) and *fee folay* (*feu folie*) are popular orthographic representations of French words and terms brought into English rather than translated. A few "dialect" pronunciations (*bad* for *bed, chiren* for *children, gaff* for *gulf, chune* for *tune*) are represented, as are apparent eye-dialect forms like *Emmet N. Domangue* (*eminent domain*). Such materials are, of course, far from descriptive; their utility lies in their attesting to the persistence of popular attitudes about the dialect. Also, they attest to the existence of a dialect about which one would be hard-pressed to find any information in more academic sources.

The ambiguous status of "Cajun English" is almost duplicated by that of "Cajun French." The latter has now become recognized and even receives some support from CODOFIL (*Conseil pour le Developpement du Français en Louisiane*), whose programs on Louisiana Public Broadcasting ("*En Français*") feature a moderator who is notably a speaker of "international" French, but occasionally have "Cajun" French speakers. (To this ear, almost all of them sound extremely English-dominant.)

In the recent past, "Cajun" status has become more acceptable; in the last two or three decades, humor about Cajuns has tended to lose its malicious tinge and even to become benevolent. The term *coonass,* once a proscribed and even a taboo form, has become a badge of membership in a group which has boasted a state governor and other prominent figures. (The preferred form, however, is still *coonie* in "mixed company.") Southwestern Louisiana University, at Lafayette, even calls its football team the Ragin' Cajuns — to the chagrin of some of the new Black majority among holders of athletic scholarships. Across the Texas border, on the other hand, there is — or was until quite recently – a tendency to confuse "Cajun" French speakers and "Black" (Creole) speakers.

Driven more or less by economic (or some other) necessity, the groups discussed so far came to the United States to some extent at the own volition; they remained in contact with their own countrymen and their own ethnic groups; they never entirely lost contact with their native languages. All of these factors change drastically when the black Africans brought in as slaves come to be group under discussion.

From the time the first slaves were brought to Virginia in 1619 – overlooking some theories that the process began earlier – African slaves were brought to the Americas in an international pattern which only *ex post facto* thinking assigns originally or exclusively to the South. Mixing of tribal and language groups by slavers, despite the counteractive factor of selective purchasing in the New World, meant that the vast majority of the slaves had to use a new language and to adapt to cultural patterns which, although they might be similar insofar as other slaves from West Africa were concerned, were to a great degree unfamiliar. There are relatively early records of the use of Portuguese Trade Pidgin and even Lingua Franca (Barbot 1732) along the west coast of Africa during this period, attestations of the use of West African Pidgin English (although it is arguable just what the relationship is to "Cameroonian" pidgin or to Krio of Sierra Leone), and evidence that the creole developments from these pidgins were used from Surinam to Nova Scotia Dillard (1973). These factors are the bases for the "creolist" theory of the development of the American BEV (Bailey 1965; Stewart, 1967, 1968; Dillard 1972a). Preliminary work on Gullah (Turner 1949) and some rather modest claims about the English of Blacks in the United States (Pardoe 1937, Haman 1939) preceded these works; but from them stems the furor over the history of BEV as well as over the claim that differences between Black English and ordinary English are more than superficial (B. Bailey 1965; Loflin all references).

Insofar as counterclaims have been rational, they are represented by D'Elioa (1973). She indulges in some obvious misunderstanding in trying to refute the creolist position by gratuitously dismissing African "substratum" influence; more importantly, she poses a demographic objection: Black slaves were isolated in small groups among whites on Southern plantations. They would not have been able to develop an ethnic dialect. They would rather have been forced, as the conservative position has long held, to learn the whites' dialects, which they may now retain in an archaic form. Widespread use of [æ ks] for [æ sk] and occasional use of *hit* are probably the soundest arguments for Black archaism, and the arguments probably have some validity. It may well have been a form in *aks* rather than *ask* which served as the model for *(h)akisi* in Surinam.

There are, however, objections to that presentation. First, Black English was not limited, in colonial times, to the South. It was spoken in New England (Dillard 1972b) in New York state (Dillard 1975), and even in Nova Scotia (Dillard 1973). Porter (1970) points out how an African day-named (Felix) Cuff established a "maroon" settlement near Waltham, Massachusetts, in 1780 and how another named Quock (Walker) sued his master at about the same time, also in Massachusetts. (For Cuff[ee] 'Friday' and Quaco 'Wednesday', with variants, see DeCamp [1967], Dillard [1972a], Dillard [1976].) Such occurrences are not emphasized in conventional histories, but they are not for that reason less significant.

For the sake of argument, however, it is just as well to cope with D'Eloia's demographic claims within the somewhat artificial confines of the ex-Confederate states. Except for the low country where Gullah was spoken and Lousiana where French Creole was used, "the vast majority of slaveholders held twenty slaves or fewer" and "this small plantation pattern was clearly dominant throughout the eighteenth century and the pre-Civil War period'. (1973: 92). Apparently, she assumes that the communication networks of the plantation slaves were made up of slaves on the same plantations – or farms, in the case of fifteen slaves or fewer – and that effective communication and cultural relations were restricted to these slaves and whites on the same plantations. (Although she does not deny interaction with slaves of other owners, she apparently minimizes it.) A corollary would be, apparently, that the white speakers were dominant on those small units and transmitted their dialect forms to the Black slaves. Although it does not follow that those dialect forms followed British "regional" dialects, D'Eloia (and McDavid) have apparently made some such assumption.

Far from attempting to refute the demographic data – which, however, I accept from D'Eloia and her stated sources, without independent investigation – I welcome the opportunity to examine the consequences of such a distribution of the slave population. It has been observed that contemporary writers reported that "every large plantation had a distinctive dialect" (Whitney 1901). While the sources from which Whitney worked were likely to exaggerate those individual differences (as do West Indians today insofar as the differences between the dialect of their own island and other islands where English Creole is spoken are concerned), there may well be significance in those reports.

Let it be assumed, then, that both D'Eloia and Whitney are partly right: Few plantations had more than twenty slaves, and *large* plantations all developed distinctive dialects. It should then be possible to argue that the basic uniformity of Plantation Creole arose not *in spite of* the typical small size of slave populations but *because of* that demographic fact.

To make that particular counterassertion, it will of course be necessary to demonstrate that communication networks existed *between* these relatively small slave groups and not only *within* them. The operating assumption of the adherents to the "creolist" theory has never been very different. Another assumption has been that cultural survivals in general (in the sense of Herskovits and Herskovits 1936, Herskovits 1942) have been responsive not to the brute facts of demography but to the finer aspects of interaction. In particular, it has been assumed that density of interaction, as of communication, has been less important than qualitative factors.

There is very early evidence of inter-plantation visiting and intimate interaction between slaves of different owners. Governor Nicholson of Maryland wrote on August 20, 1668 (Thompson 1907: 165):

> Their [the Negro slaves'] common practice is on Saturday nights and Sundays, and on 2 or 3 days in Christmas, Easter and Whitsuntide is [sic] to go and see one another tho' at 30 or 40 miles distance. I have, several times both in Virginy and here met negros, both single and 6 or 7 in company in the night time.

Davis's report from Virginia in 1799 or 1800 is "On the Sabbath the Negroes were at liberty to visit their neighbors" (1909: 400). Reports of this type are fairly easy to find, from these early examples up to the writings of Olmsted and Ingraham just before the Civil War.

In the ex-slave narratives to be considered here, the evidence is that considerable movement took place between plantations. Narratives from the unpublished Louisiana collection at Northwestern State University, Natchitoches, Louisiana, have statements like this:

> [In Christmas week] we had singing, dancing, an visitin among ourselves an on udder plantations.

Mrs. Elizabeth Ross Hite, interviewed by Black fieldworker Robert McKinney, reported:

> I rem'member [sic] one day another master brought one of his slaves over wid him when he came to see my master's daughter.

and

> Master took Jolley to a plantation to dance against a slave of one of his friends.

Julia Woodrich reported, on May 12, 1940:

> Me an' my older sister would have to go across the bayou in winter time to make grinding at the cane mills.

and

> I used to deliver notes to the neighbor.

A report in May 1940, probably from the same Mrs. Woodrich, is that the slaves of other masters were whipped within earshot; "some of the other massas was mean."

It is true that there were restrictions on slaves' movements, but control over movement to other plantations was not absolute prohibition. An ex-slave who used the interesting name of Hunton Love reported on January 8, 1941:

> We didn't leave the place often. When day's work was over, we wuz too tired to

do ennythin' but go to sleep – and besides we didn't know any outsiders. But if we did go, we had to have a pass or we'd be taken up. They wuz strick in those days.

Another such disclaimer, with the same kind of modification, was made by Rebecca Fletcher on August 21, 1940:

> In slavery days, we were not allowed to visit another plantation. The onliest way was to go to ol' master an' gitten him to write a paper with his name signed to it sayin' we could pass. Those paddyrollers wuz mighty bad about pickin' you up. They used to be a song:
> Run nigger run, the paddy-rollers ketch you.

Obviously, if there was a system of passes travel from one plantation to another must have been fairly frequent.

The infamous patrollers were not alone in restricting the slaves. Elizabeth Ross Hite reported:

> Roger an' Abraham Rugless, po white trash, would wait at night to catch de darkies an' bring 'em to dey masters. Some of de masters would pay dem for dis but not mah master.

A little later she says,

> All masters had different laws. I nebber heahed nuthin erbout patrollers an' rollers. News? We carried news by stealin off.

Apparent contradictions most likely have to do with "allowed visits" and "surreptitious visits" (stealin off). An Alabama former slave identified only as "Uncle Ben" told Mary White Covington in 1910 (Blassingame 1977: 539):

> My marster wouldn't low us ter make no visits. We couldn't go nowhere, but I jes' put off and made my visit. I thought nobody see me, but de marster did, and he tole de overseer to whip me. I weren't going to be whipped, so I runned away.

One way or another, slaves on one plantation always seemed to know a great deal about what went on in others. Flossie McElwee reported (May 27, 1940), "I knows they used to whip dem awful at the next plantation," and Francis Toby (December 6, 1933) was one of many to make comparisons:

> Of course some white folks were kine to dere niggahs an' some were bad.

Cade (1935) also cites several such statements. Mrs. Emma Gray of Morehouse Parish is quoted:

> Our old master was supposed to be the best in the neighborhood, but he sometimes whipped.

Among the activities which encouraged the mixing of slaves from different plantations were religious ceremonies. Cade (1935: 330) cites Joseph Young:

> Most times, however, the slaves held their meetings in the woods under (brush) arbors made by them. The preacher came from some other plantation; he preached about heaven and hell.

And he quotes Kalvin Woods (1935: 330):

> . . . he always would try to preach to the other slaves and would slip about from plantation to plantation preaching.

He further cites a Mrs. Channel (1935: 331):

> . . . the slaves would steal away into the woods at night and hold services.

Fisher (1953) relates these services to the African cult and Nat Turner's rebellion rather than to Christianity as such, although it seems rather extreme to deny religious intentions to all such meetings.

Whether by "stealin' off" or not, slaves from one plantation seem fairly often to have formed romantic attachments with slaves on another. Cade (1935: 304-5) quotes Mrs. Sarah Skinner:

> A man slave would tell his master: I want to marry Sal over on Marse Jones place, and if the master thought it necessary he would consent. If Sal was a good work hand she would have to continue with her own master and her husband could get a pass to see her two or three times a week. Sometimes the masters would make exchange of slaves and let the man take his wife with him to his own master's place.

Cade (1935: 307) also quotes Lueantha Mansfield:

> If one man saw a fine woman or man on another plantation he would buy him or her for breeding purposes in order to continue to have good able workers. If he didn't bring them on the same farm, he would arrange for them to breed from each other. When this man wanted to see his so-called wife, he had to get special order (permit) from the master.

According to Genovese (1974: 462) this state of marriage between slaves on different plantations was so commonplace that the term 'broad wife *(abroad wife)* was current. Gutman (1975: 107) analyzes how the small plantation condition affected inter-plantation marriage:

> The size of slave ownership, together with the prevalence of exogamous marriage taboos among the enslaved, greatly encouraged inter-owner slave marriages

Since smallness of plantations tended to promote interaction and personal interchange between plantations, it is likely that dialect leveling between plantations was greater in the small plantations. Since the interaction patterns were largely between Blacks, it is no surprise that a relatively uniform *Black* dialect should develop.

Interaction of slaves from different plantations included, according to the records, the following activities, although these are not necessarily the only ones:

1) The African cult and revolt
2) Marriage and more transitory sexual arrangements
3) Sermons and religious meetings
4) Religious holiday activities
5) Parties and entertainment
6) Acquiring and sharing information
7) Errands for the master
8) Working away from the plantation
9) Being sold

The seventh and eighth purposes above are familiar from the history of slavery but have not been documented herein because it seems improbable that the communication engaged in for those purposes could have had any great effect on the formation or maintenance of a uniform Plantation Creole, whether between large plantations or small ones. It is interesting that three of these — mating arrangements, religion, and amusements — appear to be among the domains of greatest distinctiveness in the modern Black English vernacular — especially if "music" is substituted for "parties and entertainment." (Dillard 1977 — see however Hirshberg 1982a.) It would be interesting, especially from the viewpoint of language, to have more indications of young children's inter-plantation associations. The sad fact of children being separated from their home plantations and even from their families is, however, one of the most recurrent themes in the ex-slave narratives.

The intimate sharing, which the slaves clearly practiced, in domains such as these is an important factor in developing and maintaining a relatively uniform language variety like Plantation Creole. It would seem to be much more important than the demographic factors concerning the average number of slaves on a plantation. In terms of Fishman (1973), the variety would have had the function of "symbolic integration" — a much greater force than mere density of communication.

Blasingame (1977: 537) quotes a former runaway slave named Isaac Jones who had been fed and protected by slaves on various plantations during his absence from his own master's plantation: "Colored folks was more together in dose days dan dey are now." (The context seems to indicate that *together* is used in its traditional English sense, not in that of the slang of the ghetto.) It is this "togetherness" that we must look to in the study of the history of the Black English vernacular, not to the geographism of the owner units. The failure of dialect geographers to consider this slave-developed "togetherness" at least equally with the plantation boundaries gives a ready explanation of why their techniques failed to make any progress in the description of Black dialects even after Turner (1949). Works like Labov (1973), which still reflected the work of the New York projects with verbal games ("the dozens," "sounding," or "joning") in one or two large East Coast cities, also failed to capture the syntactic distinctiveness of Black English. The games, as anyone can discover for himself with a little effort, are used in places like Shreveport, Louisiana; the basic syntax is also used in small towns and in rural areas. Labov (1980) reflects awareness of these facts.

Once the demographic prohibition has been dismissed, the linguistic facts themselves can be examined. Probably the most difficult single item to deal with in an Anglocentric framework is preverbal *been* (*I been had it a long time, you must be been rake leaves*), used as a kind of anterior time marker.[2] Bickerton (1979), who calls it a "past before the past" for nonstative verbs and more or less a simple past for statives, compares Guyanese Creole, Sranan Tongo, Nigerian Pidgin English, and even Fula. Alleyne (1980: 85) derives *bi* of Saramaccan, the "deepest" of the New World creoles, from *been* by an independently motivated optional nasal deletion rule.

The problem is not, of course, the raw use of *been* itself. It is the merest commonplace that Middle English *been* had a non-participial use:

Some been of tree, and doon hir lord servyse.
I sey nat this by wyves that been wyse.
(Chaucer, Wife of Bath's Prologue)

The significant matter, obviously, is that the Middle English use is nonpast. Herndobler and Sledd (1976) discuss some extremely elaborate conditions of raising which would derive BEV *been + V* from the grammar of ordinary English, not from a Plantation Creole or general Creole English. There is, however, no reason to assume that the same "raising" process did not take place in the English Creoles. To say that rather complex raising rules may be written for Black English which do not apply to ordinary English is, it would seem, simply to say that the two have some differing syntactic rules.[2]

For that matter, it is quite possible that the analogous French Creole *té* (probably from *était*) and Papiamentu *taba* developed (either in some historical sense or more likely in the sense "are generated") from the same kinds of raising rules. Creolists who have pointed out this peculiarity of, particularly, the Afro-Caribbean varieties, have used the words as a kind of shorthand for "a set of syntactic rules." There is no Creolist, it seems safe to say, who does not know that French has *était* and Spanish *estaba*. (In fact, anyone worth his salt could cite *staba*.)

Feagin (1979) found eight examples of preverbal *been* in an investigation of the speech of whites of Anniston, Alabama. (Three other examples, apparently outside the main body of data, seem "to be used as in Standard English.") Four of these examples are *been V+ing* (in fact, all are *been knowing*); it is interesting to compare this with Bickerton's observations on stative and nonstative distinctions (1979: 309). These probably represent reduction of *have* to *'ve* and then deletion of /v/; or, rather, their interpretation matches utterances produced by that process in the less formal styles of ordinary English. The same can be said about

... I been quit about 15 years.

This *quit*, applied to smoking, may quite possibly be adjectival here. It would be quite different if Feagin had a white example of either

I been quit my job

or

I been had it a long time.

Another example,

That was the last time I been

is a marginal case of *have* (or rather *had*) deletion. The remaining example sounds even idiomatically Black:

... ever since I been born.

As Feagin says (1979: 256) "Eleven — or eight — examples do not prove that Southern White English has the same special *been* found in Black English." Neither does the one example cited which is unambiguously not *have* deletion.

Williamson (1970) reported

I been had it

from a Southern white bus driver. In addition to the obvious argument that a busy bus is not a good place for linguistic observations, there is the factor that Southern White English has been strongly influenced by Black English, and that a person in an occupation like bus driver would have had abundant opportunity to learn the structure from Blacks. As Feagin's data rather unintentionally show, the truly Creole *been* is quite rare in Southern white speech.

Those more oriented toward phonological tradition than either Feagin or the "Creolists" were most excited by "zero copula," as in sentences like

They good

Who that?

(you don't know) who Brenda Weston.

The theory of phonological deletions (Labov 1969), although important in the early history of variable rules, encounters difficulties with *Doris stupid* (where a hiatus between /-s # s-/ would seem to be favored phonologically) and *Im is* (varying with *Im am*). The term "zero copula" has by convention included finite auxiliary deletions (if such they are) before *V+ing*. The deletion (or, looked at from the other end of the telescope, insertion) of /z/ and /Vz/ is subject to the same constraints. Like the true copula, this form is negated with *ain't* or less frequently with *not*.

It is interesting that copula is not one of the features which causes most troubles to learners of English. Jenson (1980: 132) reports:

Overall, Cop[ula] is a high performance functor, consistently ranking at the top both in accuracy and in the longitudinal orders of acquisition . . .

The experiment referred to here deals with Indonesian, which "does not have copula," in the manner of many languages often referred to in the literature. Contrastive analysis with the native language would probably not explain Jenson's results — with a student population — and many linguists have grown skeptical of "interference"; the answer can be sought either in "language universals" (which Jenson's results do not seem to support) or, in the case of BEV and Atlantic Creole forms, in WAPE and Creoles related to it. WAPE is not copula-less (see below), but it does use a "zero copula."

Stewart (1965) very early called attention to how this "zero copula" (and the zero auxiliary) contrasted with an invariant *be*:

He sick   ≠   He be sick

He going   ≠   He be going

and pointed out how the forms in the left-hand column co-occur more readily with time adverbials like *right now* whereas those in the right-hand column fit more naturally with *all the time* or some equivalent. (This does not amount, in either case, to an absolute prohibition.) Both can occur with past-time expressions like *last Friday*; on *be* with such a co-occurrence see

116   Immigrants

Loflin, Sobin, and Dillard (1969). Early designations like "durative" and "intermittent" were applied (Fasold 1969), and early note was taken (first of all, apparently by Stewart) that *be V-ing* negated with *don't* whereas the zero form (and the occasional form with inserted *is, am, are,* etc., not always with the "agreement" conditions of Standard English) was negated with *ain't.* This was one evidence of a fairly elaborate system, and pedagogically it helped to refute teachers' notions of the "disorderly" usage of disadvantaged Black students. Similarities in West Indian English are greater than the familiar literature, which focuses on "basilectal" rather than "mesolectal" varieties, tends to indicate. Comparison was soon made to the Anglo-Irish "consuetudinal" or "habitual" copula. It was pointed out that Irishmen acted as overseers on the large plantations at a time when influence on the English of the slaves was a strong possibility.

It was not necessary to go to Anglo-Irish for such occurrences of invariant (non-infinitival, non-subjunctive) *be.* The King James Bible is a more easily accessible source. In fact, if italicized finite forms (representing presumably non-existent auxiliaries in the Hebrew original or the Old Testament) are equated with zero copula, something like the BEV verb system in two particulars (one more than usually adduced) can be found. The King James translation is, obviously, an unlikely source – but no more unlikely than Anglo-Irish.

Attestations of a simply invariant *be* can easily be discovered for white Americans.[3] Davis (1909) reports (c. 1800) an "oaf" (apparently white, since Davis usually identifies Negro speakers) who says, "You be in the pan now." This kind of thing is easy to find but simply irrelevant.

Two factors seem to be necessary to any serious claim about the BEV *be* ≠ $\emptyset$. The first is historical continuity of the population concerned (Stewart 1967, 1968). The second has to do with the full nature of the copula subsystem, not just with the occurrence of the forms (Loflin, Sobin, and Dillard 1969). The last citation shows the ability of *be* in the BEV to co-occur with past-time adverbials, like *last Friday.* Actually, the $\emptyset$ form also has the potentiality of that co-occurrence. Non-systemic factors (like the nonoccurrence of *ain't* as a negator of the italicized auxiliaries in the KJB) could be cited almost without limit, but to no purpose.

Within the framework of documentary differences, it seems significant that the attestations of the English of those who came from England and of Anglo-Irish immigrants have never been shown to contain either "zero copula" or "invariant" *be.* On the other hand, such attestations abound in the literature which cites Black speakers. Dillard (1972a) was strongly influenced by written representations of slave speech like Hugh Henry Brackenridge's *Modern Chivalry* (1792): *I be cash [catch] crab* ... Within the nineteenth century and later, evidence accumulates for the obligatory nature of *-ing* after the verb. In Gullah, a recognized creole variety of the low country or Sea Islands of South Carolina, Georgia, and Northern Florida, there is an apparent parallel in the variation between *NP de V* and *NP de Ving*. Turner (1949) recorded [sʌmpm̩ de kʌmIn], for which the meaning is either 'something is coming' or 'something was coming'. That is, there is a verbal category which marks something besides tense — perhaps "aspect" — and which may exist even in the absence of tense marking. (In the discourse unit, as distinct from the sentence, 'present' or 'past' seems always to be marked.) The historical claim is that *be* in the Brackenridge citation has replaced *de*. Here is where the real claim of difference from Anglo-Irish or other varieties is based: The creole system has an aspect-over-tense system not described for ordinary English at any of its historical stages but common-place within Afro-American varieties (Alleyne 1980).

Apart from systemic considerations, the uniqueness of the BEV verbal auxiliaries is not supported — whether in historical documents or otherwise. Humphreys's *The Yankee in England* (1815) presents a white visitor in England who uses both the auxiliary *been* and non-subjunctive, non-infinitival *be*:

What be you . . .? (p. 31)

This *be* negates

Suppose I ben't . . .

unlike BEV

Suppose I don't be . . .

Non-systemic considerations were, however, of no importance to investigators like B. Bailey (1965), Stewart, Loflin, Fickett, and Dillard (all references).

In the flurry of attempts to derive BEV invariant *be* from something British, it seems to have been overlooked that — if systemic considerations are overlooked — even a Dutch "origin" is possible. Veltman (1940: 82) cites *That's the one we be looking for* and reports that "*Be* is often substituted for other forms of the verb *to be* [in the Dutch-influenced English of Holland, Michigan] ." The implication is that "invariant" *be* can be derived from almost anywhere — a *reductio ad absurdum* which I gleefully accept. Perhaps attention can now be diverted to systemic factors.

Any attempt to reconstruct earlier historical stages of the BEV verb and to take into account documentary evidence would seem to need to deal with the relationship to the West African Pidgin English and Surinam varieties, among others. The set of verb forms would include, but not be limited to, the following:

(1) NP Ø V   John go
(2) NP de V   John de go
(3) NP Ø Adj[4]   John sick
(4) NP de Adj   John de sick
(5) NP be NP   John be a man

Both *NP been V* (Saramaccan *NP bi V* by a nasal deletion rule [Alleyne 1980]) and the locative construction would presumably be present in all the relevant varieties but can be omitted here.

There are some restrictions in present-day Afro-Creole varieties and probably always have been. Alleyne (1981: 82) reports how Krio informants refused to accept *a de sick* 'I am getting sick', although he cites Hancock's report of the acceptability of *a de Adj*. Alleyne (1980: 87) is also struck by the lack of clear meaning difference between *u de bunu* and *u bunu*, both 'we are good' in Saramaccan. It should certainly not surprise anyone that co-occurrence restrictions of this type complicate the picture.

Under the pressure of decreolization (leveling toward other varieties of English), it seems plausible that *de,* an auxiliary with possible origins in African languages, should be the first to go. According to Alleyne (1980: 211-2), in Trinidadian English, *d∧z* is attracted into the same function as *de.*

The *be* of (5) would be under some systemic pressure to spread, especially to replace *de.* The "zero" of (3) would be a somewhat less stigmatized form, falling together as it does with phonological deletions of *is* and *are* in some environments.

It should be noticed that this hypothetical set is still "copula rich." Early emphasis on "zero copula" did not mean — certainly not in the works of B. Bailey (1965) and Stewart (1965, 1966, 1967, 1968) — that creole languages were assumed to be "without copula." The Ø of (1) and (3) is not meant to dominate the set in any sense. There would seem to be little spread of the zero feature in the stage conveniently called the second:

(1) NP Ø V
(2) NP be V
(3) NP Ø Adj
(4) NP be Adj
(5) NP be NP

The common nineteenth century rule

(2) NP be Ving   John be going

would involve taking on a new feature, perhaps borrowed from ordinary English — whether or not under the influence of Irish speakers. On the other hand

(5) NP Ø N   John a man

May come from phonological deletions, language universals (if a *form* can be generated directly in that manner), or the ship's jargon stage of the formation of the pidgin.

In *Modern Chivalry* (1792), a relatively early attestation of this type, Cuff (whose name is based on the Ashanti day name for Friday) uses *NP be NP* five times in a relatively short speech and zero copula not at all except for *an de hair long,* which may contain an elliptical *come* from the last clause. Like the Irish servant Teague, Cuff also uses *was: de first man was de black a man.* Teague's *He was a good master* overlaps with Cuff's grammar in the area which they both share with ordinary English. Cuff's *I be cash* indicates perhaps an action of long duration, perhaps something of reportable consequence; quite incidentally, it is concerned with a past action. Today, non-subjunctive, non-infinitival *be* co-occurs in the same tale with (for example) *was Ving.* More than simply replacing *de,* however, this particular *be* has apparently acquired – or always had – a function as a kind of marker of importance. (The difference between *she was settin'* and *she be settin'* in a folk tale seems to be that the latter comes at the climax of the story, where it is also important that she [the wife] has been there all along.)

Whatever the source of this particular *be,* however, the earliest observers did not find it equally in the speech of Black and Irish speakers in the United States. That its occurrence in Black speech in opposition to zero copula is attested from the plantation literature (Stewart 1967) seems to be some argument for its provenience in Plantation Creole, which has virtually unbroken attestations from the late seventeenth century. It should be said, however, that Stewart, with whom I am in agreement on most things, has wanted to look at this *be* as a "relexification" of something like Gullah *blan* rather than of *de.*

If Black speakers borrowed specifically Irish *be* in the continental United States, in the West Indies (C. – J. Bailey 1982), or at some other place, why did they not also borrow *used be*? Why are there no Irishisms in the Black lexicon? Now, from the *Dictionary of American Regional English* – rather closely allied to the Linguistic Atlas itself – Hirshberg (1982b) says nothing about any, although he does insist that there are uniquely Black items in many domains.

As Wolfram (1974) and Feagin (1979) tend to indicate, Southern White English seems to have borrowed this *be* from the Blacks. Feagin (1979: 154) says only, "That is what has probably happened, at least in recent years."

Like Dillard (1972) and Wolfram (1974), Feagin points out the contact between whites and Blacks in childhood (1979: 71):

Most upper-class whites born before World War II had a Negro nurse, a 'Mammy', who served as surrogate mother.

See also Parkhurst (1938).

Looking at Anniston, Alabama, Feagin (1979: 77) finds about what the others concluded for the entire South:

The contact between white and black in Anniston varies according to age and class. The older upper class had intimate contact with blacks, more so than with working class whites. Teenagers of the upper class have had some contact with blacks . . .

Partly in response to the argument in (e.g.) Dillard (1972a: Chapter V) that Southern White English reflects strong influence from Black English rather than the speech of the Blacks being an extreme relic form, a kind of catch-all from many British dialects, Feagin writes:

> I see Black English and White Southern as ranging along a continuum, similar to the creole continuum in the Caribbean. In most areas of syntax, Black English and working-class/rural White English overlap, but Black English extends further in one direction, toward the Atlantic Creoles, and Southern White extends in the opposite direction, toward Metropolitan English.

For something of the same in the Bahamas, see Holm (1980).

Feagin's last statement seems unexceptionable, and perhaps it would represent the compromise called for — somewhat unusually for the controversial discipline of linguistics — in meeting after meeting of the 1970s. (Surely the controversy between the creolists and the dialect geographers is not so threatening as, say, a nuclear war!) The trouble is that forms which do occur in a large corpus of Black English may be overlooked if one is not constantly aware of the non-white English end of the continuum. One may find sequences like

NP would be is $\left\{ \begin{array}{c} \text{NP} \\ \text{Adj} \end{array} \right\}$

If one takes

> You my baby

as a true example of zero copula, and

> Is you my baby?

as the derived question form, overlooking the movement rules of ordinary English and simply considering *is* "a . . . surface, empty constituent like the supportive *do*" (Mufwene 1983: 26), then he may be able to see that

> You ain't my baby

can be questioned by

> Is you ain't my baby?

The last would be approximately the equivalent of ordinary English emphatic negative question: *AREN'T* you my baby?

Although, like most extremely complex potential syntactic sequences, seldom realized, the possible structures deviate more and more from ordinary English. Putting another *is* in as emphasis marker, we derive

> Is you is my baby?

where the first *is* is a question-marking constituent as above. With a single conjunction we get

> Is you is or is you ain't my baby?

This is actually the title and recurring refrain in Louis Jourdain's song from the 1930s.

Operating on an equivalent set of premises, one could produce

> You my baby
> You is my baby (emphatic)
> You would be my baby (hypothetical)

and

> You would be is my baby (both hypothetical and emphatic)

Sentences of the type

NP would be is $\left\{ \begin{array}{c} \text{NP} \\ \text{Adj} \end{array} \right\}$

actually turn up, although rarely, in compositions written by Black students at Northwestern State University of Natchitoches, Louisiana. The rarity of such sequences would seem to be explicable in terms of the constant awareness of the students that standard usage is to be observed as well as the relative infrequence of hypothetical emphatic statements.

The material discussed immediately above has not been reported from Northern big city projects, but the syntactic principles by which the sequences are produced are present in the descriptions of Loflin, Fickett, and others. To refer all the Black evidence to the South is to place an intolerable limit on the evidence which can be brought to bear on the contact picture in the United States. New York City, for example, figured prominently in the early slave trade, although most of the slave ships probably sailed out of Massachusetts ports. Stokes (1915-28: 347) reports:

> The negro quarter of the slaves of the West India Co. is also laid down on the Manhattan surveys. Its location apparently was in the East River shore, just North of the Saw kill, in about the present 75th Street.

Flick (1933: 402) states that New York had a larger percentage of Negroes in its population than did Virginia. Leonard (1910: 201) and Szass (1967: 217) report on the repressive elements of slavery in New York City at the end of the seventeenth century. Ottley and Weatherby (1967) trace the general history of Blacks in New York. These circumstances might not be important if the slaves did not use some special variety of English, but there is evidence that they did.

Perhaps the most interesting of the non-fictional writings about the speech of slaves is that of Justice Daniel F. Horsmanden in *The Negro Plot* (1744). He reports of Jack (i.e., Quaco), one of the ringleaders in the alleged conspiracy,

> his dialect was so perfectly negro and unintelligible, it was thought it would be impossible to make anything of him without the help of an interpreter.

In this case, interpreters were available in the persons of two young white men who had known Jack long enough and well enough to have learned his dialect. Among other things, Horsmanden's materials reveal that this "Negro" variety was learnable by whites. Horsmanden quoted the prisoner, "His master live in tall house Broadway. Ben ride de fat [i.e., white] horse." Horsmanden also recorded *backarara*, a variant of *buckra/bakra* 'white man', a form of wider distribution than is usually thought (see 135-140). He further documented the use of the day names like Cuffee and Cudjo in New York and commented several times on "the negroes' dialect." Benjamin Hobart, in *A History of Abidngon, Mass.* (quoted in Greene 1942: 247) and Sheldon (1895-6: 55) quote Massachusetts slaves who use the ubiquitous *massa, by and by*, and double negative – forms at least consistent with these slaves' speaking Black English. (See Mather [1721] for almost undeniable evidence of the use of West African Pidgin English in Massachusetts.) Added to the fictional representation of creole-like Negro speech in the Northern colonies (Krapp 1925; Stewart 1967, 1968) and to the evidence from Nova Scotia (Dillard 1972), this amounts to a rather impressive amount of evidence that the early stages of the BEV figured in a general picture of American language contact.

In spite of frequent pronouncements about the exceptionally small number of African etymons in American English (Mencken-McDavid and Maurer 1963: 125), the surface has only been scratched in dealing with such matters. Major (1970), Dillard (1977), and Hirshberg (1982a & b) offer some indication of the distinctiveness of the BEV vocabulary. One would think that Vass (1979) overstates the case somewhat, especially in giving attention to rare forms like *holla ding* "expression used in work songs" and *mafoobey* "exclamation of amazement." In a citation like *diddy-wa-diddy* 'legendary place of plenty to eat', however, she has merely scratched the surface in citing Kennedy's *Palmetto Country* (1942). It is reported from a 1929 song by bandleader Phil Harris, a self-conscious promoter of a Southern accent and of Southern living styles ("That's What I Like About the South" was perhaps his most characteristic number.) Harris's account of his acquiring the number links it to the Black oral tradition. The sexual suggestiveness of the term in a number of Southern and "country and Western" songs suggests a typically Black link between food and sex (Dillard 1977). There is still a great deal to be found out about this and other "nonsense" names and phrases associated with Black lore as there is — and probably for the same reasons — about "scat" singing, in which the articulation and intonation of apparently random nonsense syllables gives a suggestive undertone.

When slavery lost its economic appeal to the Northern colonies, they became strongly abolitionist in sentiment — as had Great Britain before them and for the same reason. But the states that had abolished slavery were not necessarily strong on tolerance, as Alexis de Tocqueville noted:

> The prejudice of race appears to be stronger in the states which have abolished slavery than in those where it still exists, and nowhere is it so important as in those states where servitude never has been known.

As in the case of the "plantation" states (see discussion above, pp. 110–114), social factors — in this case, prejudice and segregation — were at least potentially more important than raw demography in terms of dialect maintenance. It is not certain how long the creole stage of Black English persisted in non-Confederate states, nor how much influence could have been observed even in post-Civil War years. Nevertheless the variety existed in the Northern states in the prewar period and in fact seems never to have been confined to the Southern plantations.

With the heavy concentration of slavery in the Southern states (associated, originally, with the predominance of agriculture in those states) and with the greater density of Black (although not necessarily "African") cultural patterns, Black English became, to a great degree, a Southern dialect. It seems to have very strongly influenced the speech of Southern whites, especially those of the plantation-owning class, in a pattern more widespread in the New World than has been generally realized (Dillard 1972a, Holm 1980).

For Afro-American anthropology and Black cultural studies, the status of the Black English Vernacular (including its early history) seems of the utmost importance. It has even been suggested (Puckett 1926: 20, quoted almost as a kind of proof text by Whitten 1962) that the symbolic system of English prevented any significant African transmissions in such areas as religion and folklore:

> Apart from such isolated cases . . . the African impress upon the English language was negligible. Everywhere English became the accepted method of communication and English folk beliefs and superstitions were given an enormous advantage over African forms.

The dominance of "English" − considered as something transmitted in an uncomplicated fashion from Great Britain − has indeed made it almost the exclusive determinant of official, formal aspects of such domains; in the "intimate," or "non-public" aspects of Black culture, other factors have been important.

An analogy from naming practices may be relevant here. Except for the rash of Moslem names (Kareem, Mohammed) in the 1950s and 1960s, American Negro names have been strikingly English in nature, with Johnson well known to be the most popular surname in the Black community. Place names, with the exception of an occasional Cudjo Key in Florida, have shown an almost complete absence of African influence. When one looks at an *imaginary* place, however, like Diddy wa Diddy in blues lyrics, the ownership of which does not require economic dominance, the situation may change. Again when one looks at names for vehicles, which are not subject to official approval, there are striking similarities between Black American practices and those of the Caribbean and West Africa. And if one looks at nicknames (Dillard 1976b) or at the development of the Lousiana Black name Irchirl /ayrčayrl/ from a disguise of *Achilles* [ašil] , one sees a component which can be called "British" or even "European" only by a great exercise of arbitrariness.

African survivals, however, have never (*pace* Sledd 1980) been the primary focus of the "creolists" who have worked on the Black English Vernacular (B. Bailey 1965; Stewart 1967, 1968; Dillard 1972a). Nor have they been the exclusive preoccupation of innovative West Indianists (Taylor, Voorhoeve, all references). Nevertheless, it is almost impossible to examine the field without realizing how little attention was given even to such salient works as Herskovits and Herskovits (1936), Herskovits (1942), Jones (1963), Stearns

(1956), Stearns and Stearns (1968), and Lomax (1959). To invoke the language as a counter-argument to all that productive work is, it seems, to attribute almost magical power to a reconstructive theory of the development of American English which has not been especially productive even in the treatment of white American dialects.

The West Africans who were brought to the Americas retained traces of their original tongue, perhaps, but even more of the *lingua franca* that had developed — or spread — among slaves and slave traders. A similar situation existed among the Chinese brought in as exploited labor in the mid-nineteenth century, and the use of Chinese Pidgin English in the gold rush and thereafter is well attested. In marked contrast, Pennsylvania Germans, Chicanos, Cajuns, Jews, and certain other groups which had a great deal of integral cohesiveness from the beginning, have maintained their ethnic languages and/or dialects as a function of their group solidarity. The West Africans, on the other hand, had a bewildering diversity of languages and cultures, although some common currents have been shown or at least postulated. (In the Caribbean, Álvarez Nazario [1974] has produced a major work within this frame of reference.) The obtuseness of many whites, who saw only the skin color and heard only "foreign" speech, kept them from realizing how diverse the early African slaves were. Even Frederick Douglass showed little perception in that area. Yet tribal animosities persisted, in some cases, into the period of slavery in the New World (Goveia 1965).

For the Blacks, the complexity of the language contact situation, which included in many cases at least one Indian language, demanded the use of pidgin and the retention of creole for a long period. The visibility of black skins plus the color-caste system, which accompanied and extended far beyond slavery, further impeded assimilation. Thus, these involuntary immigrants were the furthest from the simplistic language assimilation paradigm. Their only real competitors for that little would be the American Indians, an almost equally "visible" group.

Slave labor was a major requirement of the Europeans who came to the Americas in the colonial period. As everyone knows, West Africans were the primary victims of that exploitation. But before the Africans were brought over, the Europeans attempted — usually with only marginal success — to enslave American Indians, either to work in mines or to till the soil.

Long before the appearance of Europeans, the Indians had worked out solutions to their own multilingual contact problems. There was, however, a basic difference in the solutions found by the coastal Indians and by the plains Indians.

Leaving aside Chinook Jargon of the Northwest for the moment, we find several Indian contact languages or varieties like Delaware Jargon, Occaneeche (perhaps also known as Saponey) of eighteenth-century Virginia, Tuscarora of

North Carolina, Pseudo-Shawnee or Savannah of eighteenth-century South Carolina, Catawba of the eighteenth-century North and South Carolina pied-mont, a jargon or jargons of the Creek confederacy extending down into Florida from perhaps as early as the sixteenth century, and Mobilian Jargon in the lower Mississippi Valley (Drechsel 1979 35-52). Most of these are mentioned in a few travelers' reports, but Delaware Jargon was the subject of rather extensive inquiry by Prince (1912).

Pidgin English, used in the early period from at least as far north as Massachusetts to the Florida Seminoles (Dillard 1972a; Goddard 1977, 1978), and perhaps other European contact varieties, had exerted some influence upon Delaware Jargon. In addition to *me* as the first-person singular pronoun and *paia* 'fire', Prince recorded *kabay* 'horse', obviously from Iberian. He derived *hodi* 'farewell' from English; Holm and Shilling (1982) point out its general use in the Atlantic English creoles. The Algonquian words *squaw* 'wife' and *papoose* 'a suckling child' suggest the beginnings of a pattern which would later become quite general, as frontiersmen and pioneers applied the terms to Indians of very different language families. Meredith (1932: 420) shows the incidence of compounds with *squaw* in Nebraska. Drechsel (1979) found /papos/ 'baby, child' among Louisiana speakers of Mobilian Jargon.

Although many European elements were present by the time descriptions of any type could be made, the lingua franca treated by Prince, like the others, was apparently Indian in essence. These varieties were used primarily by the coastal Indians. The plains Indians had their own solution, the well-known sign language, which frontiersmen observed and sometimes learned. Bourke (1892) reported how some Crows communicated with other tribes:

> Squatting upon the ground, with fingers and hands deftly moving, they communi-cated through the "sign language" . . . things which would astonish persons ignorant of the scope and power of this silent vehicle for the interchange of thoughts.

Campbell (1928) found that it had been "a sealed book to the coastal and mountain tribes [but] understood by all the Indians of the plains."

With the coming of the Europeans and African slaves, as well as by contact with other tribes displaced in the Indian "removal," there was fostered a replacement of the sign language in favor of a spoken variety, Pidgin English. Actually, the two coexisted. Campbell (1928: 659) described the communica-tive abilities of an Indian:

> Black Beaver's ability to hold communication with different tribes whom the exploring party met was not due to any knowledge of the oral language of those tribes, but to use of the sign language, which is universally understood by all the Indians of the plains, but which is a sealed book to the Coast and Mountain tribes.

But Campbell also quoted Black Beaver, a Delaware "living the last years of his life on the Washita" after "long experience in the Northwest" in obvious Pidgin English:

"Captain, I no tell him that Indian no fool and he know that not true, for I see heap and know that one big lie, for I live with white man long time and no see thing like that."[5]

Later, Indians found Pidgin English useful in a contact situation with the Chinese who came in from around the time of the gold rush and who, like the Blacks, were more successful in relating to the Indians as peers than to Europeans. There was also the problem of coping with Spanish and French as well as English, especially in the South and West. Richardson (1865) represents Indian squaws in Kansas who were asking for "sooker"; they could as easily have been seeking *azucar* (or for that matter *sucre*) as *sugar*, in a sense having three languages for the price of one. Danker (1959: 123) shows Indian women addressing Mollie Dorsey as "Wano [*bueno*, with characteristic disregard of gender concord] Squaw . . . Wano White squaw." Gregg (1844: 185) found a Comanche who "informed us that some of his part had a few mulas para *swap*." From the Seminoles in Florida and across the nation, Pidgin English attestations tend to be mixed with Spanish (Dillard 1972a, Bateman n.d.).

Although the earlier attestations of American Indian Pidgin English antedate those of any other Pidgin English variety (Goddard 1977), it is significant that they regularly turn up about ten years after the introduction of West African slaves into the area. The Africans had even earlier experience with the Europeans and the language contact problems which the latter introduced. Dillard (1972) argued that the Pidgin English was transmitted from the Africans to the Indians, and the possibility continues to be a live one. A contrary belief, held by linguists who do not discuss the existence of either AIPE or WAPE in the United States, is that an "interlanguage" factor has produced a situation where Native American English varieties often contain features which cannot be traced to either English (nonstandard or standard) or to the native language (Bartelt 1980: 10). Whatever the status of "interlanguage," it is well attested that AIPE functioned in the language contact situation (Leechman and Hall 1955, Miller 1967).

Certain linguistic features common to WAPE and AIPE are much more easily explained in terms of transmission than by independent 'origin. The use of preverbal auxiliary *been* (Bickerton 1979, Alleyne 1980), the *-um* post-verbal transitivizer (used approximately like New Guinea Pidgin *-im* as described by Mühlhäusler [1983: 69]), the use of *spose* in the meaning 'if', *bimeby* (often written *by and by*) as a future indicator, and familiar vocabulary items like *savvy* and *palaver* arouse the suspicions of anyone who has looked at other contact patterns. Holm and Shilling (1982) call /bay(m)bay/ Atlantic, although they also cited the "Brit[ish] dial[ect] West" form *bamby*; the notion, however, that speakers of British western dialects were in direct contact with plains Indians and that they exerted a worldwide influence seems one of staggering improbability.

There is, further, evidence that Blacks acted as interpreters for whites in contacts with Indians (Porter 1970). Among the attestations of such activity is that by Catlin (ed. Marvin C. Ross, 1959), whose Caesar spoke English, Spanish, and Lingua Geral, but who couldn't use any of them with some Pacific Coast Indians who came aboard the ship. Master of signs, "which (a curious fact) are much the same amongst all tribes, both in North America and South America" (1959: 134), Caesar is able to report, "Well, hear me, Massa Catlin . . . dem dar bery curious people. I guess you go ashore, Massa?"

Although frontiersmen and other observers (like James Fenimore Cooper) did not use the term AIPE, they recorded many examples of it. Cook (1976) reported her Arizona missionary grandfather's hearing a Pima Indian say, "Louis no Christian." Famed Indian painter Catlin recorded (1959: 000):

"You white man, where you come from?"
"How white man come to England? How you face come to get white?"
"Among white people, no body ever take your wife – take your children – take your mother, cut off nose – cut eyes out – burn to death."
"No! Then *you* no cut out eyes – you no burn to death – very good."

Another of the recorders of AIPE, Thomas Woodward (1859: 70) knew no name for the variety either. But he felt compelled to meet the objections of those who doubt the acuracy of the long passage in AIPE he quoted:

Now the above is an Indian speech, and no doubt will appear silly to some who have not been accustomed to these people. Should it, however, fall under the eye of those who were along at the time, they will recognize John's speech, and call to mind our old friends.

And even James Sledd, a self-styled stuffy old professor of *Anglistik*, tells me about two Georgia Indians, Walkingstick and Toothpick, in a family story (personal communication), one of whom said, regarding Sledd's great-grandfather Sam Candler, who married a thirteen-year-old girl, "Ugh! Old Sam raise-um up wife to suit self." Sledd himself says that the attestation obviously shows "a pidgin" in use in west Georgia well into the nineteenth century.

NOTES

1. For an interesting coincidence, note the (unplanned) change from *massa* to *boss* in the Gullah attestations (pp. 15-16). The texts were not selected with these words in mind.
2. Preverbal *been* tends to drop out of what can be called for convenience an "academic register" of the BEV. Except where the base verb contains *-ing* (*I been knowing him a long time*), I have never seen it in a student paper. Like preverbal *done*, it is rarely heard in a classroom environment. Those who base their studies primarily on school language often find that this particular register, although not identical to that desired by the school system, lacks the salient features of the BEV. Torranz and Zimmerman (1981: 10) report that auxiliary *be* was seldom used by Black students and that certain other features have become essentially standard by

about the fifth grade level. If so, there must have been something in their elicitation procedures that encouraged an extremely academic register. Auxiliary *be,* for example, is relatively frequent in college freshman composition papers from the same general geographic area. Like other such statements, the confident statement by Torrans and Zimmerman (1981: 11) that they had elicited "the most casual speech" seems greatly overstated. Their "types of language samples" (1981: 6)

    I. Repetition of sentences
    II. Repetition of a story told by the interviewer
    III. Telling a story from a picture sequence
    IV. Telling about pictures
    V. Spontaneous speech – individual
    VI. Spontaneous speech – group

do not deviate much from those familiar in the literature. The investigators show no awareness, however, that transcribing even a relatively short period of speech under "Condition VI" is a gigantic task, hardly to be undertaken except by a major project.

The participant observer technique, utilized especially by Stewart (1964, 1965) and familiar to Caribbeanists especially from the work of Douglas Taylor, yields results that are unlikely to be fully matched by formal elicitation methods. Rickford (1975) shows, however, how an innovative empirical test can validate observations made under conditions of participant observation.

3.   In spite of the received position articulated by Brooks (1935) and almost universally followed until about 1965, C.M. Wise (1933) and his students (Pardoe 1937) continued to investigate the possible effect of Black speech on whites. Pardoes (1937: 344) considers "the relation throughout the South of the Negro nurse to the white baby; the considerable amount of playing together . . . the fact that there were relatively few whites thrown in with the large numbers of Negroes in the early plantations and later in the outlying cotton districts . . ." Pardoe stresses the importance of the childhood association.

4.   Mufwene (1983: 29) assumes "an obligatory absence [of the copula] before adjectival predicates" and a generalization from that state. My own version assumed nearly the same thing: zero varying with *de/da/a* before adjectival predicates, with neutralization of the contrast as in Sranan (below). Both of us would agree with Alleyne (1980) that constructions like *you is, we is, I'm is, I'm am* are evidence of insertion of a copula by influence from another variety ("the acrolect," as Mufwene styles it, following the terminology of Stewart [1962b]).

5.   Black Beaver was also quoted by Marcy (1866: 122):

"Bob Jones [a rich Chickasaw] he say, s'pose find um copper mine, give um four hundred dollars."

"Delaware law, s'pose show um' Merican mine, kill um."

Chapter VI

Frontier Speechways — Old and New

The next stage in the history of American English–the movement of the British colonists and the ethnic immigrants, along with displaced Indian tribes, to the West–cannot be accounted for in terms of a linguistic vacuum. Movement into the frontier brought new language contacts, but something was always carried along from the preceding stages. Gradually, in the competition of languages, English won control, but there were many times when the emigrant population from England had to adjust to a language contact situation not of its own making and not necessarily made for it. This complex linguistic situation left its mark on the speech of the American frontier and, to some degree, of all subsequent Americans.

In no few ways, the multilingual situation and the other social factors of the frontier resembled what the frontiersmen's ancestors had run into at sea and in the coastal colonies. Long distances had to be covered, many new populations dealt with, and physical adaptations made to new environments. The movement characteristic of the new American society and the relationships of the frontier brought speakers of American English back into contact with the language problems which had existed and been partly solved in the European maritime expansion.

Even some of the terminology was the same. In a strikingly significant metaphor, the large wagons with canvas hoods used by the settlers entering the West were called *prairie schooners*. *Caboose*, the maritime borrowing from Dutch for 'cook's cabin or galley', only slightly changed in present-day Bahamian English to 'a hearth for cooking on a boat' or 'a camping hut' (Holm and Shilling 1982), was first used by the pioneers for the cook wagon, then for a stationary cook house, and finally for the car on the train that contained the provisions and the facilities for cooking them. There is a significant difference in British and American usage; Jensen (1981: 155) tells how it can affect standardized testing:

> In England, *caboose* means a ship's kitchen, and hence many English children fail the PPVT [Peabody Picture Vocabulary Test] item that requires pointing to the last car on a train.

Davis (1909: 10) used it in the sense of a ship's kitchen; on his trip to

America in 1799, "there was never any occasion for us to have recourse to the caboose" because he and his two messmates had brought along a stove. The rangeland name for the food carrier later became the *chuck wagon*, and a now-obsolete term for unemployment *riding the chuck line* developed; both are reminiscent of the British Navy's *chuck barge*, the bread bin or case in which the ship's biscuits are kept. Layton (1955) also identifies *chuck* as "lower deck and civilian slang for 'bread'."

More similarities between the language of the sea and that of the frontier could be cited, but few seem more interesting or significant than *sky pilot* 'parson'. That it is not an Americanism is much less significant than that it is a maritime usage. It seems to have arisen as a compound with the nautical sense of *pilot*, which functioned in several sailors' compounds. Within the United States, *pilot* (verb) came to mean 'guide a person (or party) overland or about a place' by 1649 and the noun *pilot* was applied to a guide on land. The first attestation in the *Dictionary of Americanisms* is actually of an "Indian Pilate," by whose direction a party "Set o[u] r corse." Around 1842, a short-lived application to a railroad conductor developed. Cowboys came to use the term; Bauer (1975) writes of "Cowboys and Skypilots" in the Western religious experience as though using a term thoroughly familiar in the West. It would hardly be necessary to determine whether the "sky pilot" who "praised the Lord and passed the ammunition" in a World War II popular song represented naval terminology, general Western usage, or for that matter generalized American slang. Maurer (1930-1) reported for underworld argot

Sky pilot. A protestant minister.

Mobility, not a sedentary, long-settled condition, has always been characteristic of the American population, even though the latter yields best to dialect geography as a technique for reconstructing historical developments. A statement to that effect can be found in Hockett (1958: 483) and at least by implication in many other responsible sources. In order to understand the development of American English we cannot limit ourselves to regarding the British-derived Americans as though they were alone and worked out their own language development with only minor influences from elsewhere.

Conventional histories, in their concern with the claims and counterclaims of the European nations to the "new" continent, find it all too easy to overlook the fact that two of the most prominent groups with which the "white" Europeans came into contact were the American Indians and the Africa-derived slaves.

Insofar as the Indians in the West were concerned, the first contacts tended to be made by the fur trappers or "mountain men." These men had interesting locutions, according to recorders of their speech and customs like Ruxton (1848). Common Westernisms like *savvy*, *palaver*, and the general intensifier *heap* are not only in their language but are prominent in the pidgin tradition. Other terms peculiar to the mountain men stemmed from their occupation, with a lot of emphasis on the animal which finished his staple pelt, the beaver. When one fur trapper asked another whom he was working for, he quite naturally expressed it with "Whose beaver you earnin'?" Derived from Dutch ultimately, a loan translation, *beaver pay* was used in the colonies from as early as 1662, when it is attested in the Long Island *Record*.

The spin-off from beaver-trapping terminology was tremendous among the mountain men. If the beaver swam away with a trap, all was not lost; there was a *float stick* (Ruxton 1848) attached which would tell where the trap had gone. (Adams [1968] uses the more exotic-sounding *float-my-stick*.) From this, mountain men came to use *the way the stick floats* for 'what's up' or 'what's what'. It was the rough equivalent of later *the way the ball bounces* or *the way the cookie crumbles*. Whether mountain men are responsible for *work like a beaver* or not, it comes from a time (1741) when they would have been the ones most likely to observe the beaver. *Eager beaver* apparently has no attestation before the 1940s, but the earlier phrase may have contributed to its spread and acceptance. A.B. Guthrie's *The Way West* has a trapper saying, "Worth a pack of beaver to see you, you old bastard, and if you got a dry, here's whiskey." *Dry*, associated with the lack of alcoholic drink, had been used for a long time in England although primarily as an adjective. The U.S. system of voting precincts "wet" or "dry" and designation of people favoring one ticket or another as *wets* or *dries* was well in the future. If Guthrie, who knew his mountain men, is authentic, the trapper was somewhat innovative grammatically in using *dry* as a noun. Phrases like *a gone beaver* and *a gone coon* spread from the mountain men. The latter may have had a tinge of the ethnic slur word used about Blacks, since the mountain man frequently used *this nigger* or *this coon* for *I*. Marryat (1839) reports, however:

> In the Western states, where the raccoon is plentiful, they use the abbreviation coon even in speaking of people.

Communication with the Indians was carried on at least partly in the Plains Sign Language. Sketchy frontier accounts support the generalizations of Dick (1941: 69):

> The Indians had a universal sign language by which members of the different tribes who could not understand each other's speech could converse readily for hours. Often by way of practice trappers sat conversing by this method, and it was reflected in the sparcity of words of their conversation.

Frontier observers also corroborate the statement by Taylor (1981: 194): "Signing was often accompanied by verbal language." That verbal language was often Pidgin English, Spanish, or a mixture of the two.

Since the function of the Plains Sign Language has been little studied, it is not known how much influence there was on the distinctive phraseology of the frontier. A phrase like *rubbed out* 'destroyed', may well have come from this sign language. Mencken confidently traces the phrase to Prohibition gangster talk, but Neihardt (1932) records Black Elk, an Oglala Sioux holy man, protesting in 1863 about how "the Wasictus [white men] were coming and that they were going to take over our country and rub us all out." Burton (1860) records *rubbed out* 'extinct' in a Western context. Even earlier, Ruxton (1848) derived the term from "the Indian figurative language." It figures extensively in the literature of the mountain men. The sign in Plains Indian Sign Language, made by rubbing the right hand over the left palm (Umiker-Sebeok and Sebeok 1978: I: 167) may well be the source. The same sign is used in the Lord's Prayer with the translation "rub out our works bad." The next phrase, translated "the same as we forget" involves rubbing the left hand over the right palm.

Another phrase often used in frontier literature, *gone under*, may well be a verbalization of the sign made by moving one hand from above the other to below it. Sometimes, in the literature of the mountain men, it is used to mean 'die'. There is not, however, a translation equivalence. According to Umiker-Sebeok and Sebeok (1978: xxii), "the less the individual signer has to rely upon translation from spoken language, the greater the fluency of sign language performances," On the other hand, such a statement seems to indicate that the influence came from the sign language to spoken language and not *vice versa*.

French was at least as important a language for the fur trade as English, although the English speakers got the publicity in the United States because of newspaper coverage (Isley 1939: 100). Spanish was also used, along with the kind of mixed Spanish and Pidgin English reported elsewhere on the border. Ruxton (1848) presents this scene:

> The Indian exclaimed in broken Spanish and English mixed, "*Si, si,* me Arapaho, white man *amigo,* come to camp, eat heap *carne* – me *amigo* white man. Come from Pueblo – hunt Cibola – me gun break – *no puedo matar nada: mucha hambre.* (very hungry) – heap eat.

The preeminence of French is reflected in *plews* 'beaver pelts' (from *plus,* according to Ruxton). Extreme anglicization was frequent. One of the most familiar trees on the plains, if not in the mountains, was the bois d'arc; Dodge (1874) actually spelled it *bowdark.* Others use the spelling *peraira* for the French *prairie.* The term for a delicacy made from the buffalo's intestines was boudin, also borrowed – no doubt independently–in Louisiana.

An etymological puzzle exists in *fofarrow,* the word for the finery that a pretty young squaw demanded and usually received from a mountain man. Louise Pound made the attractive but highly improbable suggestion that it was a kind of blend of French *frou frou* and Spanish *fanfarrón.* Vass (1979: 188) lists – not in this connection – *foofaraw* 'fuss, disturbance about very little' and compares "Bantu" *-fufula* 'create confusion'. In this respect, Ruxton's early quotation is strongly relevant:

"First I had a Blackfoot [squaw] – the darndest slut as ever cried for fofar-row . . ."

The trappers borrowed from the maritime contact language in the term *freebooter*, for a bandit who might *raise* (steal) their *possibles* (clothes, kitchen utensiles, etc.). They either made up or borrowed from the general American stock phrases like *not know poor bull from fat cow* [buffalo]. According to Safire (1983), the phrase *NP doesn't know* is the favorite American way of attributing stupidity to a person, with variants in many dialects. Safire, who apparently has privileged information, quotes from the still-forthcoming *Dictionary of American Regional English.*

After the trappers came wagon trains bringing farmers to disposses rather than to mix with the Indians. Especially before 1860, some of them brought slaves; obviously, the last had a very different relationship to other ethnic groups from that of an occasional Black trapper like Jim Beckwourth.

Between the mountain men and the farmers – and especially before the hated sheepherders – those who raised cattle came to the frontier, primarily in the South and Southwest. The story of how the "Anglos" moved into Texas and learned the cattle trade from the Mexicans has been told so often that one would believe there is nothing to be added to it, but Jordan (1981) has managed to find something. He shows how the cattle-tending tradition which moved from South Carolina south and west along the Gulf corridor as far as East Texas preceded the learning of the business from the Mexicans, provided a few but rather important features of the trade, and even contributed to some of its vocabulary. Bill Pickett's trick of jumping from his horse onto a cow, securing a hold, and fastening his teeth on the cow's lip gave rise to the term *bulldogging,* which could not have come about if it had not been for the cattle-dog tradition brought in by the English immigrants. (Pickett himself was, however, Black [O'Brien, 1961].) Jordan (1981: 31) points out how "the term 'bulldogging', used at least since the late 1700s in Britain, refer[red] to holding or working cattle and hogs with bulldogs." Pickett obviously gave a novel twist to the already-familiar term.

A purely Eurocentric view will never provide an adequate account of the cattle trade along the Gulf corridor or of the language contact situation there. Among other languages in the area was Yama – a name for what is also called Mobilian Jargon – used as a way of designating a contact language from the word meaning 'right, all right, indeed; this, that (in answer to "Which one?")' (Drechsel 1979). Drechsel argues convincingly that this largely Choctaw-based variety existed before the Europeans came. In an attestation from 1838-41, Gustav Dresel's *Houston Journal* typically makes the contact vernacular a "mixed" language:

> The old man understood some words of English and Spanish, and I was acquainted with some telling Indian expressions, so that with the assistance of the sign language I could make myself understood without any interpreter.

An example of the Alabama Indian's speech shows how much the contribution of English and Spanish is overestimated:

"No, gshaw, papeshillo,[1] plata, plata, shocke ma fina!" That is nothing, man; silver, silver is fine, good the sterling.

Plate may well be the only word from a European language; Dresel possibly thought *fina* was Spanish, but the word may well have been MJ *fe(:)na* 'very, especially, the best' (Drechsel 1979). Linguistic preconceptions may well have influenced Dresel's not-entirely-accurate transcription: his *shocke ma* is probably *čokma* 'good, well'.

Dresel may very well have been familiar with contact-language use of Spanish between Indians and Europeans; typically, he may have failed to understand that it is not the case that one lingua franca solution is found for every multilingual contact situation – witness the use of both French and Pidgin English in the East Cameroun. Working apart from, almost in spite of, the linguists, Jordan (1981) found evidence of a "partly Romance contact vernacular" in an area which would have overlapped partly with MJ. Like Wood (1974) stressing the importance of Blacks in the eastern American cattle trade, Jordan cites as a linguistic survival *crawl* 'livestock pen', from Dutch-Portuguese-African *kraal*. Although not involved in the monogenesis controversy (see p.   ), Jordan came independently to deal with "Dutch-Portuguese-African."

This "partly Romance lingua franca" may well be the explanation to many problems in early Southwestern English. There are a number of controversial derivations, either unconvincingly traced to Spanish or left in relative mystery.

Jordan (personal communication) tends to agree with my position that the westernism *dogie* may well have come out of this era in the development of the cattle trade, although admittedly evidence is scanty. When it was first recorded in 1888, the term was already the subject of general puzzlement:

A bunch of steers had been traveling over the scoria buttes to the head of the Creek; they were mostly Texas doughies – a name I have never seen written but it applies to young immigrant cattle.

(Century Magazine)

Apparently influenced by such spellings, the *Dictionary of Canadianisms* derives the word from *dough-guts*, "with reference to a bloated belly resulting from poor feeding." Apparently, since the putative source is plural, DCE takes *dogies* as basic and *dogie* as a back formation (not unlike the well-worn example of *pea* from *pease*). However that may be, the change $/-\partial t/$ to $/-iy/$ in the second syllable seems unprecedented. Furthermore, evidence from the 1890s shows that the term became a synonym for *barnyard cattle*, which are hardly ill-fed compared to range cattle.

Not long after the earliest attestation, Wister (1893) recorded a version of a cowboy song which sets the irreducible minimum of features for dogies, [+small]:

Sing hooplio get along my little dogies,
For Wyoming shall be your new home,
Its [sic] hooping and yelling and cursing these dogies
To our misfortune and none of your own.

Although Adams (1968) suggests spontaneous generation by an anonymous Texas cattleman, the absolute absence of the feature [+large] (*big dogies* would be ludicrous) suggests a connection to African and Afro-American *-dog-* 'little'. Somewhere in the mix of Black cowboys in the Gulf corridor or in the West there may have been a retention of something akin to Swahili *kidogo* 'a little', Bambara *dogo* 'small, short', Ga *ateké* 'short', and Twi *ateké* 'short-legged'. Turner (1949) attests Gullah *Dogo* as a personal name; if Bracketville Gullah is to be considered an importation from the Sea Islands or low country (Hancock 1980) rather than an outcropping of a generalized Plantation Creole, *dogie* might be considered to have been so transferred as easily as to have developed in some odd fashion from *dough-guts* or Spanish *adobe*, which has actually been suggested. Wister elsewhere (1893: 159) recorded *doga* 'anything in stock that's trifling', and the connection between [+small] and [+trifling] would seem to be a reasonable one. DJE lists *dogi* 'short, small' and the typically Afro-Creole reduplication *dogi dogi*. It also attests Jamaican compounds like *dogi fowl* 'a small fowl', *dogi hen* 'a small hen', and *dogi man* 'a short man'. Adams (1968) records Western *dogie lamb*, a direct parallel, and *dogie man*, not directly comparable.

Mason's (1960) suggestion of another Africanism in the cattle trade vocabulary has been strongly attacked by Cassidy (1978).[2] Mason suggested that *buckaroo*, conventionally derived from Spanish *vaquero*, came rather from Gullah *buckra*. This form, common to the Atlantic English creoles although there is the prominent variant *bakra*, is attested in Turner (1949). It appears, however, never to have been uniquely characteristic of the low country or sea islands; Horsmanden (1744: 128) points out that in New York City "Backarara . . . Negro language, signifies white people" and Benjamin Franklin (1782) gives *boccarorra* in a slave's speech in Philadelphia. These are only the beginnings of the spelling variations which Mason depended on. Hancock (1980) finds that *buckra/bakra* "has acquired an extended meaning in A[fro] S[eminole] C[reole] . . . 'outsider' or 'non-Seminole'." Whether the Bracketville Gullah form was borrowed from white westerners or transmitted directly by Blacks – which is of course more likely – it reflects the pejoration which also characterizes *buckaroo*.

Once the cattle industry was established among the Anglo Texans, there were many terms for *cowboy: cow-puncher, cow-poke, (cow) waddy*, and *vaquero* (probably /vakerow/ or /bakerow/), the last frequently a different form from *buckaroo*. The pejorative feature differentiates *buckaroo*; Harvey (1913), although giving only the glosses 'a broncho-buster, cow-puncher', offers the illustrations:

That night the buckaroos shot up the town.
He is some buckaroo all right.

Wentworth (1942) repeats Harvey's sentences, probably in support of his unconvincing attempt to derive the suffix -*eroo* from *buckaroo*. A tinge of the meaning 'frontier rowdy' seems, however, to be associated with the word.

If the first citation in DA is indeed an attestation of *buckaroo* — and that assumption will be called in question below — then Texas would seem to be the natural locale for the word. Dewees's writings, the first citation, are styled *Letters from Texas* (1827), although the one quoted actually originated in Saltillo, Mexico. Atwood (1956: 53) reported:

> *Buckaroo*, supposedly a widely used western term has never caught on in Texas.

Braddy (1937) anticipated Atwood's judgment and asserted that *buckaroo* was frequently used elsewhere in the West, especially in Montana. The word seems, in fact, best acclimated in the Northwest, where it has spread, with new technical meanings, to at least two other occupations (Mencken 1936).

Mason asserted that *buckaroo* had acquired the "surface meaning" 'cowboy', imposed apparently from *vaquero* on Afro-Creole *buckra/bakra*. He offered no phonological arguments except those based on the many spelling variants of the word. His attribution to white writers of the belief that "a Negro might confuse sounds, particularly *v* and *b*" is, in light of the merest commonplaces of Spanish phonology, best forgotten. Cassidy, on the other hand, has a set of roughly ordered rules: weakening of the initial, unstressed (after borrowing, presumably) vowel of *vaquero*, stress shift to the first syllable (in support of which Cassidy has to invoke the word *buck*, which otherwise has no etymological relevance), and finally, raising of the last vowel to /uw/. It should be noted that Cassidy does not link this final change to any kind of stress shift but sees it rather as a development by analogy to the -*eroo* suffix popular in such Americanisms as *flopperoo* and *switcheroo* from about 1942 (Cassidy's date).

There are many difficulties with this last step. For one thing, spellings which indicate a raised-vowel pronunciation for *buckaroo* date back to 1889, 53 years earlier. Bentley (1931) has *smokeroo*, which would narrow the gap by eleven years, but the resorting to -*eroo* brings many problems with it. Wentworth (1942) derived the suffix from *buckaroo*! A fondness for biological metaphor in expressing linguistic change could lead one here to an intriguing speculation: In some wondrous way, the suffix -*eroo* and the word *buckaroo* begat each other! At any rate, the kind of etymological purity which is served by tracing the phonological, morphological, and semantic components of a word to a single source is compromised in Cassidy's treatment. Before discarding either Mason's or Cassidy's solution, one should do a great deal more investigation.

Mason was strongly influenced by spellings like Dewees's earliest-discovered *bakharas*. From Cassidy's point of view, that spelling would have to be considered some kind of distortion of *vaqueros*. But Dewees, like Stephen F. Austin (with whom he corresponded), was a student of Spanish. He rejoiced in the opportunity to hear no other language for days at a time, and he recorded a number of Spanish words. He even indulged in a bit of Hispanist pretension: "the Escoses or Scotch." He has *empresarios, haciendas, Ayuntamiento, rancho*, and *rancheros*, all in correct Spanish. Except that he uses *h* for graphic *j* and *e* for graphic *i* in *havalenas* (the peccary), Dewees makes no other mistake in the individual words of undisputed Spanish origin which he cites. He spells *rancheros* – parallel to *vaqueros* in syllable and stress patterns and in the vowel of the initial syllable – in the standard Spanish way. Can it be said that his *bakharas*, contrary to his other patterns of Spanish usage, is a mistake for *vaqueros*? Dewees glosses the word as 'herdsmen', but does not say that it is Spanish – and he often calls attention to his own use of that language. The attestation *bakharas* is not unambiguously an occurrence of *buckaroos*; DAE gave a separate entry to BAKHARA, with only this one instance.

Another apparently anglicized form in Dewees's usage is *mustang*, usually traced to Spanish *mesteño* and assumed to belong to the Texas cowboy period of borrowing. Bentley, however, traces it to a strange blend of *mesteño* and *mostrenco* 'that which belongs to no one'. In the "reduction" of the initial vowel and (presumably later) shift of stress to the first syllable, *mustang* is the closest parallel to the supposed development of *vaquero* in the cowboy Spanish vocabulary. One should not conclude, however, that there are no problems with *mustang* other than its doubtful Spanish source and its date, at least twenty years before Dewees's *Letter*.[3] For one thing, why did it lose the "inflectional" vowel rather than turning it into /-uw/ (*mustangoo* or *mustanyoo*)? The palatal or non-palatal nature of the nasal is an additional problem (cf. *canyon* from *cañon*).

Still another word ordinarily traced to Spanish and used but given no special indiation of being non-English by Dewees, *calaboose*, is first attested in J. Pope's *Tour of the South and West* (1792). The title here is misleading: Pope got no farther west than New Orleans, and the *callibouse* [sic] that he refers to was in Mobile. The dictionaries derive the word from Spanish *calabozo*, and it sometimes occurs in that spelling in the English attestations. Pope's spelling suggests, however, French – a language not unknown in the area where he was traveling. It is interesting that British traveler Sir Richard Burton, in an 1860 attestation not used by the dictionaries, traced the word in these terms:

> The Spanish is *calabozo*, the French *Calabouse*. In the Hispano-American countries it is used as a "common jail" or a "dog hole"; and as usual is converted into a verb.

Calaboose, it happens is also a widely known Pidgin English term, attested in various literary sources like Herman Melville (Tahiti) and Margaret Mead (Manus, near New Guinea). Ingraham (1835) gives an early attestation from a port city:

> ... the famous Calaboos, or Calabozo, the city prison, so celebrated by all seamen who have made the voyage to New Orleans.

On the same page is, "That is the Calaboos." Ingraham, in the same work, stresses the linguistic complexity of New Orleans; as the company approached the calaboose, "the chattering of half a dozen languages all at once, as we rode along, assailed our ears." Like other vocabulary of the cattle trade, *calaboose* seems to be Romance, but not necessarily Spanish.

Calaboose, if derived from *calabozo,* would be an example of the raising of Spanish /o/ to cowboy /uw/, but the derivation is far from convincing. Hill (1979) also cites the older pronunciation of *lasso*/læsuw/, but Adams (1968) derives *lasso* from Portuguese *laço* 'a snare', and raising of the Portuguese *-o* would be much more likely.

As Dewees's spellings (regularly *-o* and *-a* for masculine and feminine Spanish nouns, "correctly" in every case except those cited) and a minimum of comparison to other borrowings of the period will show, Mexican Spanish final *-o* in the cowboy words of the first two quarters of the nineteenth century does not become English /-uw/ but /-ow/ in borrowed words. The words are well known, but here are some final *-o* words from Adams (1968):

amigo	cuidado
arriero	paisano
arroyo	rodeo
caballo	. . .

The last has shifted the stress from the second to the initial syllable in South-western English (of some speakers) but did not before that reduce the vowel of the first syllable as *vaquero* must be assumed to have done in the formation of *buckaroo.* Neither has it raised /-o/ to /-uw/. The only variant pronunciation, outside of the slight possibility of *buckaroo,* of a Spanish-derived word pronounced in English with /-uw/ is the above-mentioned *lassoo.* (Hill [personal communication] has cited *San Berdoo* as a familiar name for San Bernardino [California], but it is not at all clear that this form belongs to the same tradition.)

There has been even more of the giving up of the conventional constraints of historical phonology in the derivation from Spanish of *wrangler* (from *caballerango)* and *cavvyard/cavviard* (from *caballada).* Both contain an etymon for 'horse', and it is perhaps not completely amiss to remember *kabay* from Prince (1912). DA first attests *cavvyard* from the writings of Stephen F. Austin — a strange mistake for a man who was meticulous about his Spanish. In context, both of these words appear, in their first DA citations, to be familiar English words rather than Spanish borrowings. The rather clear implication would be that they are borrowings from before the period of major Southwestern contact with Spanish. Now John (1983) cites a Louisiana manuscript from 1808 which supports that conclusion, at least insofar as Spanish borrowings are assumed to come from Texas. The exact derivation of *cavv (y)* from /kaba(C)/ remains in doubt, as does the apparent suffix /-(y)ard/. But there is no longer any need to speak of mere distortions of Spanish.

When Stephen F. Austin uses *mustang horses* in an 1821 citation, he also does not appear to be using "Spanish." The first attestation, from Pike in 1808, is rather inconclusive; but those from Austin and from Dewees (1852) leave a distinctly non-Spanish impression.

In light of these considerations, it seems relevant that there were several Portuguese (or, as Alleyne [1980] would have it, Iberian) contact varieties (e.g., Papiamentu) which were later swamped under Spanish vocabulary, which were once spoken in polities governed by Spain, and which are popularly considered varieties of Spanish. They were spoken in coastal and maritime areas, which may give some significance to the fact, often pointed out by historians of the Louisiana area, that the early migrating "Anglos" going across the Spanish/French border into Texas often referred to topographic features by nautical words like *cove* and *island,* and that the immigrants frequently indulged in lyrical comparisons of the prairie to the sea. It might help explain, also, how a folklorist like Jan Brunvand (1965) was able to find so many common points between the folklore of the American cowboys and that of sailors. Branch (1961: 164) confirms this: "The real kinship of the American cowboy is with the men on that everlasting frontier the sea . . ."

Some of the same knowledge about the writings of the early immigrants into Texas prompted Jordan (1973) to question the traditional derivation of Texas *mott* from Spanish *mata*. Jordan pointed out that the loss of inflectional *-a* is not the regular pattern in such loanwords. (He may not have been aware of the treatment of the inflectional vowels in some severely altered borrowings like *chaps, wrangler,* and the less drastically altered *tank* and *cinch*.) Jordan tried to find an Irish source for *mott*, and at least his objection to the Spanish source does seem well taken.

Two further deletions of the "inflectional" vowel seem to constitute important evidence: *lariat* from *la reata* and Louisiana French (and English) *lagniappe* from Quechua by way of Spanish *la ñapa*. DA credits the first attestation to "our Creole Negroes." Both have a historical definite article now incorporated into the word itself, so that an English *the* can easily precede what is historically the Spanish word for *the* (*the lariat, the lagniappe*). There is one other such American English word, *alligator,* precedable by *the* but from words that mean 'the lizard'. *Alligator* is not a "cowboy" borrowing but came into English earlier from maritime contact with Spanish, first recorded by British travelers to describe American reptiles. The use of *lariat* is less clearly international, but attestations sometimes take the form *lariette*, as though the word were French.

Combining the article with the noun is a common word-forming device in Papiamentu (*lareina* 'queen', not 'the queen') and Haitian Creole (*lakay* 'house', not 'the house'). *Lagniappe* has been conventionally traced to *yapa*, the added article explained no more adequately than with the phrase "from Spanish." Nasalization of the initial palatal glide is observable even in varieties in which the article has not been incorporated into the noun, as in Puerto Rican Spanish *la ñapa*. /ɲ-/ is relatively rare in Spanish; the great majority of the words in Puerto Rican Spanish that begin with it are Africanisms (Álvarez Nazario 1974: 168). Alvarez Nazario also cites the occurrence of *la ñapa* in Colombia, Venezuela, Central America, Mexico, Cuba, and Santo Domingo as well as in Trinidad, where he apparently considers it to have been transmitted to the English of that island from the Spanish which is now of restricted distribution there. Earlier contact with Arabic, yielding *alcohol*, *algebra*, *alférez* by a roughly analogous article incorporation, is often adduced, but it is hard to see what relevance that undoubted historic fact could have for the New World situation.

With all this evidence of a special Romance (or Iberian) contact language, it seems difficult to believe the derivation of *buckaroo* from *vaquero* with *ad hoc* phonological developments and the collaboration (as Cassidy would have it) from both *buck* and *-eroo*, especially since the latter cannot be proved to have had an independent existence at the time it supposedly performed such a helpful service. Mason's derivation from *buckra* is almost as bad as either of those procedures, but it does have the advantage of having brought into the picture an attested and respectably studied language contact pattern.

Southwestern cowboys used *vaquero* with varying degrees of phonological accuracy, but *buckaroo* is not a believable result of that process (whether in the traditional sense of interference or as "interlanguage"). *Buckra* was, also, probably around; folklorists found it in Louisiana, along with *niam* 'eat', *brawtus* 'something extra', and *pinda* 'peanut' (Strecker 1926) in the nineteen twenties. Dewees's *bakharas* is not, considering his orthographic practices, convincingly like any of these. It might have come from some third, still unknown, source – as DAE apparently assumed. The suggestion by Rollins (1936) and Adams (1968) that *boyero* is the source of *buckaroo* introduces, however, a totally unnecessary and unproductive complication. The only thing that *buckaroo*, *vaquero*, and *bakharas* have in common is that at one time or another, in the same general geographic area, all of them might be applied to a man who by profession tended cattle. But surely not all words that can have the same referent must be assumed to be etymologically related.

There are, in short, many complications to the pattern of borrowing from Spanish into English in the Americas. It might be well to consider the overall picture, with special reference to the Southwest. Sawyer (1959) provides a key to the interpretation of the southwestern Spanish borrowings: There was an early period of free borrowing from Mexican speakers whose mastery of the cattle trade gave them prestige and then a later period of "aloofness." In the later period, Anglo Texans used no Spanish except for some badly pronounced food names like *chili* (which was thought to refer to the meat, making a bilingual absurdity of *chili con carne)* enchilada, tamale (from *tamal,* with metanalysis from the Spanish plural *tamales),* *taco,* etc. A striking example of the ignorance of Spanish by many Texans is the town name Refugio, pronounced [rlfyuwrɪow] by those who live in the immediate vicinity. A very recent change in the trend may be heralded by the wide-spread use of *macho,* especially in the feminist movement, and of *Chicano.* It only remains to add an earliest stage (not dealt with by Sawyer) even before the clear-cut borrowing of ranching terms like *chaparral, hacienda, corral, peón, reata,* and *rodeo.*

This earliest stage must have borne some resemblance to Jordan's partly Romance contact vernacular; possibly the two were in essence the same. Ever since at least as early as the seventeenth century, English-speaking Americans had been using something like Spanish in their contacts with Indians. Traveler Jonathan Dickinson, who wrote an account of his journey from Port Royal, Jamaica, to Philadelphia with slaves, a journey interrupted by a shipwreck in Florida, recorded *totus,* which may well just be a non-native-speaker's way of rendering Spanish *todos* 'all, masculine plural'. But Dickinson also recorded an Indian's saying *Nickaleer no comerradoe* 'Englishmen were not his friends', with an apparent zero copula with past-time reference. This seems, like the frontier variety under consideration, Romance in at least part of its vocabulary but not Spanish – and not necessarily Romance in grammar.

Folk typologies for special varieties of Spanish used by English speakers have not been wanting. The term *cow-pen Spanish* has been recorded (Marcy 1855, cited in Drago 1965: 59). In this case, it was John Bushman, a Delaware Indian guide who "spoke English and Comanche and what has been called 'cow-pen Spanish'."

Even a fictional account, like Dion Boucicault's *The Octaroon; or, Life in Louisiana* (1861), might represent an authentic tradition. In Act I, a white reports of the Indian Wahnotee, "He don't understand; he speaks a mash-up of Indian and Mexican." The same character addresses Wahnotee, "*Wahnotee Patira na sepau assa wagiran.*" The second word seems Spanish (a version of *partirá* 'leave', third person singular future tense) and the last three seems unfamiliar enough to be believably "Indian," at least for dramatic purposes. But *na*, which, coming after *patirá*, ostensibly means 'to', is strikingly like the most common preposition in the Portuguese pidgin/creole tradition (cf. also Haitian Creole *nan*). Elsewhere Wahnotee uses a great deal of French vocabulary. Threatened with a gun, he begs another character, "No tue Wahnotee," where *tue* is obviously a form of the French word for 'kill', but the grammar is not marked as French in any special way. (Compare Haitian *NP pas VP* for French *NP ne V pas.*) He also objects to a weapon on the grounds, "*No, carabine tue.*" Still another character informs Wahnotee that "*Closky tue Paul,*" reporting an incident in past time with a zero marked ("present") form. (Cf. Prince's Negro Dutch informant, p. 101.) Wahnotee uses the term *firewater* to describe rum. He even uses sign language to some extent. At least some of these traditions may be literary; but it does not follow, as has so often been assumed, that they are thereby necessarily wrong.

To this "partly Romance contact language" could belong *lariat*, just possibly *alligator* and *lagniappe, crawl* (which, according to Jordan [1981: 28] would have facilitated the later adoption of *corral*), *lassoo* (later Hispanized to *lasso*), *mustang, galoot, caboose,* and *(kit and) caboodle. Vamoose,* with the familiar correspondence of /-uw/ to Spanish /-o/, would be more likely than *mosey* (putatively also from *vamos*) in this variety.[4]

Cattle-trade terms from English and some of the words usually explained as strangely mangled Spanish may also have been features of this trade language. Of the former, some may have received a special twist like *bulldog*, which received a different sense when Black cowboy Bill Pickett made his special contribution (O'Brien 1961). It makes little difference, of course, for the trade language itself which language is the source. The "Spanish" terms very likely would have included *cavvyard, cabestro,* and *wrangler.*

This hypothesis would entail the claim that the contact variety functioned west of Louisiana in the early Texas period, since some of the terms may not be attested west of Louisiana. Given the situation of immigration and trade, however, such a notion is not unlikely. Not having John's earlier attestation from the Natchitoches-Natchez area, the *Dictionary of Americanisms* attests *cavvyard* first from Stephen F. Austin, in 1821; an 1824 citation from Dewees (*DAE*) tells of "driving a large cavvyard of horses and mules to Louisiana."

Given the polyglot situation which prevailed in Florida (Bateman n.d.) and elsewhere along the Gulf Corridor, not even an occasional Africanism is impossible. *Buckaroo*, if from *buckra*, might join *dogie* and a slightly larger number of West-African-derived words not attested in the meager records. On the other hand, there is as much in the relationship

vamos : vamoose :: vaquero : buckaroo

as there is in other suggestions for the background of *buckaroo*. It just might be the Gulf Corridor reflex of *vaquero*, /vakerow/ or /bakerow/ being the Texas version.

In an area where Cajun French and "Gumbo" French Creole were spoken, the variety could have served an important communicative function; that function may have been as important in its maintenance as its standing as "bad" Spanish across in Texas. The Spanish, who called Texas the "New Philippines," would also have adapted better to the use of this Romance-based variety than to English, at least in the early stages of the cattle trade. Spanish contact vernaculars have played an important role in the Philippines since the early eighteenth century, according to Frake (1971). (See also Whinnom 1956). Taylor's review of the latter (1957) was perhaps the single most important step in linking the entire tradition to a Portuguese (which perhaps should have been Iberian) contact variety.)

Working in a different tradition, Jordan concluded that *lasso, lariat,* and *calaboose*

> . . . may instead [of being adopted from Hispanos in South Texas] have entered English in Louisiana or even Georgia and Florida, in which case the words may have passed from Spanish to Creole French and then to English.

This would make the "partly Romance lingua franca" related to Creole French, and there may have been at least a very strong resemblance. It is noteworthy, also, that Jordan stresses the ethnic diversity of the herdsmen who spoke the variety:

> The bloodlines of the herders themselves had become more diverse [than the original mixture, which included Black and Indian] in transit through the pine barrens and prairies, a result of intermarriage with Cajuns and Indians. A few herder families crossing the Sabine into Texas were "redbones" – a mixture of white, black, and Indian.

The late Margie I. Dillard (personal communication) hypothesized that *redbone* was somehow related to *red Ibo* cited in the *Dictionary of Jamaican English* with reference to relatively light skins associated with some slaves. Holm and Shilling (1982) attribute the use of *red* in the sense 'light-skinned person' or 'light-skinned with Negroid features' to the Atlantic Creoles and cite parallels in Twi, Yoruba, and other West African languages. The second etymon in *redbone* poses, however, more of a problem.

If there was a pidgin variety in the area at the time of formation of the word, the form *redi* with enclitic vowel could have developed; the vowel would have later been taken as belonging to the second etymon. An optional nasalization rule like that postulated by Alleyne (1980) might have reduced *bone* to *bo*, or rather have caused the general group of whites who observed the pidgin to analyze *bo* as *bone*. White observers in the area did report the use of Pidgin English by Indians. Eskew and Eskew (1954: 93, 145) reported, in direct quotation of an eighteenth-century Indian:

"Big Leg [Robert Jussereau de St. Denis], me damn rascal."
and, in indirect discourse, some trading Indians of the same period:
    . . . the traders asked for heap-big pelt.
    Next, they wanted -um teepee, you betchum.
Just across the border from where the Texas cattle trade was launched, on
or very close to the path of the earlier Gulf Corridor trade, there existed
Romance etymons not easily traceable to French or Spanish, probable
Africanisms, and some contact varieties. The strangely distorted Spanish of
the early Texas cattle trade very possibly comes from just that lingua franca
that Jordan postulated.

Such a re-evaluation of the early language of the cattle business has far-
reaching implications for the history of the English of the West. Other vocabulary of the same occupation, with perhaps less exotic origins, has entered
the general vocabulary of American English. *Cow camp* came into use around
1885, according to DA; *cowhands,* in 1886. As a designation for workers,
hands is another of the obvious nautical parallels of the frontier. Some of the
vocabulary is fairly recent; the compound *cowboy song* seems to go back
to about 1908; *cow pony,* to 1874. Unlike the familiar movie cowboy with
his one devoted and super-talented white horse, the working cowboy had
circle horses, roping horses, cutting horses, a night horse, and one or two
broncos, all these making up his *string.* To lose one was a great misfortune,
and to be deprived of one by the foreman who assigned the mounts was the
worst possible insult. The descriptive term *breaking the string* came to mean
losing after a series of victories; e.g., in baseball. The talents of the horses
led perhaps naturally to the phrase *horse sense,* attested from the West as
early as 1870. The gap between real and fictional usage is sometimes great;
bite the dust, a favorite term from cowboy and Indian movies, is first attested
from William Cullen Bryant's translation of the *Iliad.* Adams traces the
general pejorative *stinker* not to cowboys but to buffalo hunters, specifically
to newcomers who skinned the buffalo and, perhaps partly because of their
inexperience which caused them to become afflicted with unpleasant scents,
were held in contempt.

Wister (1958) recorded *like getting money from home* in the the West in
1893. Cow-punching was a young man's occupation, and a lot of those
attracted to it may have been runaways or other adventure seekers with
limited independence from their parents. Wister also recorded *hot in the
collar* (ostensibly the same as *hot under the collar*) 'angry', an obvious
development from the presence of the bandanna which formed a regular part
of the costume. Mencken (1948: 761) points out how *tenderfoot* first used
by cowboys for a cow new on the range, was transferred to mean an inexperienced westerner and then popularized by the miners. It should be
remembered, however, that the meeting place of the Anglo-American and

Spanish-American herding traditions was "not uniquely in Texas, for they mingled in California as well" (Jordan 1966: 85). Some of the borrowings from Spanish regularly treated in works on American English (Marckwardt/ Dillard 1981) were probably made independently in the two places.

Across the western rangeland, compounds from already-existing English words were made or adapted to new situations. *Cow brute* was a euphemism for *bull* in the East but meant 'a wild cow, difficult to manage' on the range. *Cow path* and *cow pen* were both originally American but not Western, neither being a term involved in taking care of stock on the open range. *Cowkeeper* (1619) 'a person employed to look after the cows of a village' obviously had no place in the large-scale cattle business of the West. *Cow town*, on the other hand, fits the scale of the Western cattle trade and originated in that area (1888). *Cowhide* as a noun meaning 'a handwhip' (1818) and as a verb meaning 'to use such a whip' (1820) are not necessarily Americanisms but they were appropriate to the life style of the West and were adopted there.

The railroads and the ranches frequently argued over the right of way, which may be one reason why public sympathies as expressed in folklore often went to outlaws like Jesse James. *Cow-remover* (1948) was a term for the railroad's attempt to keep the range cattle off the tracks. In 1838, it had been *cow-* or *horse-remover*. *Cowcatcher* was more appropriate to the Western idiom and has become a part of the national stock of metaphors; Packard (1957: 157) characterized the three- or four-minute speeches by minor local candidates that were tacked onto the President's speeches as "cowcatchers on the Prexy's talks." He was apparently thinking in terms of a city dweller's reactions to the locomotive appendage as something visible but not obviously useful.

The partly Romance lingua franca may have become lost in the process, but the effects of mixing on the language of the West have been frequently reported. Bourke (1892) commented:

> Tucson was as foreign a town as if it were within Hayti instead of within our own boundaries. The language, dress, funeral processions, religious ceremonies, feasts, dances, games, joys, perils, griefs, and tribulations of the population were something not to be looked for in the region east of the Mississippi River.

Hulbert (1929: 155) said that the cowboys carried their "intriguing, half-Spanish lingo" as far north as Montana. And Adams (1968) acknowledged their profound influence:

> When the Texan rode over the long trails north, he carried his customs and his manner of working all the way to the Canadian line ... Montana, Wyoming, and other northern and central states adopted much of his Spanish-influenced language. In exchange, the northern cowman gave the Texan that which he had appropriated from the northern Indian and the French-Canadian, words strange to the man from the Riọ Grande.

If all these statements about the Texans' influence are true, then it becomes a matter of some importance that not all of the influence on the language of the Texas cattle trade was Spanish.

The receptivity to French and "Indian" words may also have been strengthened by the early contact language nature of the cowboy's talk. According to Adams, an example of the cowman's words traceable to French is *hiveranno:*

> A trapper's name for someone who had passed several winters in the Indian country. From the French *hiver,* meaning winter, and *année,* meaning year. Also called *hiverant.*

Adams seldom bothers with phonology; otherwise, one might expect him to invoke Spanish to explain the strange final vowel of a word with such a derivation. Or were there still some contact language traditions which could be applied independently to various Romance languages?

By the time the frontiersmen got close enough to the Pacific Northwest to pick up French words, no matter how questionable the etymology, they were getting close to still another special variety, Chinook Jargon. Since the Jargon got mixed up with Pidgin English, it in a sense entered into the same kind of mixing as Spanish in the Southwest. At any rate, its use drew a lot of attention from observers; Browne (1934) was like many who were somewhat imprecise linguistically but still pretty good indicators of what was going on:

> The prevailing languages spoken are the Clallam, Chinook, and the Skookum Chuck, or Strong Water with a mixture of broken English.

Chinook Jargon seems to have remained largely out of the reach of the cowboys, but the loggers were obviously a different story. McCulloch (1958) recorded a large number of logger words he traced "from Indian." Most of them turn out to be actually from Chinook Jargon;

> cultus — no good
> potlacher — a generous man [from the Indian custom of competitive gift-giving]
> Skookum block — actually a trade name [based on *skookum,* 'strong, tough, big, good'] but used especially to mean a big heavy main line block.
> *Skookum chuck* — fast, dangerous or tricky waters, as falls narrows, or tide rips.

No etymologists, the frontier occupational groups took their terms from any contact language which happened to be around. Mencken (1943) pointed out that a number of terms from Chinook Jargon were still familiar locally in the Northwest:

klootchman	'a woman'
wawa	'talk'
muckamuck	'food'
tenas	'small'
hyas	'big'
chechako	'a stranger'
keekwilly	'house'
kla-how-ya	'How are you?'

Mencken did record attempts to derive *hooch* from Chinook Jargon, but asserted that they were "without much success." Both Mencken and the OED believe that the word came from Alaskan *hoochino*, for which a Jargon transmission would be far from impossible. Mencken also felt that the derivation of *hike* from Jargon *hyak* was unlikely because the word "did not come into common American use until after Chinook influence had died out." But McCulloch seems to indicate that Chinook Jargon influence still has not "died out" among the Northwestern loggers. *High muckamuck*, from a Jargon phrase which the OEDS somewhat tentatively renders as 'plenty food' has a rather widespread use as 'a self-important person who imagines he is more exalted than he is'. Some folk-etymologizing — the phonetic similarity between *hiu* and *high* — seems obvious. So does the kind of jocular alteration that has occurred to *mugwump* in its change from 'an important official' to 'a fence sitter'.

Not all the loggers' terms "from Indian" were local developments in the Northwest, however, McCulloch calls *wanigan*, 'bait boat' or 'the eats boat', "a borrowing from Indian word in Maine, meaning bait." Dick (1941: 40) reported the use of *wanigan* in a semantically related sense, 'the camp commissary', for the frontier around Pierre, South Dakota. In *Dialect Notes* III, Part 1 (1909: 418), it is said to mean 'A woodsman's storehouse and stock of supplies . . .' in Aroostock, Maine.

Both *wanigan* and *no-see-um*, the latter obviously from Pidgin English, seem to have found their way to the logging camps of the Northwest in a northern path from coast to coast. The latter, 'an almost invisible fly found in the north woods' is first cited from Thoreau's *Maine Woods*. McCulloch reports an old friend, in *savey* 'know-how; the difference between the old-timer and the greenhorn', from the logging camps. *Wrangler* apparently came in from the cowboys, changing to the meaning 'a teamster on a log skidding job' in the logging camps. Whether from Spanish or from the partially Romance lingua franca, *vamoose* also reached the lumbermen in the meaning 'get out, make yourself scarce'.

Phrases from the logging camps have been adopted into the general American vocabulary. *To drag one's feet* was to ride a two-man saw and fail to do one's share. It still means 'to fail to do one's share', although an associated meaning of 'delay' has developed — and of course more than two persons may be involved. But probably no logging term has a more interesting history than *skid road*, especially if *skid row* be taken as a development from it.

In the simplest version of the history of the term, it is said to have come from the logging camps (McCulloch 1958). Logs were skidded along·a "road," at the site of what is now Yesler Way in Seattle, and establishments designed for the "entertainment" of the loggers soon became abundant. (For the possibly parallel development of *skid row* for a section of Dennison, Texas, see pp. 184-5). Given the tendency of such sections to develop on the frontier, it is obviously a great oversimplification to assume that other cities did not participate in the development and spread of *skid row.*) The logs going down the road were *on the skids,* a phrase which has been applied often to a person going from respectability to the gutter. To facilitate the movement of the logs, loggers used to *grease the skids.* An 1983 citation from Oregon refers to the *skid-greaser,* who "lubricated the skids with oil so the logs would slide easily." Metaphorically, the term spread as far as the big Northern cities, in the sense of helping someone along the road to ruin. There is, as often, a nautical predecessor *greasing the way.* In a typically British development this phrase acquired the more general sense of 'making preparations in advance to secure influence to get an appointment or the like'. The British and American expression *to grease the palm* 'bribe' is another development in the same complex of terms. Eventually, *skid row* lost its logging associations as completely as its final consonant. In *Notes and Queries* for 1944, it was defined as 'a district of cheap flophouses, employment agencies, etc.'

Like other frontier groups, the loggers developed a number of compounds with *squaw.* Probably the best known is *squaw man* 'consort of an Indian woman'. These compounds with *squaw* were transported all over the frontier. A report of an interview made in 1844 by the Reverend John Dabney Shane with an aged pioneer woman yields three (Hench 1937: 75):

> Malumphy [the old Indian Chief] said: he commanded there that day. Well, McGary said, he would give him *squaw play.* It was a *squaw ax* he did it with [killing the old chief as he was surrendering]. The Indian women laughed and said it was a squaw trick [and not a warrior's act].

Carrance (1959: 80) reports redwood region loggers' *squaw hitch* 'the bite of the choker . . about the corner or corners of the log for the purpose of turning or changing the position of the log'.

Chinese as well as Indians were important language contacts for the loggers, especially in earlier times when there were Chinese working in the camps. They were very widely used as cheap labor in the West; for the railroads, see Nee and Nee (1972). Pidgin English is convicingly attested for many of those workers (Dillard 1972a: 164-178; Dillard 1980: 403-416). There is little doubt that some of the loggers found the pidgin very useful in communicating with the "yellow" men. It is not surprising that McCulloch should record *cookee* 'second cook or kitchen helper' and *chokem* 'cheese' along with less obviously pidgin lexical items:

> *China boy* – a Chinese logger, at one time quite common in B.C. camps. One boss China boy would contract to put out logs, and did all the bargaining for the whole crew.

and *Q,* a Chinese logger, from the queue worn by the "many Chinese fillers and buckers in the B.C. logging camps."

McCulloch's derivation of *cumshaw,* a word known in the logging camps and many other places, from "Indian" is extremely doubtful. The OED considers it to be derived from a Chinese verb meaning 'to be grateful'. It came to mean, in Chinese ports and obviously in Chinese Pidgin English, 'a present or gratuity or baksheesh'. By the time of World War II, it had become a part of general U.S. service slang. It is possible that discharged soldiers or sailors took jobs in the logging camps and brought the word along, but the conditions for transmission through Chinese Pidgin English itself were highly favorable in the late nineteenth century.

Americans in various occupational groups and in differing places came to know Chinese Pidgin English, at least receptively, after the gold rush immigration began in 1849. Rusling (1875) has a characteristic expression, "John Chinaman turned up again." Rusling was amazed at the behavioral Americanization of the Chinese, despite their lack of linguistic assimilation:

> They engaged in all household duties, ran errands, worked as traders, performed all kinds of manual labor, and yet as a rule their only dialect was a chow-chow of "Pigeon English."

Other observers of about the same time, like John H. Beadle, quoted Chinese workers in the West. He attested (1873: 173) "their universal no sahvey" (don't understand) to every question and included that pidginism in a longer reported conversation (1873: 182):

> "Oh, velley Melica man, me believe [in] him [God]."
> "All Chinamen believe in him?"
> "Oh, China like Melica man. Some believe him, sahvey; some think him all gosh damn."

Furthermore, Beadle's footnote identifies this as Pidgin English, "a language used in the ports of China."

The astonishing assimilative powers of these Chinese included some regrettable traits, like apparent anti-Semitism in this attestation from Richardson (1865: 390):

> Their chief deity is called "Josh;" in a violent quarrel between a Chinaman and a Jew, the former wrathfully said, "Oh, yesee; I knowee you – you kilee Melican man's Josh."

A joss house or two is still to be found in almost any city in the United States which has a Chinatown. And some traditions of Pidgin English used by Chinese are still found in cities which do not meet those criteria. In Baton Rouge, Louisiana, the Crimson Dragon, a Chinese restaurant, advertizes *Takee Outee Special Lunch*. This is probably stereotyping, which is one way in which the pidgin has been preserved. The supreme example of all Chinese Pidgin English stereotypical sentences, "No tickee, no laundee; alle samee to me," is as unlikely as *Furiously sleep ideas, green, colorless*.

Influence from the usage of the Indian is easier to demonstrate, provided that it is not expected to conform to what has been conventionally observed of the influence of (e.g.) Dutch. As suggested above (pp. 44-45), the "fifty or so" American Indian loanwords are only a small part of the story. When we take into account phrasal compounds like *take up the hatchet, bury the hatchet, Great White Father* and the collocational function of *big, great,* etc., the influence begins to be seen in the light of its true importance. It should be borne in mind that Indian-influenced forms which no longer survive were characteristic of the periods of contact. In-depth analysis, however, may show more influence on present-day English than has usually been assumed.

There has been great resistance to the suggestion that *yankee* is the result of an Indian attempt to produce *English*. Pyles (1954: 56) even went so far as to say, "There is no evidence that they [the Indians] ever attempted to use the word *English*." Nevertheless, there is considerable documentary evidence of such usage. Armstrong (1971: 7) records how in 1682, at a treaty-signing with William Penn near present-day Philadelphia, a Delaware chief with the historic name of Tammany said:

> If Yengeesman come, he pass and do no harm to Indian. If Yengees man sleep in path, the Indian pass and do him no harm. Indian say, "He's Yengees; he loves sleep."

Derivation from Cherokee *eankee* (in the unflattering meaning 'coward') is another, if perhaps remote, possibility. And Herskovits (1966: 284) pointed out that Yanke is the name of one of the *Winti* worshipped in Surinam.

Insofar as the palatalization of the initial vowel in *Eng-* is concerned similar developments are far from unknown in Chinese Pidgin English. Leland (1900) has

Ink-eli	'English'
Ying-kwo	'English Nation'
Yin-ke-li	'English'

Similar processes may well have been active in AIPE. The first attestation of *Yankee* in the dictionaries is from 1758, but the form accredited to Tammany is clearly earlier.

Pyles (1952: 50), who reported that Indians never attempted to use the word *English*, also reports — and rejects — the theory that *Yankee* comes from an Indian pronunciation of *anglais*. As a unique source, *anglais* is probably as much to be objected to as the others cited above. What seems unavoidable, however, is the conclusion that *Yankee* came out of a multi-ethnic, multilingual contact situation, in which several languages including Pidgin English were involved.

Much more came from the American Indians than the place names and the relatively short list of plant, animal, and food names usually attributed to them. Many of their contributions were in the area of idiom, where quantitative evaluation, especially in the terms of conventional etymology, is difficult to make. No one would call *medicine* as borrowing from the Indians; in fact, they almost certainly got it themselves from the French. Catlin (1874: 83-84) gives a representative statement from a frontier observer:

> These Indian doctors were called by the Frenchmen, who were the first traders on

the frontiers, *"Medecins,"* the French word for physicians, and by a subsequent frontier population "Medicine Men . . ." The meaning of *medicine* to the Indians seems, however, to have been quite different from the French meaning. To the Indians, it involved concepts more religious and philosophical than that of mere remedy and treatment. (See Vogel, 1970.) If *medicine man* was indeed the first compound, there were soon many others like *medicine drums, medicine rattles, medicine dances, medicine books, medicine fire, medicine animal, medicine bag, medicine hunt, medicine arrow, medicine pouch, medicine song,* and *medicine stone.* Few if any of these terms derived their meanings from either the French or the English etymon most closely related. The frontier whites picked up many Indian usages; Adams (1968) lists *no medicine* 'no information', and other such phrases are familiar from the frontier literature. Folk etymology made *power doctors* out of *powwow doctors,* which itself apparently developed sometime after 1624 from the simple designation of the "medicine men" as *powwows.*

Many figurative expressions, like *firewater,* have found their way into the popular stereotype of Indian talk, but they are also well-attested from genuine historical sources. One of the first was Jean-Bernard Bossu's *Travels in the Interior of North America,* 1751-62, which lists:

prayer chief	missionary
cloth that soaks	paper
flat wood	table
firewater	brandy
fire warriors	Spanish warriors with guns
the great lake	the sea
big canoes	ships

There are also quite late reports; Crofutt (1871) writers:

Infantry soldiers are called by the Indians "heap walk men." Indians call Major Powell's boats "water ponies." Long trains of cars are called by the Indians "Heap wagon, no hoss" . . . The Indians call the telegraph the "whispering spirit."

Campbell (1928: 660) gave a conventional summary:

When the white man introduced new objects, words had to be coined to describe them to those who had never seen them. The first railway train became at once a "fire wagon."

This is quite in accord with the popular viewpoint, as well as perhaps being consistent with a fantastically over-simplified version of a "naturalness" theory for language. Nevertheless the reader who sees familiar terms in *firewater, great lake,* and *big canoes* will perhaps begin to suspect some kind of transmission.

From the viewpoint of the speaker of ordinary English, these expressions are highly figurative, and it is one of the commonplaces of the treatment of the frontier that figurative language abounded there. The interesting, if somewhat over-emphasized, feature called "tall talk" may be a sort of culmination of that tendency toward extreme metaphor. Perhaps simply as a kind of bizarreness reaction, British observers sometimes attributed the same tendency to all Americans; Candler (1824) wrote of "that fondness for high-sounding words for which Americans, notwithstanding their Republicanism, have long been marked." Although some exaggeration is to be expected, given the circumstances of the observations, the attitude is persistent enough to require some explanation.

Convincing sources for these verbal tendencies have been hard to find. Orthodox students like Marckwardt (1958) have tended to compare Elizabethan English, with its tendency to hyperbole, but there are flaws in that approach. An obvious one is the two-hundred-year gap between Shakespeare's "rude mechanicals" and frontier characters like Mike Fink and Davy Crockett, with no record of intermediate stages (Laird 1970: 353).

Looking outside the England-to-America framework, we can easily find such figurative language, often criticized or condemned, depending primarily upon the personality of the observer, as "exotic" or "picturesque" – or perhaps as "unrestrained" or "imprecise." Hancock (1973) gives these examples from Sierra Leone:

Jakas-os (jackass plus *horse)* 'a glutton for hard work'
cher-cov (tear plus *curve)* 'take a stroll'
han beli (hand plus *belly)* 'palm of hand'
swit mot (sweet plus *mouth)* 'flattery'
do klin (day plus *clean),* 'daybreak'

In comparison, Hancock cites Trinidadian *beli-han,* with the same meaning as Krio *han beli. Sweet mouth* is very similar to *sweet talk* and *bad mouth,* well known in Black English and perhaps now in general American English. *Do klin* is paralleled in Gullah and other English-based creoles; DBE calls it "Pan-Creole", compares French Creole *ju netyé,* and calls it "a calque on an African idiom."

As a general principle, this kind of highly figurative language is characteristic of many special contact situations. Hancock, in his treatment of the relationship of pidginization to Anglo-Romani (1979), deals with what he calls "incoining," a process of combining existing morphemes with no exterior model. For example, the Romanes word for 'new' is combined with the word for 'lights' for the meaning 'electric lights'. Other examples are 'iron + 'bird' for 'airplane', 'salt + dirt' for 'sand', and 'running' + 'iron' for 'bicycle'.

Mühlhäusler (1983) provides the most recent and in some respects the most complete of "circumlocution" as a vocabulary-forming device "to come to grips with the new concepts and objected encountered," in this case by plantation workers who use Samoan Plantation Pidgin. The circumlocution *he white fellow man bilong cocoanut stop no grass* is used for a bald-headed European', *big fellow bokkus white man fight he cry* for 'piano', *spia bilong laus bilong kokonat* 'a comb', *stima bilong bus* 'railway', *glas bilong longwe* 'telescope', *bokis bilong devel* 'camera', and a number of others. These circumlocutions are the most "exotic" or "bizarre" of all largely because they represent plantation workers from very different language and cultural groups adapting to very new circumstances.

The apparent innovations in the American West were not so extreme, probably because the innovators themselves did not undergo so complete a separation from their own group. Innovations, or at least forms for which no source has been found, were nevertheless fairly commonplace on the frontier. Crofutt (1871) calls these "Western Travel Talk":

"Hash houses" —roadside restaurants. Waiters are called "hash slingers."
Telegraph operators are called "lightning shovers."
On the plains bacon is called "sowbelly."
Teamsters on the plains call a meal a "grub pile."
Old settlers on the Plains call Emigrants "Pilgrims";
. . . Ox drivers, "bull whackers"; mule drivers, "mule skinners"
Utah whisky, "Valley Tan." To be out of money is "in the Cap"; "on the bed rock," etc.

Generalized use away from the frontier developed for *bull whacker, hash house,* and *hash slinger.* Technology probably caused the disppearance of the first; *hash house, hash slinger,* and the derivative *to sling hash* were more appropriate to the depression of the 1930s than to affluent later periods, especially to the 1980s when "gourmet" sections are to be found in ordinary supermarkets.

Miners also had their characteristic figures of speech. A familiar one is *Long Tom,* known from Western fiction as a term for a rifle and to sports fans as Satchel Paige's name for his *really* fast ball. (For the pitch that was "only" blindingly fast, Paige formed by analogy *Little Tom.*) In the mining camps, however, according to Adams (1968), it was "a type of trough used for washing gold-bearing dirt." Hulbert (1929: 187), who defined the term as meaning "an artificial wooden sluice for washing 'pay dirt'," also commented how

The lingo of the mines is fascinating to newcomers when they hear it, and mere boys on the trail talk airily about "long toms" . . .

The term came to mean 'rifle' among buffalo hunters, and the rifle metaphor seems dominant in the use by Paige. The early distribution was apparently West-wide; differences in use, including frequency and precise meaning assigned, correlated with occupational groups.

The "lingo of the mines" included *prospector* (1851) and a large number of phrases with metaphorical extension. *Pan out* meant 'to obtain gold by washing ore in a miner's grub pan' when first attested in 1851; the general sense 'be successful' had developed by 1873. *Stake a claim,* referring to the process of establishing one's exclusive rights to a potentially rich piece of mining land, ad *claim jumper,* one who ignores the marking of such rights, can be figuratively applied to many other activities – not necessarily by people who are fully aware of the origin of the phrases. Much the same can be said for *make a stake* 'earn some money, make a fortune, obtain enough money to finance future operations' and *grubstake* 'advance money needed for living expenses'. According to Mencken (1948: 761) the miners themselves were the ones to make metaphorical application of *tenderfoot*, first used by cowboys for a cow new to the range.

Chinese were surprisingly ubiquitous. In the mines they were given *a Chinaman's chance* to dig in a mine which the whites were pretty sure was worked out. When middleweight champion Bobo Olsen rashly scheduled a fight with light-heavyweight champion Archie Moore, who had been fighting heavyweights and doing pretty well, those who really knew about boxing said that the former "didn't have a Chinaman's chance." (The phrase was actually used by Walter Winchell, in a 1950s column.)

Blacks were also plentiful on the frontier, among the cowboys (Katz 1971) and elsewhere (Porter 1971). But the primary contact was with the Indians, and it seems important to establish their influence.

Many frontier commentators, some of whom have been quoted above, noted both the existence of "picturesque" Indian English expressions and the prevalence of tall talk. Could there be a link? Is it possible that frontiersmen took a hint from Indian talk? Records indicate that they used it seriously, in communicating with the Indians. They may have used it playfully or facetiously among themselves, even to the point of caricaturing the Indians. Guthrie's mountain men seem to be doing just that. But the Indians' own figurative uses may well have been what started the whole thing.

There is little direct evidence of the influence of sign language, despite its importance to both Indians and frontiersmen; *rub out* and *go under* are the only strikingly obvious phrases with such influence. This is not to say, however, that the flowery, highly figurative language which was used on the frontier and which has been the subject of so much discussion could not have been influenced by the sign language. An example of a translation from the sign language into English is offered below as an indication of what could be produced. This is the Twenty-Third Psalm, said to have been translated by a white missionary, Isabel Crawford, at the suggestion of "a bright Indian."

The Great Father above a shepherd Chief is. I am His and with Him I want not. He throws out to me a rope and the name of the rope is love and He draws me to where the grass is green and the water not dangerous, and I eat and lie down and am satisfied. Sometimes my heart is very weak and falls down but He lifts me up again and draws me into a good road. His name is WONDERFUL.
Sometimes he makes the love rope into a whip, but afterwards he gives me a staff to lean upon. He spreads a table before me with all kinds of foods. He puts His hand upon my head and all the "tired" is gone. My cup He fills till it runs over. What I tell is true. I lie not. These roads that are "away ahead" will stay with me

through this life and after; and afterwards I will go to live in the Big Tepee and sit down with the SHEPHERD CHIEF *foreover.* *

"Psalm One in Indian" is attributed to Mrs. Ioleta McElhaney:

Glad in his heart is he that walks not in the ways of those who know not God, that does not share the paths of those who have evil in heart, nor does he sit in the place of those who laugh at the good way.

But he finds joy only in the rule of the Lord, and on this rule of the Lord, he thinks and thinks a long time.

This man is like a tree that grows by flowing water, that brings the fruit when it is due. His leaves shall not become dry, and all that his hands touch is made good.

Those who do not fear God are not strong, but they are like the waste of grain that blows away.

Because of this, those who do not fear the Lord will not be able to stand before His face; nor will those who do evil, stand with those who walk right.

For those who walk the evil path will become lost forever, but the One above who rules and knows, will keep safe the hearts and ways of those who walk His road.*

Sign language, pidgin English, Indian languages, other foreign languages — all these were part of the frontier context. Mixtures of these produced unconventional, "colorful" language. Bourke (1892: 152) reported:

One could pick up not a little good Spanish in a pack train in the times of which I speak — twenty-one years ago — and there were many expressions in general use which presented all the flavor of other lands and other ideas.

Gregg (1844: 189) gave the speech of a Frenchman:

"Foutre de varment! he butt me down!" exclaimed the exasperated Frenchman. "Sacré! me plenty scart; but me kill him for all."

Both Pidgin English and foreigner talk are identified in frontier attestations, and sometimes — obviously — they were mixed. Malapropism and outlandish formations are associated with both of them. Such formations, perhaps playfully exaggerated, may well have produced terms like *splendiferous, absquatulate,* and *snollygoster.* DeQuincy (Works VI: 147) showed English awareness of that kind of American creativity:

. . . (as in America they say) teetotaciously exfluncticated.

Snollygoster is a kind of symbol of the whole frontier tall-talk process. It is regularly treated in works on American usage, a great deal being made of the fact that President Truman once used it in a public speech. None of these works call attention to the fact that the first use recorded in DA is from Dan Emmett's "Black Brigade" (1861): "We am de snollygosters and lubs Jim Ribber oysters." Emmett, who is most famous as the composer of "Dixie," was one of the popularly best-known writers in Negro dialect (Black English) of the mid-nineteenth century. His dialect has, perhaps, few claims to perfect authenticity; but, like other commercial writers, he adapted a genuine tradition. Meredith (1931) pointed out how writers of fiction could use the "Negro patois" for humor without completely distorting the "idiom" itself. From Alton, Illinois, painter Catlin reported the speech of a Black servant (1856, II: 93):

*Property of Cook Christian Training School 708 S. Lindon Ln, Tempe, AZ 85281.

My good massa, Massa Wharton in dese house, just dead ob de libber compliment.

Compliment here is obviously a "malapropism" for *complaint,* such relationships being abundant in the contacts of Black English and more ordinary English. Richardson (1865) records a servant woman who had been trying to prospect for gold and who answers her master's queries about the rocks she carries with, "Speciments, mass'r, speciments." Tape recordings made in Samaná in the Dominican Republic, where the descendants of freed slaves have maintained a dialect of Black English since 1824, contain a form *paragolized* for *paralyzed.* It probably is not a performance error; the speaker repeated it three times.

The Blacks were a linguistically important group on the frontier. In the Southern states, which were more or less the point of origin for most of them, observers had long reported the high-flown fancy talk in which they indulged on special occasions. The observer might be a Yankee critic of the Southern system like Ingraham (1835) who recorded:

> "Mighty *obligated* wid it [a sermon], master, de *'clusive 'flections* werry districtive to de ignorum."

The reporter might, however, be a defender of the Southern tradition like Molloy (n.d.: 245), which includes a section entitled "How They Do Talk," which quotes a Gullah speaker:

> "He tell me a lot o' who-kill-John" means, for instance, the speaker was employing corroborative detail to lend verisimilitude to an otherwise bald and unconvincing (and probably quite untrue) narrative.

Beadle (1890: 6) gives a more baldly fictional example:

> Gentlemuns, fur de purpose uv *'vestigation'* de *finity 'twixt* sugar an' salt, I takes dis case *'visement* tell turmorrow evenin'; meanwhile, de court would thank you fur any *'thority* yer can show on de pints at issue.

Harrison (1884), an article much maligned because of its formal linguistic inadequacy but one which deserves some credit as a pioneering attempt, reports:

> The humorous and proverbial character of many of these expressions shows a distinct feature of the Negro mind. The talk of the African abounds in metaphors, figures, similes, imaginative flights, humorous delineations and designations, saws and sayings. These have so interwoven themselves with his daily speech as to have become an unconscious and essential part of it.

Contact language situations seem to produce this kind of fanciness, especially if the contact remains in existence long enough to be effectively permanent. Green (1962) reports on the island of St. Helena:

> Occasionally they invent words with amusing results . . . All rights, "said the islander, "I'll leave the wordification to you." . . . in the islander phrase, "in the before days."

The same kind of influence apparently worked on the frontiersmen. Dick (1941: 69) reported that

> . . . [the Northwestern trappers] developed a spoken language which was so interspersed with idioms that it was difficult for the uninitiated to understand.

Semi-outcast frontier groups, tending to make a display of their unconventional language in something like the way they reacted against the conventional life style of the East, with the mixed and exotic co-occurrence patterns of multilingual groups and special contact languages serving as models, may well have made a kind of game out of spectacular linguistic innovations. Notice – especially disapproval – by more conservative users would only give impetus to the activity. Something of the same thing was probably involved in the creation of Cockney rhyming slang and Harlem jive talk. Occupational and other idioms which the occasional outsider found strange would have a positive value in producing and preserving the linguistic image which the frontiersman almost consciously desired.

Boatright (1949) provides possibly the most complete description of what he calls the "free speech" of the frontier. He includes "lawless coinages" like *to absequatulate, combobbolate* and *discombobbolate;* "typical similitudes" like *as ragged as a sheepherder's britches* and *like hunting for a whisper in a big wind;* the boast in the *more . . . less* formula, like *Texas had more trees and less timber, more rivers and less water, more preachers and less religion* [than any other place] ; "mild asserveration" like [if I don't, then] *grind me up in a mill for tanbark, there's no snakes in Virginia, take my eyes for green grog bottles;* "hyphenated compounds" like *do-good-itiveness and frightened-to-death-a-tive-ness;* "placing of unsanctioned endings on recognized roots" like *indignitorious* and *unscruplocious;* "humorous euphemisms" like *bottled courage, bug juice, gut warmer* for 'whiskey'; and "lawless coinages" like *absquatulate, combobbolate,* and *discombobbolate, explunctify* or *exflunctify, antigodlin, catawampus, peedoodles, phildoodle, ramstugenous, rumsquaddle* or *ramsquaddle, flumex, hornswoggle, spondulicks, squadlification, wapper-jawed,* etc. There were, as Boatright himself asserts, many others. The frontier has been better known for these oddities than for the genuine communicative strategies operative in a complex linguistic environment. In a sense, they may be the surface of a sociolinguistic situation which has much to reveal beneath that surface.

The one fully constant factor in the history of frontier English is contact with one or another Indian tribe and language. It would seem, then, that more attention should be given to their usage than the conventional list of borrowed words and phrases. There has been, however, a distrust of sources hardly paralleled except by the case of Black English. Familiar expressions like "Ugh!" [uʔ] , "How!" and "heap" have all too easily been taken as the fabrications of novels or of Hollywood. Reports of the same forms are, however, commonplace in the historical literature. They go back at least as far as Jean-Bernard Bossu's travels in 1751-62 (trans. Feiler 1962: 114):

> The [Indian] audience replied with shouts of "How! How!" which means, "True, true!"

Ruxton's account of the 1840s, praised universally for its authenticity, represents a Sioux greeting the party of whites with "Howgh" (ed. Hafen 1951: 69).

Apparently authentic, the expression entered the stereotype. Fanciful explanations, as often in such cases, abound. This one is from Clayton (1983: 96):

> . . . every time the Indian met a white man, the white man commenced to ask him: *How are you feeling,* or *how are your people,* or *how are you getting along* . . .

Overt statements about the Indians' use of sign language are much easier to find than those about the use of Pidgin English, although as expected actual pidgin attestations are far more numerous than explicit documentation of the sign language. It was fairly easy to record "bad" English with at least some accuracy but completely beyond untrained observers to describe the signs in a recognizable way.

An occasional coincidence tells more than the observers realized. For example, more than one source reported about the Indian named Black Beaver and his communicative abilities. This one comes from Campbell (1928: 659):

> Black Beaver's ability to hold communication with different tribes whom the exploring party met was not due to any knowledge of the oral language of those tribes, but to use of the sign language, which is universally understood by all the Indians of the plains, but which is a sealed book to the Coast and Mountain tribes.

But the same sources also quoted Black Beaver, described as "a Delaware living the last years of his life on the Washita" who "had long experience in the Northwest":

> "Captain, I no tell him that Indian no fool and he know that not true, for I see heap and know that one big lie, for I live with white man long time and no see thing like that.

Historian Campbell is, as a matter of fact, a kind of textbook case where observers of the Indians' communicative strategies are concerned. He defends sign language as "more than an elaboration of gestures, ordinarily used by every person" and stigmatizes Pidgin English in terms of the Indians' inability to correlate the pronouns used by the white man with the subject:

> My sister, he say.
> Bob Dunlap, she mighty good man.

English gradually came to replace Spanish as the primary language for governing and dealing with the Indians, as Anglo-Americans took the leading roles in planning campaigns against the "wild" Indians (the Navajos, for example) and in planning for the future of the "civilized" ones (like the Pueblos). Under the influence of Indian scouts like Kit Carson and William Donovan, even the making of treaties came to be in English. Of course, a treaty was an official document which might be sent back to Washington and which would be in the most formal, school-like English of which its framers were capable. Such informal records as we have tend to show, on the other hand, that Pidgin English was the variety in which Anglo-Indian interaction most often took place.

Formal government sponsorship of the use of English among the Indians of the Southwest began about 1870. Before that, American policy with regard to the area had been limited to consolidating its military position. It was necessary not only to cope with the Indians (and their refusal to see the pattern of "Manifest Destiny") but also to plant bulwarks against possible Confederate power in the West. Not insignificantly, some of the first attempts at responsible administration of the area — favorable to the Indians in a way, despite paternalism — came under President Grant, who had been a part of the army most concerned with preventing the Confederate spread.

In the days before cultural relativism had penetrated even most academic circles, the primary concern (besides that of conventing the Indians to Christianity) was with "educating" the non-whites — that is, with bringing the white man's school and society to them. Missionaries as teachers had a tradition going back to John Eliot and Roger Williams in using the Indians' own languages in their teaching and preaching; non-missionary teachers were probably somewhat less tolerant.

Missionary groups have shown an interest in the sign language (see pp. 154-155), and it is likely that they were more tolerant than other teachers of American Indian Pidgin English. The difficulty is that AIPE was not known to be a genuine language variety; therefore, even the most well-meaning teacher might stigmatize it as "bad" English.

How much attention the Anlgo-American teachers gave to the language backgrounds of their Indian students is, in an absolute sense, unknowable; but the records that we have make us believe that it could seldom have been very great. John Beadle, in *Western Wilds,* gives an account of the activities of the Reverend W.S. Robertson, at a mission where the teachers of the Creeks (Uchee, Natchee, Alabama) were selected and paid by the Presbyterian Board of Home Missions. For Beadle's benefit, two Uchee boys were set to conversing in their native language while Beadle sat and played the virtuouso phonologist by watching their lips:

> It [the Uchee language] is entirely devoid of labials; for five minutes they touched the lips together but once. It also rarely requires the dentals; and thus to a Uchee it is almost impossible to distinguish between *b* and *p, d* ant *t,* or *a* and *e.* This inability produces most ludicrous results in spelling. Pronouncing the words to be spelled orally, the teacher can not possibly determine in the quick sound whether the spelling is correct or not — that is, with Uchee beginners. But, when they come to write it on the slate, bat becomes *p-e-t,* that *h-e-d,* bad *b-e-t,* etc.

It would seem from this account (Beadle 1878: 201) that most teachers knew no more of the Indian languages in dealing with Indian children than Shakespeare learned of Welsh to develop the character of Fluellen (see pp. 6-7).

Elsewhere, we are told of teachers who had to teach Indian children, not one of whom knew a word of English. The dominance of English was, of course, not questioned; not until the 1960s, in the bilingual education programs, was much serious thought given to having teachers speak the Indian languages. In some cases, the use of English was fostered – although one may wonder what variety of English was used in the dormitories – by bringing Indians to boarding schools. According to Spicer (1962: 437) the first was Hampton Institute in Virginia. By 1881, Hampton had Pimas, Papagos, and Apaches from the Southwest. There were also Negroes at Hampton; the Indians' and the Blacks'struggles with the dominant English have often been in common. Carlisle Institute, founded in 1879 by General Pratt, had some two hundred students from the Southwest (Apaches, Navajos, and Pueblos) by 1885. Nearer to home in the Southwest, boarding schools were established at Albuquerque in 1884, at Tucson in 1888, at Santa Fe and Fort Mojave in 1890, at Phoenix in 1891, and near Riverside, California in 1892. These tribally mixed boarding schools were probably happy hunting grounds for Pidgin English. Some educators still report how it is "springing up" in tribally mixed boarding schools today. Spicer (1968: 440) reports'

A sort of boarding school dialect of English developed, recognizable as a "foreign" version of English, but still perfectly intelligible to non-Indians.

Harvey (1974) offers some more recent evidence for "dormitory English."

According to Spicer, the great majority of all Indians who attended the white man's schools from 1878 to 1900 were in those boarding schools, with their mixed-language environment. And, although Spicer doesn't say this, such environments are excellent for the spread and perpetuation of Pidgin English. In 1917, there were 6,949 young Indians, at a linguistically impressionable age, from New Mexico, Arizona, Utah, and Nevada in the broading schools. Spicer guesses that within fifty years of the inauguration of the church-dominated school program, at least one-tenth of the Arizona and New Mexico Indians had been enrolled for greater or lesser periods.

For the other nine-tenths, there were different kinds of contact situations with potentially different results. Cremony (1868: 173) quotes a typical Indian conversation:

You good man. You stay here long time and never hurt Apache. You want the 'yellow iron'; I know where plenty is. Suppose you go with me, I show you, but tell no one else. Mangas your friend, he want to do you good. You like 'yellow iron' – good! Me no want 'yellow iron.' Him no good for me – can no eat, can no drink, can no keepee out cold. Come, I show you.

Brandt and McCrator (1979) confirm the existence of AIPE among Southwestern Apaches.

The Bureau of Indian Affairs was blissfully unaware of the linguistic realities and conviced that all those Indians were receiving the "civilizing" influence of (Standard) English, being taken away from their "vernaculars." Spicer (1968: 301) quotes a rule of the commissioner in 1887:

Instruction of the Indians in the vernacular is not only of no use to them but is detrimental to the cause of education and will not be permitted in any Indian school over which the government has any control . . . It is believed that if any Indian vernacular is allowed to be taught by missionaries in schools on Indian reservations it will prejudice the pupil as well as his parents against the English language . . . This language which is good enough for a white man or a black man ought to be good enough for the red man. It is also believed that teaching an Indian youth in his own barbarous dialect is a positive detriment to him. The impracticability, if not impossibility of civilizing Indians of this country in any other tongue but our own would seem obvious.

In more recent times, especially the 1970s, bilingual education programs have brought some sophistication to that narrow linguistic view. But they, like the Bureau of Indian Affairs in an earlier century, have failed to realize what variety there is within English, especially in the aftermath of the frontier contact situation.

It is, of course, not possible to be absolutely certain about the import of such reports. It is, for example, not certain whether "dormitory English" represents American Indian Pidgin English, perhaps mixed with more ordinary English as in some of the attestations given above, or the newly popular "interlanguage" (Schumann 1975). Many of the writers on the subject obviously had a normative view of the language and reported on "deviations" rather than seeing the Indians' variety or varieties as something to be reported and described. It is probable that many of the statements are made by spokesmen who are more proficient than the average in Standard English.

Pidgin English, however, has its charms. It crops out in the writings of people like War Bow (1930: 224), described as a "Cherokee poet, philosopher, and farmer," who wrote:

WAR BOW HEAP FARM

By War Bow, Blanket Indian
Colony, Oklahoma

War Bow think he goin' to farm;
Like country life, got plenty of charm;
He goin' to raise it, plenty of corn
Will heap much plow in early morn.

War Bow, who was obviously educated and knew Standard as well as Pidgin English, addressed the accompanying letter to "Honorable Commissioner, Indian Affairs, Cato Sells," whose Standard English instructions are reproduced verbatim.

Pidgin English and literacy were not, in spite of the frequent assumptions, mutually exclusive. Bourke (1892: 339) reported how an Apache proudly showed off his literacy by writing:

MY WIFE HIM NAME KOWTENNAY'S WIFE
ONE YEAR HAB TREE HUNNERD SIXTY-FIBE DAY

For other examples of AIPE in the Southwest, see Dillard (1972a).

With the considerable aid of pidgin, English progressed rapidly in displacing Spanish among Southwestern Indians. According to Spicer, the knowledge of English was much more extensive after seventy-five years of contact, even among the Sonoran tribes, than knowledge of Spanish had been after two hundred years of exposure. What is missing from such a statement is obviously an evaluation of what role contact varieties – even of other languages – may have played in the earlier situation. The school could, in a sense, claim some of the credit for the spread of English; but, to a degree hardly realized by anyone, the language contact in the dormitories was a more effective agent than the contact in the classroom. Spicer estimates that the learning of Spanish ("except for the acquisition of a few Spanish words by Navajos in a largely hostile situation in Northern Arizona") had ended by 1850.

Other Indians in the Northwest found another solution to the language contact problem, the variety that is generally known as Chinook Jargon. Again, there was a competing and perhaps complementing use of sign language:

> Salishan tribes who did not go much to the plains probably continued to use the older or plateau form of the sign language until the Chinook Jargon came in. It is said that the Coeur d'Alene did not have much trouble in talking by means of signs with people of any tribe. Some time after the arrival of traders the Chinook Jargon began to supersede the sign language along the upper Columbia River and west of it, and later along Fraser River and in other parts of the north, west, and south, but it never took much hold east of the Colville and Lake tribes.

A picture of mixture of solutions to multilingual problems, depending on location and direction of trade, emerges from what is reported by Bailey (1980: 408-9) about the Flathead:

> The Flathead were noted as adepts in the sign language and all the tribes used it extensively in talking with strangers. The Chinook Jargon was unknown except in recent times among some of the Spokane and a few other Indians who had traveled extensively in the West, or who had been associated with the fur traders of Fort Colville. However even at Colville and other interior trading posts, Chinook was not used a great deal, the principal language being French. Some Indians spoke a little French. The sign language was also employed to some extent by the traders, who had learned it from the Indians.

Like other contact varieties, Chinook Jargon picked up words from other sources with relative ease. One of its better known derivatives, *siwash*, seems to have come from French *sauvage*. Chinook Jargon also mixed with the AIPE which moved west and north, so that one cannot always be sure whether an early text from the area is Pidgin English or translated Chinook Jargon. On the other hand, one can be virtually sure that it made no practical difference to the speakers. Bailey (1980: 169) reports that a passage from R.D. Symons, *Many Trails*, shows how "Chinook Jargon underwent the process of relexification as its speakers were more and more dominated by anglophones." The passage is:

> "One tam," Jack told me, "me see um that Akiti Siwash – me hyu scare – all he

dlad hy tall – he helo shirt his back: he helo mocassin his feet; helo hat his head stop – just plenty hair like brush. Me no savvy see-um that fellow before – me hyu comtux him Ankiti Siwash. Me go way that place all same cultus couless."

Some influence of Pidgin English is obvious in forms like *-um, savvy, me no Verb, all same*. There is also a fairly high incidence of Chinook words in Pidgin English texts in the attestations from the Northwest collected by Miller (1967). Chinook Jargon has been, in a sense, one more rug under which Pidgin English influence could be swept, but even the most unwilling observer must be able to see that the lumps are showing.

NOTES

1. Drechsel (1979: 105) gives Mobilian Jargon *babesele* and interprets Dresel's form as "a Hispancized version." Mistaking of an Indian language /b/ for /p/ presumably presents no difficulty. Even so, it may be idle to speculate about any connection to Trinidad-Tobago English *pappyshow* (verb) in Ottley (1965) with the example
    You pappyshowing me 'You are making fun of me'
    and noun in the example
    He is a pappyshow 'He is a fool'
    Ottley also cites the probable folk-etymological form for the noun *puppet show*. Although continued use of *pappyshow* in Trinidad could be checked with a consultant (Lima Mendoza, who also was able to report on St. Crucian English and Trinidadian Spanish) there is little that can be said about the historical relationship except that the change 'man' to 'fool' is hardly impossible over nearly 150 years.
2. The material in this section was reproduced and distributed by the Interdepartmental Program in Linguistics of the University of North Carolina at Greensboro, North Carolina, under the title of "In Defense of Julian Mason." An earlier version had been read at a meeting of LASSO in Phoenix, Arizona, in 1978.
3. Zebulon Pike, the source of the first attestation in DA, is in his own way as explicit about his Spanish as Stephen F. Austin and Dewees. He was, however, far less proficient than either. In fact, Pike's expressed ambition about Spanish extended no further than to someday be able to read and write it.
4. The adherents to the etymology of *vamos* for *vamoose* (that is, "deformed" Spanish) have surely noticed, although they have not commented upon, the fact that an extremely naive version of a historical naturalness condition would be fatal to that derivation. It is, obviously, not *vamos* but *vamonos* which is most natural for 'Let's go'. The DA obliges by listing "the well known *vamanos*" as the first citation (1844) under *vamoose*. The phonology becomes even more impossible – unless someone has a hitherto unknown rule for deleting internal /-on-/ in Spanish loans to English. In fact, the earliest citation in the DA in any kind of possible phonological source for *vamoose* comes in 1847, from McHatton and Ripley's *Rough and Ready*, in what was for a time an idiomatic expression or even a cliché, "they . . . 'vamoosed the ranch'." The next DA citation under this idiom, from 1891, is "was now ready to vamoose the ranchy," where the final *-y* could easily be the enclitic vowel. The second DA citation, from the *Oregon State Journal* in 1868, cites *vamoosed*. The expression moved east rather quickly, if west-to-east was indeed the direction of movement; the Natchez [Mississippi] *Courier* for October 7, 1862, has "*vamose the Ranche*" – where the final vowel letters are certainly non-Spanish and may mean almost anything or nothing. Meredith (1919: 293) asserts that
    "vamose" and vamose the ranch" were brought from Mexico by the Santa Fe traders.

It is not apparent, however, where Meredith got either the information or the spelling *vamose*. Humorous pseudo-Spanish was apparently not unknown in Mississippi during the Civil War. Bettersworth (1961: 237) reports:

The Spanish language must also cease to be used in court and the Americano Africano dialect be substituted in its stead.

Colcord (1945) traces *vamoose* to Spanish, but "probably brought home to the coast by sailors." She also lists as "a whaler's terms" *foo-paw* (*faux pas*.) These and certainly *calaboose* are cases of English /uw/ the usually cited Romance languages (French and Spanish in these cases) have /o/. Another obvious example from French is /pUlduw/ from poule d'eau (Read 1963: 61). A generalized Romance of the maritime trade − that is, Lingua Franca − still seems the most likely source for these English words in /uw/.

Chapter VII

The Effect of the Frontier on the Lexicon of Gambling, Drinking, Smoking, and Other Vices

The trapper and, to a much greater extent, the cowboy had an influence on the developing American English of the nineteenth century. So, too, did other occupational groups like the railroad men and farmers. Loggers and miners both carried on earlier traditions and developed terms of their own. Work was certainly important to the development of American English, but it would be sanctimonious to claim that our ancestors devoted themselves entirely to work − except, perhaps, for a Sunday turned over to religion. In small towns on the Fourth of July, it has not been unheard of in the past for the claim to be made that "The strong back and the weak mind built America." But there were always those who, no matter how strong their backs, preferred some kind of hustle to outright labor. And even the sailors, cowboys, railroad men, and farmers looked to the time when they could get to town and escape the monotony of their work.

It would be equally unrealistic to say that the frontiersmen got away from civilization only to work or that those who followed them never had pleasure and relaxation in mind. Just what they had in mind, a lot of the time, can be seen if one considers the prominence of the term *squaw man* 'one who consorts with an Indian woman' in the vocabularies of groups like the mountain men and the loggers. Escape from the constraints of civilization often meant the opportunity to indulge in activities which the staider part of the population might have objected to. When those seeking to escape the restraints were protestant and even puritan in background, it is not astonishing that they sought escape in contact − including, incidentally for the seekers, language contact − with heterogeneous groups of other types.

In the process by which "the frontier moved away from the seaboard" (Allen 1959: 30), the rum of the West Indies gave way to whiskey as the staple liquor used for that kind of indulgence in pleasures to which the Puritans would have objected. Nor was even this kind of indulgence devoid of its economic aspects. The distilling of alcoholic liquors is one of the more effective devices for control of surplus grains. The "Whiskey Rebellion" during Washington's second term is a well-known historical event illustrating the economic importance of alcohol. At least to certain unscrupulous individuals, sale to the Indians, who had no traditions of moderation and were therefore greatly harmed, was a source of quick income. It may be true, as Allen (1959: 30) points out, that alcohol did not have "as catastrophic effects on the Indians as it was to have on the [Australian] aborigines," but the damage was great for all that.

Adapted economically through the use of corn instead of other grains or sugar cane for rum, whiskey had a far-reaching effect on the life of westerners. It would be a mistake, however, to assume that a different material base meant that the cultural development was isolated from more general patterns. In behavior and in language, the effects were apparently as great in Australia as in the American West. Allen (1959: 31) says:

> In the lore of the Far West among the cattlemen, "blowing your pay," principally on drink, was a common enough phenomenon, but it did not assume the proportions of the universal, as did that of "drinking," or "knocking down," "your cheque" in the pastoral legend of the bush.

Activities concerned with drinking alcoholic beverages produced a fair amount of terminology in the United States. They brought in *saloon, firewater* (possibly an Algonquian loan translation in the East, but spread throughout the West through English), the relatively short-lived *Indian whiskey* and the seemingly permanent *bootleg.* The last originally described the process of smuggling whiskey to the Indians, but was adapted to mean any kind of illegal sale of alcoholic drinks, then extended to the domain of illegal sales in general. In football, the *bootleg play* became a trick in which the T-formation quarterback, after faking a handoff to a running back, hides the ball on his hip and runs with it himself. The football usage discards the meaning feature 'illegal' and replaces it with 'tricky' or the like. (There may be some influence from *quarterback sneak,* virtually the only other play in which the professional quarterback – a player of great value to his team, who usually serves a four- or five-year apprenticeship before becoming the starter for his team and who is often regarded as somewhat delicate – carries the ball.)

Legal or illegal drinkers needed to be able to order their whiskey *straight* (not *neat,* like the British) and they needed to be able to describe the quality of the whiskey usually available on the frontier as *rotgut.* Even if a host of transitory expressions like *tanglefoot whiskey, snake poison, chain lightning,* and *Hoe Joe whiskey* are thrown in, however, there is nothing comparable to the influence of faro and poker. One can throw in tobacco terms like *roll your own, ready rolls, coffin nails, bite off more than you can chew,* and even Easternisms like *corncob pipe, chewing tobacco,* and *plug tobacco* and still not match the productivity of the gambling games.

As is the case of most Western innovations, the terminology of poker builds on a base constructed elsewhere. The most common and influential of the card games, poker is traceable – as a game and as a term – to New Orleans, where the common passion of master and slave was said to be gambling. Among the heterogeneous users of the port of New Orleans, a European game called *poque* combined with the Persian *As Nas,* played with five cards in each hand whereas poque had only three. There was also some influence from the English game of brag, especially the introduction of certain *wild cards,* originally known as *braggers.*

The new game which had caught on in the dives of New Orleans eventually spread up the Mississippi (Searight 1973: 29). In *Domestic Manners of the Americans* (1832), Mrs. Frances Trollope reported that "no boat left New Orleans without having as cabin passengers one or two gentlemen whose profession it was to drill the fifty-two elements of a deck of cards to profitable duty." Although poker eventually reached the big Eastern cities, it did not until well after its spread into the West. In 1835, a reform administration in New Orleans drove out many of the professional gamblers, and some of them emigrated to cities like New York (Asbury 1933: 156). Since the terminology had already been established on the frontier, the movement was essentially from West to East, South to North.

The spread of poker and its terminology was facilitated because New Orleans was the supply base for movements up the Mississippi and to the West, including the Army's movement into Mexico for the war of 1845. As a consequence of our involvement in that war, poker was not only introduced into the Army but went with the soldiers as far west as the California gold fields.

Poker soon became such an integral part of the West that its foreign origin and even its association with New Orleans and the Frenchmen of that city were forgotten. The western players were nevertheless operating in a linguistic environment in which both French and Spanish were prominent. This is reflected in the names of some of the cards: no poker player would ever say *two* and *three* for *deuce* and *trey.*

The West's own contribution to the game was the invention of stud poker, played with one card down and four cards up. There has been a great deal of speculation about the origin of the name, but the easy explanation – that it comes from *stud* 'a stallion', which was the bet when the game was first played – belongs strictly to etymological folklore.

Today, *passing the buck* is more generally associated with politics than with poker, perhaps because of Harry Truman's famous slogan: "The buck stops here." (Television comedy programs and commercials are almost sure to resort to some paraphrase of that slogan wherever there is a character who is, or can be, called Buck.) The term came into existence on the western frontier in the 1860s. A player who did not care to deal passed an object on to the next player. The object was frequently, if not always, a knife made with handles of buck horn. The one who passed it on was thus "passing the buck."

Deal, a word that had been around for a long time in English, took on a special meaning among the poker players of the West. The basic meaning of 'share' or 'divide' makes it natural to call the distribution of his share of the cards to each player a *deal* and the distributor a *dealer*. *Deal* (verb) 'to apportion the cards' is a back formation from *dealer*. The noun *deal*, referring specifically to the apportioning of cards, can be looked upon as a specialization of the original noun. In American usage, *deal* came to mean any transaction or arrangement, a regeneralization that was helped along by the faro meaning 'twenty-five turns'.

Compounds like *square deal* and *new deal* developed from that general sense. The former, long familiar in the West and on the Mississippi, was an important slogan in the 1904 presidential campaign of Theodore Roosevelt. It would be a suicide slogan today, or at any time since the 1960s, when *square* 'naive' or 'out of it' moved from jazz and popular music terminology to the general vocabulary. But to Teddy Roosevelt and other Westerners of his day, it simply meant 'honest'. TR's distant relative, Franklin D. Roosevelt, was surely aware of the American fondness for poker when he chose the slogan *New Deal*.

There was a long tradition of using the term in political slogans when Harry Truman, a poker player and great practical folklorist, chose to call his own program the Fair Deal. The term was prominent in the 1948 presidential campaign, in Truman's famous upset victory over the highly favored Republican candidate Thomas E. Dewey, and it figures rather prominently in his *Memoirs* (Truman 1955). Republican sympathizers, much more prominent in the press than they had been during Roosevelt's terms, parodied it as the *Queer Deal*. The cynical expression *big deal*! and *What a deal*! and the sarcastic designation for a braggart *big dealer* seem to have been current around the time of the Truman administration. OEDS lists *big deal* from 1928 (Zane Grey) and 1949 (Arthur Miller), but the sarcastic import of the attestation is not apparent until J.D. Salinger's *Catcher in the Rye* (1951), a work justly admired for its representation of the contemporary slang of an adolescent.

Other poker terms that have passed into the general vocabulary include *dealing from the bottom of the deck* 'taking unfair advantage' or 'not acting in accordance with the rules', *deal me out* 'I don't care to participate' and its reverse *deal me in*. The cowboy who sat around hoping for a game was, again according to Adams, *sweating a game* – as a participant in other activities one might "sweat" the grades for last semester's work or the results of an X-ray. Poker rules often require a hand of minimal quality (a pair of jacks, for example) to open the bidding; thus the phrase *for openers* by extension means a beginning action in any domain.

In poker as in other gambling games, a *piker* is one who is inclined to make small bets. The term apparently comes from Pike County, Missouri, immigrants from which came as small farmers and were less willing to risk their all on a card game than were the mountain men and the cowboys. Such a person would be more at home in a *penny ante* game; the use of *ante* specifically for making a bet is an Americanism (1835), as is the compound. A term for the poker *pot* (hence the expression *to sweeten the pot* 'to increase the stakes') was *kitty*, which came to mean any kind of collection fund.

Poker terminology is also reflected in the expression *to go someone one better* (*five better/ten better* in the 1840s, when the expression originated). British usage had known *to go a crown* (or other sum of money) 'to bet a crown, etc.', but the addition of the indirect object and *better* seems to be American.

In poker, the ability to bluff is almost as important as skill in playing or luck in drawing the right cards. The term *bluff* itself may have come from card playing in the first place, the first use on record being from Barton's *Comic Songster* of 1838:

Those who play at pharo bark
At poko [sic], brag, or loo or bluff
Must all be sure to lose enough.

By 1845, the game could be identified either as "bluff" or as "poker." Too much bluffing is characteristic, however, of a *four flusher*, one who tries to make four cards do the work of five or who by extension vaunts his abilities beyond what he can really accomplish. By 1876, Bret Harte could provide the *locus classicus* of such expressions, ". . . he sees that little bluff and. calls ye."

To call or *call one's hand* has spread perhaps even more extensively into other domains than *call one's bluff*. OEDS list *call* "Also in poker (orig. U.S.) 'a demand for a show-down, the show-down itself'" from 1850; the DA's first listing had been from San Francisco in 1857:

Finally after floating him through a list of metaphors, his good nature gets the best of him; and he concludes to 'call our hand' . . .

To prevent one's bluff from being detected, one tries to assume a *poker face*, usable in other domains for putting on a good front. But the sportswriters who commented endlessly on Joe Louis's poker face knew he wasn't bluffing; so did those who wrote about Helen Willis Moody, the "Little Poker Face" of women's tennis in the 1920s.

Like the faro expressions, the terms of poker have had metaphorical applications far beyond the gambling table. The dream of a stud poker player *aces back to back* (the "hole" card, turned down, is an ace and the first card turned up is an ace), provides a term that has been extended to other fields. The New York *Post* music critic wrote on May 23, 1975, how a noted conductor had presented "back-to-back performances of *Tannhäuser* and Schoenberg's *Gurrelieder.*" Improbably enough, the expression turns up in religious contexts; the Christian Broadcasting Network's Sunday School lesson on July 16, 1983, called Samuel and Samson "back to back" judges! Some have called this a "natural" development, having nothing to do with poker, but Russell (1955: 284) did not think so. He cites a 1952 use from baseball as, in effect, a change of domain. The *ace in the hole* is a hidden resource of some kind; *an ace up the sleeve* (or *something up one's sleeve*) originally indicated cheating, but now perhaps it means trickery or some hitherto-undetected plan.

A *full house*, three cards of one kind and two of another, is extended to such domains as having a sold-out performance or producing a large family. One who holds full houses consistently is likely to wind up *in the chips,* although Asbury (1933) notes that poker originally had *checks* and *chips* was borrowed from faro. *Blue chip*, the most expensive color, now is more readily used of market stocks than of poker. To *cash in one's chips* was to leave the game, but poker assumed so much importance for some players that the term became a synonym for 'die'.

A poor player tends to *draw to an inside straight* 'take a chance that has little probability of success'. A dealer may *stack the cards* (arrange them so that he receives better cards than the other players) and a person in any kind of futile endeavor may find *the cards stacked against him.* A *shuffle* is supposed to scramble the cards so that the dealer does not know which ones he is dealing, but the victim of any kind of cheating may be given a *fast shuffle.* The oldest form of trickery is *dealing from the bottom of the deck.* If a teacher gives his students a test this week from the lesson assigned for next week, he can be accused of "dealing from the bottom of the deck."

Once the cards have been shuffled and dealt, draw poker allows the player to discard probably useless cards and to "draw" others still unknown to the drawer or to the honest dealer. A really confident player may, however, choose to *stand pat* – that is, leave his hand "in the way it fell." *Pat* in the sense of 'unchanging' is not an Americanism, but the poker expression is. The term is used, generally in a favorable sense, in many domains, notable among which is politics. "Stand pat with McKinley" was one of the most successful presidential campaign slogans in American history.

Simple draw poker has a basis of bluff, call, and showdown (when a player is required to reveal his cards and the game is settled). The last term can be applied to, among other things, the last game in a playoff series in sports or a military confrontation. The most famous variant of the basic game, aside from stud poker, is to set up some comparatively low-valued card, like the deuce, as a *wild card.* This term, too, has other applications; the National Basketball Association's and the National Football League's playoffs involve a "wild card" team, which has a poorer won-lost record than the other teams in the playoff, and the position enjoyed by such a team is known as the *wild-card berth.*

Faro was almost as popular as poker in the West, although it was a simple game of luck based on what happened to be the second card turned up and lacked the combative appeal of poker, especially the bluffing. Asbury (1933: 117) asserts that it made "a very considerable philological contribution to American culture." A person proud of his predicting ability may endeavor to *call the turn* without thinking of card games at all, but the phrase originated in faro and meant 'guess correctly the order of appearance of the last three cards'. (The DA lists the earliest occurrence as 1889, but faro terms in general were current as much as twenty years earlier.) To *play both ends against the middle* is to engage in something analogous to a dealer's method of providing a kind of double bet by a faro player. There was also a system of playing a card to win and lose an even number of times, called *breaking even*. Today a businessman may well calculate *a break-even point*. No historical dictionary seems to have a separate entry for this phrase, but OEDS contains it in the first citation (1938) for *break even*.

On a shoestring 'with a small amount of money or capital' is first listed by DA from 1904, but like most faro terms it must have been current forty years earlier. If the faro player who starts with very little is lucky, he can wind up *on velvet, velvet* being the faro term for money won from the house. By 1901, Westerners were using the term for 'profit or gain beyond what is usual or expected', and the term can be used in domains other than gambling.

To *string along* 'go along with' was a term applied to continuing in a faro game, but it was applied to other domains. In the 1940s, it had a certain currency in popular songs; "stringing along with" one's romantic interest was virtually the same as being faithful – or at least persistent.

The phrases *in hock* and *hock shop* also stem from faro. The last card in the box was the *hocketty card* and later was said to be *in hock*. The player who bet the card that turned out to be the last one was at a disadvantage and, by transference, was "in hock." Since faro was a gambling game, losing cost money; *in hock* rapidly came to mean 'at a financial loss'. Among professional gamblers the meaning 'beaten by a smarter man' developed; among thieves, it came to mean 'in prison' (Matsell 1859). But for the average player it simply meant a situation in which a debt had to be paid and he might have to pawn ("hock") some of his possessions. The place where one might get a loan (at exorbitant interest) on the collateral of a watch or a wedding ring became a *hock shop*. The phrases associated with one game transfer easily enough to another, and now a person can get in hock as easily in poker as in faro.

With the precedent set in the West by faro and poker, American English easily absorbed expressions from other card games. Bridge has been one of the more productive. It is, however, a more cosmopolitan game than poker, and its terms are not so likely to be Americanisms in the narrow sense. The game reached England and America at about the same time, around 1892, after having been popular in areas like Russia, Turkey, and Egypt. A relatively simple Anglo-Saxon game, whist, was its predecessor in the English-speaking world, but bridge is far more sophisticated and has influenced our terminology more.

A *long suit* today does not necessarily have anything to do with bridge; it may refer to a decathlon athlete's ability to broad jump better than he runs the hundred-yard dash, or to a linguist's ability to transcribe supra-segmentals better than he does generative semantics. The noun *bid*, in the bridge sense of *a bid of seven spades*, has spread to any attempt to gain an advantage, as in *a bid for fame*. Spades are the highest suit in bridge, so *in spades* has become a general term for the high quality of whatever is under discussion. One *makes points* at the bridge table but also with a woman or a professor, depending upon the direction of one's interests.

Every bridge player must *follow suit*, play a card of the same suit that has been led, if he can, and thus do what someone else has done: *John ordered a martini and Bill followed suit*. Other terms, including *finesse* 'take a trick with a lower-valued card while holding a higher-valued one in reserve', applied in sports to the triumph of skill over strength, and *duck* 'back out or default' may have been influenced by their similar use in bridge, although the contribution is disputed.

The simpler gambling game blackjack ("twenty-one" or "twenty-one or bust") was also popular in the West. *Hit me*, an injunction to the dealer to add a card to one's total, has some figurative currency as an indication of willingness to continue. *I'm busted*, appropriate when the player has more than twenty-one points, can also indicate that one is out of money or otherwise *hors de combat*, but the term could also come from bridge, where a *bust* is a hand with nothing. In more recent slang, *busted* meaning 'arrested' has virtually displaced the older usage.

Dice playing was not equally important in the West, and Asbury (1938: 205) tells us that it "never became very popular on the rivers except among the Negro deck hands." Yet Rollins (1936: 79) assures us that the dicer's *at the first rattle out of the box*, a way of expressing prompt action, was important to cowboys. Other terminology has become widely general. *Snake eyes*, two ones, is the symbol for any kind of impossible predicament. To *crap out* or *craps* is even more widely current for any failure. *To load the dice* is a virtual synonym for *to stack the cards*.

Many of the forms discussed in this chapter so far were westernisms first which later moved east. But the frontiersman was like the other Americans in that he tended to mix his gambling with drinking, and in that he cared little for the origin of the terms he used. Drinking and gambling terms mixed in the speech of most men. Mrs. Trollope, who sailed for America in 1827 and returned to England in 1831, was apparently not concentrating on frontiersmen when she wrote:

> During my abode in the country I not only never met a literary man who was a tobacco chewer or a whiskey drinker, but I never met any who were not that had escaped these degrading habits.

The western terms for alcoholic drinks came into sometimes ludicrous contact with those from further east, as when Rollins (1936: 189) tells of the Easterner who said to the frontier bartender, "I guess I'll take a cocktail," and was told, "You don't guess, you drink, and you gets it straight and in a tin cup." Terms which came to be used for whiskey-based drinks were partly indigenous, partly foreign, as in *julep*, a word with Arabic and Persian origins which had been in British English since 1400 but in the meaning 'a sweet drink prepared in different (usually non-alcoholic) ways'. In the sense of an alcoholic mixed drink, it is first attested from Virginia in 1787. The word and its derivative compounds spread quickly: *julep-drinkers* was applied to habitués of bars in San Francisco in 1859, *mint julep* was in existence by 1809, and *mint sling*, a name for another drink involving a sprig of mint, was current by 1804 but out of fashion by 1840.

What Mencken (1945: 260) called the "Gothic age of American drinking as of American word making" was between the Revolutionary and Civil wars. Fantastic drinks were, during that time, given fantastic names. Marryat (1839) observed that there were "many other compounds [for mixed drinks] which only the luxuriance of American English could invent." Examples from the period are *cobbler* (1890), *stone fence* (made of ginger beer and brandy — 1809), and *cocktail*. *Cobbler* caused apparent confusion to Dickens's Martin in *Martin Chuzzlewit*, who assumed that a shoe repairman must be involved. But few words have caused so much speculation as *cocktail*.

On May 13, 1806, the Hudson, New York, *Balance* defined *cocktail* as "a stimulating liquor, composed of spirits of any kind, sugar, water, and bitters." Washington Irving provided an 1809 citation including also *stonefence* and *sherry cobbler*. But the most intriguing attestation is by Irishman Tyrone Power, concerning a Black man with the typical slave-owner-bestowed name of Cato:

> For Cato is a great man, foremost among cullers of mint, whether for *julep* or *hail-storm*, second to no man as a compounder of *cock-tail*, and such a hand at a *gin-sling*.

Power (1836: I: 57) gives an interesting fact about the bartender:

> Cato is a gentleman of colour who presides at a little tavern some four miles from New York.

It may be no accident that a Black bartender of at least transitory fame is associated with the early history of the cocktail. The first non-American record of the word is from Alexander (1833), in a narrative of a voyage to

West Africa; the attestation is rather early, considering the times, for a term originating in the United States to be transported to Africa. Etymological fantasies have compared the pre-existing *cocktail*, descriptive of the feathery appendage of a male chicken. But in Krio of Sierra Leone *kaktel* means 'scorpion' (Hancock, personal communication). The sting in the creature's tail may be what motivated the comparison to the drink; compare modern *stinger* – or, for that matter, *firewater*. Without any impressive attestations, New Orleans tradition runs contrary to the dictionaries and celebrates the Crescent City as the place where the cocktail was invented (Searight 1973: 248). Either African or maritime origin could support independent trans-mission to New York state and to New Orleans.

These terms are not western, but certain drinking terms like "Here's how" are attested from more frontier sources. Burton (1860) made one of the many reports:

> "How! How!" the normal salutation [of the Indians]. It is supposed to mean "good" and the Western man, when he drinks to your health, says "Here's how."

Cook (1854: 188) reports how Indian approbation was expressed: "Yells of 'How!' came from all sides." Rationalization of the Indians' exclamations as abbreviations of "How do you do?" seems to be a matter of folklore. It is hardly necessary to cope, in a serious context, with their authenticity or lack of it.

Regarded as a vice by observers like Mrs. Trollope, subject to a kind of guilt-by-association with liquor and gambling, and with an Indian component of its own, the use of tobacco also played a major part on the frontier. Some-what like whiskey, tobacco was supported by imaginary remedial qualities. Texas scout Bigfoot Wallace is supposed to have said (Duval 1870: 294):

> These [his boots] don't protect you against the stinging scorpions, 'cow-killers', and scaly-back cinches that crawl about at night when you are asleep! The only way to keep them at a distance is to 'chaw' tobacco and drink whiskey, and that is the reason the Temperance Society never flourished much in Texas.

Where tobacco was concerned, the cowboy preferred *store tobacco* (1884) to the less-desirable *niggerhead*. The use of *store* in compounds was a develop-ment of the late nineteenth century: *store-bill, store-goods, store-bought, store boots, store candy, store cheese, store dress, store medicine, store pants, store sugar,* and *store teeth* are for the most part attested between 1851 and 1889.

To smoke store-bought cigarettes was less usual in the West, however, than to *roll one's own*. Although the dictionaries do not seem to have it, *ready rolls* was current in Texas by the 1930s. The *corncob pipe* (1829) was charac-teristic of the farmer rather than the Westerner.

The threat which Mrs. Trollope observed to the health of the non-literary American was chewing tobacco rather than anything smoked. *Plug tobacco* goes back to 1814; *chewing tobacco*, to 1835, with *chaw tobacco* having a vogue from Kentucky to California between 1834 and 1858.

Given the potency of plug tobacco, it was a real problem for the chewer to avoid *biting off more than he could chew,* a phrase still used (far outside tobacco-chewing circles) for taking on something beyond one's capabilities. Although there was an Eastern predecessor *bite off* – meaning 'shut up' – the phrase seems to have developed entirely in the West. *Chaw* was used rather than *chew* in the first attestation (Beadle 1878).

The term *dipping snuff* is first recorded in 1848; it is, however, probably much older, the practice itself having been observed by Columbus's men among the Carib Indians on Cuba. *Up to snuff* is not an Americanism in the narrow sense, but it is now regarded by Englishmen as the approximate American equivalent of *quite acceptable* (Schur 1973: 320). Obviously, users of the language are more aware of cultural patterns than are the dictionaries, and many times their impressions have a validity which the dictionaries cannot capture.

It is not usual to think of advertising as a frontier activity, and yet there is more of the frontier in the occupation, when it is carefully examined, than one would have thought. And frontier motifs like the vaguely Western characters pictured on horseback with cigarettes or chewing tobacco or in some other "western" type of consumption are a staple of newspaper, magazine, and especially television advertising. (Impressionistically, one would say that there was a hiatus during the period that radio dominated advertising, but there is no known study of the matter.) The prominence of alcohol and tobacco – down to the specific prohibition of cigarette advertising on television – in the advertising business is also noteworthy.

Even before the end of the eighteenth century, American housewives were being tempted to extravagance and husbands driven to despair by advertisements in newspapers. In "Account of a Buyer of Bargains" (Carey 1787) a husband reports:

> I had often observed that advertisements set her [his wife] on fire, and therefore
> ... I forbade the newspaper to be taken any longer.

In the *Monthly Magazine* for 1804 (XIV: Supplement: 626) an "English gentleman lately returned from America" reported his "Animadversions on the Present State of Literature and Taste in the United States":

> One third of the American newspaper is filled with uncouth advertisements written, in general, in language, and abounding in phrases, wholly unintelligible to the English reader.

Many other observers reported the prominence of advertising in the public functions of American English, that being one of the domains in which it gained an early advantage over competing languages. Benjamin Franklin (*Works*, ed. Jared Sparks, Vol. 7: 71-2), for example, had complained about the persistence of German in Pennsylvania, but English had obviously achieved almost complete *public* domination even in that area.

To replace the lacking electronic media, early Americans had methods like the traveling medicine show. A certain amount of entertainment was thrown in so that a crowd would gather to listen to the advertising pitch. Some of the shows involved the services of minstrels, white and black. Where the commercial theatre used white performers in blackface, the medicine show was multiethnic and multicolored. It included an Indian component from very early times. It often peddled "Indian" herb medicines, with Indians arriving in, for example, a New England town and boiling medicinal herbs in front of their tents.

The term *medicine show,* which obviously belongs in this period, surprisingly does not appear in the historical dictionaries before the citation from Asbury (1938). Asbury's method itself, however, almost ensures that he is quoting a phrase from the past rather than creating one. The shows themselves utilized Indian *medicine men* (attested from 1806), who did a *medicine dance* (1805), sang *medicine songs* (1791) smoked *medicine pipes* (1833), carried *medicine bags* (1805), talked *medicine talk* (1791), and even lived in *medicine lodges* (1814). If the shows themselves were not called *medicine shows* something is strangely amiss.

Medicine in the European, not the Indian (see p. 151), sense was important in early American advertising, partly because of the scarcity of physicians on the frontier. Many people tried to cure their own illnesses or resorted to whatever remedies might be offered. There was a remarkable growth of medical quackery in the second half of the nineteenth century, producing strange and strangely named medicines (J.L. Curtis's Original Mamaluke Liniment, Dr. Williams's Pink Pills for Pale People, Dr. Godbold's Vegetable Balsam of Life). Tobacco was counted among Indian herb medicines (Kell 1966: 104-5). In view of the recent injunction that each smoker must be informed that the Surgeon General had determined that cigarette smoking was harmful to his health, it is striking that some of the earliest advertising of tobacco presented it as a cure for many ailments.

Until recently at least, tobacco consumption was the subject matter of perhaps the biggest, best-planned, and most expensive advertising campaign in American history. When in 1952 Harriet van Horne wanted to compare the "selling" of the Eisenhower-Nixon Republican presidential team to an especially effective advertising campaign, she referred to "patently rehearsed ceremonials borrowed from the tobacco ads" (Packard 1957: 168).

After tobacco and medicine, politics may just be the biggest customer of American advertising. Packard (1957: 200) put it rather strongly:

By 1952 the Presidency is just another product to peddle through tried-and-true merchandising strategies.

If this is "merchandising," it is no new phenomenon. The 1840 campaign slogan of General William Henry Harrison, "Tippecanoe and Tyler, Too," is squarely in that tradition. Martin Van Buren, called "Old Kinderhook" because of his birthplace, used the chance similarity of his nickname's initials to the newly popular colloqualism *O.K.* in a clever but ultimately ineffective attempt to profit by some sloganism of his own. Dalby (1972) makes a good but bitterly resented case for African origin of the term, citing similar expressions in similar meanings from Wolof, Mandingo, Dogno, Djabo, and Western Fula. The aggressiveness of Van Buren's campaign caused even some etymologists, however, to think that his adherents had invented and popularized the expression. Harrison's victory revealed amazingly the effectiveness of frontier sloganism. His campaign became known as the *hard cider campaign*, his adherents as *hard cider Democrats* or *hard ciderites* (both from 1840), his program *hard ciderism* (1841), and his congress the *hard cider congress*.

It turned out, however, that the log cabin, which also came into use during the 1840 campaign, was a more potent political symbol. The term *log cabin* was originally used to describe a type of housing that seems to have been first used, perhaps by Swedish immigrants, around 1750. Thanks to politicians, it came to symbolize solid American frontier virtues. The fact that Abraham Lincoln was born in one added to his appeal; his administration interrupted a long succession of generals and wealthy landowners in the presidency. In the late Al Capp's *Li'l Abner* (personal memory), there was a wealthy candidate who had been reared in the world's largest log cabin by his politically ambitious parents. As in other cases, Capp's caricature captured the spirit of American political ballyhoo much better than .a "realistic" portrait.

Ever since 1840, a slogan has been almost essential to a presidential campaign. It seems likely that "Fifty-four forty or fight" contributed a great deal to the 1844 campaign of James Polk. It hardly matters that Polk neither extended the Oregon Territory to that parallel nor fought. Americans are accustomed to the failure of both political and advertising slogans. Both Woodrow Wilson and Franklin D. Roosevelt won second terms as presidents who "kept us out of war," and war was declared during the second term of each. In both domains, politics and advertising, slogans have become a kind of phatic communication. The catchiness of the slogan is the important thing, not the semantic content – and certainly not the truth value – of the words.

Both Abraham Lincoln and Franklin Roosevelt, facing reelection in wartime, made capital of the rural proverb, "Don't change horses in midstream" as a campaign slogan. Horses were, of course, a much more important part of American life when Lincoln ran than when Roosevelt did. FDR used them as part of the rather self-conscious appeal to frontier life that has remained a part of the apparatus of politics. Rather than stressing the supermodern, as other public relations efforts usually do, politics often depends largely on allusion to the past and its methods of life. Ronald Reagan's ranch, especially in contrast to Jimmy Carter's peanut farm, didn't hurt his 1980 campaign at all. Politics is full of the homey vocabulary of the backwoods: *pump priming, slice of the melon, log-rolling.* "Distribution of governmental largesse to political adherents" is a pale term alongside *pork barrel.*

The last expression, meaning 'a barrel in which pork is kept', was used as early as 1804, but even that citation refers proverbially to "minding our pork and cider barrels" — thus symbolically to property in general. The figurative meaning 'funds for local improvements designed to ingratiate congressmen with their constituents' is not attested before 1913, but it must have existed earlier since *pork barrel bill* is recorded for the same year. Contacting his most important constituents is *getting back to the grassroots* for the American politician, even one whose voters are predominantly urban. The *full dinner pail* is one of the few expressions appealing to urban and rural workers equally.

Both rural and urban voters expect the politicians to *talk turkey.* The phrase is attested, although with little explanation, from 1835. Beckwourth (published 1856 but reporting events of twenty years or so before) quotes a Pawnee Loup Indian whom a white man was trying to swindle in a proposed treaty as saying that the document "talked all turkey" to the white man and "all crow" to the Indian tribe. *Talk turkey* in the sense 'tell me what's in it for me' could very easily have developed from that kind of usage.

In keeping with these emphases of political terminology, Indians have retained an important place in the vocabulary. Tammany Hall, for example, was named for a Delaware Indian chief, although most Americans may never have heard of him. The original Tammany was famous for his love of liberty and for his wisdom. William Mooney, who founded the Tammany organization and named it after the Delaware Tamanend, introduced this affectation of using Indian titles in 1789. The thirteen trustees of the organization, called *sachems,* symbolized the original thirteen states; the president of the organization was the *grand sachem*; and the President of the United States, up to the time of Andrew Jackson, was the *great grand sachem.* In the 1920s Al Smith was known as "the Tammany brave."

Words like *caucus* and *mugwump,* despite the absurd and well-known semantic change of the latter, still play an important part in national politics. There are, in fact, enough Indian terms in politics to make them seem quite normal. It was nothing unusual, for example, when the powerful New Orleans Ring organization, which had kept the city under white supremacy rule throughout almost all of the third quarter of the nineteenth century, regrouped under the name of the Choctaw Club after being defeated by a reform group.

Like our politicians, our soaps, medicines, cigarettes, and even automobiles have sold better when they were advertised in a vocabulary reminiscent of older times. Most of our really big promotional schemes, whether in business or in politics, have been rural- and frontier-oriented.

Why should this be so, when the American society boasts of its technology above all else? Why do we go to the automatic teller at the bank in an automobile whose name commemorates the premechanical days of the frontier? Despite names like Grand Prix, El Dorado, Riviera, Monaco and Malibu, automobiles sell better under names like Bronco, Pinto, Charger, Colt, Mustang, Maverick, Cougar, Wildcat, Bobcat, Hawk, Falcon, Skylark, and Rabbit. Hornet, the old Hudson, was so much in the spirit of things that the American Motor Company revived the name. The Indian past is also evoked in automobile names. Pontiac, the name of an Indian chief, has long been with us, and Chevrolet recently came up with a Cheyenne model. Ford's Thunderbird — with sensational inappropriateness — is nevertheless named after a mythological creature of the Haida Indians.

It would be easy to explain this phenomenon in terms of "the American spirit" or "the enduring ideals of the frontier," but the answer is probably more mundane — culture lag. The frontier itself was the biggest promotional scheme up to that time. We have carried over the habits of the past rather than consciously innovating.

Those who moved westward did not do so simply because they spontaneously felt the urge. It may not have been only Horace Greeley's "Go West, Young Man", that did the trick, but his and other slogans probably had as much to do with it as the desire for adventure. The real advance guard, like the mountain men, was motivated both by the desire for what gain could be realized from the sale of furs and by the lure of pleasures restricted back East but more openly to be enjoyed in the wilds. But for the larger groups who ventured out toward the Oregon Territory and other areas, it took a promotional scheme of fantastic proportions to instil any urge to move away from the comforts of the East.

With the movement for territorial expansion and free land, the country entered upon one of the greatest advertising campaigns in history — the booming of the West. (For the term *boom*, see p.102.) This was a campaign in which orators and politicians participated as much as railroad companies and land salesmen, departments and bureaus of agriculture and other farmers' organizations, boards of trade, and chambers of commerce. Countless speeches were made in support of it, and promotional activity included inspirational literature in immigrant handbooks, railroad guides, state and regional gazetteers, rural almanacs, real estate directories, and government reports.

The people involved in these activities were *boosters*. This term, in the sense of 'one who supports or promotes given interests', arose in the West in the 1890s and soon spread to general advertising and chamber of commerce activities. The opposite of the booster was, of course, the *knocker*, who dared to see that every money-making or expansion scheme wasn't perfect. Lincoln Steffens had one of his cartoonists do a picture of a burglar, caught in the act and menaced by a policeman's club, saying "Don't knock; boost." The novels of Sinclair Lewis, like *Babbitt* and *Main Street*, and no longer regarded as models of sophistication, but the innocent booster continues to be the target of a lot of American satire.

No matter what appears in *New Yorker*, ordinary Americans have continued to revel in the kind of ballyhoo by which the West was sold — if not won. Historically, there can be little doubt of the importance of this promotional rhetoric. Botkin (1944: 276) put it exceptionally well:

> Besides manifest destiny, free land, and state pride, the West had another string to its bow — the long bow which it drew in order to live down its wild and woolly reputation and to attract settlers. It was the myth of a land flowing with milk and honey — part of the American dream of a promised land of plenty, opportunity, and "beginning," which had first attracted settlers from the Old World to the New and was now transferred to the fabulous, far-off West. To make its assets outweigh its endurances, orators, promoters, and guidebooks painted this unknown country in the rosy hues of fairyland.

It is not customary to call attention to the fact, but the fabled tall talk of the West was nearly contemporaneous with this advertising hype and was perhaps a contributor to it. It is, at any rate, not in the least surprising that advertising and ballyhoo continue to stress the frontier spirit, the cattle country, and rural activities. The commercial, particularly on television, continued the tall talk tradition in American society, and it is as irrational to expect the strict truth in the latter as in the former. One may, on literary grounds, prefer the tale of the prodigious buffalo in Mark Twain's *Roughing It* to the seemingly endless running gags of the Miller Beer commercials ("Everything you ever wanted in a beer, and less," with often obscure ex-athletes engaged in absurd combat over whether it's more important that Miller Light be "better tasting" or "less filling"), but it's a better bet than a draw to an inside straight that more Americans will know about the latter than the former. The disconcerting thing is that, in our heart of hearts, we feel that Jim Beckwourth, Davy Crockett, and Daniel Boone would have shared the tastes of the American public of the 1980s in preferring the beer commercial.

Chapter VIII

The Changing Relationship between Movement and Innovation: the Railroads

The early settlers in the United States came by way of the sea, and the sea had an important influence on the way they talked, including the strategies for dealing with multilingual populations who spoke no English unless it was a special variety. That influence was retained, although somewhat weakened, in the westward spread by wagon train and river boat, and in the great commercial activity of the cattle drives. Nor was it lacking in the coastal cotton trade (Berger 1980). Whatever waning of that influence took place during the inland trip westward was partially restored by new maritime contacts on the West Coast.

If all of these had their influence on American English, it seems self-evident that what followed them — the railroads, the automobile and trucks, commercial air traffic — would be the creative domains for the late nineteenth and twentieth centuries. However, it begins to seem that a major change of pattern began taking place at about the time the railroads became dominant in transportation.

It cannot be said that the railroads were unimportant. They began to reach their peak about a generation after the wagon trains (Masterson 1952: 4) and at about the same time as the cattle drives.[1] They are in a sense a dividing line — the end of the frontier (except for persistent metaphorical use and for its continued function in advertising) and the beginning of "modern development."[2] The railroad represents the transition between a transportation system like the ships on which the passengers lived for at least a space of time and the airplane which one occupies for only a few hours, often spending as much time in getting to the airport and boarding the plane as in the actual travel. (It is perhaps symptomatic that there was much friction between the railroads and their passenger traffic until the railroads managed to achieve their desire to carry only freight, with a very few remaining passenger services mainly for commuters.)[3] Linguistically, the railroads may turn out to represent the mid-point between a situation in which one needed to learn a new variety in order to travel and the present condition in which one's attention even while in transit is on the printed and electronic media, with their use of the leveled and standardized dialect. (See the next chapter.)

In the early days, the railroads borrowed a great deal from the maritime trade. Chase (1942) has pointed out how *ship* and *bill of lading* are terms "nautical in origin" as is the "causative use of *run*" (the conductors *ran* their trains), as are *trip* (and *round trip*), *passenger, fare, freight, berth,* and *cabin* (on a sleeper). *Caboose,* the most obvious of all, has been treated before (pp. 129-130). *To board* (a train) and to be *on board* are also phrases borrowed from the sea. Even the *railways* (or *ways*) were originally what the keel of the ship was laid upon in order that the ship might slide into the water when finished. A locomotive is said to *tie up* even in inland cities. The conductor on the passenger trains was sometimes called the *skipper* (Colcord 1945:   ), and the transfer of that name to the manager of a baseball team may have been influenced by railroad usage, although it seems to have come basically from the language of sailors.

Most of these terms seem to have remained in use with little change by the trainmen. *Crummy,* perhaps from the disorderly state which it is likely to have come into from time to time, occasionally substituted for *caboose.*[4] According to Mencken-McDavid and Maurer (1963), what outsiders have called the *cowcatcher* was called the *pilot* – an obvious nautical term. But neither the Pidgin English of the maritime trade nor the partly Romance lingua franca of the cattle trade seems to have been used on the railroads, and borrowings from other languages (like the cowboy Spanish loanwords) apparently were not a factor.

Students of American English searching for a large lexicon of permanent new words produced by the era of American railroading will be disappointed. It is certainly true that the *iron horse* (and, thinking of transfers to the domain of baseball, consider one of the nicknames of Lou Gehrig) and the engineer in the cabin with one hand on the throttle and the other on the whistle affected the American imagination for well over a hundred years. It is also true that the railroad men imbedded some words and phrases into the American consciousness. However, a large number of these terms, like the physical parts from which the railroad was constructed, were already in existence prior to the arrival of the locomotive and its "train" of various cars. There was change or specialization of existing terminology, especially in terms of phrasal compounds, but the number of even these is not very large when the magnitude of railroading as an industry is considered.

Dominant in railroad talk is not the kind of borrowing which the cowboys practiced from Spanish or the mountain men from the French and Indians but the development of new compounds. The word *rail-road* stands as a potent symbol of what happened when people in this new industry searched for "talk" to describe the new physical elements and processes of the industry. Examples of this process of word development are numerous: *loco-motive engineer, sleeping car, box car, hot box, flat car, switch engine, call boy, brake-man, fire-man, hand-car, rail-car,* and the list goes on.[5] Reinhardt (1970: 107) cites the "slang of old-time railroading" in which a fireman was a *tallow pot,* from his duty of climbing out onto the boiler of a moving locomotive with a pitcher of tallow to oil the valves. Phrases singled out by consultants in 1983[6] included *yard office* 'place where the paper work is done', *dead man's pedal* 'a device on the floor for safety; if the engineer should happen to keel over, it would engage the brake', and *bull of the woods* 'a locomotive with a tendency to run off the tracks'. They told how the passing of trains going in different directions could be a *meet* 'crossing at a given milepost', a *meet order* being the directions as to where the two freights were to cross paths and a *cornfield meet* a crossing far from town. If the crucial job of preparing those orders was not carried out effectively by the dispatcher, a *pile-up* or wreck could occur. None of these seems to constitute any important contribution of the railroad to the general vocabulary.

A somewhat greater influence can be seen in the wider use of the phrase *to sidetrack* 'to divert, as from a planned course of action'. The phrase for completely leaving the rails, *to jump the track,* also can be used figuratively for a catastrophic failure in following plans. The phrase for the condition of an overworked engineer, *asleep at the throttle,* is not unknown; the better-known term, however, is *asleep at the switch.* It illustrates the perhaps rather basic point that the terminology which came from the railroad had generally the perspective of those who observed from outside the train itself rather than from inside. The *switch tender,* in the days when he performed his job manually, could easily be responsible for a major pile-up, a matter of interest not only to the train crew and to any passengers but to anyone who happened to be within miles. Seemingly, the further the phrase was from the actual business of railroading the more likely it was to become part of the public vocabulary.

Thus it is not surprising that *to hop a train* became part of the general American English lexicon but that *mud hop* 'the clerical worker whose job it was to check the yard cars even under conditions which would have made him prefer not to be walking around' did not. *Dining car* or *diner* or *Pullman* became known because of the obvious involvement of the passenger. A term like *gandy dancer,* for the "sniper" or track worker who "danced" around loading the railroad (*cross*) *ties,* caught the public imagination at one time, but it quite possibly belonged to the language of peripheral workers more basically than to that of the train crew itself. A *high baller* was a good train, to which a superior engineer was assigned, and *high-balling* the process of getting there in a hurry. The latter is well known outside railroading, but there is no certainty that either originated within the industry. Wentworth and Flexner (1960) accept the probably related *balling the jack* as "orig[inal-ly] logger." A very fast train would be known as a *blue streak*, but again the phrase is appropriate to those standing by the right of way rather than to the crew; furthermore, there is no indication that it originated with the railroad. *Fast roller* (Throm 1952) may have had some currency with the general public, but the phrase *on the card* to designate how a fast roller would keep his train on schedule seems not to have been widely known. The public knew *fireman*, but not the alternate names *fireboy* or *coal shoveler*. In at least some local railroad jargon, a *788* was a train that didn't steam well, needing a *class five overhaul*.[7] None of these terms seem to have reached the general public. Neither does *hog* for locomotive or *hoghead* for the engineer, unless perhaps the former is reflected in ghetto slang for 'a Cadillac'. Passenger train crews developed their in-group vocabulary, like *fourth cook* or *Forty* 'dishwasher' (Moore and Pearl 1971: 200-201), but those who rode the passenger trains seldom learned those phrases and terms.

Some of the language of the railroad became just well enough known to permit a certain amount of allusiveness. Daughen and Binzen (1971) use the terms *wreck, red and green, sidetracked, end of the line,* and *caboose* (the last chapter!) in chapter titles, obviously with such a purpose in mind. Perhaps only the second, a reference to railroad lights, would seem obscure to the most casual observer of the railroads. It would be hard to add half a dozen other expressions, however, with as much suggestive power for the general reader.

In striking contrast to the cowboys and mountain men, there seems to be little evidence of drinking, gambling, or wenching terminology among the train crews. It seems almost counter-intuitive that nobody at all should bring a deck of cards into the caboose on a long haul, but trainmen (in our experience) stress the arduous nature of the work and the lack of any opportunity for such vices. They also stress the 125-mile trip and return nature of the work; such a trip may have taken a week of much more than eight-hour days in the early period of railroading, but the trainmen themselves seem not to have gone much further from home. These factors would take the trainmen out of the class of sailors and, especially given the greater speed of the trains as compared to the cattle herds, the cowboys. The railroads eventually made the trail herds obsolete, but there is no indication that they took over the function of lexical innovation.

It is probably in such a context that we should interpret the case of Masterson (1952: 186-7) for a railroad contribution to *skid row*. Dillard (1976a) subscribed uncritically to the insistence of McCulloch (1958) that *skid row* was a corruption of the loggers' *skid road*, a term taken from their occupation and applied to Yesler Way in Seattle. Masterson makes a fairly good case for the contribution of Skiddy Street in Dennison, Texas, named for a very respectable Mr. Skiddy. It seems quite likely that what was "originally" *skid road* should have changed under the influence of an important railroad town. It is not necessary, however, to assume that the change — or the transmission — was due to the train crews as such. A major difficulty is that the trainmen themselves insist that they spent "no" time in such sections, and they show no signs of directly comparable linguistic play *(row* for *road, skid* for *Skiddy).*

It is not that the trainmen did not have — or do not still have — the special vocabulary which goes with any profession or occupation, from plumber to linguist. Botkin (1953: 514) quotes *The Railroad Magazine* for 1900 in a reported speech:

> "The 'con' was flipping the tissue in the doghouse; the hind 'shack' was freezing a hot tub, near the hind end; 'tallow pot' was cracking diamonds in the tank; 'Eagle Eye' was down greasing the pig; and I was bending the rails, when they hit us.[8]

It is rather that this quite conventional occupational creativity produced lexical items or usages which either never reached the general public or — much more likely — never caught its fancy.

One cue to the group actually responsible for *skid row* comes from the name of a group which is more or less casually brought up in treatments of railroad talk, the *boomers.* A term ultimately from the sea (for the maritime origin of *boom* and some inland developments, see p. 102), *boomer* was far from unknown outside the railroad business. It meant, in that context, a man who moved around a great deal. (The semantic feature of mobility was already inherent in the name of the *boom* said.) Boomers were so expert, whether as telegraph operators or as workers on the train itself, that they could get jobs wherever the railroads operated. There might be some reluctance to hire them; an article by Laurence Bell in the *American Mercury* from the 1930s (quoted in Reinhardt 1970: 161) describes such an attitude on the part of an "Old Man McCormack" of a "Texas town":

> He would wait until the last possible source of help had been exhausted before he began hiring "boomers," as migratory trainmen were called.

The boomers had a reputation for drinking and general shiftlessness, despite their expertise, and they may well have had tendencies to spend time on skid row. They traveled much more than the average trainman; one linguistic consequence of that travel was the term *thousand-miler* (shirt), because [the boomer] was reputed to wear it on about a thousand miles of rail travel before sending it to the laundry" (Hubbard, *Pennsylvania Songs and Legends,* quoted in Botkin 1953: 164).

The boomers, the section hands, and the hoboes were certainly casual enough in their relationships and imaginative enough linguistically to have engaged in verbal play. One of the names for a type of hobo (see below, p. 187) was *gandy stiff,* which linked him to the section hands. This kind of *stiff* or *gink* "occasionally labored, a day or two at the most" (Anderson 1923: 101), and his labor was hardly as engineer. Part of that same nonestablishment fraternity of the railroads was the boomer. Botkin (1953: 235) quotes a 1946 publication:

> In boomer days, an unemployed switchman or brakeman who was broke was not too proud to stop in at a hobo *jungle* (camp) to eat, sleep, wash up, or merely stick around between trains.

The picture that emerges is rather that boomers and hoboes, along with the Black section hands, were extremely creative, especially in contrast to the almost stodgy trainmen. Otherwise, the lore of the railroads is primarily the reaction of people who observed the iron horse on its rails, were affected by it (not always favorably by any means), and reacted to it without being railroad employees. Not a little of the lore of the railroads has to do with those who robbed the trains rather than with those who operated them, and it would be rather extreme to say that even Casey Jones was as famous as Jesse James. Even the movies found it easier to interest their audiences in *The Great Train Robbery* (1903) than in driving the engine and collecting fares.

For those who did not attack and rob the trains, the most creative activity has not always been in praising them. Botkin (1953: 505) points out how "Railroad employees and travelers have long enjoyed concocting humorous and often scathing nicknames by misinterpreting the initials of the company."[9] Among thirty-three such names Botkin includes *Cough and Snort* (Colorado and Southern), *No Omelettes, No Eggs* (New Orleans and Northeastern), *Gophers, Frogs and Alligators* (Georgia, Florida and Alabama), and *Damned Small Salaries and Abuse* (Duluth, South Shore, and Atlantic). He asserts (1953: 506) that "travelers and hoboes may have had a hand in devising *Narrow, Crooked, and Ornery* (Nevada-California-Oregon)" and finds that they were certainly responsible for twenty-two names, including *Bumpy, Rocky, and Peculiar* (Buffalo, Rochester, and Pittsburgh), *Leave Early and Wait* (Lake Erie and Western), *Never Did and Couldn't* (Newburgh, Dutchess, and Connecticut), and *Take Your Parcels and Walk* (Texas Pacific and Western). Botkin cites names of locomotives, passenger trains, sleeping and parlor cars, freight trains, and railroads, in addition to the humorous play with initials, but there is hardly a case where a proven naming by an engineer, conductor, fireman, or brakeman — or all of these in concert — is as exotic and imaginative as those which seem to have been concocted by "travelers and hoboes."

Despite cavils by Holbrook (1981: 438) about "sociological documents that are preliminary to the bestowing of the degree of Doctor of Philosophy" which overrate the hobo and his scorn of the "preciosity [that] has gone into these erudite studies," many have been generous to the creative abilities of the hobo, granting him the authorship of "The Big Rock Candy Mountain" and "Hallelajah, I'm a Bum" (or "Hallelujah, Bum Again," to the tune of "Revive Us Again"), "Pie in the Sky" (a parody on "The Sweet Bye and Bye"), and the country and western standard "The Wabash Cannonball." His linguistic creativity is also capable of being argued.

Although trainmen may never have been aware of any sub-categories at all, hoboes went far beyond the popular threefold division of *hobo, tramp,* and *bum.*[10] (A popular typology of the pre-1950s had it that a hobo would work from time to time but wanted to keep moving, a tramp would work only as a last resort, and a bum wouldn't know how to work.) Botkin (1953: 237-9) reprints a 1918 classification into no less than forty-seven distinct sub-groups in "The Rating of the Tramps." These designations dealt with factors as various as the begging styles of certain tramps, their trades like mending umbrellas (a trade learned in a penal institution by a *Mush Faker*) or selling shoestrings, court plaster, or pencils, to a series of terms for young hoboes held in various states of bondage by a *jocker* 'male homosexual, experienced tramp [who] taught minors to beg and crook'. The categories include *punk* 'lad discarded by jocker' and *gonsil* 'youth not yet adopted by jocker'. (OEDS traces this to Yiddish *genzel*: apparently the hoboes were linguistically more diverse than the trainmen.) The non-specialized literature has fairly frequent references to *bindle stiff* 'a hobo who carried bedding'; the hoboes' own language had *pokey stiff, phony stiff, proper stiff, alkee stiff* (a confirmed user of alcohol), and the already mentioned *gandy stiff* — who worked at least sometimes with the section gangs.

As a kind of fraternity, hoboes "accepted and took care of each other . . . through their graffiti" (Reisner 1971: 78). Like highly effective ideograms, institutionalized drawings informed hoboes-to-come about the nature of a town and its police, the probability of securing a handout at a given house, and other practical matters. The obvious motive was to achieve a communication for hoboes but a disguise from others. Reisner (1971: 78) observes:

> Many are probably still in use, and others may well have changed, as does all small group secretive communication. When the hobo code is broken by the feds, the squares, the johns, the slanguage or signs must be a step ahead and new symbols invented.

Mencken-McDavid-Maurer (1963: 677) attribute the following "terms . . . familiar to most Americans" to the hoboes: *jungle* (an area, usually outside a town, where hoboes lived); *blind* (the front of a baggage-car, directly behind the engine-*tender*); *flop* and *flop-house*; *mulligan* (stew); *slave-market*; *main stem* or *drag*; *mooch*; *hand-out*; *panhandle*; *ride the rods*; *bughouse* (crazy); *barrelhouse* (a low saloon); *pound the ties*; and *rustle a meal*. Mencken felt that the last was related to *rustler*, the enemy of the honest cowboy, although he was not sure of the exact relationship. He also thought that *hoosegow* from *juzgado* (with a typically Spanish collapsing of the last two syllables in rapid speech) was transmitted through the agency of hoboes who had been in Mexican jails or who at least had heard of their terrors. The probabilities are certainly greater than those of deriving *calaboose* from *calabazo* or *buckaroo* from *vaquero*. Also, there would be an interesting parallel between the borrowing of *calaboose* by sailors and of *hoosegow* by hoboes who were to some extent their landlocked counterparts.

The term *hangout* just may have come from the hoboes; the attestations using it as the rough equivalent of *jungle* for a temporary base of operations are as early as any others in the dictionaries. If the hoboes did not innovate the term, they probably appropriated it when it was still new. The same could probably be said for *out of sight*, in the sense 'too good to be true', frequently applied to (e.g.) jazz soloes in the 1950s or thereabouts. It has apparently never been traced to hoboes, but Jack London's 1907 use in "The Pen" (Foner 1947: 360) is closer to that meaning than is the same phrase attributed by Majors (1970) to the Afro-American slang "of the 1950's." In London's account, a prisoner who attributed his arrest to taking food from a garbage can speaks:

"It was good bread," he often assured me, "and the meat was out of sight."

The hobo slang seems to preserve some awareness of the relationships between ships and trains. London's 1908 use of the verb *deck* 'to ride on the top of a passenger train' (Foner 1947: 332) is the only citation in DA. London's account reads:

"I am on top of the train – on the 'decks', as the tramps call it, and this process I have described is by them called 'decking her'. And let me say right here that only a young and vigorous tramp is able to 'deck' a passenger train . . ."

If these are traceable to the hoboes – and there seems to be no doubt that some of them are – the "tramps" (London apparently did not learn that distinction) seem like a linguistically innovative group. Their in-group language, with an oft-cited but apparently never systematically explored relationship to cant and the language of the "Gypsies," was in itself fascinating, even if it had never supplied a word to the common vocabulary. The hoboes may be linked rather to innovative outsiders, however, than to the mainstream. Links to the Blacks are probably not entirely fortuitous. Their use of the term *barrelhouse* will suggest the vocabulary of jazz – or at least that of a type of music closely related to jazz. The hoboes have then been overlooked for the same reason that the Blacks and other groups have been overlooked in work on American English: they associated with and belonged with the minorities, and a middle-class-oriented dialectology would take little account of them. They were not completely ignored, but rather relegated to the status of interesting oddities.

It was certainly from the Blacks that at least part of the American population got its railroad lore. Green (1972: 345) reports how the "mountain whites would sit for hours watching and listening to the [Negro] steel drivers and other gang workers."

Steel driving was the occupation of the title character in "John Henry," arguably the greatest American folk ballad. He represents the Black laborer striving to maintain his occupational validity in the face of mechanization — a problem which increasing numbers of workmen have had to share at varying stages of industrialization and which is now an important one in the time of automation. Somehow, perhaps coincidentally, the name John Henry (as in *Put your John Henry on it*) worked its way into American folklore as a less bland version of John Doe. Probably there is some connection to *John Hancock* (*Put your John Hancock on it*) from the signature of the bold first signer of the Declaration of Independence. Can it have been the railroad ballad through which the substitution was made?

Green (1972) reports that Black laborers on the railroads taught phrases like *go down the line* to mountain youngsters, some of whom became recording artists. For example, he relates (1972: 344) how Charles Bowman put together "Nine Pound Hammer" "directly from locutions and a melody used by Black railroad-construction laborers early in the [twentieth] century." The nine-pound hammer was, of course, the type used by John Henry, the "steel-drivin' man."

It may also be from Black railroad influence that the phallic significance of *hammer* in American folk usage came about, although a certain type of comparative folklorist would carry it all the way back to Thor's hammer — or further. College students listening to a recording of "John Henry" in one of my classes once broke into laughter at the last line, "He died with his hammer in his hand." I feel that the laughter may have been just exactly the reaction aimed for by the "original" composer of the ballad; what better way is there for a real man to express his independence? (It is well known that John Henry's woman, Miss Polly Ann, "drove steel like a man" when John Henry himself was incapacitated, but the function of the phrase *like a man* is surely to retain the male-dominant status.) Certainly neither the Black rail gangs nor the blues singers, who often sang about the railroad and its trains, were squeamish about sexual terminology and suggestion (Dillard 1977: Chapter Two).

The steel driver had his share of that type of terminology. Green (1972: 339) reports that the "shaker held and turned the steel drill, which was frequently given a phallic name such as *bull prick.*" The work of one driller striking the drill while a co-worker turned was known as *single-jacking*; "when two drillers worked with a solitary turner the appropriate term was *double jacking.*" What these phrases have to do with *balling the jack*, both a Black and a railroad (and a marginally obscene, at times) term for getting things done in a hurry is not completely clear.

Blacks were, except for the section gangs, consumers rather than producers where the railroads were concerned. Black trainmen were unusual enough to be the subjects of special remembrance, but the section gang itself and the boss, who "called" the work much as such calling was done at the cotton press or on plantation work gangs, were almost exclusively Black.[11] Blues lyrics, like those in Sackheim (1975), deal extensively with either taking a passenger train or hopping a freight to leave the scene of one's sorrow. But perhaps there is no more characteristically Black reaction to the railroads than the prisoners' name, Shorty George, for the train which brought women for conjugal visits. The term *wheelers* has had many uses in other domains (as in *sixteen-wheelers* in trucking), but Green reports the use of the term by Negroes "moving dirt" in railroad gangs to mean 'wheelbarrows'. Green also (1972: 340) notes the absence from DA of *levee camp*, 'either as a river-bank or general construction site'. Green traces French *levee* 'a river embank-ment' to New Orleans "before 1719" and notes that the phrase "also acquir-ed a secondary meaning as a lively place swarming with saloons and brothels" – a skid row, in other words.

If a quick survey of blues lines shows rather less importance of railroad lyrics than one would have expected, Blacks were still very active in music about railroads. The song which Holbrook (1981: 429) calls "without a doubt the most popular railroad song ever written" was apparently the work of Wallace Saunders, a Black who worked in the roundhouse of the Illinois Central at Canton, Mississippi. The song commemorating the death of John Luther Jones, "Casey Jones," on April 30, 1900, was thus written by a member of the same ethnic group that produced "John Henry" and, like the other ballad, by a peripheral worker for the railroad and not by a train-man. Other memorable railroad songs are by Negro writers like Gussie L. Davis ("In the Baggage Coach Ahead"), "the first popular Negro songwriter in the United States" (Holbrook 1981).

It begins to appear that the trainmen had rather little to do with what we usually style the creativity of the domain of the railroad. It is striking that Holbrook (1981: 442) disparaged just the two somewhat inauthentic railroad songs which our consultants at Natchitoches in 1983 cited in opposi-tion to the notion that railroad songs were usually sad:

> But in Tin Pan Alley, the realm of the "popular" song, song writers and song pluggers are well aware of the popular appeal of the railroads. The "Chattanooga Choo-Choo" and "The Atchison, Topeka, and the Santa Fe" are two fairly recent gems, but any reader who is a radio fan can probably name a dozen others.

One does not mean to be too hard on the railroads. It was perhaps in their nature to serve purposes other than the creative. One of them was being on time, and the folk frequently referred to a passenger train by the time at which its schedule called for it to come through ("the ten-ten train" in Terrell, Texas, in the 1930s. Jelly Roll Morton sang a characteristic lyric which surely even he would not have claimed to "compose":

Two-nineteen train done took my baby away
REPEAT
Two-seventeen bring her back some day.

More important than the involvement of the American public in the work of the railroad or its relatively short-term stays on board when traveling was the way in which the locomotive stood – for the public, but evidently not for the trainmen – for unrestricted travel and freedom from cares. The boomer knew that use of the railroad to leave his troubles behind – even if he had to ride the rods sometimes like a hobo. The hobo knew it, and in the process often became a well-traveled man. This escape was not the lot, however, of the engineer, the brakeman, the firemen, or of most of the passengers.

With the rapid transit of the railroads, it became possible to travel long distances without actually living that travel. By World War II or shortly thereafter, it was not unusual to receive the answer, when asking if someone had visited Colorado (or Iowa, or New Jersey), "Only out a train window." There were many who had changed stations in Chicago, or in New York for that matter, who had not seen the city at all. The railroads were probably the first type of traveling about which it could be said with conscious or unconscious irony, "I never left home."

Such travel did not demand adaptations like learning a new language or a new variety of English. It was not really necessary to have one's old variety reshaped greatly, although the railroads probably participated as much as any transit medium in maintaining the leveled dialect of American English.

There seems to be a linguistic watershed here. From the time of the railroads until the present, linguistic change in American English – vocabulary change, at any rate, including the formation of new phrasal compounds or the reviving of old ones – has not been an overland matter but a matter of other kinds of transmission. The railroads mark, linguistically, a rather unspectacular mid-point between the cattle drives and the coast-to-coast hookups of the electronic media. For all the railroads' economic importance, it seems impossible to accord them any great linguistic significance. (In fairness, it should be said that the same limitations seem to apply to the riverboats.) Linguistically, they seem to stand as a kind of intermediate point, contributing little but pointing in their own way to an important transition.

Up to this point, innovation in American English seems to have come from multilingual contact of a rather special kind. (The particular type does not, however, appear to have much in common with the conventionally studied stable bilingualism.) The railroads did not promote that kind of multilingual contact – unless, by some great fluke of history, such activity existed but somehow escaped being written down. Neither did the flowery, exaggerated diction which has been called, somewhat scornfully, "peculiarly American" seem to thrive among the trainmen. One can hardly imagine anything called "Railroad Tall Talk." Fancy, exaggerated diction and pleasure in outlandish, even shocking, speech probably existed among the hoboes, but they were lacking in just that economic status which was becoming indispensible to influence in the nation.[12] If the hoboes, in some bizarre reversal of history, had had money and prestige, one can well imagine that the development of American English might have been vastly different and that railroad terms of much more significance might have developed. But it seems that, in that respect at least, the hoboes missed the train.

NOTES

1. The fourth annual folklife festival at Northwestern State University, Natchitoches, Louisiana, July, 1983, had as its theme the importance of the railroad to the development of Louisiana. Four railroad men were kind enough to participate in a long, public discussion of "Language and Lore of the Railroad" with me at that festival. The public was greatly entertained by their accounts of railroad life; my somewhat curmudgeonly comments in this chapter represent an attitude toward the history of American English and not toward those men or to the railroads they represented.
    Donald Hatley, professor at NSU and director of the festival, first undertook to wrote this chapter for me but was unable to complete it. In several places, I have used Hatley's materials – even, in a couple of places, his exact wording. Hatley is not, however, responsible for mistakes or for infelicities of style or of taste in this chapter.
2. One of our consultants at the festival, who placed this development "between 1800 and 1869," commented explicitly that "the railroads made this country great." Although this is an extremely conventional comment, made – *mutatis mutandis* – at many type of gatherings, the audience seemed to be in agreement.
3. One of our consultants at the folklife festival admitted, *off microphone*, that passenger-train personnel had been rude to the passengers. It is matters like these which motivated my decision not to reveal the names of any of the four consultants.
4. At my prompting, one of our consultants volunteered this form. When a source is not specified, railroad terms in this chapter come from those consultants. It is, of course, possible to go to published sources for a much greater amount of railroad vocabulary. Since, however, this work aims to advance a historical thesis and not to be a full compendium of American English forms, it was thought that the sample provided by those railroad men would serve the purpose equally well.
5. The hyphen is used in these terms as a way of calling attention to simple compounding processes.
6. These are the same four railroad men referred to above.
7. This term was volunteered in the context of considerable pleading on my part for specifically railroad vocabulary.
8. Botkin (1953: 316) also reprints an excerpt from *Early Day Railroading from Chicago* (1910) in which an impostor trying to ride free (*deadhead*) on a train as a railroad man is spotted because he says "twenty minutes past nine" when any true member of the profession would say "nine twenty." Our Natchitoches Folk Festival consultants stated and reiterated that they could identify a stranger as a railroad man from his talk and his gestures, but they proved unable to describe any specific features.

9. Although not specifically questioned about such humorous onomastics, our consultants had abundant opportunity if they had wished to tell about – or had known about – such practices. My impression was that they struggled earnestly to provide what was wanted, and that they were at most marginally aware of such developments.

10. On direct questioning, our consultants denied knowledge of even this rudimentary classification.

11. Mr. Clifford Blake, whose songs, stories, and calls for the cotton press are recorded on LFRS – 001, was our consultant for this activity. Unfortunately, Mr. Blake's experience in calling the rails turned out to have been for a few days at most. In an informal session. Mr. Blake proved much more willing to discuss "bawdy" usages of the section hands than the trainmen were – even after the audience had gone – for the train crews. Some of the forms were, however, undoubtedly "shockers" provided in the absence of understanding of the purpose of the elicitation.

12. Anderson (1923) stresses, as did our Natchitoches Folk Festival consultants, the surprising intelligence and "education" of the hoboes. They and other sources emphasize that there was and is probably a great deal less enmity between trainmen and hoboes than is popularly thought. Both Negro and white blues contain well-known stanzas in which a brakeman asks for money and callously ejects the hobo who has none. Our consultants, on the other hand, stressed the protective function of the trainmen against the dangers of "hopping a freight." They reported some of the ghastly sights which they had encounted, especially when an inexperienced person had attempted to get a free ride on a train. It is obviously only a difference in viewpoint which makes the same action of a trainman seem protective (to himself) and harshly prohibitive (to the hobo).

Chapter IX

The Special Variety and the Norm

Despite the attractiveness of an east-to-west presentation on a map, it seems necessary to take into account the much more complex cultural paths of linguistic change in order to deal effectively with American English. Not much of our population has ever been composed of the kind of settled peasantry that gave a special character to European dialects, and attempts to find patterns of the same kind in the United States have been far from success-ful. It is noteworthy that they have missed Black English, but they have also missed many other developments. Recent attempts (Butters 1983) to explain away Black English influence on the speech of the 16-25 year age group as southern ("Sun Belt") seem to seek out blindness in quest of a praiseworthy but misguided color blindness. The influence of rock music and its vocabulary has been at base Black.

The American population, not even excluding – as we so habitually do – the American Indian tribes, moved from east to west. The more settled and agrarian parts of the population perhaps carried its dialects with it, although there is little or nothing to link the dialects correlated with region in the United States to the geographic dialects of England. The leaders in the west-ward movement were not the members of those settled, agrarian populations. The major innovations seem to have come from the ethnic groups with which the British immigrants were mixed and from the occupational and other cultural groups which preceded the main body on the frontier. These groups were different enough to attract attention and to be recorded at almost every stage.

Professional and religious affiliation were, given the nature of the British migration to the American colonies, much more likely to differentiate the American groups than the mix of dialects from the mother country. Since religious freedom was often the slogan, if not necessarily the effective force, that united a group of immigrants, the linguistic influence from religious groups could have been of paramount importance. It is striking how the speech of the coastal colonies, populated largely by dissenters, resembled, in being "strikingly uniform" and "pure" English, the literary standard pro-pagated by Wycliffe and the Lollards (pp. 4 – 6). Yet there is relatively little evidence of direct religious influence on the language of the frontier. The shepherd symbolism of the Bible met a poor reception from the sheep-hating cattlemen, and miners like those in Mark Twain's "Buck Fanshawe's Funeral" were apparently as little at home with the lexicon of the "gospel sharp."

Notwithstanding the difficulties which organized religion had with the advance guard of frontiersmen, it had an extremely strong influence on the more settled parts of the population, and preachers were not too far behind the trappers and cattlemen (Phares 1964).

Unfortunately, there seems to have been no study which broke down religious "Americanisms" by population groups. (Dillard 1977 makes some attempt with the Black population; see, however, Hirshberg 1982a.) Writers like Dickens, in *Household Words*, were content to label *religious revival* and *anxious seat* as Americanisms, that being the ultimate in opprobrium in at least a pose which Dickens took. Mencken (1945) pointed out how American *Holy-rollers, Dunkards, hard-shell Baptists,* and *mourners' bench* were as foreign to English as *vicar, curate, dissenter, benefice, almoner, dean,* and *pluralist* are to the great majority of Americans. Presumably some of these terms are distributed according to denomination (even Christians are more likely to refer to others as *holy-rollers* than to themselves, and Episcopalians self-consciously use *renewal* rather than *revival*), and some of them (*dunkard*) may be obsolescent or have regional limitations.

What emerges rather clearly is that there is a great deal of difference, in religious terminology, between the United States and England. A work like Nelson (1945: 131) will go so far as to say that the two English-speaking countries "have gradually developed a marked difference in religious vocabulary." Nelson also points out other Americanisms like *anxious seat, camp meeting, circuit rider, come-outer, foot-wash, pounding, to get religion,* and *to shout.* The last has a special function and perhaps history in the Black church (Dillard 1977: 55ff). See also the Black extension of *member.*

Certain special Christian groups, like the Baptists, had different terminologies on different sides of the ocean. The term *Particular Baptist,* said to have been applied eventually to the little group of Separatists who formed up in London in 1616 (McBeth 1983), seems not to have come to America; their doctrine of salvation of an elect only is also not characteristic of American Baptists. There was, then, no need for the contrasting term *General Baptists,* although their anti-predestination beliefs are characteristic of the denomination in the United States. Of course there are some generally regional implications from the predominance of Baptists in the South; it is perhaps no accident that the Southern Baptist Convention is the largest protestant organization in the United States.

Evangelical protestanism passed on to the Black community almost from the time of arrival of the first slaves, with a still-controversial amount of influence from the revivalist movement of the late eighteenth and early nineteenth century. Fisher (1953) found a lot of influence from African traditions in slave religious ceremonies and even a reflection of the Nat Turner rebellion in the early spirituals. Work (1940) reports how a colony of some two hundred freedmen from Kentucky, Pennsylvania, and South Carolina migrated in 1824 to Samaná Bay in the Dominican Republic. According to Work, the group preserved its spirituals, not in church services but at parties for corn huskings. Hoetink (1962) points out the link between the Protestant religion and English (as opposed to Catholicism and Spanish) in preserving the distinct culture (and language) of the group. Dillard (1977: 50-57) claims peculiarly Black status for a large number of religious terms and expressions; Hirshberg (1982a) offers rebuttal only for *amen corner*, *setting-up* 'wake', and *breaking exercise*, although a generalized claim is made that Black protestant terminology came from the white revivalist movement. Expressions like *to be a seeking, still in de open fiel', coming through*, and a number of other terms (see especially Dillard 1977: 51) are not dealt with by Hirshberg, and it is impossible to tell whether they figure in his general disapproval – or whether there is an objective basis for that general disapproval if it exists.

More recently, perhaps, the Catholic church has made linguistic adaptations. Some of them, as in the shift from Latin to modern languages, are spectacularly obvious. But terms and compounds in use in the Catholic community are also changing (Stern 1979). While phrases like [*he's*] *in our church* remain typically Protestant (against Catholic *in our parish*), phrases like *faith community, parish family, fellowship, involvement*, and *caring relationship* are increasingly heard among Catholics.

At any rate, it is certain that Protestantism, and particularly the revivalist movement, left its mark on American English. Whether Black church terminology represents retentions or innovations – and it does not seem safe to assume either – their terminology, like the style of their sermons and of their church music, is strikingly different today in "ghetto" and rural Southern environments. Regardless of ethnic composition (and *de facto* segregation is still strong today), Southern Protestant churches exercise considerable freedom in terminology, with frequent apparent innovation; the "Religion" page of the Shreveport *Times* for March 20, 1983, yields the forms *scripturecise* and *singspiration*.

To an appreciable extent, the innovative varieties of American English are still those more easily characterizable as "special varieties" rather than as "dialects" in the European Atlas tradition. If, as the above chapters suggest, such varieties were the most important developments in colonial times and on the frontier, and if such "lects" (in the sense of C.–J. Bailey) remain the most influential in American English, then it becomes somewhat difficult to identify the time at which those more traditionally conceived influences were dominant.

In particular, the tracing of American dialectal variants to regionally distributed variants in British English seems unproductive and even alien to the pattern of development of the language in the United States. It has been rather easy to observe (Laird 1970) that, in marking the alleged westward spread of colonial American dialects, a different set of forms (largely words) must be used than can possibly be used to trace early American dialects to England. Not even the special Atlas Worksheets list, to which many have objected as placing unnecessary limitations on American dialect work (Underwood 1974), provides any special connection with British dialects. And, although those Worksheets have not usually been claimed to relate any more to Standard English than to nonstandard dialects, they tell almost nothing about special varieties.

When special varieties of American English have engaged attention in the last two or three decades, they have tended to be those spoken by "inner city" youth from minority ethnic backgrounds. A major cause is that such children and teenagers brought new problems to the school systems of the large Northern cities, including language problems of a type not hitherto encountered even in cities where large immigrant populations had brought foreign language problems. The rather obvious early answer was "language deficit," but closer examination showed that the "deficit" groups had complete and non-pathological grammatical systems which, insofar as objective linguistic analysis could determine, provided as much communicative potential · as any other language variety, including Standard English (Stewart 1969, Labov 1972, Baratz 1969).

The speech of Blacks was so often the variety examined that an occasional protest from a Black scholar was voiced (Williamson 1968).[1] In addition to work on Black English as a dialect or "lect," a flood of works dealt with the picturesque slang of the inner city, the majority of the speakers of which were very often Black. Whether the "argot" of the inner city was picked up by Blacks or whether Blacks brought it to the inner city turned out to be a question not susceptible of any easy answer. It might well be easier to answer the venerable riddle about the chicken and the egg. Nevertheless, a careful and elaborate study like Folb (1980: 121) showed, in the Los Angeles "ghetto," "a small segment of the glossary . . . known almost exclusively by . . . Blacks."

Many of the works on the lexicon of inner-city Blacks have been ephemeral; it would seem that every popular magazine has had at least one. Some have been educationally oriented and highly responsible, like Foster (1974). A few have been anthropologically sophisticated (Mitchell-Kernan 1969), and some lexicographically sound to a greater or lesser degree (Major 1970). The last and Dillard (1977) make an extreme case for the separateness of the Black lexicon; see now Hirshberg (1982a and b). In most of the academic studies (Mitchell-Kernan 1969, Labov et al. 1968) preoccupation with striking language behavior like the dozens (also called *sounding, joning,* etc.) diverted attention from grammatical or lexical analysis.

Perhaps even more unfortunately, the language of the inner city reflected ghetto activities like prostitution and the selling and consumption of narcotics. Perhaps because of the discovery of Beck (1969), there was a rash of studies of Black pimps and their prostitute victims (Milner and Milner 1972, Hall 1972). Robert Beck ("Iceberg Slim") provided enough data for a seminal paper by Kochman (1969); it was about this time that *rapping* and *to rap* became familiar terms to the academic and linguistic communities, although it is very unlikely that the term was new. The advantages of discovering a literate and intelligent treatment by a (presumably reformed) practitioner of a trade that many were tempted to consider exotic were many. The fact that he recorded in detail a few discourse strategies of which he claimed convincingly to be master was of great interest to anthropologically oriented linguists. Although Beck's primary interests were not lexical, he tended to provide information of a first-hand nature which one cannot attribute to writers like Gold (1975).

Out of this line of investigation developed the theory that Black "use" of English differed in some greatly significant way, although the actual items (including lexicon and syntactic rules) were almost identical to those of Standard English (or, in an occasional statement, white nonstandard dialects.) Intuitive reactions from Black speakers tended to favor this hypothesis, particularly since few inner city Blacks were impressed with the similarities between their speech and that of Jamaicans, Antiguans, Trinidadians, or West African English speakers with whom they came into contact. On the other hand, few historical linguists would argue that a speaker's intuitions about his own language history are any especially reliable guide to that history.

There is not much doubt that the language-functional approach which Kochman (1969, 1970, 1972), Abrahams (1964, 1976), and others brought to the language of the ghetto provided a useful corrective to the overly historical approach of the neo-Herskovitsians (Dillard 1975). At about the same time, however, a reaction against the facile assumption that only nine or ten words in American English could be traced to West Africa was led by Dalby (1972). He demonstrated that more than one West African language might figure in the background of an American English expression like *O.K.*; treatment of this specific expression led rather to angry rejoinders in the New York *Times* than to serious academic consideration.

Dalby's presentation made a strong case for deriving Black slang *cat* 'person' and *hip* 'aware, *au courant*' from West Africanisms like Wolof *hipicat* rather than from some elaborate metaphorical processes with now homophonous English etymons. (One deservedly forgetten amateur suggested that *hip* came from the first syllable of *hypodermic* [*needle*] and thus reflected the very great influence of drug terminology on jazz.) Most of his really impressive demonstrations, however, involved phrasal compounds like *eye water* 'tears' and *big eye* 'greed'. Coupled with Beck's phrases like *pull one's coat* 'orient, provide pertinent information', such compounds seemed to demonstrate that the significantly Black element in the lexicon was not individual words, even though a few like *mojo* were much more widely current in the Black culture than conventional treatments would lead one to believe, but slightly variable fixed phrases which might be three or four or even more words long. See now Dillard (1977) and Hirshberg (1982a and b), who would seem to agree on that principle if not on much else.

The amount of work to be done before any serious conclusions can be reached is staggering. Vass (1979) provides a provocative list of possible Bantu derivations for etymological puzzles like *ballyhoo*, *brotus*, and *goofer*. The first has interesting nautical associations; Holm and Shilling (1982) derive the Bahamian English form meaning 'a beaked fish' from Puerto Rican Spanish *balajú*, and the DA suggests Spanish *balahú* 'schooner' as a possible source for the American English word. OEDS simply calls the word "originally U.S." with "etymology unknown." DA finds a rather unconvincing "British dialectal" source for *brotus*; OEDS apparently ignores the whole thing. The latter does, however, consider *goofer* "of African origin," and would probably agree with Vass that *goofer-bag*, *goofer dust*, and *goofer-doctor* are extensions of that African influence into compounds. DA agrees with Vass in offering *kufua* 'to die' as a source. Under any circumstances, semantic changes are required, since *goofer* is not used exclusively in order to produce the death of the victim. Robert Thompson (personal communication) suggests that the verb *goof*, the adjective *goofy*, and perhaps even slang expressions like *goof off* and *goof on* may come from some transferred sense like 'be dead' or 'dead-headed'. OEDS opts rather for "apparently a use of dialectal goof, GOFF. 2" Although *goofus*, as a musical term, is called an "arbitrary formation" by OEDS, it is tempting to find some connection. The broadside approach by Vass cannot be ultimately convincing, but it is not, on the face of it, inferior to the traditional assumption of influence from anything but African languages.

Somewhere between the extremes of the one viewpoint that Black English differs only in "use" (discourse strategies, affective devices) from Standard English and the other that large numbers of Bantu or other African language words have survived must lie the truth about Black slang. A balanced viewpoint, it is suggested, would give as much attention to the Black church as to inner city vice, even though the latter has a kind of popular appeal which the former may lack. Mitchell (1970) and Pipes (1970) give abundant evidence that Black churches and Black preaching have a character of their own, and even the influence of a Martin Luther King should be some indication of the importance of religion to Black people. Fairclough (1960) and Noreen (1965) pointed out some naming practices which appear to be peculiar to Black churches; Dillard (1976) has attempted to show how, without any unusual lexical elements, Black church names like

> The United House of Prayer for All People of the Church on the Rock of the Apostolic Faith ("Daddy Grace's Church")

and

> Sacred Heart Spiritual Church of Jesus Christ, Inc.

are unlike the names of white churches anywhere in the United States and rather like those of some African churches (Parrinder 1953). Hirshberg (1982a) criticizes Dillard (1977) for including *amen corner* in the Black lexicon and observes that "*much* [emphasis added] of the lexicon of the Black religious experience derives directly from the revivalist movements of the late eighteenth and nineteenth centuries" (1982a: 56). Since "much" is not all — and conceding the matter of *amen corner* — it would still be nice to know *how* much of the "thoroughly nativized" Black church terminology is, from the vantage point of the Dictionary of American Regional English, white as well. As a white Southern Protestant, I have never heard *seeking [re] ligion, sinner man (boy, girl), still in the open field, setting on the sinner seat, coming through, shout* (in the well-attested sense of a religious *dance*), *mourner's bench, tarry service,* nor several other terms listed in Dillard (1977), nor is there any immediately obvious reference work which classifies them as non-Black. Hirshberg cites, unusually for him, the "history of black conversion to Christianity" (Frazier 1964, Williams and Brown 1977) rather than dictionaries or the publications of dialect geographers.

Nor does it seem fair to dismiss the possibility that a lot of musical terminology, especially that of the blues and jazz, is specifically and historically Black on the grounds that the lyrics "are highly conventional, at times even formulaic; and they are metaphorical" or to object to jazz and blues texts as sources for domains like religion and lovemaking on the grounds that "To the extent that the language of the blues is conventional, it may operate within one linguistic domain only, that is, the domain of musical lyric" (Hirshberg 1982a: 57). Historically, expressions like *juba* and *pat juba* are undoubtedly Black, and *swing, blues,* and *blue notes* do not have convincing explanations as terms derived from older English. These and many other Black musical terms (*gate/alligator, riff, break, gutbucket, scat, ragtime, boogie woogie*) were the first Black words taken into the speech of many

American whites. From the so-called Jazz Age of the 1920s to the rock and roll of the 1980s, music has been the domain of probably the greatest Black influence. Whatever other "ghetto" language forms and communicative processes have come to the white community have generally been preceded by some of the terminology of music.

Having become aware of the language of the Black community and at least some of its cultural values through music and popular entertainment, whites (especially teenagers) have borrowed Black slang from those domains quite rapidly as such things go. The probably African *hip* gave birth to *hipster* (using a suffix that, except for *trickster, youngster,* and a few others even if *punster* is allowed, is rare), which in turn seems to have spawned *hippie*. The originally diminutive connotations of the new suffix seem to elude the white youngsters who so aggressively contrast themselves to *rednecks* (as a hipster would once have contrasted himself to a *square*). *Cool* is the term of universal approbation; according to Thompson (n.d.) that is the African function of the term, not the temporary meaning (opposite in musical value to *hot*) which Charlie Parker, Dizzie Gillespie, and Miles Davis attached to it during the bop revolution of the 1950s. (*Bop* itself was soon appropriated by teenagers to mean a loud music with a fixed beat like rock and roll rather than the innovative music of Parker and his followers.)

The phrase *rock and roll*, apparently referring to an alternative between relaxed and sustained physical activity and frantic activity which can only be sustained for a short time (Dillard 1977), soon became shortened to *rock*. There have been a variety of styles of that music: *hard rock, punk rock, rockabilly,* etc. The terminology of rock music reached England; indeed, groups like the Beatles and the Rolling Stones added to the terminology and re-exported it (Hellman 1973). The function of rock music in the "counter-culture" and in adolescent rebellion is well known. Insofar as it is the music, as parents, teachers, and clergymen often claim, of the vice world, rock and roll has contributed to the near-fusion of Black slang and the less innocent aspects of inner city culture.

While there may be some controversy as to the use of rock music to foster Satanic cults, illicit sex, and certain other vices, there is little doubt that the music has almost from the first been background for drug consumption. A condition labeled *stoned*, seemingly taken over from an intensifier widely used by Blacks in phrases like *stone blind* and *my stone friend,* is the aim of the participant − and, to some, the only condition under which rock music can be tolerated. There is no necessary Black connection to the LSD connotations of the Beatles' "Lucy in the Sky with Diamonds," nor to the "downer" (depressant) associations of "Yellow Submarine." Nor is there any necessarily Black component to the title "Eat a Peach," which younger Americans at least can relate to the consumption of hallucinogenic mushroom.

These drug associations are far from new. The jazz scene of the 1920's had *roach* 'a marijuana cigarette' long before the hippies discovered, or less probably invented, *joint*. The term *viper* 'marijuana user' seems incredibly old-fashioned and almost innocent today. The multiplicity of terms for marijuana (*Mary, Jane, pot, grass*) reflects a very large number of influences, including probably some Mexican and South American terms. Users of the early 1970s were high in praise of *Colombia gold*, and some even expressed an interest in migrating to that country in order to be near the high-quality supply.

What is Black about the "hip"slang is probably not so new as is often believed; a serious lexical study of plantation documents (Hirshberg 1982b) might well reveal slightly different usages on the plantations of the nineteenth century. There is, for example, the participle *busted*, long familiar in white slang in the sense 'broke, without funds'. In the 1960s, that sense was almost entirely displaced by the meaning 'arrested'. Although the hippies and their associates might be *busted* for even such minor infractions as traffic violations, the most characteristic use of the term was for being picked up by the vice squad for prostitution or drug use. Harrison (1880) records the expression *to get busted* 'to fail', which could lead by easy semantic transference (the subject *failed* to evade the fuzz) to the later meaning.

In jail, the member of the counter-culture was *on ice*. I do not have the faintest notion whether or not that expression is originally Black, although the temptations to associate it with *cool* and *cooling it* are so obvious as to demand resistance. Eldridge Cleaver's almost archetypical Black protest book. *Soul on Ice* (1968), combined the expression with a term usually applied in the Black community (*soul music, soul food*), but Cleaver's associations were not exclusively Black by any means.

The contemporary use of *heavy* to mean 'arcane, profound' also has its plantation and even Creole progenitors. *Heavy knowledge* had a vogue associated with racio-political lines of reasoning and with a certain occultism (Labov et al, 1968: II, 146). Herskovits and Herskovits (1936) reported the use the term in a strikingly similar sense among the Blacks of Paramaribo, Surinam:

Thus comment is made that *Kromanti* dancing is *hebi* − "difficult" − that is "strong," or "dangerous.". . .

Gonzales (1922) lists *hebby* 'great' in his Gullah glossary and cites *uh hebby complain* 'a great outcry'.

This transfer across (perhaps accidentally) related domains is hardly a function of geographic proximity. To adapt a statement by Folb (1972: 85), "race, economics, or geography alone do not determine a person's [language usage]." An extremely important factor is what Eastman and Reese (1981) call *subcultural solidarity*. This is expressed

by speaking like our cohorts – be they ethnic, professional, or some age grade for
example. People who participate in a sport have their own common vocabulary,
jargon, and mutually defined ethnosemantic domain, as do urban nomads . . .
streetwalkers and the like . . . . Teenagers often try to adopt the argot of their
rock music idols as an effort to be "in."

The television set, the radio, and, most especially, the phonograph now assure
a much more rapid transmission of this sub-cultural "argot" than would have
been possible even in the days of the Western nomads.

In the early days of attention to Black English, people often wondered,
with unbelievable naivete, why the constant television watching which
ghetto children were supposed to engage in did not teach them Standard
English. The reason seems altogether too obvious: "Subcultural solidarity"
does not emerge nearly so effectively from the television set as from the
phonograph record. Representations of dialect and argot on television are so
patently stereotyped, where they are not so reduced as to be completely
washed out, that not even pre-teens can find much to identify with. For
better or worse, television is essentially wedded to Standard English; the
most standard speech in the United States – not necessarily the "best" –
is that to be heard on national network newscasts. Tucker and Lambert
(1969) found that Black college freshmen in the Deep South and their largely
white counterparts in New England showed an overwhelming preference for
that type of speech over other American dialects. The television networks
provide employment for speakers with leveled dialects, although they do not
themselves create those dialects.

One of H.L. Mencken's most cherished insights was his perception of what
he called General American. This was, incidentally, something quite different
from what he called the American Vulgate, a kind of conglomerate of all the
"bad" English forms Mencken found in use by Americans. (One would have
to say that the latter lacked the validity of the former.) It has been asserted
that there is no *geographic* locus of this ultimately leveled dialect – which is
probably exactly what Mencken meant to claim for it.

The treatment so far has perhaps been lacking in purely geographic factors,
the movement east-to-west which seems like the one indispensable element in
a history of American English. One reason for this omission is that such
treatments have frequently been done before. A more serious objection is,
however, that I cannot find any evidence of such purely geographic transmission which does not appear to be totally circular: Form X is found in
regions A and Z, the latter much further west, therefore it must have been
transmitted there – apparently *by all English-speaking groups* who made the
trip. Such a formulation does not appear to be believable, although it has
been the basis of most historical work done on American English.

Pickford (1956) was one of the early works, and perhaps the most important, to question the empirical foundations upon which the work of the

Linguistic Atlas of the United States and Canada, the sponsor in effect of the traditional historical viewpoint, rested. She criticized the way in which the Atlas workers overlooked complex American migratory patterns and their consequences. Referring to work in California, she wrote:

There has never been enough stability of population or homogeneity of origin in California to establish the cultural dominance of an aged native sector . . . . Out of fifty-three interviews completed, where aged, life-time Fresnans of American stock were sought, only six qualified – from a community of 150,000 population first settled by white men in 1849. These six showed a complete lack of homogeneity in their individual backgrounds. Their parents and grandparents migrated from over sixteen states, in varying proportions and combinations. The fact that these six were unacquainted with one another further demonstrates that native Californians do not necessarily comprise a cohesive group – do not, indeed, comprise a group at all. (ibid., p. 226)

Pickford's critique did not focus on the linguistic forms apart from sociological sampling, but the same results come from a thorough examination of those forms. As Pickford pointed out, the rural emphases exemplified by studies of the spread of words like *mudworm, angledog,* and *snake doctor* cause an underestimation of the effects of urbanization in the United States. In a few cases, relatively homely terms suggest more complex distributions than the framers of the Atlas questionnaire may have suspected: *Johnny cake,* far from being a U.S. localism, turns out to have distribution in the Western Caribbean as well (Holm and Shilling 1982).

The issues of urbanization and of British origin are not related in any simple way, even though dialect studies have traditionally sought English dialect survivals in rural vocabulary. The Black dialect, considered in terms of its grammatical system and of the distribution of grammatical forms (Feagin 1979), can no longer be considered the amalgam of British regionalisms which it was considered to be by Brooks (1935). The opposite mistake would be to consider all "urban" slang, or even all "Black" slang, as somehow Creole in origin.

A good example is provided by *bread* 'money', widely used in the inner city. It very probably comes from the rhyming slang which is associated with the Cockney *stairs: apples (and pears); money: bread (and honey).* Since not even those who have insisted that Black English vernacular forms were acquired primarily from Irish overseers on the plantations have suggested much contact with Cockneys, the transfer was probably made through generalized street talk. Specifically Black reflexes of *bread* are much more like to have had sexual rather than monetary connotations (Dillard 1977, Holm and Shilling 1982).

The media have had a great deal of influence in determining what the American population in general has thought about dialects. Even before television's *The Jeffersons,* radio's *Amos and Andy* gave use an identifiable Black dialect more concerned with impressionistic identifications that with historical validity. Although many of the forms attributed to Blacks – or to any other group – by the entertainment media are suspect and others may be outright false, some genuine transmission of the vocabulary of ethnic slang has taken place thereby.

Nor is that influence limited to Blacks or other minority groups within the United States. During World War II, for example, newspapers and magazines brought a great deal of German vocabulary to American English – temporarily in some cases. While some German words may have spread out to the surrounding areas from Grundy County, Illinois, the flood of Germanisms during the war did not come from any such rural groups. *Blitzkrieg, panzer, Luftwaffe, Stuka* and other such military terms came into our vocabulary even without direct personal contact. In like manner, those who learned the Russian word *Sputnik* around 1957 did not need even to know any Russians.

Words from another language (e.g., German) often have a national life history in the United States that deviates greatly from any use in the original language. There is probably no better example than *hamburger*, which has departed so far from its German source (*ein Hamburger Wurst*) that a World War II correspondent could claim that Hamburg had been "hamburgered" after an Allied bombing raid. The element *-burger*, far from meaning 'resident of a city', soon became a suffix meaning 'a sandwich made of meat and other ingredients between two buns'. There was a fad, now largely past, or making new compounds: *nutburger, crabburger, cheeseburger, steakburger*, etc. There even developed *beefburger*, although the original hamburger was allegedly made of beef. When the spread of fast food chains resulted in a smaller selection of items quickly prepared, *fishburger* became *whaler*, a large hamburger became a *Big Mac* (from Burger King and McDonald's, respectively); the latter (and *quarter pounder*, etc.) tended to replace even the original *hamburger*. The formative devices used by McDonalds involve generally the use of the prefix *Mc*: *Egg McMuffin* and *McRib*. If it had developed in the 1940s or even the 1950s, the latter would probably have been a **Ribburger*.

Even virtually separated from the domain of food, *-burger* continues to function in the American vocabulary. In the 1980s, Helen Gurley Brown coined *mouseburger*, apparently a blend of *mousy* 'unspectacularly female' and *burger* 'typically American'.

A similar vogue and relatively quick decline was observable in *cafeteria*. Undeniably from Spanish, it may have come from the Southwest – that is, anywhere between Texas and California. Analogous words proliferated, but the 1980s. (See Marckwardt/Dillard 1980: 53-54.) Phrases like *cafeteria feeding* (letting a child choose whatever he wished to eat) spread far beyond the domain of commercial food service. Perhaps nothing sped the disuse of *cafeteria* quite so much as the dominance of nationally syndicated fast-food chains.

Certain groups may be more influenced by national factors than by local contacts, by the very nature of the social relationships in the area of contact. Thus, in the very areas where "Anglo" Texans picked up somewhat distorted Mexican food names but virtually nothing else from Mexican Spanish since the mid-nineteenth century (Sawyer 1959), Latin bilingual speakers were more likely to know the national *corn husk* and *wish bone* than *corn shuck* and *pulley bone*, although those are the forms used by the local Anglos. They are also unlikely to know /rows ñiyrz/, a form of *roasting ears*, although Texas whites and Negroes as far away as North Carolina (Farrison 1936) used the term during the period of contact studied. Geographic proximity had been outweighed, as very frequently, by social considerations. (For other examples, see Blanc 1954 and Gumperz 1958a and b.) Since the Latins and the Anglos did not mix on kitchen levels of intimacy, they did not learn the same words for those homey food items. It is more likely that the Latins picked up the national terms from newspapers and magazines than from books, but in any case printed sources were much more important, in those specific domains, than geographic proximity.

An interesting case of transmission through contact, parallel in many striking respects to the development of inner city street slang, was the development of heavily English-influenced Spanish spoken by Mexican-American "ghetto" residents in the Southwest (Coltharp 1964). As Alvarez (1967), who had apparently been a member of the Calo-speaking Mexican groups, pointed out, Mexican-American adolescents used Spanish with their parents, English with the official world, and Calo (with enough disguise or "jargon" features to be unintelligible to the other two groups) with their peers. Alvarez explicitly compares the linguistic preferences of the Calo speakers to those of (Black and) Anglo-American hipsters. Notably, again, this linguistic result of direct contact does not seem to have any of the localisms that have been used for drawing isogloss boundaries.

More assimilated "Latins" in the Southwest, like their "Anglo" counterparts who had an interest in (e.g.) recorded music might learn a great deal of the same vocabulary from newspapers and audio magazines, or from audio (formerly *high fidelity*) stores. In English (and sometimes in the Spanish of the Southwest in border areas or even in Puerto Rico) they would refer to the *turntable, tone arm,* and *cartridge*; to *monophonic, stereophonic,* and *quadrophonic* reproduction; to *solid state, preamp, amplifier, woofer, tweeter, mid-range (speaker), damping, moving coil, electrostatic, crossover network, hysteresis, synchronic, elliptical* and *conical (styli)*, and to *tracking force*. Their records would be *33-1/3's (LP's)*, less frequently *45's*, and only as a relic of the dim past *78's*. They might be very much concerned as to whether the recordings were made at a *live* or *studio performance.* There is much more likely to be a generational difference in these terms (many of the oldsters not knowing them at all) than local variation.

Words relating to radio and television are, also, very unlikely to have local distributions. *Radio,* itself an "Americanism" in the narrow sense from at least as early as its adoption by Congress in an act of 1912, furnishes some excellent examples of national but not regional usage. Of course, it is true that from the early days of radio a great deal of the program material has come from either New York or Los Angeles. In radio, much was made of the *coast-to-coast hookup.* The phrase itself does not seem to be represented in the dictionaries, but OEDS calls *hookup* originally U.S. colloquial. Further, the citation of *from coast to coast* from Tennyson does not seem to have the technological associations of the phrase in radio usage. At any rate, attributive use of the phrase does not seem to be earlier attested than the American *coast to coast aviator* of 1911 and *coast-to-coast chain* of 1926.

At one time, it was considered quite a trick to have the engineers of a station broadcasting from New York "try" to get Los Angeles, or vice versa. Especially after techniques were perfected, the city on the other coast may have "been there" all along, but the phrase had a certain impressiveness before the whole business became commonplace. If there's a geographic locale for *coast-to-coast* in the 1920s and 1930s, it's New York-Los Angeles, an area spread over 3,000 miles. An electronic medium like radio simply made available to the non-erudite, even to the illiterate, user of English the same kind of shared communication and non-local vocabulary which had long been available to the reader of poetry, philosophy, or philology.

No matter where he came from or where he lived, the radio listener of the period heard about and talked about *soap opera* (1927, OED Supplement, but *horse opera,* which may have been the model, is attested as early as 1857), *quiz show, static* (for the radio listener, a sound and not a type of electricity), *announcer* (not an Americanism – but it isn't certain that British announcers played as important a part in the programs as Don Wilson did for Jack Benny or Harry von Zell for Burns and Allen), *station break, sign-off, comedy hour,* and *give-away program.* No claim is made here that all of these are Americanisms, although a spot check of the OED Supplement will show that the last is labeled "orig[inally] U.S." It doesn't necessitate any looking in the dictionary to garner the information that phrases like *Fibber McGee's closet, Jack Benny's Maxwell,* and *Bob Hope's nose* were familiar phrases among American listeners – and early viewers of television – except perhaps for the most selective. On the semi-technical side, and somewhat later, we learned *AM, FM, transistor,* and *portable.* It is hardly worth checking to see whether these are technically Americanisms.

Some of the terminology of radio, like *serials* (neither that term nor *daytime serials* in the use as a more dignified term for *soap operas* seems to be in DA or OEDS) may have come in from the movies. The two media certainly shared some terms. For small boys in the 1930s and 1940s, a *serial* with a cowboy or a jungle man was a *continued piece*. Perhaps this may have been specific to rural Texas, but in all parts of the country movie fans at one time or another talked of *bank night* (DA entries for 1936 and 1948), *double features* (DA 1932), or even *triple features* (perhaps not an elegant enough term to make the dictionaries). Those in the hinterlands read about *sneak previews* in the newspapers and heard about them on the radio, although the previews themselves may have been actually available only to the residents of big cities.

Like the radio terms, the words and phrases characteristic of the movies were national and to some degree international. The word *movie* itself is said to have entered the folk speech from New York or Chicago around 1906-1907; the first DA attestation is 1913, and the OEDS calls it originally U.S. With movies went *previews of coming attractions, newsreels, selected short subjects, westerns* (DA 1929, although it is probable that it was used earlier of novels), *shoot-em-ups* or *gangster pictures* or *cops 'n' robbers* ("originally U.S." as a children's game around 1903), *musicals, tear-jerkers, screen credits, Academy Award, Oscar* (DA 1936), *Oscar winner, supporting cast, character actor, Technicolor* (DA 1944), *black and white, 3D, Todd A-O, Cinemascope, sound track, on location* (DA 1914), *stunt man, star*, and *starlet*.

From 1932 onward, movie makers were very sensitive to what was called the *Hayes Code*, and any moviegoer – depending more on his morals than his place of residence – would be in favor of or against that code. With the screening of Edward Albee's *Who's Afraid of Virginia Woolf?* in 1966, the phrase *suitable for mature audiences* began a temporary vogue. The greater freedom of European movie makers, combined with the at least temporarily higher artistic standard of foreign directors like Ingmar Bergman, led to the popularity of *foreign movie* and *art movie*. Unfortunately, both tended to become confused with *adult film*, about which it was cynically commented that no real adult would bother to see one. The whole movement, reminiscent in some ways of periods of insistence upon artistic freedom, soon led to Hollywood's use of *G, PG, R*, and *X*.

Television carried on a great deal of the national media vocabulary of radio and the movies and added some of its own. Whether he would be caught dead eating one or not, any American knows the meaning of *TV dinner*. Even aficionados know that the set is often called *the boob tube* – sometimes *the tube* for short. The very slightly technically minded learn of the *teleprompter* and of *telstar*, the artificial satellite used in transmission. (It is, incidentally, highly improbable that the meaning of Greek *tele-* figures in the derivation of even the second of those.) All viewers know of *prime time*, *talk shows*, *the late show* (OEDS has apparently only heard of *late, late show*). Even though *rerun* may not have originated with television, the term probably has that connotation to an American viewer of today. And a *channel* is a number on a dial, not what a river runs through. The British may abbreviate the name of the medium as *telly*, but to Americans from any part of the country it's *tee-vee*. (One who is less than an ardent fan of the medium may be pardoned for suggesting that *tee-bee*, for *tuberculosis*, was the model.)

The number of new terms created by the medium is amazing, especially if temporary developments are included. *Bunkerism* may disappear when the last spinoff from *All in the Family* disappears from the networks. *M*A*S*H*, a fairly literate treatment of the experiences of doctors and nurses during the Korean war, left only its own title as a linguistic legacy; but consumption of water in the big cities is supposed to have risen to record highs as audiences went to the bathroom after the end of the well-publicized last broadcast. (Mickey) *Mouseketeers*, by analogy with *musketeers* understood not as Dumas wrote about them but as 'any group of especially close friends', has spawned *Grouchketeers* on *Sesame Street*, for an organization based on the character Oscar the Grouch. Other cases of entertainment media inbreeding are probably observable by habitual viewers.

Spectator sports have been taken over to an amazing degree by television. A *commercial time-out* is a routine occurrence in contests which are not exclusively and sometimes even primarily for those actually in attendance. The *instant replay*, especially as it permits second-guessing of the call of an official, often figures in post-game discussions for days afterwards. A wartime word, *blackout*, has been transferred to the situation in which a game will not be *telecast* (*television* + *broadcast*) to the immediate area in which the game is played, apparently in order that spectators might be encouraged to go to the stadium. *Closed circuit television* has other uses, but in sports it refers to a broadcast for theaters only, all in attendance having to pay a rather high price. Heavyweight champion boxing matches are the most usual features of such presentations; ordinary commercial television will normally show the match, or excerpts from it, some weeks later.

Much of the terminology of sports remains unaffected by media presentation; *play-by-play* and *blow-by-blow* go back to the days of radio. The *winner* and the *loser* remain the same; *win, place,* and *show* are specific to horse racing, whether through the electronic media or at the track. A racing fan whose only exposure to the "sport of kings" was through the electronic media might, on the other hand, never become familiar with *claiming race, plater,* and a few other terms not characteristic of the *triple crown* (Kentucky Derby, Preakness, and Belmont Stakes for three-year-olds) and *handicap* races.

Baseball, long the self-styled *national pastime*, has adapted perhaps best of all the sports to the commercial demands of television. Unlike a boxing match, a baseball game will not end quickly with a *knockout* or a *TKO*. Commercials can be offered at the end of each half inning, traditionally the time at which concessionaries sold hot dogs, soft drinks, and beer. The home watcher often uses this time from a trip to the refrigerator. Baseball terminology, like many other areas of American speech, had a heavy maritime cast in the beginning: *skipper* for 'manager', *on deck* 'entitled to bat next', *in the hole* (originally *hold*) 'next after the on-deck batter'. The *minor leagues* (groups of teams made up of players who have not qualified for the *big* or *major leagues*) may have suffered from the spread of network television, but the majors thrive on electronic exposure. One may wonder what will happen to *bush league* and *bush leaguer*, figuratively usable in almost any domain for 'a performance of marginally professional quality' and 'one who so performs', respectively.

With rapidly changing technology, there is bound to be some obsolescence. One obvious example was *wire report*. In the non-visual days, the *sportscaster* might have only the information that player A had flied out to player Y in right field, but he might embroider it with imaginative details down almost to the blades of grass over which the outfielder ran to make the catch. Nobody's imagination works much on televised sports; an announcer tells the viewers, who have presumably seen, what has happened, and a "color" commentator (usually a former athlete) is on hand to explain any technicalities that may come up. Fans often have strong opinions about the personalities of these announcers, a factor perhaps as important in some cases as the information they dispense.

The stage appears to have supplied certain terms like *Bronx cheer* and the virtually synonymous (*get* or *give one*) *the bird* which were appropriated by baseball and other sports. There have been a few other contributions from the stage. *Lay an egg* 'to flop', called "orig[inally] U.S." by OEDS, is first cited from 1929; however, the *Variety* headline, "Wall Street lays an egg," about the stock market crash of that year, obviously depends upon the stage meaning's having been established and become well known. One meaning of the phrase *play down*, 'to underemphasize important dialogue or action', has achieved currency in other domains and may quite possibly be an Americanism. Nevertheless, the stage never had the impact on the general American public that the electronic media have had.

Before the entertainment media, the telephone brought us an essentially national vocabulary. Something of the history of American English may be mirrored in the vocabulary of the instrument. Inventor Alexander Graham Bell originally had the instrument answered with the significantly nautical "Ahoy." It was Edison who replaced that with the more prosaic "Hello"

(Bryan 1926). A somewhat gruffly professional "Yes" may be replacing even the latter now. What the British call a *telephonist* and Americans a *switchboard operator* are both going the way of automation, with most functions now performed by direct dialing. An earlier usage called the girl (which she was, *pace* feminists) by the now obsolete term "Central."

Most Americans took up *operator* and dropped *central* at about the same time. "Hello, central" had been so commonplace that Mark Twain made a joke of it as one of his conscious anachronisms in *A Connecticut Yankee in King Arthur's Court*, but it became obsolete soon after the invention of the dial telephone. The telephone has brought us (and in some cases the British) *long distance, person-to-person, station-to-station, local call, toll call, direct dial, area code, dial tone, busy signal,* and even *obscene call* and *nuisance call.* (*Heavy breathing* has a special telephonic significance.) *Third-party-call* may be on its way out, having been replaced by *calling card,* a familiar phrase but in a much different meaning before the 1982 change in the telephone system of the United States. (The use of the trade name *Bell* to refer to the telephone seems to be in for considerable reduction.) Without the telephone, *unlisted number, party line,* and a few other terms including *directory* and *yellow pages* would have a very different significance. Few of these are Americanisms in the narrow sense, although DA does cite *long distance telephone call* from Mark Twain in 1904.

The dictionaries do not inspire great confidence in the domain of telephones. OEDS cites *wrong number* from 1972, but any American can supply it from memory from thirty or forty years earlier. (*Older* Americans, at any rate!) James Thurber's 1943 cartoon ("If I called the wrong number, why did you answer?") was earlier, and so was the "Chinese" joke about the city which removed all telephones for fear someone would Wing the Wong number (at least as early as 1967).

The most important recent development may be the computer; it is already a cliché to call this the "computer age." Youngsters play PacMan or Atari, and almost everyone is exposed to some of the terminology. Covington (1981) reports on the slang of computer programming. Covington deals with sixteen words, most of them common words in different meanings because of the use in the new field. They include *burnt out* 'terminated because of programmer error', *computer bum* 'compulsive programmer', *garbage* 'useless information on a printout', and *number crunching* 'mathematical computation'. *Software* 'programs, especially those sold commercially [and in implicit contrast to *hardware*]', *bit* 'minimal unit of information, corresponding to one binary digit', and *byte* 'larger unit' seem to be entering the general vocabulary quite rapidly. *G[arbage] I[n], G[arbage] O[ut]* is already a cliché. Either there is a singularly effective conspiracy, or for almost the first time the use of *garbage* is not a euphemism for the working computer operator's *shit*. It may be, however, that the quasi-reduplication has been a more effective pattern than the competing scatology. At any rate, it would be interesting to have a report on the terminology used by computer operators in the armed services.

One of the most frequently commented upon traits of American English in the twentieth century has been the development of "freedom" in discussing formerly tabooed topics, especially sexual intercourse and the sexual parts of the anatomy. Marckwardt (1958) made a good case for that kind of change, where the former avoidance of words like *bull* (substituting *seed cow, yearling,* or the like) and *leg* (substituting *limb* or, in the case even of cooked chicken, *dark meat*) has given way to an almost contrived openness and frankness. Marckwardt inadvertently gives an excellent illustration of changes between 1958 and the 1980s: With an apparently straight face, he refers to *unmentionables,* a word which seems inexpressibly quaint in the 1980s.

In 1939, the movie *Gone with the Wind* titillated audiences with Rhett Butler's parting line, "Frankly, darling, I don't give a damn." The moviemakers hedged somewhat, however, even on this; there just might have been someone among the writers who knew that the phrase was originally [*tinker's*] *dam.* It has been frequently commented that this mild essay into profanity seems extremely mild in view of today's freedom. There is, however, very little profanity and little explicity sexual talk on network television, and virtually none in movies rated "G" or "PG." The pay television *H[ome] B[ox] O[ffice]* offers somewhat more, along with a certain amount of nudity and explicit sex. Nevertheless, the four-letter words, known to virtually everyone over the age of about eight but not generally used in "mixed company" (a term they were using in the days when *unmentionables* was really current), are not blatantly imposed upon the public ear. Nevertheless, there has been a striking increase in public use of relatively explicit terms for bodily functions, apart from the taboo words. Maurer (1976) does an exemplary job of describing that change. The big watershed insofar as explicit terminology was concerned was probably World War II; many of America's readers were shocked at the realistic reporting of serviceman talk in Norman Mailer's *The Naked and the Dead* (1948) and in James Jones's *From Here to Eternity* (1951).

Discharged members of the armed services, especially in organizations like the American Legion and the Veterans of Foreign Wars, are notorious examples of subcultural solidarity. While they are still in uniform, these men (and women) have both officially encouraged and rebelliously non-regulation ways of expressing solidarity. Language may take either course. The U.S. Navy, for example, encourages members of that branch to use *deck*, not *floor*, whether at sea or not. The use of *rifle* (abstaining from *gun*) is part of the lore of all the branches. Enlisted men, especially, compensate for what they feel to be excessive restrictions by linguistic practices which, while not officially approved, are generally no secrets to even the higher-ranking officers.

From the descriptions which we have, the Korean War (which also brought *police action,* as an extremely ironic term, into the national vocabulary) was typical of these processes of language production. Whether this was "transmission" or "innovation" remains susceptible to interpretation. Algeo (1960: 117) reports:

> The slang of the Korean GI was time-honored army talk with a gilding of Japanese and Korean borrowings. This traditional army slang sometimes suffered a sea change in its transit across the Pacific and acquired new uses in its new environment. In addition, many of the GI's had prior service in Japan and had there learned the elements of Bamboo English [Norman 1955], a Japanese slang which was intelligible to the Koreans because of the long Japanese occupation of the peninsula.

If this statement reads somewhat like quotations about Pidgin English in Chapters I and II, there may be no great coincidence. Algeo also reports (1960: 122) that the Korean variety "had begun to move in the direction of a genuine Pidgin English." Not in this connection, Algeo cites (1960: 120) the development of *gook* from the Korean *-guk* in *Han-guk* 'Korea' and *Mi-guk* 'America'.

> The latter word, when used by Koreans, gave rise to some confusion on the part of the GI, who interpreted it as 'me gook', 'I am a Gook'.

This is not a claim that "the slang of the Korean GI" or even "Bamboo English" was "really" Pidgin English. By the time of the Korean War, Pidgin had been so extensively used in pulp novels and in B movies that almost any American would have been embarrassed to use the very real pidgin of the eighteenth and nineteenth centuries. This does not mean, however, that Pidgin had not had some formative influence on the "time-honored army talk" which became useful in the Korean conflict. There are even reports of the enclitic vowel being added to native English words in order to make the natives or "Gooks" understand. (It is perhaps significant that, in the television series *M*A*S*H**, set in the Korean conflict, the highly unsympathetic character Major Frank Burns was assigned the behavior pattern of using pidgin-like English. He was also represented as the sort who would call Koreans "Gooks.")

Aside from, possibly, *gook* and a few terms which had a temporary vogue, like *skoshi* or *skosh* 'little' or 'few' from Japanese and *moose* 'Korean mistress' from Japanese *musume* 'daughter or very young girl', none of the words and phrases cited by Norman (1954, 1955) and Algeo (1960) seem to have had any real effect on American English. They are, on the other hand, useful in characterization of a certain military group with shared experiences. (*M*A*S*H** occasionally gave some emphasis to the use of *moose.* Its users were primarily enlisted men, although the "good Joe" officers of the mobile hospital were familiar with the term and used it in a jocular fashion. Those enlisted men who actually had "mooses" were characterized as rather irresponsible, although perhaps charmingly opposed to the military system.) These temporary developments in a special variety of American English illustrate, however, the way in which old elements and old tendencies can be reshaped as ways of expressing sub-cultural group solidarity and identity.

Such trends are of course dwarfed by that of the one largest American group to lodge a protest against being a "subculture," women. With the working woman and Women's Liberation, a reaction against the sexism allegedly inherent in the language has taken place, to some degree modeled after the attack on the color bias of English metaphor (Davis 1967). There has been a reaction against the assumption that a man rather than a woman is likely to be the chief of a department or an operation, as evidenced in the term *chairman*. The replacement *chairperson* cannot be described, however, as wholly successful; if a letter is signed by J.B. Doe, Chairperson, one can be almost sure that Doe is a woman. Otherwise, the title *chairman* would probably be used. There has been even less success for *s/he*, a far-fetched attempt to eliminate the use of *he* as a universal pronoun for any human noun antecedent that is not certainly female. Dubois and Crouch (1983: 208-210) collected examples of inconsistency, disturbance, or inaccuracy in the use of this somewhat artificial pronoun with results that are, sometimes unintentionally, funny. *They*, the almost universal solution of the non-academic register, is generally rejected, at least by people who are likely to write books. Marckwardt and Walcott (1938) presented abundant proof that the principle of agreement in number with disregard of gender was often violated by even outstanding writers, but few who are brandishing the feminist axe will risk lifting that one at the same time.

The feminist movement is, of course, international rather than American, and certain aspects of the linguistic prescriptions supported by the movement are well known in England as well as in the United States. Lawson (1983) treats the rallying epithet of the movement, (*male*) *chauvinist* – a term which has tended to become almost synonymous with *sexist* within the movement. For some reason, Lawson does not include *pig* in her treatment; *male chauvinist pig* was perhaps the most striking form of the epithet, and the three-word from links the name-calling to teen-age, counter-culture, and ghetto language practices better than perhaps anything else.

Another change, toward use of "objectionable" language by women, has taken place as a by-product of the same movement. Erica Jung's *Fear of Flying* was a striking example of writing by a woman in a genre which had been almost the exclusive property of men and in which even they had exercised considerable restraint before World War II. (Around 1970, the New

York Public Library still required that a reader use Herbert Asbury's now-innocuous-seeming *The Barbary Coast* "under supervision." Much more salacious works, of more recent authorship, could be used freely.) An occasional female speaker at a scholarly conference very pointedly, aggressively, and rather self-consciously uses one of the "four letter" words in order to demonstrate her freedom to do so. In such a case, however, the calling attention to the usage is tantamount to an admission that it is not really commonplace for women to use such words in public. Impressionistically, it seems that such speakers choose their taboo words from the domain of either scatology or sexual intercourse, but not both; profanity in the narrower sense seems never to be a feature of such demonstrations.[2]

Again on a national scale, the attempts of brand-name companies to make their products household words have often been strikingly successful. In some cases, the success was so great that the proper name became a common noun, to the loss of the advertiser. The Eastman Company promoted *kodak*, only to find to its dismay that the word was being used for any camera, except perhaps more expensive Japanese and German imports. Likewise, any kind of "facial tissue" (as distinct from "bathroom tissue") became *kleenex*. *Frigidaire* and *Hoover* encountered the same problems of being likely to be used for any refrigerator or vacuum cleaner. What happened to the Coca Cola company was even more typical; it was soon found that *coke* could mean any soft drink and that "Have a coke" might not serve as a slogan to sell only that company's products. The word *cola* itself was subject to use by other companies; the 1930s saw Pepsi Cola, Royal Crown Cola, and for a time even Cleo Cola — with a picture ostensibly of Cleopatra on the bottle. Even drinks with fruit flavors had a nationwide vogue as "cokes." Everything seems to feed an advertising campaign in the United States, however; the Coca Cola company has recently pitched its advertising around the phrase *the real thing*. A more recent fad has been to preface the name of the carbonated drink with *Diet* or *Low Calorie*.

Trouble with the national vocabulary was primarily a problem for the companies; the people adjusted marvelously well. Here and there a vernacular usage superseded a national or commercial vocabulary form. Experienced carhops in the roadside cafes of East Texas and perhaps of part of western Louisiana in the 1930s and 1940s had to explain to new employees that the occasional Black customer on the still-segregated highways who asked for "a Ah See Cola and a spreadwide" wanted a R[oyal] C[rown] Cola and a large candy bar which the carhops themselves called a *peanut patty* and which their modern replacements call a *praline* — if any are sold in the fast-food establishments which have almost entirely replaced the old drive-ins. The large cola drink of the time (now commercially obsolete) made enough for two (who usually had to be really good friends, ready to drink out of the same bottle) and the sugary candy bar could be broken in two and made into a stopgap meal not entirely devoid of protein.

With the increasing mechanization of the electronic media and thereby of most entertainment, defense mechanisms against the constantly repeated slogans of the advertisements have had to arise. The television show *Saturday Night Live* has been perhaps the leader in satirizing the obvious abuses of advertising terminology. And when one of the stars of that show, John Belushi, died of a reported overdose of cocaine, it was a national joke that Belushi had not survived because he failed to use the tag line from one of his most popular skits, "no coke – Pepsi!"

Even with middle-class teenagers adopting inner city slang wholesale and educated women self-consciously destroying the attitude that certain words are not to be used when they are present, the most public varieties of American English have a great deal of homogeneity. As Blanton (this volume pp.   –) points out, "standardization" is relative to the culture concerned, and greater deviation from an idealized norm may be more "standard" in Appalachia than elsewhere. Nevertheless, the idealized norm is fairly well agreed upon, and public utterance is much more likely to approach that norm than private communication.

Although there is a great deal of ethnic group diversity, every ethnic group has a number of spokesmen whose English is rather close to Network Standard. On another continent, this same tendency is apparently what caused Palenquero to be left out of the Colombian picture until different elicitation procedures were used (Bickerton and Escalante 1970).

The relatively recent opportunities for Blacks to advance in public life and to obtain responsible jobs exposes them to public attention and even causes Black English to be considered a recent development in some quarters. The employment of many Black girls as telephone operators in New York City in the 1960s prompted many complaints that "The telephone company should give those Black girls speech training before putting them on as operators" and inspired the production of an educational recording concerning the nature of Black English (Western Electric n.d.). But a spokesman like Adam Clayton Powell (1967) seemed to have little in common with ghetto or Southern Black speech; on his recording, he depends upon the vocal mannerisms of a Black preacher to establish solidarity with other members of his group. In spite of eschewing nonstandard English, however, Powell leaves little or no doubt as to just which group it is that he wishes to achieve solidarity with. And not even the most cautious dialect geographer of them all would call that group a "Sun Belt" population.

In some extreme circumstances, group solidarity factors can produce some rather extreme linguistic behavior. One of the most interesting examples has been described by Adams (1971). The speech of Boonville, California, features but apparently is not limited to a special speech style, something like what is often described as "cant" or "jargon," except that, within the limits of the town at any rate, no special disguise purposes seem to be served. It is built, it would seem, entirely on conventional English grammatical and phonological processes but with considerable special use of the vocabulary. In that special variety, *speak* has become *harp* (by now dozens of philologically inclined persons have compared Polonius's statement that Hamlet was "harping" on his daughter), *Boonville language* has become *Boontling* or *Boont*, and the noun *burlap* has been turned into *to burlap* 'to make love', reportedly in memory of a general store clerk who was found with a young lady on a pile of burlap bags. It is the number of these developments in one small locale, rather than their unusual nature, with the unusually overt recognition of the distinctive characteristics of the variety which sets "Boont" apart from many other developments. And, even in these, it is not at all unlike some of the contrived utterances in Harlem jive talk which are now thoroughly familiar.

Group solidarity of a less exotic output in sofar as language is concerned is nevertheless an important factor in the dialect situation on Martha's Vineyard, as described by Labov (1963). In the pronunciation of the /aw/ diphthong, Labov found a regular correlation between the speaker's age and the frequency of centralization to /əw/. It was concluded that the centralization of the diphthong served to mark native status on the island. The least centralization was found among high-school-age youngsters who planned to find work on the mainland.

The change, according to Labov, began in a not-surprising group, considering the pattern of influences on American English we have seen already. Yankee fishermen were apparently the first to use the centralized diphthong, and the changes spread first to others of the same ethnic group regardless of other factors. Later, this change spread to the neighboring Indian groups and finally to the Portuguese who lived on the island. As "foreigners," the last were, in a familiar pattern, eager to conform to the native norms of the area. They became linguistically more Yankee than the Yankees.

Another such change, so far not studied in such an exemplary fashion, is the use of a special vowel nucleus where English spelling has a vowel followed by *r*: *bird, thirty-third, church, Murphy*. Pronunciations of /əy/ and /ɛ/ are considered to be closely related by almost everyone who has studied the matter and to be part of the same phenomenon. Kurath (1864: 120) has told us that this vowel pattern

> is used in America in several areas along the Atlantic Coast and the Gulf of Mexico, Eastern New England, metropolitan New York, eastern Virginia, and an extensive belt extending from South Carolina westward as far as eastern Texas and Arkansas.

Although Kurath adds that these areas contain some one-third of the population of the United States, it is obvious that by no means all of the speakers in that area use the vowel nucleus. In metropolitan New York, this nucleus is perhaps the most prominent feature of what is known as "Brooklyn dialect."[3] In New Orleans, popular dialectology assigns it to the "Irish Channel," frequently with the comment that the channel isn't as Irish as it used to be.

This vowel nucleus, distributed as Kurath says along the Atlantic Coast and the Gulf of Mexico, is not unknown elsewhere. It has been reported for Liberia and for Watling Island, formerly San Salvador. Berger (1980) shows how the similarity in New Orleans and the port of New York (Brooklyn") is probably to be traced to pre-Civil-War commercial contacts, primarily in the cotton trade, between those two largest eastern ports. In inland Texas, as in inland Georgia, users of that vowel nucleus are often of an older generation. These speakers may be relatively upper class, although they tend to be somewhat restricted in their travel and outside contacts.

Of all these special varieties, none except the "slang" of the inner city seems to be making any great inroads on general American usage. It is probably too soon to make any kind of statement about how the "computer revolution" is going to influence the language, but there seems to be little chance that it will be felt outside the lexicon (a slightly different meaning for the verb *program*, a rather widespread metaphorical use of *interface*, and relative familiarity with technical words like *cobol* and *Fortran*).

There has been a recent rash of popular books on the "crisis" in American English. Newman (1966, 1974) and Simon (1980) have been the best-known such treatments, with Simon's deserving special attention because of the brilliant erudition of the author, if not for his linguistic sophistication. We should probably conclude with Daniels (1983), however, that the "crisis" is nothing new and that our present state is not really much worse than it has been in the past. Since 1954, white (and some middle-class Black) teachers have come in contact with working class Black students of a type with whom they had never dealt before. Those Black students are turning in papers to (e.g.) freshman composition classes with grammatical structures of a type that the plantation literature shows to have been in Black English all along. Black students who would not have had a chance to take the NTE examination to qualify as teachers in past decades are making low grades on that examination.

In spite of some apparent concern over the survival of dialects (O'Neil 1972), none of these strictures against modern trends represents any alarm over dialects or special varieties or attempts to eradicate them. If anything, there appears to be some embarrassment over the leveled dialect; the familiar metaphors are that it is lacking in either "flavor" or "color." A reluctant nod to Walter Cronkite as the primary representative of Network Standard (not the term used) is given by Roy Peter Clark in the New York *Times* for March 24, 1975 (p. 33). Writing from Montgomery, Alabama, Clark laments "a feverish urge to sound like Walter Cronkite" which has caused the South to surrender "a rich heritage." He specifically faults "prominent newscasters" for having "cast off their regional dialects."

It would be unfair to television, however, to say that it creates these attitudes toward dialects; it simply reflects American attitudes that have been around for a long time. The stage operated in this way before the electronic media were technologically feasible. Bowman and Ball (1961) list

> Stage English A "standard" form of the English language used conventionally for stage purposes, free of peculiarities of place, and in pronunciation generally resembling the educated usage in Southern England.

How much this stage variety transferred to the United States — and what concessions were made to an "educated" variety in this country — may not have been studied at all yet.

On a descriptive basis, it has been argued that many nonstandard speakers are heard on television. Aside from comedians and former athletes, there are certainly superordinated speakers like politicians. John F. Kennedy's use of *idear of it* and analogous locutions was exaggerated in the public mind; an actual count from a recording showed that he used "intrusive *r*" about one-third of the time. Ronald Reagan, a former radio announcer himself, and former president Richard Nixon come much closer to Network Standard than did Lyndon Johnson.[4] Television preachers are also chosen for reasons other than their dialects. Louisiana evangelist Jimmy Swaggart, whose own extensive publications call his program the most widely watched religious program in the United States, regularly says *Newnited States* and it probably would not occur to anyone to correct him.[5] Pat Robertson of the Christian Broadcasting Network and the *700 Club* is transparently a Virginian, but his job does not rest on his dialect. (Regional characteristics are observable primarily in his articulation of the vowel nucleus of *about* or *doubt*.) Co-host Ben Kinchlow, a Black from Texas, fits the pattern of a Network Standard speaker much better. Billy Graham's speech, after many years of a primarily radio- and television-based ministry, is still quite conspicuously "r-dropping." Graham has, however, dignified his speech somewhat since the days when he used to close his radio sermons with "God bless you all, real good."[6]

Specifically Protestant religious terminology seems to have been combined with a passion for "correctness" in language which may go back to the Wycliffite sermons and tracts (Samuels 1963, Warner 1982). Samuels, especially, insists that the Wycliffites spread a "written," not a "spoken," standard, but one may doubt that the distinction can be made so easily. It is, however, far from characteristic of American Protestantism to think of virtues in speech apart from writing; cf. the very use of the term *Scripture*.

After some improvement in the national situation with regard to racial segregation, television networks began hiring Black former sports stars on their broadcasting teams and thereby inadvertently producing a diglossic situation in which one sportscaster is, even when unseen, obviously white while the other, who is the "color" commentator – giving background information and personal data about the players – is just as obviously Black.[7] Former Pittsburgh wide receiver Lynn Swann, on the USFL broadcasts for ABC, is an outstanding exception, with strikingly standard usage and pronunciation; recognition that he is Black comes only from seeing him. White former quarterback Don Meredith utilizes his Texas accent as part of a comedian's role, a kind of relief from the businesslike delivery of Frank Gifford and the (some say phony) erudition of the idiosyncratically speaking Howard Cosell. Cosell's language, particularly his academic vocabulary, has probably contributed to his disfavor with the public; in late 1983, it is rumored that he is leaving "sportscasting."

Blacks who appear regularly in the movies and on television are usually masters of Standard English and sometimes have to make a special offort to speak in dialect when the part requires it. Those who were privileged to be present at the making of Western Electric (n.d.) saw several of them recalling the "ghetto" dialect and enjoying doing so. Some dialect forms still come through inadvertently. When Ben Vereen appeared on *Tony Brown's Journal* on March 17, 1983, he used *suffrage* five times when he obviously meant *suffering.* (On derivational problems in Black English and related varieties, see Dillard 1983.) Apparently Vereen, as an actor, has needed to learn Standard English pronunciations for parts he learns rather than a completely standard system. Dialect shibboleths like *ain't* and the "loss" of /-s/ in third person singular, non-past verb forms are generally avoided by dialect speakers who get on television.

Although emotional attachment to Black English tends to take the form of allegiance to ethnic slang rather than to the Vernacular's grammar, fondness for regional features dies hard – especially among those whose speech is very little marked by such features. Anyone who dares to write of supraregional norms may be subject to a lot of sanctions, not the worst of which is to be excluded from that select company of linguists who have displayed proper contempt for the schoolmarm and her notions of "correctness." American literature has been crowned with the efforts of certain regionalists, and it is not surprising that students of Faulkner should be opposed to the notion of "a single standard" and in favor of "a number of regional standards" (Esau, Bagnall, and Ware 1982: 276). Nevertheless, there are ongoing developments in American English – and have been in the past – for which regionally-oriented techniques are grossly inadequate. Some of these developments are and have been normative, it would seem unfortunate to omit the national, or at least supraregional, norm.

In a context of emotional support for regionalism (on a more subtle and scholarly level, see J. Sledd, all references) the attempt to deal with special varieties and with the norm meets with little support. Many seem afraid that regional dialects will be lost. It is really hard to explain why there is no such concern expressed over whether special varieties of other types may perish. With increasing standardization, a nostalgia develops for all regional features of American life, and identifiable dialects are the only elements of the language which are enough within awareness for such nostalgia to be expressed linguistically. On the other hand, it would seem to be a responsibility of the historical student of American English to report that such tendencies toward standardization, however "bland" or "colorless" the result may be, have been with us since at least as early as the eighteenth century.

NOTES

1. In the 1960s especially, the focus upon Black English was linked to pedagogical innovations like Standard English as a Second Dialect. Some observers, like Sledd (1972), objected that Blacks were singled out for attention as the group most needing to learn Standard English. The charge that such recommendations were politically motivated was answered most extensively by Stewart (1970).
   It is unfortunate that this educational singling out occurred barely a decade after the 1954 desegregation decision by the U.S. Supreme Court. It was, however, just that desegregation of the schools which really brought the Black dialect problem to the forefront of educational concerns. American Blacks are by no means the only ones who face this dialect problem, even in the English Creole tradition. Holm (1983: 100) writes of Miskito Coast Creole speakers:
   > Spelling aside, most of the deviations from standard English . . . can be easily accounted for by referring to MCC phonological and syntactic rules. Unfortunately on the Miskito Coast – as in most other Creole-speaking areas – the literary language of North America and Britain is taught with no reference to the profound differences between it and the pupil's mother tongue, Creole English. It is therefore not surprising that the exotic inflectional systems of the written language often remain only half understood, even after many years of study.
   To "inflectional systems" might be added "derivational systems" (Dillard 1983).
2. It is sometimes difficult even for older Americans to remember how different the attitude toward public expressions about sex were before World War II. In the comic strips, for example, it was not considered generally respectable for children to be born. Both Donald Duck and Mickey Mouse had nephews who lived with them, but they were not the offspring of their girlfriends – Daisy Duck and Minnie Mouse, respectively – who were not married to their male counterparts and who *certainly* were not living with them! Uncle Walt and his wife Blanche, of *Gasoline Alley*, acquired their first child by finding Skeezix on their doorstep. The movies of the 1920s and 1930s may have been more daring, but not by much. There is an excellent satire of the "secrecy" of the times in James Thurber and E.B. White's *Is Sex Necessary?* (1929).
3. The degree of association of this formerly maritime dialect with taxi drivers is astonishing. The New York *Times* for April 9, 1975, contained an unsigned article, "Class Aims to Loin [sic] Cabbies Proper Speech." Dillard (1976b: 44-50) gives

an anecdotal example concerning the impressions of one who first hears a Brooklyn-like dialect from a cab driver in New Orleans. There are obvious differences. Linguistically, the New Orleans driver may say *y'all,* which the Brooklynite would never use. Culturally, the resident of New Orleans, if he has lived in rural South Louisiana, may be addicted to such activities as alligator wrestling, which the Brooklynite would probably never engage in. (The editor of Random House cut this information out of Dillard 1976b on the grounds that alligator wrestling is an absurd activity. Even so, it is no more unusual – and probably no more dangerous – an activity than bull riding, which is practiced about as extensively in, say, South Texas as alligator wrestling is in South Louisiana.)

4. Note that Nixon is a Californian (see Pickford 1956) and Reagan a former actor whose communication skills are highly praised, at least by his admirers. And probably neither of them had the political "connections" that Johnson had as protégé of "Mr. Sam" Rayburn, one of the most powerful politicians ever to come from Texas. That is, Nixon and Reagan were probably under some pressure to level their dialects; Johnson was not.

5. Swaggart's rather extensive writings, particularly in his periodical called *The Evangelist,* emanating from Baton Rouge, Louisiana, are seemingly well-edited and generally in a good expository style of formal standard English, although there are some departures from standard usage.

6. Graham's Christian names appear in *Who's Who in America* (1976-77) as William Franklin. The use of Billy may date back to the evangelist's early ministry, which was primarily to rural Southerners, long before he became internationally known and attracted much secular attention because of a well-publicized trip to Russia. It is noteworthy, however, that Graham, who is entitled to use the title Doctor, does not do so. Television ministers Robert Schuller and D. James Kennedy not only seem to encourage the use of the title but wear academic robes.

7. Statistics of Black former running backs and linemen who have enjoyed brief careers as television sportscasters are not available. The impression is that turnovers since about 1969 have been very rapid. A syndicated comic strip, "Tank Mac-Namara," gently ridicules the "jock" who has gone on television.

Chapter X

Puerto Rico: Bicolonialism and Bilingualism

The history of American English does not stop with the establishment of the language on the Pacific Coast and the filling in of the frontier areas between that coast and the East. In addition to the internal developments like borrowings and innovations, and the discoveries of "new" dialects which had been around for hundreds of years, there have been important recent external developments. Noteworthy among these is the participation of Americans in the world-wide increase in numbers of speakers of English. The British inaugurated the use of English as an international language, and they were to a large degree the ones who had carried it around the globe by the nineteenth century. But in the second half of the twentieth century, Americans are the most effective agents in spreading it. To some extent, then, it is American English that is becoming a world language.

Holm (1983: 7) points out that there has been "a struggle between Spanish and English for dominance in the New World which has been going on for some 350 years." Holm's work shows that Central America, "the front line" in the struggle, reflects a history of English Creole as well as Spanish and ordinary English. The same struggle went on in formerly Spanish colonies like Guam, the Philippines, and Puerto Rico. Like Guam, the areas where Spanish remains in competition for dominance came under the influence of English around 1898, at the end of the Spanish-American War. (For a convenient summary of the language situation in Guam, see Bruce and Walsh 1983.) There was, in fact, a considerable overlap between the dominance of English in the American Southwest and its imposition on the overseas territories. Hispanics in the United States, like Cubans in Miami (Fernández 1983) have comparable language tendencies.

The proximity of Mexico in the Southwest supported the persistence of Spanish in that area, and many Spanish-dominant speakers remain in Texas, New Mexico, Arizona, and California. An Associated Press dispatch for December 11, 1982, concerned a nineteen-year-old graduate of the public schools in Brownsville, Texas (on the border), who had not learned to speak English. The lack had apparently not been noticed until the young man was tried for burglary; part of the probationary sentence was that he learn some

English. A Puerto Rican acquaintance of mine once told me that he had spent fourteen years in Buffalo, New York, without having to learn any English. In reply to questioning, he asserted that it is possible to live very well (*"Se puede vivir muy bien"*) in that city without using any English. Wölck (1972: 4) reports "some [speakers of foreign languages in Buffalo] have never really managed to pick up the new one [English]." The contact between Spanish and English, examined carefully, still yields some surprises.

The pidgin phase of the contact relationship was, by the twentieth century, essentially a matter of the past. As elsewhere, the person in the Southwest who asked another "You savvy?" might be in physical danger. (Banfield [1908] quotes, "What for you say savie? You take me for a blurry Chinaman?") For this and other reasons, the history of American English has been considerably different in the twentieth century, one result being that those who reconstruct from the present without using documents have missed several developments.

With westward continental expansion hardly completed, the year 1898 marked perhaps the greatest step in American colonialism. English was soon imposed upon areas like Cuba, the Philippines, and Puerto Rico, where Spanish was already one kind of colonial language. The relationship between English and Spanish in the Puerto Rican schools underwent eight changes of policy between 1898 and 1948, and a 1925 study showed that "80 percent of the students failed both English and Spanish and dropped out of school" (Zentella 1981: 220). The relationship outside the formalized environment of the schools is perhaps more difficult to study, but it might well be more revealing.

The political imposition of English did not necessarily constitute the first use of the language on the Spanish-speaking island. There is evidence that Pidgin English was not unknown in the Caribbean colonies of Spain. Murray (1857) recorded a Chinese speaker in Havana saying, "Belly great swell; much wind; pain all around."

Puerto Rico makes an interesting test case of the effects – linguistic as well as political – of the extension of American English overseas. It is somewhat closer to the United States than Guam or the Philippines, it has not broken relations like Cuba, and it is bigger than the Canal Zone. Furthermore, the millions of Puerto Ricans on the North American continent bring home to Americans the problems and complications of trying to assimilate a population with a different culture and a different language. The ability to return to the island gives the Puerto Rican, in many ways, a greater freedom to hold onto his own language and culture than other Hispanics have.

As a commonwealth, Puerto Rico enjoys – or suffers – ambiguous status. In Spanish the term is *Estado Libre Asociado*, 'free, associated state'. *Independentistas* have long since seized upon the punning possibilities of such a self-contradictory term: *No es estado, no es libre, pero sí es ensuciado* ('It is not a state, it is not free, but it is dirtied' [a pun on the slight resemblance between *asociado* and *ensuciado*].) A 1958 poem by Cuban Nicholas Guillén calls Puerto Rico "you associated associate of society."

The adoption of English was never wholehearted in Puerto Rico. The islanders still vary between resentment at being expected to learn English, with concern at what may happen to their Spanish, and pride in being able to express themselves in a second language. It is not difficult to detect the influence of this ambivalence in what has happened to English in the Caribbean commonwealth.

Just what has happened to Spanish is a matter of some controversy. So is the state of the total communication situation. Linguistic consultants have had an important source of income from Puerto Rico, and one of their primary activities has been to assure the islanders that bilingualism "won't hurt them." Politically oriented traditionalists (see Gonzales, below) haven't been so sure. Educational researchers have been impressed that some 25,000 Puerto Rican children in New York City failed both the English and the Spanish test administered in compliance with the consent decree, with many youngsters evaluated as lacking dominance in either language. Elderly Puerto Ricans, monolingual in Spanish, with whom I talked, complained about the language of bilingual younger islanders, although I never heard a serious claim that intelligibility had been lost.

Zentella points out (1981: 233) the code-switching behavior of Puerto Ricans, a shift "for entire sentences or parts of them." My more proficient (in English) students at the University of Puerto Rico did just that, and some of them articulated the belief that this was "natural" behavior for proficient bilinguals. Dulay, Burt, and Krashen (1982), who strongly question the importance of any first language on the pattern of acquisition of the second, cite a Spanish-English bilingual saying:

I'd get desperate [for a cigarette], y ahí voy al basurero a buscar, a sacar, you know.

Such utterances are produced by Puerto Ricans, but by the more proficient bilinguals. There are relatively few Puerto Ricans with this degree of proficiency, except for those who have lived for long periods in the United States. The case for interference may have been weakened greatly in the last few years, but the final decision should not be made on the basis of exceptional speakers.

More ordinary speakers adopt English loanwords with the local Spanish pronunciation. The bus stopped at [ehtop] *Dieziocho,* even though the street signs (before they were removed in the 1960s) read *Parada 18.* (In the 1970s, bilingual signs with both *Parada* and *Stop* and the numeral were introduced.) The waiter in a restaurant brings *el ticket* 'the check'. A word like *pie* is almost fully nativized, although the English spelling is usually retained. I have heard a waitress in a tourist-frequented coffee shop, having been asked for *pastel de moras* ('blackberry pie' in some forms of Spanish), turn to an older woman and ask, "Señora, como se dice en español *pie de blackberries?*" ("How do you say *blackberry pie* in Spanish?") Actually, the customer, an "Anglo" trying to show off his Spanish, had a continuum of forms to deal with if he wanted to communicate with Puerto Ricans:

pastel de moras
pie de moras
pie de blackberries
blackberries pie
blackberry pie.

The topmost and lowest forms above are not usual in Puerto Rico. The first would be used only by a self-conscious Hispanist — say, a professor at the *Departamento de Estudios Hispánicos* of the University of Puerto Rico. (*Pastel*, in fact, is not characteristically Puerto Rican at all, although *pastelillo* is used for a kind of pastry which is not a pie in the same American sense as Mom's apple pie.) The last might be used by an unacculturated *gringo* or an *agringado* Neorican (New York Puerto Rican). The three inner forms come closer to what an ordinary Puerto Rican would use, with distribution which could be accounted for rather easily in terms of variable rules.

Notably, the English noun-noun modification pattern is difficult for Puerto Ricans. Guillermo's Restaurant in the very touristy beach area called the Condado once advertised *Aples Pie* and *Pineaples [sic] Pie*. (In pronunciation, *aples* contains two syllables; *pineaples,* three.) A bar is usually a *Cocktails* [not cocktail] *lounge*. Pluralizing of the first noun in the compounds is also seen in store names like SUITS CITY, THE BARGAINS CORNER, and 500 COFFEE SHOP CLAMS HOUSE.

This kind of mixing of languages has some comic possibilities which are perfectly harmless if done in the right spirit. A newspaper writer and night club comedian named Eddie Lopez made that kind of language mixing a regular part of his career. He developed a fictional character named Candid Flowers (Candido Flores), who said things like, "You are the brassiere of your family," to his friends. In Spanish, *el sostén* means either 'brassiere' or 'support'; the pun is quite a meaningful one to the even partly bilingual Puerto Rican. Lopez's characters also did things like thanking benefactors for "overcoating" them. Spanish *abrigar* means 'protect, support. and *abrigo,* a derivative noun, means 'overcoat'. It is used in Puerto Rico instead of the perhaps more familiar Spanish *sobretodo* (Zentella 1981: 229). Perhaps imitating Lopez, Puerto Rican students in linguistics classes rather freely improvise mixed sentences like

I have the grasshopper (*la esperanza*) that everything will turn out all right.

Even children produce macaronic hieroglyphs like

T K 2	'ice cream'
(man)	(te-ca-dos)	mantecado(s)

where the Puerto Rican Spanish change of /-s/ to $\emptyset$ is irrelevant because English *ice cream* is only marginally a pluralizable noun. This kind of mixing is under conscious control and seldom evokes resentment, although Puerto Ricans may be inordinately surprised that an English speaker could understand the little joke.

High-spirited (if low-browed) good humor – along with the possibly inevitable bits of anger – can come out of the bilingual situation. One Edwin, who cartooned for *El Mundo* until the early 1970s, committed in print such outrageous puns as *"puse un HUEBO* [sic] *en la* EGGS *plicación"* [30 November 1962], matching in a sense island *gringos* who learned to accuse each other jocularly, "You put one egg" – 'You made a mistake'.

Not all of the mixing is intentional, however. An American teaching English at the University of Puerto Rico was disconcerted when a young man called to say, "Eight boys are coming over to see your daughter." When they arrived, seven of the "boys" were girls. Spanish *muchachos,* in the masculine form, influenced the English *boys* even if seven of the eight were *muchachas/ girls.* And the young lady who once spoke of a meeting of the UPR faculty "cloister" (Spanish *claustro*) should have known that many of them are not very cloistered.

The English verb-preposition compounds like *pick up* and *fill out*, which are difficult even for Spanish speakers whose English is relatively fluent, produce such confusers as

Please fill this form
I have to pick my children

It is of course commonplace that Spanish and the Romance languages in general do not use these compounds to the extent that they are used in English and some other Germanic languages. Such sentences usually succeed in conveying their meaning, but it is very likely that this success can be partly explained in terms of the English-speaking interlocutor's having learned something about the Puerto Rican "hybrid."

Essentially monolingual English speakers who have resided on the island for a long time show a great deal of accommodation. The word *lamp*, for example, can come to mean 'light, electric bulb' on the order of Spanish *lámpara.* After a few years, one begins to lose one's grip on just what is English rather than Spanish. El Monte, an apartment complex in Rió Piedras, near the university, with a largely *gringo* clientele, advertised in the San Juan *Star* (the English-language newspaper) that it offered "Elevated buildings," and some residents were not quite sure whether or not that was "continental" English for 'buildings with elevators'.

The most extreme mixing of English forms into Spanish probably takes place in the tourist area of Santurce (a kind of sister city to San Juan) called the Condado. There continental tourists give orders, in English exclusively, to Puerto Rican waiters, who relay them to the cooks in some weird combinations. I have heard

"Tengo dos cheeseburgers trabajando" ('I have two cheeseburgers working')
Un jamón sandwich ('A ham sandwich')

and other combinations uncharacteristic of unmixed English or Spanish. These are, of course, extreme examples; the same waiters who used them would probably not speak in the same fashion away from the job.

Around the touristy area of the Condado, there is a somewhat pretentious use of French names, strictly for their snob appeal since French is not a language much used in Puerto Rico. In the 1960s and 1970s, one could find a smattering of stores and other establishments with names like MAISON BLANCHE GUEST HOUSE, or:

MATTY'S BOUTIQUE
BRUNNY'S BOUTIQUE
CARMEN CHIRINO'S BOUTIQUE
INTERNATIONAL BOUTIQUE
TU-TU BOUTIQUE
SAN JUAN BOUTIQUE
PETIT NIGHT CLUB
DA VINCI BOUTIQUE
PINOKKIO BOUTIQUE
JUL D'OR BOUTIQUE

The apostrophe in the first three examples illustrates graphically the association with English. In fact, these names and others like them should probably be said to be pretentious English rather than French, even though Jul D'Or Jeweler does advertize *parfums*. Perhaps the all-time champion insofar as rampant apostrophes were concerned was the crudely hand-lettered sign on the small bar in Santurce, SAN'S SOUCI'S. It had some competition, however, from CHARLIE'S MELODIE'S BAR in Loiza Aldea.

The English graphic tradition complicates the vaunted phoneme-grapheme match of Spanish, although the folk Spanish phonology contributes to the same result. The apostrophe comes in, with not always predictable results. One guest house had a circular with approximate Spanish on the side:

CELEBRATE LAS TRADICIONALES DE
SAN JUAN BAUTISTA EN LOS GARCIA'S
BRISAMAR GUEST HOUSE

and parallel English on the other suggesting that the traditional festivities be celebrated

AT THE GARCIA'S BRISAMAR GUEST HOUSE

Examples are everywhere on the island.

Anglicization affects certain words that have similar spelling in English and Spanish. *Garage* is regularly used in Puerto Rican car repair establishments;

I have never seen the fully acceptable alternative *garaje*. Although *Restaurante*, which would also evoke continent-based linguistic snobbery, is used, the more familiar device is the abbreviation REST (KIKI'S BAR & REST). *Dry Cleaning* has displaced *Limpieza en Seco* or *Lavado en Seco* completely in San Juan, judging from the entries in the yellow pages of the telephone book. And *Lavandería* has been almost completely displaced by *laundry*, giving rise to one wonderful name LAUNDRY EL BROTHER and motivating the student reaction that this is a "pretty" name unlike the "ugly" LAVANDERÍA EL HERMANO. Somewhat more frequent use is made of *Laundromat*. (For reasons which will appear in the next paragraph, the suffix -*tería* never became productive in the formation of words like *Washatería*.) Laundries and dry cleaning establishments display the familiar signs "ONE DAY SERVICE" and even "ONE HOUR SERVICE" − claims, apparently, imported from the States and quite as meaningless as they are in New York City.

Because of its homophony with the Spanish word meaning 'coffee', *Cafe* is hardly used at all. And Anglicization cannot displace the meaning 'coffee house' for *cafetería*. An establishment like Cafetería Sixto in Rio Piedras (the proprietor apparently being a sixth son) is a more likely place to procure alcoholic beverages than coffee. (Around 1970, it has changed to be Club Bambu.) For what continentals call *Cafeterias*, which have become abundant in the larger cities, Puerto Ricans had by the early 1960s adopted the name *self service* (La Ronda Self Service, in Miramar). This element is frequently combined with Spanish words: La Española Self Service or El Típico Self Service. One could probably find *self service* in restaurant names in most cities in the United States; it seems, however, to be much more frequent in Puerto Rico. *Cantina* is familiar from Mexican movies, but *bar* or *cocktails lounge* is a preferred usage even in the *barrios* where one would think that tourists would be seldom found.

A somewhat greater mystery is the abundance of small cafes with the designation *Quick Lunch*. It is almost a prestige designation on the island, with names like Bankers' Quick Lunch, Time [sic] Square Quick Lunch. It is often explained as being a transfer of New York City practices, but there seem to be no such names in New York. Furthermore, lifetime residents of New York have assured me that it was never very popular there at any time they can remember.[1] Zentella (1981: 232) points out that the verb *lonchar*, obviously formed on English *lunch*, means to eat a quick sandwich or a hot dog, whereas *almorzar*, the native Spanish word, means to take a long, heavy lunch. The former fits into the pattern of *Quick Lunch*, which may even be a replacement for Come y Vete ('Eat and Go'), an older naming pattern still seen in some parts of the island. In the *fiestas patronales* of Loiza Aldea, temporary shacks from which food and drinks are sold often bear the designations *come y calla* ('eat and be quiet') and *toma y dame* ('take [food] and give me [money]'). Whatever the relationship, there is no phonological problem between *lonchar* and *lunch* (often spelled *lonch*), since [ə] is not present in the English of more than a few Puerto Ricans. The lack of [ə] and [ɔ] contrast is reflected in one tourist publication's invitation to tour the bay "in a lunch."

Looking not so much at language forms as at interaction patterns, Morris (1981) in an anthropologically-oriented study developed a theme by Salvador Tió Montes de Oca that "The only thing clearly defined in Puerto Rico is lack of definition." Morris (1981: 109) reports:

> It is not that there are no sophisticated users of the Spanish language, but that the lack of these skills is sufficiently broad and at a sufficiently high level in society that the "ethnographer" is surprised by it again and again.

The most immediately obvious victims of the undefined relationship between English and Spanish are residents of the continental United States who come to the island either in the hope of learning Spanish or to do business in that language. Even with past experience in using Spanish for the same purposes in another country, these people may find their attempts to use Spanish rejected. For a person who fancies himself an interpreter, to be told "Mister, I will traduce for you" is sobering if not outright humiliating. The "continental" (the Puerto Ricans' name for what is called an "Anglo" in the Southwest) who remains on the island for very long is sure to hear many a "traduction." Yet it is not possible to rely entirely upon English, unless one wishes to remain entirely in areas frequented by tourists. A popular typology is, "If you speak to them in Spanish, they answer in English; if you speak to them in English, they answer in Spanish."

The hybrid language which most Puerto Ricans think of as English contains, at the level of idiom at least, a large amount of Spanish influence. (Zentella [1981] criticizes Nash [1971] and Dillard [1975] for introducing no statistical data and for not using formal elicitation techniques to verify this claim. The best answer I have is that it would be like using statistics to prove that the sun shines in the daytime. The evidence surrounds one, all over the island.)

The new arrival on the island is frequently asked, "Is this the first time you are ever outside the states?", in a pattern easily traceable to the slightly different use of the present and perfect in Spanish. The English speaker may well understand this, as he might later in his stay on the island understand "You can stay with the original [copy of a report] " if he happened to know the Spanish idiom *quedarse con* 'keep'. When it comes to the direction, printed on a rental office,

See Mr. Alfaro on the Yellow House

realistic expectations of behavior (a rental agent does not usually climb up on houses) are perhaps as useful in interpretation as the knowledge that Spanish *en* translates English *in* or *on*. In the Christmas season at any rate, *Greetings Seasons*, a sign actually observed in a small store in Hato Rey, will probably be understood. Here the context carries a large part of the communication, and there are no critical distinctions to be derived from the language forms.

When the information in the linguistic signal becomes critical, however, problems can develop. Can one understand the direction that a building is "six apples down Mahogany Street" if he does not know the idiomatic usage of *manzana* (literally 'apple') to mean 'block'? In this case (a similar event was actually reported by a friend of mine), the street was Calle Caoba. In a city where streets often have English names (Calle Washington), my friend might not have known whether he had reached "Mahogany Street" or not.

Overtranslation of this sort is a phenomenon which occurs in many countries where rapid acculturation is taking place. Among other things, the tendency to overtranslate illustrates how social factors can complicate, if not override, simple linguistic factors like the ability to speak or understand a language. As Morris (1981: 132) reports, English is becoming, and is to some extent already, a "language of reference" in Puerto Rico. Puerto Ricans quite demonstrably do use English where no native speakers are present, and hyper-Anglicism is everywhere apparent. Morris (1981: 124) reports an incident in which a clerk confirmed the Spanish name Coll with "Coll – ¿de llamar en inglés?" Phonolgoical factors – the mismatch between Spanish contrasts and those of English in the [a] [ɔ] [o] area – would explain the lack of distinction between *Coll* and *call*, but apparently not the confusion over the Spanish name itself.

The case of Puerto Rico provides fuel for those who say that when bilingualism exists on a societal level there is a strong tendency for diglossia to develop. The vacillating nature of the language requirement in the schools, where Spanish was denied the status of "medium of instruction." then reinstated to that status, with attempts to define the exact relationship between the two (Zentella 1981) was probably less important than the growing economic ties. There was an increasing tendency to use English for public functions and to reserve Spanish for private activities. Militant action by Hispanists has brought about some changes, but the tendency toward diglossic distribution is by no means a thing of the past.

Although even some *Independentista* political leaders make speeches – not without irony – in English, there is a point beyond which even the Puerto Rico insistence upon that language will not go. When Jose Torres, light-heavyweight boxing champion in the 1960s, fought on the island, the announcer thought it appropriate to begin, "Ladies and gentlemen." After a few minutes of booing, he corrected his error and produced the correct form of address, *"Damas y caballeros."* If a Puerto Rican figure in whom there was some local pride had not been a participant, the change might not have been necessary. The situation seems to be diglossia, up to a point.

Diglossia has its more unpleasant as well as its lighter side. A typical Puerto Rican bar may have the sign:

WELCOME. HAPPY HOUR 5 TO 7

along with:

NO SE ADMITEN DAMAS SOLAS.

The second sign, written in smaller letters, means 'unaccompanied ladies are not admitted'. It is a flagrant proclamation of the harsh socio-economic fact that girls who are able to speak (and read) English are not so likely to be forced into prostitution as are those who know only Spanish. Or a store significantly named BEBITA'S SUPER LIQUORS [sic] STORE may have a sign:

PARKING PARA CLIENTES SOLAMENTE
EVITE SER DENUNCIADO

which suggests that customers are more likely to speak English but that people who park in the wrong place and risk getting tickets are more likely to be restricted to Spanish. Whether the proprietor of the liquor store chose *parking* rather than *estacionamiento* as a means of communicating with English monolinguals is an issue not to be decided *a priori*. The English term is probably as common as the Spanish one throughout the island.[2]

Spanglish originated as a jocular term to describe a certain kind of language activity easily observable in Puerto Rico. If it should be taken as a designation for a language variety, it would have to be a basilect (in the sense of Stewart 1968). Neither "pure" basilect (in the U.S. Black community) nor "pure" Spanglish (among Puerto Ricans) is likely to be observed in a discourse of any great length. The producers of the nearest thing I have ever heard to pure Spanglish were English-dominant professors at the university, who would indulge in joking conversations like: "Mister, you want one cigarette?" "No, sank you, mister. I no fume." The use of English *fume* to translate Spanish *fumar* 'smoke' is an extrapolation according to a principle, not a report of an actual usage by Puerto Ricans.

The mixing of English and Spanish in Puerto Rico is a highly variable matter, obviously. "Basilectal" Spanglish would be as rare as basilectal Black English Vernacular, and without the external justification that basilectal Black English resembles Gullah, Sranan Tongo, and other English-based creoles.[3] It is not true that everyone on the island mixes the two languages, but it happens more frequently than that they remain unmixed.[4]

There are many Puerto Ricans who speak "standard" English, in a dialect which is very close to Network Standard. It is quite noteworthy that children of English speakers who grow up on the island do not even approximate the dialects of their parents from the States. Many of these speakers have attended private schools, and they are often almost intolerantly critical of both the dialects of their American parents and the language mixing of the less fortunate Puerto Ricans.[5]

These speakers exist, and it would be a distortion to omit them, just as it would be false to omit the nearly "perfect" bilinguals of pure Puerto Rican parentage. But it would be a serious mistake to use such exceptional cases to dismiss the more typical (and, to some, rather embarrassing) Hispano-English of the majority of Puerto Ricans who usually migrate to the United States. Yet those who are so preoccupied with the Puerto Rican image that they will not tolerate any talk of "Spanglish" are likely to do just that.

William A. Stewart (personal discussion) has pointed out to me how much the Puerto Rican situation resembles that of the Black American. Whenever the Black English Vernacular, he says, is discussed by linguists or by educators, there are always those who will point to the examples of Blacks who speak totally standard English, as if the existence of this minority somehow did away with the necessity of dealing with the nonstandard dialect of the vast majority of Black Americans.[6]

The similarity is not solely linguistic. Maldonado-Denis (1972: 136-7) finds similarities between the Puerto Rican struggle for independence and the Black Power movement. In lexical function, he compares Puerto Rican *pitiyankee* to *Uncle Tom* in Black slang. People who have lived both in Puerto Rico and in the American South are often struck by the similar ways that islanders and Blacks decorate their cars (icons or puppets dangling in front of the driver, lacy pillows in the rear window) and certain similarities of body language like the averting of eyes to show respect. Luis Palés Matos, whom Maldonado-Denis calls Puerto Rico's greatest poet, drew large-scale comparisons which are generally agreed to have been overwrought and even occasionally sensational but correct in principle.

The analogy goes further in that those who would avoid the issue of class and ethnic-group differences often invoke geographic factors or temporary failure to achieve a goal about to be realized (Jackson 1976: 154) in explanation. Despite listener reaction tests (Bryden 1968; Tucker and Lambert 1969; Baratz, Shuy, and Wolfram 1969; Baratz 1969) which show the opposite, Black-white differences have often been explained as the difference between Southern dialect and Northern dialect. (To judge by Hirshberg 1982 a and b, this will not be the point of view of the Dictionary of American Regional English.) In like manner, public statements (especially tourist literature like *Qué Pasa in [sic] Puerto Rico?*) often refer to the alleged fact that Puerto Ricans speak (or, in the case of some educators, "soon will speak") both Spanish and English, without reference to the immediately obvious differences in the speaking of English by different groups of Puerto Ricans. In both cases, there is a somewhat less prominent but still not uncommon tendency to refer still observable language patterns to the past.

Inaccurate as some of these statements are, they are still preferable to the statements that either the Black English Vernacular or the Hispanized English of Puerto Ricans is simply "bad," or even incompetent language use. The very existence of Puerto Ricans and of American Blacks who speak "standard" varieties is for this reason important. Both groups can be shown to speak as they do for social, not genetic, reasons.

Those who have regarded Puerto Ricans as incompetent users of language have given explanations either in terms of the effects of growing up in a lower-class rural or slum environment so that language learning is impeded, or in terms of the psychological effect of domination by Americans. (Sellers [1972] refers to the "mispronunciations, the poor vocabulary, the phonetic distortions ... that America stamped on her black refugees from impoverished rural areas of the South and the neglected slums of the cities of the North.") While the explanations that these factors have denied the children the opportunity to learn a standard dialect (or "good" language) may be preferable to some other statements (e.g., those based on genetic factors) they are of questionable value as explanations as to why the children do not acquire language patterns prescribed for them by the school system, their parents, or some other authority.

For this reason, the attempts to explain the language situation in Puerto Rico in terms of historical, social, and political factors by Maldonado-Denis and others are important. It is possible to support the validity of these explanations even though in most cases they are not linked to a single linguistic form. At a more mundane level, the historical linguist has to work with the familiar assumption that language varieties are the product of normal social processes and to continue to look for non-pathological explanations. For just this reason, it is important to look at other colonial language situations. It is not fair to compare the Spanish of Puerto Rico to that of Mexico or Colombia, where colonial influence has been more nearly obliterated (cf. Zentella 1981: 224).

At first blush, the comparison to another language contact situation may not support a relativistic interpretation. Those who take the mixing of languages by Puerto Ricans as evidence of incompetence in language often cite the fact that, while Puerto Ricans mix their two languages, others in somewhat similar language contact situations do not. It is certainly true that natives of Curaçao, often with no more than a high school education, manage to speak Papiamentu, Spanish, Dutch, and English without much mixing. Papiamentu, the home language for the vast majority of them, is strikingly appropriate for consideration of language contact matters, being an Iberian creole in origin (Navarro Tomas 1951, van Wijk 1958, Birmingham 1976, Baum 1976). Why does a new variety of English (Nash 1971) emerge in Puerto Rico and not in Curaçao?

A number of possible answers suggest themselves, and perhaps all of them are partly true. The most obvious is that, as the institutional dominance of one culture and language wanes and that of another increases, there is a period when, for either one or both of these, the prestige of the "pure" form will not be great enough to insulate it against influences from the other. A familiar example is the Middle English of the period after the Norman Conquest, where there was an abundance of vocabulary borrowings; and arguably the two situations were similar enough to make study of the Puerto Rican situation useful in interpreting that of England. The degree of comparability might depend partly upon whether "Puerto Rican Spanish" was as unified, at all points in its colonial history, as is generally assumed. How much comparison can be made with the centuries of domination of English by both Norse and Norman French, considering that in Puerto Rico not only has English been superimposed upon Spanish but an Iberian contact variety may have figured in the total picture as early as Spanish?

In comparing Curaçao, Aruba, and Bonaire to Puerto Rico, it is well to remember that one of the four languages used there does tend to undergo a special type of contact change, "decreolization" (Wood 1972, Baum 1976). Papiamentu constantly incorporates Dutch and Spanish lexical elements as well as some English. An advertisement in the the newspaper *La Prensa* for April 17, 1962, for example, reads:

> Haci BO CAS bunita pa PASCU di RESURECCION cu un DINETTE SET y un set di SALA di Curacao [sic, without cedilla] Trading Company. Prijsnan drasticamente reduci. Condicionan di pago mash faborable y bo por scohe por diferente model.

In this passage, besides the obvious English of "Dinette Set" and the mixed English-Spanish-Papiamentu of *set di sala,* there are Hispanized words (*resurección, drasticamente,* the article *un*), and "model," a word it would be difficult to tie down to any one language. Such passages, along with ads and articles in Dutch, Spanish, and English, were commonplace in *La Prensa* until about 1968, when puristic and standardizing attitudes toward Papiamentu began to exclude other languages from the paper.

It should be stressed that this is no invidious comparison between Puerto Rico and Curaçao. The latter is by no means a linguistic paradise, and educators have not found that problems have disappeared because of the prevalent competence in up to four languages. There is no reason to believe that the literacy rate is any higher than in Puerto Rico, that literary culture has advanced any more, or that any other great advance has been accomplished. Educators in Curaçao frequently complain that too many of their people are "semiliterate in four languages." One Ph.D, educated in Holland and eminently successful, was almost bitter when, on returning to the island for the first time in many years, he realized what had happened to his childhood classmates who had failed to solve the multilingual problems as well as he had. One instructive experience is to watch ordinary airport workers in Willemstadt buying magazines in English: comic books and movie magazines.

It is also noteworthy that Papiamentu, which has some interesting similarities to varieties of Puerto Rican Spanish, is a creole language in contact with relatively standard varieties of European languages. Since language mixing, in some sense of the term, is at the historical root of the creoles, the tendency of Papiamentu to "hybridize" more than Dutch, Spanish, or English might be explained in part by a continuation of the language attitudes which made possible the "initial" mixing.

Last, although in no sense an "African" language, Papiamentu is the native language of the mostly African-derived (at some remove) Curaçaoans, theirs to do with as they please. There are no outsiders — like the Dutch, Spanish, and English speakers who are often dominant economically and even politically — to specify how the language should be used. (This is not to say that there are no prescriptivist tendencies, but these recommendations tend to be limited to the Papiamentu to be used in newspapers and the electronic media.)

Returning to the Puerto Rican situation, it may be more accurate to compare the use of Spanish there with the use of Papiamentu rather than with Spanish in Curaçao. Just as Dutch was previously superimposed upon Papiamentu, English has been superimposed upon Puerto Rican Spanish. This dominance by English is only partly the product of political domination by the United States; there is also the rise of English as a world language to consider. Spanish tended to lose prestige and to "destandardize" (Zentella 1981), so that it could be modified with impunity by its speakers — in many situations, in the direction of the more prestigious English. The counterattack by Hispanizers has not been strong enough to reverse this trend.

It is also distinctly possible that the same kind of creole language-mixing tradition as that involved in Papiamentu is a motivating factor in the hybridizing tendencies of Puerto Rican Spanish. Although most Hispanists (e.g., Navarro Tomás 1948) have treated Puerto Rican Spanish as a direct and virtually unmodified extension of the Spanish of Spain to the Caribbean, the historical and linguistic accuracy of this view is open to a great deal of doubt.

Socio-historically, the argument would have to be primarily in terms of demography. The greater proportion of Iberian Spaniards (than in, for example, Cuba) has often been adduced as a reason why the Spanish of Puerto Rico has been relatively "pure." This demographic situation was not, however, characteristic of all periods. Maldonado-Denis (1972) cites a tax list from 1673 revealing a population of 820 whites, 667 slaves, and 304 free mulattoes. Spain was almost immediately asked for a shipment of "white" people and the proportions became different, but there seem at all times to have been concentrations of Blacks in certain parts of Puerto Rico — primarily on the coast (Diaz Soler 1974: 148).

In a work comparable in effect to that of Turner (1949) in reversing the opinion about the number of Africanisms in Gullah, Álvarez Nazario (1961; 1974) demonstrates a large number of African survivals in Puerto Rican Spanish, particularly that of certain coastal areas. Even the "white" Spanish of Puerto Rico has more affinities with that of the Canary Islands than with Iberian Spanish dialects (Álvarez Nazario 1972). Álvarez Nazario demonstrates that the emigrant population from the Canary Islands became the dominant one in the Puerto Rican population. There appear to be many affinities between Puerto Rican Spanish and that of the "*isleños*" of Louisiana (Álvarez Nazario 1972). As in the case of the Caribbean creoles, including Papiamentu, African influence is an important but not a unique factor.

The demonstration of an African component in Puerto Rican Spanish (paralleling demonstrations of African forms in creole languages) by Álvarez Nazario and others has been an impressive one, and there is no longer any historical or linguistic reason for doubting that African languages influenced the formation of Puerto Rican Spanish. With the added evidence of Canary Islands Spanish, there is no longer any need to view the language as "pure" continental Spanish in Caribbean mouths, as has always been the sentimental view.

This is not to say that Iberian Spanish influences have not been great in Puerto Rico. There are still in the twentieth century socially prominent families who send their children to Spain to be educated — sometimes to the university after other schooling in the United States. But these are again the special cases, capable of being used to "prove" a point but not numerous enough to have any great influence on the "folk" Spanish of Puerto Rico. Like the residents of other Caribbean islands, Puerto Ricans are pathetically eager to find a high incidence of physiological pathology in the speakers of folk Spanish. One of the brightest students in my first year of teaching at the University of Puerto Rico assured me solemnly, "A lot of our people have speech defects." The language of a very nonstandard speaker is not infrequently explained, whether in Jamaica or in Puerto Rico, by "He's tongue-tied."

As long as the issue is treated as one of African influence pure and simple, few advances are likely to be made beyond Álvarez Nazario (1974). There is certainly no use of actual African languages in Puerto Rico (unless artificially, as in some of the French-speaking islands, by practicioners of *négritude*) — certainly not as there is in Cuba (Cabrera 1971) and Trinidad (Warner 1971). It is not to be expected that African linguistic influences in Puerto Rico should be the most important influences — or even the only non-Iberian influences. We can look at African-derived *chévere*, roughly equivalent to the possible Africanism *okay* (Dalby 1972) and think of African influences, but we can look at older *ñapa* 'something extra given with a sale' and surmise that such a word, although culturally almost obsolete, reflects a different historical situation. Starting with Quechua, according to most accounts, the word spread to several South American countries, Cuba, and Louisiana, where its first attestation is attributed to "our Creole Negroes" (DA). It could "pass for African" in Puerto Rico, where the "Black" dialect has *ñami-ñami, ñeñeñé, ñinga,* among other *"vocablos de origen africano que tienen* tal /ñ/ en *su comienzo"* (Álvarez Nazario 1974: 168).

"Africanisms" are not, however, necessarily the real issue here, but rather a polyglot environment. There are some attestations of the realization that Puerto Rico, even in the nineteenth century, was recognized as a multilingual island. The 1868 incident known in Puerto Rico as the *Grito de Lares* ('Cry [for independence] of Lares') is central to the ideology of many Puerto Rican patriots. In Lares, a small town in the mountainous interior where folk belief places a large group of people of Indian ancestry, a few South Americans gathered a following, a large portion of which may have been Black, or Black and Indian. The agitators, who were said to have a special appeal for groups of Blacks (*negradas*), could appeal to this group because *"A cada individuo se le hablaba en su lenguaje . . ."* ('Each person was spoken to in his own language') (Marís and Cueto y Gonzalez, 1872: 75). Álvarez Nazario (1974: 217) quotes an 1843 letter to the effect that *"los negros"* were accustomed to ask for Christmas gifts *"en un lenguaje especial, que suele participar de varios idiomas confusamente amalgamados"* ('in a special language which customarily partook of various languages mixed together in confusion').

A polyglot situation of this type would be an ideal place for a lingua franca, perhaps a pidgin. Creolized (made the first or "only" language of a speech community), the hypothetical variety need not have been the language of all Puerto Rico but only of one group – perhaps the Black slaves. Change toward ordinary Spanish would be "decreolization," a process observed in many other situations. The "decreolized" variety would in turn become the "folk" dialect, used primarily by "disadvantaged" people like plantation laborers but having some capacity for influencing the speech of the more privileged classes as well.

This pattern is fairly well documented in Hawaiian Pidgin English, Hawaiian Creole, and Hawaiian Island dialect (Tsuzaki 1971). It seems to have been the pattern in the history of several varieties of Creole English and of Papiamentu. Tracing the last to an Iberian contact variety rather than to Portuguese or Spanish should resolve a number of conflicts. The later-acquired Hispanicity of a great deal of Papiamentu vocabulary, together with apparent traces of an Iberian Creole in the present-day Spanish of Puerto Rico and other Caribbean islands, especially among the Black populations, suggests that there was once a "Spanish-affiliated [read *Iberian*] pan-Caribbean Creole" (Wood 1972b). *Pace* Zentella (1981: 228), not even Dillard (1975) suggests the *entire* development of Puerto Rican Spanish from this "unattested" Creole.

Although there is no really early documentation, the "Spanish" (or Iberian) Creole is attested in Puerto Rico itself. In *La Juega de Gallos, o El Negro Bozal* (1859), José, the "*Negro bozal*" ('muzzled Negro', but apparently institutionalized in the sense 'Negro fresh from Africa') speaks a "bad" Spanish which is as Creole as it is Spanish or African:

> Yo ta lucu lucu 'I was very crazy' = (*yo*) *estaba loco loco,* although standard Spanish might prefer *completamente loco*

For the /u/ vowels where standard Spanish has /o/, see the discussion on pp. 136-138 concerning the lingua franca of the Gulf Corridor cattle trade. José's speech has also the Romance Creole characteristic that the object pronoun follows rather than precedes the verb, although not with perfect consistency:

> Yo ta queré mucho a ti 'I love you very much' = (*yo*) *te quiero mucho,* to which *a ti* can be added for emphasis.

but

> Yo te sembrará mai,
> y fufu te jaserá
> 'I will plant maize for you, and will make *fufu* for you'

Bickerton and Escalante (1970) make the position of the object pronoun after the verb an important characteristic of Palenquero, a "Spanish-" (read *Iberian-*) based Creole of Northern Colombia.[7] The variability of the rule in José's speech may well indicate that decreolization had proceeded further in Puerto Rico by 1859 than it had in Colombia by 1970.

Variability in José's speech is not limited to this feature. His *Yo ta queré mucho a ti* and *mi corazó ta sufril mucho* and *Ella ta jasé bula* is balanced by *seño Manue ta jabrando mal de mí,* where the Spanish present participial ending is present as usual in the "present progressive" tense. Papiamentu speakers, especially in the city, vary the same way in "decreolization" (Wood 1972). Some admittedly inadequate fieldwork in Puerto Rico leads me to believe that such variation still exists in some special styles. Many Puerto Ricans describe a more nonstandard variety of Spanish used in spiritualist meetings, attended primarily by Black Puerto Ricans and poorer whites. One informant, a close acquaintance, told me that she believes *NP ta pensando* would be used in such meetings and perhaps even *NP ta pensá.* Informants represented those meetings as closed to someone like me, so that only second-hand evidence is available.

Another of the many "creole" features of Jose's speech is the preposition *nan*:

> Ahi ta nan galería, nan covesació con uno músico 'There she is in the gallery, in conversation with a musician'

Álvarez Nazario (1974: 197) points out parallels to the Negro Portuguese of

Guinea, to Papiamentu, to Martiniquan and Haitian Creole, and to Cuban Spanish. For this book, the more interesting comparison may be to Wahnotee (p. 142).

Until the broader historical issue is settled, it seems fruitless to cope with other matters – at least for one who is not a specialist in Spanish. Phonological factors like the interchange of [r] and [l] and the realization of non-prevocalic /s/ as [h] or $\emptyset$ have any number of possible sources, although Álvarez Nazario (1974) makes a good case for at least possible Afro-Creole origin among Puerto Rican speakers of areas like Loiza Aldea, where many African cultural practices survive (Alegriá 1954). Not even for the sake of controversy should it be said that *no* influence of continental Spanish dialects is found in these patterns.

A few other texts, from the nineteenth and early twentieth centuries, assembled by Álvarez Nazario, leave approximately the same impression. These are, admittedly, gaps between the seventeenth-century attestations of a pan-Caribbean Iberian Creole (Otheguy 1973) and the nineteenth-century attestations like *El Negro Bozal,* not to mention the lack of anything surviving which is comparable to Papiamentu or Palenquero. But the abundance of Africanisms and nonstandard forms in coastal areas heavily populated by Blacks suggests, even if it does not conclusively prove, a history of Puerto Rican Spanish which parallels that of Southern English (including what Feagin [1979] calls "white" and "black" dialects.)

The important consideration here is that the Puerto Rican language may preserve certain language-mixing tendencies from this earlier stage, in which creole coexisted with more conventional Spanish. If this was the case, then the "hybridization" tendencies of Puerto Ricans have a sound historical background and are not the result of any kind of pathology. U.S. colonialism in Puerto Rico is an established fact – like the easily forgotten colonialism of Spain – as is the guilty conscience that a great part of the mainland feels when it thinks of the island – if it ever does. But it is not committing oneself one way or the other on the issue of Puerto Rico's status to assert that no pathology has been produced in the language-mixing process. If the Curaçaoan situation is assumed to be normal, at least, the Puerto Rican must also be so considered.

Neither the speech of the *Negros bozales* in Spanish-colonial Puerto Rico nor the Papiamentu of Curaçao would have been possible had it not been for a colonialism going back to the seventeenth century or earlier. It should be remembered that colonialism in Puerto Rico did not begin with the United States's entry in 1898. Even a anti-American work like Maldonado-Denis (1972: 23) stresses the nineteenth-century "presence of the *independentista* or separatist sector, determined from the very beginning to liberate Puerto Rico and also Cuba from the colonial condition of which each was a victim."

As Juan M. Garcia-Passalacqua wrote in the *New York Times Book Review* in October 1973:

The Puerto Ricans are a people born from the wedlock of hunger and colonialism. These two forces have shaped our 500 years of history. During three centuries of stagnation under Spanish rule, the local population clawed a subsistence living from the land while a Spanish elite in the capital guaranteed the island's perpetuation as a strategic military bastion in the Pacific.

The island was one of the few colonies of Spain which did not revolt in the mid-nineteenth century, despite a strong attempt at bringing Puerto Rico into the general Latin American independence movement. Thus the history of the island is virtually one of colonialism unrelieved except in the aspirations of its heroes like Albizu Campos.

Where the language is concerned, there are also physical matters which may be of relevance. It is a large island – not so large as Cuba, but still large. Its size permits a certain amount of socioeconomic diversification, including a great deal of subsistence agriculture by the *jíbaros,* as the country people of the inland mountains are known. This is not possible on a small, arid island like Curaçao. As on Jamaica, which is more nearly the size of Puerto Rico, mountainous terrain has made possible fugitive and hide-out groups; even in the late twentieth century, there are rumors of uncontrolled groups in the mountains. In the early period, surviving groups of Indians, perhaps joined by escaped slaves who ran away like the Jamaican Maroons, would not have wanted the attention of the Spaniards and would have felt quite the opposite of neglected if European visitors to the island had failed to write about them.

Quite apart from Spanish-English bilingualism, there is considerable linguistic diversity – probably, as Zentella (1981: 223) seems to believe, more than has emerged from studies of geographic dialect like Navarro Tomás (1966). The extremes would be the Hispanized intellectuals in the cities, especially in the universities, and the Blacks of the coastal area, with the *jíbaros* of rural and mountainous areas between them. With all these, there is more dialectal variation within the Spanish of Puerto Rico than there is in the Papiamentu of Curaçao; in other words, there is a different kind of diversity in the language of Puerto Rico, not necessarily less diversity than there is on the quatrilingual island. A monolingual Puerto Rican who may know several dialects is not necessarily less proficient in languages than a Curaçaoan who uses three or four languages.

There is also the less-tangible matter of a feeling of national unity. In spite of bicolonialism in its history, there is a more independent national spirit in Puerto Rico than in Curaçao. One of the obvious reasons is Puerto Rico's lesser dependence upon such economic windfalls as the tourist dollar. "One Nation, One Language" is far from an absolute; but there are tendencies in that direction. In some sense, "the mixed language," "hybrid," or "Spanglish" may express the Puerto Rican national spirit better than either "pure" Spanish or a "perfect" bilingualism.

When Puerto Ricans became the latest major immigrant group to New York and over thirty cities in the American North (Zentella 1981: 218), a rather different situation developed from that which had obtained with other groups. Instead of planning to go back to the "old country" on retirement, Puerto Ricans could go back to the island on any one of several flights a day for a comparatively cheap fare. For this and other reasons, their assimilation into mainstream American culture has not been especially rapid.

Not being graduates of expensive private schools, the Puerto Ricans who migrate to the States do not have a near-native command of English, for the most part. They have had to adopt other strategies of linguistic survival. One of them was to live in nearly all-Spanish *barrios*, where their separateness was emphasized and maintained.

There is a tradition among older Puerto Ricans who lived in New York immediately after World War II that they found it easier to communicate with Italians, speakers of another Romance language, and sought out this older group of immigrants. Italian-Americans in cities like New York had developed neo-Italian forms like *minuto* for *minute, ponte* for *pound, storo* for *store, barra* for *bar, giobbo* for job, etc. Italian-Americans have even reported the amusing example of *baccauso* 'toilet', from *back house*, which a born-in-America generation found to be English and not Italian only after visiting Italy. Puerto Ricans may possibly have imitated the Italians somewhat, in the early days, producing every Puerto Rican's example of "Neorican" Spanish:

Está reinando sobre el rufo, 'It is raining on the roof.

Residence in the *barrios*, however, was in effect residence in the ghetto, and Blacks were moving into the same sections of the city. Being dark-skinned, even Black, in many cases themselves, Puerto Ricans were less prone to color prejudice than other ethnic groups, although it should not be assumed that there were no conflicts between them and Blacks. The linguistic upshot was that Puerto Ricans tended to add Black English to their own type of "hybridized" English, or Spanglish.

Wolfram, Shields, and Fasold (1971) collected many sentences like the following, which show influence from Spanish:

I didn't meant it.
We didn't called it a game.
Take slow the car.
The Jets win again the Super Bowl.
It doesn't matter the age.
It doesn't make any difference the outcome.
She's married with my cousin.
He did a mistake.
He has much friends.

He's baseball player.
The Los Angeles has a good team.
The onion is good with a meal.

Particularly among those New York Puerto Ricans who have a lot of contact with Black playmates, Wolfram, Shields, and Fasold found many Black English Vernacular sentences:

He took five book.
The other teacher, they'll yell at you.
I want to know did he go someplace.
They were hoping to go someplace, which they didn't succeed.
The cannon say boom.
I been here for hours.
He gone home already.
Sometime he be here and sometime he don't.
He be here in a few minutes.
If he could, he be here.
The boy hat.
This is mines.

Many of these forms, like the possessive pronoun and the "absolute" possessive in the last two examples, are strikingly different in ordinary English and in the Black English Vernacular. Puerto Ricans pick up the Black forms if they play with Black peers, as do, especially, those larger Puerto Rican boys who play basketball with the high school teams that are dominated by Black players (Silverman 1971; Wolfram, Fasold, and Shields 1971). They also exhibit the same kind of hypercorrection: *Jack's Johnson's car.*

Various differences in the Black English Vernacular and "Spanglish" from the verb system of ordinary English lead to verb forms like those in the following sentences (from Wolfram, Fasold, and Shields):

He speaked to the man.
He taked his money and left.
I seened the man.
He tooked a long ride.
He threwned the ball at me.

Both Blacks and Spanish speakers have trouble with English past-tense forms, for different reasons. Spanish speakers have special trouble with past-tense questions, often refusing

Did you hear me?

in favor of

Did you heard me?

After modeling the "correct" English sentence for a group of Puerto Rican students, I have been told, "Mister, you are wrong. It is past tense: *Did you heard . . .?*" Blacks, on the other hand, mark tense (past or present) nonredundantly, as in this sentence elicited by Marvin Loflin from a Washington, D.C. informant:

And so I comin' down and she out there blabbin' her mouth told my sister I playin' hookey from school.

Given poor instruction in the standard English past tense system, Blacks in an acropetal (Stewart 1968b) situation will often double- (or, in the case of *threwned* above, even triple-) mark the past tense. Of course a Puerto Rican who learns Black English well will pick up the same tendency.

Like the Black American, the Puerto Rican in the States has tended to keep his own linguistic identity even under considerable pressure to do otherwise. The constant switching to English, about which Spanish-speaking visitors to the island often complain, may be partly a (probably unconscious) attempt to keep his individuality even in the company of other Hispanics. Pressures to conformity have included colonialism (by two colonial powers), but the Puerto Rican has managed to retain a kind of uniqueness.

He still suffers in the schools, however, both from Hispanists who used to post (up to 1964) the sign on the University of Puerto Rico campus:

DISTINGUASE. HABLE BUEN ESPAÑOL.
('Distinguish yourself. Speak good Spanish")

and from sometimes over-enthusiastic American English-as-a-second-language teachers who assure everyone. "They *need* English."

There are prophets of doom insofar as Spanish in Puerto Rico is concerned. Author José Luis Gonzalez, for eighteen years a resident of Mexico and now a citizen of that country although born in Puerto Rico, recently reported (San Juan *Star,* November 3, 1973, p. 1) that, although he had published short stories in Spanish, he felt that he had begun to learn the language only after he moved to Mexico. According to Gonzalez:

Mexicans know the language much better than Puerto Ricans because they're taught the language much better. Also there's not such an [sic] interference by a foreign language.

Although some exaggeration for political and rhetorical effect may be suspected, remarks by people like Gonzalez do perhaps indicate something about the differences between the not-unmixed Spanish of Puerto Rico and that of other Latin countries. There is very frequently a note of protest in the writings of successful literary men who have a special feeling for the Spanish language and for Hispanic culture. In a way, it seems a pity that so much of Puerto Rico's educational effort is devoted to something they decry, the fostering of the use of English.

As seems to emerge from a closer study of Texas and the Southwest, the intrusion of English into Spanish-speaking Puerto Rico cannot be accurately described in simplistic terms. Other language varieties, some of them not even recognized in the official histories, must somehow be taken into account. As Zentella (1981: 227) asserts, there is a need for sociolinguistic work not "fraught with partisan judgments" and utilizing the best modern methodology.

In the interval before such studies are performed, it is easy to see that the battle between English and Spanish in Puerto Rico has been a real struggle, not without damage to the speakers of both languages if not to the languages themselves. The easy, familiar paradigm of monolingual (old language) first generation, bilingual second generation, and monolingual (new language) third generation simply will not work where there is the complicated sociopolitical setup that obtains in Puerto Rico. It would be interesting to study some of the same struggles in, especially, the Philippines, where Iberian creoles and native languages complicate the simple "bilingual" picture even further. And one wonders whether there were not many of the same patterns, on a perhaps smaller scale, in the Southwest when English first moved in.

NOTES

1. Masterson (1952: 119) cites the term from railway depots at the end of the nineteenth century. No earlier use seems to be recorded. There is, however, no other usage of specifically railroad English in Puerto Rico. Given the restricted influence of railroad language (see pp. 181-186), such a source seems unlikely. The writing of the history of Puerto Rican immigration to the continental United States apart from emotionally and even politically colored argumentation has not, however, been done.

2. Lloréns (1968) shows how English permeates the Spanish vocabulary of drug addicts. He cites words like *chutazo* 'shot', *chutiar* 'shoot', *esnifiar* 'sniff', *estofa* 'stuff' *juquearse* (from *hook*) 'inject oneself', *cortar* (translating *cut*) 'adulterate the drug'. These borrowings apply strictly to the domain of narcotics; it is very unlikely that *chutazo* would be used in the sense 'shot (from a gun)'. Lloréns explains the use of this terminology as the result of a *germanía* ('brotherhood') relationship. Other gang terminology, not necessarily associated with drugs, participates in the same relationship: *deque* 'deck' (of cards), *jolope* 'hold up', *pana* 'parnter', *tofete* 'tough', blofear 'bluff'.

3. A basilectal speaker of Spanglish would use *fabric* for *factory*, dropping the final vowel of Spanish *fábrica; packet* from *paquete* or *bult* from *bulto* for *bundle; note* from *nota* for *grade* at the school which he *assists* (Spanish *asistir*) under the supervision of a *mister* 'teacher' (Spanish *maestro*). Note that [mihtɛl] also fills the function of Spanish *señor*, notably as a noun of address. He will give one his *direction* 'address'; to call him, one needs his *telephone* (Spanish *teléfono*) 'telephone number'. Vocabulary items of this type are basically Spanish nouns without the "inflectional" vowel. Since final unstressed vowels are reduced in Puerto Rican Spanish (Zentella 1981: 224, quoting a story of Rosario), the folk Spanish might be said to be closer to "Spanglish" than more standard Spanish, Notice especially how the dropping of the inflectional endings of (e.g.) *blofear* will produce *blof,* phonologically identical to *bluff* in the usual Puerto Rican pronunciation.

4. Because this chapter is concerned primarily with the spread of American English to Puerto Rico, the interesting issue of whether English has affected the structure of Spanish in Puerto Rican is not really relevant. Perez Sala (1973) made a limited investigation which tended to indicate English syntactic influence only in a few isolated cases like ¿*Como le gusta Puerto Rico?* for ¿*Le gusta Puerto Rico?* 'How do you like Puerto Rico?' Fieldwork, with a Puerto Rican student as helper, in 1973 seemed to establish the almost complete acceptability, at all social levels, of sentences like *Nadando es un buen deporte* (for *Nadar es un buen deporte*) 'Swimming is a good sport'; in other words, the typically Spanish infinitival subject

can readily be replaced by a "gerund" in Puerto Rican Spanish. Nonce forms like *No* (for *Ningunos*) *Vehiculos Pesados* 'No Heavy Vehicles' are easy to observe, although Zentella (1981) objects to this kind of collecting. Again, as Zentella suggests, nothing meaningful can be done in these areas without utilizing the concepts of domains and speech communities. Either "Puerto Rican syntax is affected by English" or "Puerto Rican syntax is not affected by English" is near to being nonsense unless it is specified what persons are talking and to whom, in what styles they are speaking, and in what domains they are conversing. Having used it myself, I can say with some confidence that *buenas nights* has been used for leave taking in Puerto Rico, but it is not a very frequently used form.

5. Two such speakers are my stepsons. Through them, it has been possible to observe the English and the rapid Spanish-English switching practices of several youngsters who were teenagers in their 1970s and are now in their twenties.

6. William A. Stewart was kind enough to criticize and to amplify this section in Dillard (1975), from which much of this material is taken. As the first book was eventually printed, this section contained more of Stewart than of Dillard. Stewart is not, however, responsible for any mistakes or for any infelicities of style, particularly in this later version, which has been revised considerably.

7. Bickerton and Escalante (1970) eschew historical documentation of Palenquero, as is usual in Bickerton's work because of his theory of the relationship between synchronic variants and historical change. Alvarez Nazario (1974) cites, however, M. Chávez Franco, *"Crónicas de Guayaquil, Folklore Costeño," Revista de las Españas*, 1919, nums. 36-37-38, pp. 334-336: *"Los primeros trabajos de aprovechamiento del caucho por dicha region [el pueblo del Palenque] se llevaron a cabo con 'negros esclavos o libertos, cimarrones del Ecuador y de Colombia,' hablantes de una 'jerga' or 'pichilingue'."*

Chapter XI

A World Language
— and How to Understand It

In the past few decades, the story of how English has become the world's second language has been told many times (Baugh 1957; Laird 1970; Krapp/ Marckwardt 1969). So far as the nineteenth century was concerned – and even part of the twentieth – this worldwide use could be traced to the colonial expansion and naval might of Great Britain. The world looked basically to British English, although only a small part of the people who spoke the language really passed for British. Even today some West African nations send the sons of their most affluent or most powerful families to Oxford and Cambridge; even among the working classes, a person may pretend to the status of a "been to" (i.e., been to England). An "Oxford" accent is still prized in India, but the emphasis has been shifting with the decline of British military and economic power. More and more, American power and influence are being felt throughout the world; and it is American English that now provides the initiatory power for the world's lingua franca.

The spread of English, whether British or American, had to do primarily with the military and commercial might of England and then of the United States, rather than with any special characteristics of their language. The day when even popular language histories contained statements about the "simplicity" of English compared to Latin and Greek is surely over. It is even necessary to cite Bantu languages with their prefixed morphological system, on speakers of which the "simplicity" of a language like English that still depends somewhat on suffix morphology would be lost.

Difficulties with any second language remain, but there is controversy about the cause of such difficulties. The older question of native language "interference" on a second or foreign language has given way to a new orthodoxy in which it is asserted that the speaker of Chinese or Portuguese learning English goes through exactly the same processes as the monolingual English-speaking child in acquiring his first language (Dulay and Burt 1974). One of the most influential books on TOEFL, Burt and Kiparsky (1972: 3) asserts:

Because we have not found "foreign syntax" to be a major factor in describing learner goofs *The Gooficon* is not language specific. Instead, it simply displays some parts of English grammar which cause speakers of many different languages difficulty.

Dulay, Burt, and Krashen (1982) hint that hearing a French (it could be a Spanish) speaker say "I have seventeen years" does not prove that *J'ai dix-sept ans* (or *Tengo diesisiete años*) has figured in the generative process. Basically, they seem to mean that the "major" part of this utterance is universal, a "minor" part of it French- (or Spanish-, etc.) specific. Actually, it would be difficult to find outright contradiction of this viewpoint even in the older works on English as a Second Language. The chief difference is in the statement process: The contrastivists have focused on what is unusual and reportable; the universalists, on the whole process. That this latter involves progress is almost undeniable; it also represents a more precise version of what an academic profession is supposed to do. All this does not, however, eliminate the existence of the "reportable" element, nor does it totally invalidate amateur observers' accounts where nothing else is available (e.g., in the early American colonies, or on the frontier). And most of us feel that these non-universal, superficial differences have been involved in those cases where we have run into difficulty in understanding the English which is spoken outside those countries where it is the official language.

Nor is there a lack of countries where English has an official status but the English encountered can be confusing at times. (See the last chapter, on Puerto Rico.) English is official in Liberia, but an American can encounter varieties there which are greatly puzzling to him, as he can in Nigeria and the West Cameroon. The transmittal of English to Liberia is usually explained in terms of the repatriation of Black ex-slaves in the nineteenth century. There were cavils even at the time about "repatriation'; Winks (1971: 154) reports that "the majority of the Negro leadership agreed . . . the Negroes of the United States had become North Americans and should remain so." If their English was "North American," then it is pretty obvious that pidgin and creole English were North American. It seems inescapable that, in a real sense, a variety of English that was in some sense "American" was transported overseas before the period of British domination had ended (Berry 1961; Hancock 1971).

Although not identical to any Afro-American variety, Liberian English of today has striking resemblances to several of them. Holm and Shilling (1982) classify Liberian (after Hancock 1969) among the "Atlantic" varieties; they also have the category "Pan-Creole," for forms found not only throughout the English-based creoles but in varieties based on Portuguese or French. (They cite [1982: xi] the use of Bahamian English *foot*, Papiamentu *pia*, and Guine Portuguese creole *pɛɛ* to refer to the leg from the knee down as an example of Pan-Creole tendencies presumably derived from West African languages.) The casual observer should perhaps not be deprived of his innocent amusements. The traveler who knows that he has heard *stay* 'dwell' in both West Africa and among American Blacks may be too quick to advance a theory of the direction of influence, but his observations are not for that reason less accurate. And some of his observations may well parallel, in less exact form, those of Hancock (1970-71).

The casual observer under discussion would be somewhat enlightened, but not surprised, to find that expressions like *bad mouth* and *sweet mouth* are used in West Africa, in the Caribbean, and in the United States, with West African language analogues; that *dollbaby* 'doll' falls into the same category; or that *carry* 'conduct, escort' is classified by Holm and Shilling (1982) as "Atlantic," even though they cite British dialectal Northern and Ireland occurrences. The traveler who observes that *humbug* is more usually a verb meaning 'annoy' in West Africa than a noun meaning something like 'fakery' has made an observation which would stand him in good stead wherever the "Atlantic" creoles are spoken, whatever he thinks of the OEDS designation as "a slang or cant word which came into vogue about 1750." If he uses his knowledge of Atlantic *fufu* 'a starchy dish' to try to impress a caller with his knowledge of Black U.S. slang – this happened to me one time, on a radio-telephone interview with presumably numerous listeners – he is likely to be judged sadly lacking in knowledge of hoodoo terminology. (Vass [1979] cites *foo-foo* 'a new person, an outsider; disliked person, one not accepted'.) The humiliated "expert" could always retaliate·that he had been over-influenced by Caribbean Spanish (Holm and Shilling 1982). "Pan-Creole" forms like *one-one* 'separately', *one-time* 'immediately', and Atlantic *josna* 'right away' add to the impression that there is a kind of Afro-American language community, whatever the precise direction of influence may have been in any given case. A few Liberian terms like *stink-mouth* 'abusive or bad talk', although not paralleled in Bahamian, apparently, are reminiscent of wider-flung varieties – in this case, Hawaiian Pidgin English *talk stink* (Kent Bowman n.d.)

The Pidgin-English-related varieties are, however, a drop in the bucket in the world picture, however interesting they may be in themselves. Although Melanesian Pidgin English seems quite healthy as does that of New Guinea, Pidgin English is in disrepute in many parts of the world. The variety of English used as a lingua franca has changed, and Pidgin is sometimes even regarded as the invention of fiction writers.

Whether the cause has anything to do with the relative speed of air travel compared to sea voyages or not, there is a greater approximation to prestigious varieties of English among the non-native speakers who abound in many parts of the world. Great differences can be observed, however, from the varieties spoken in the United States and in Great Britain. Each of us has his own rogue's gallery of almost incomprehensible "English" utterances and even writings. My own favorites include an item on the menu of the Hotel Torarica in Paramaribo, Surinam, which advertised "Selectable French Toast," along with "Golden Brown Waffers." Friends have tried to help me with that one, but we haven't been very successful in riddling it out. One thing I'm sure of: The English word aimed at couldn't have been *delectable* – I ordered the stuff one morning.

A rather typical incident at the same hotel showed what is happening to English on a nearly world-wide scale. At the table next to me were a Belgian gentleman and his young son. It happened that they were talking together in French, but the man – like many Belgians – was quite as proficient in Dutch. The waiter, who was also proficient in Dutch, could just struggle along in English (as distinct from Sranan Tongo, the English Creole which probably should be called his native language). Nevertheless, the waiter, like many others in today's world, insisted on using English with *all* his customers. He and the Belgian had a terrible time communicating, even at the level of ordering meals, and the Belgian threw up his hands in mock-despair after each such encounter, but the waiter's decision that English must remain the language of ordering was irrevocable. The same kind of insistence is to be observed in many kinds of activities in widely dispersed areas.

"Growth" is the familiar metaphor for such spread, and "growing pains" is a perhaps equally apt figure for what often takes place. As a user of English, one can be addressed in the strangest conceivable ways. In Bujumbura, Burundi, I was hailed from a passing truck by a man I never saw again who was probably a laborer being carried to his job: "You Spinglish?"

We all understand things like that without any real trouble. We can all interpret *no got change* to mean 'Don't you have any change?' or 'I don't have any change' or 'He doesn't have any change', depending upon the context and speaker. But, theory aside, it helps to know something about the other fellow's language. A Spanish speaker's *He threw me with a rock* is sure to be confusing unless the hearer knows *Me tiró con una piedra* 'He threw a rock at me'. The pattern of the dialogue will probably tell us that *He likes to take coffee* has no reference to stealing, but it helps to know Spanish *tomar* 'drink' (in the right environment).

The prestige of English and its lingua franca function have caused a situation in which great numbers of people are striving to learn the language and are eager to use what they know. Such eager practicers of English may be disappointed, even resentful, to find that their efforts are not appreciated, even that the English speaker knows their own language. Cornelius (1955) corroborates these experiences and gives expert advice to Americans who want to swim against the sociolinguistic tide. One such chapter, "You Stink," deals with the familiar insistence that the speaker of the other language cannot understand and that it is necessary to resort to English. A subtler ploy is described in the subchapter, "You Speak Beautifully" — an often insincere compliment tending to make one believe that further improvement in the language is unnecessary.

An occasional change of language may be "illogical" if the desire to acquire English as a lingua franca is not taken into account. I know of no research on the matter, but anyone who has traveled a bit knows that a speaker of another language will sometimes approach an obvious "American," request that the English speaker use the other language because "I can't speak English," and then halfway through a long interview begin insisting on English — even pretending that he can no longer understand the "American's" version of his own language. A slight variation of this pattern is the bargain that each will give the other practice in his non-native language, with insistence upon constant use of English becoming stronger as the two talk together longer.

Historically, it would seem that the speakers of the dominant language (e.g., the Romans in Gaul or the Norman French in England) have yielded to the wishes of the speakers of the less prestigious language. Many of the latter hope to make some money by translating. (This applies, of course, to American English and not to Latin, since there are no known records of such activity in the latter.) Other, more pleasant, relationships prosper when the American directs his efforts toward understanding the foreign-accented English rather than expressing himself in the other language. American capitalists abroad have undoubtedly had a better reception because they knew enough to boost the linguistic ego of the citizens of the host country. And many an American abroad with an eye for female beauty has found that he gets more attractive dates if he throws in an English lesson as an inducement.

If English "enjoys" the position of being virtually the "H" language in a world diglossic situation, it is — or rather its speakers are—exposed to some suffering as well. Any person who *can* speak English is expected to speak it in many cases, even though his interlocutor may know very little. The traveler who is getting along quite well in French until someone examines his passport, discovers that he is a U.S. citizen, and begins the familiar insistence that only English be used is only going through one of the little agonies that beset a speaker of a world-wide lingua franca. It undoubtedly happened to the Romans during the great days of the empire, as well as to the Greeks earlier and to the French in the early modern period. It often seems almost mysterious how the rules for the use of a given language develop, but they are real and there is often amazing unanimity about them among the speakers in a multilingual speech community.

There is, however, no guarantee that, even with the best of intentions and determination to remain passive and non-ridiculing, the native speaker of American English will understand the foreigner's English at all. The eagerness of Japanese, for example, to learn English has become almost proverbial in the twentieth century − except perhaps during the years of World War II. But their confidence in their own linguistic achievements has been misplaced at times. Narita (1983: 133-4) writes, in not perfectly idiomatic English, of how "cultural based mistakes tend to bring smiles and laughter both to the speaker and the listener." Anyone who has read the instructions that come with a Japanese transistor radio knows that such amusement may be mixed with frustration. The *New Yorker* used to run selections of Japanese English under the heading "The Mysterious East." The following selection was printed on November 29, 1947, p. 114:

> Explanation
> Name: Picture and Letter match.
> Maker: No. 1 Toys Industrial Co. Ltd.
> Shiozaki-Muri, Sarashina-gun, Naga
>   Prefecture, Japan
> Materials and Quality
> 1. This toy is made of the best qualified wood (ho tree), grows in cold region, which has been Carefully dealt with an artificial drier, so that if it is used for a long time no strain will be occurred.
> 2. In paintiny, we never used chalk powder on the wooden basis but directly painted the wood three times with lacquar and enamel. Discolouration or dispainting will not be seen. Euen if a child is happened to lick it absolutely caused no harm.
> How to Play
> 1. Picture match
>   Children can take out 30 cubic pieces (we calls it a pawn hereafter) from a box scattering them on a table and arrange a piece to piece to form the original picture. Several children can play a game at the same time counting required time to make the picture complete. A child who needs the shortest time is a winner.
> 2. Letter match
>   Children can learn English words in playing with this toy. An alphabet letter is on each side of a cubic pawn, We arrange letters in order on serial pawn in such a way that theletters of A. B. C. D. are on the birst pawn, B. C. D. E. on the second, C. D. E. F. on the third and so on.
> 3. Building blocks
>   We painted the building bricks set around a box and back side of 30 pawns in a box with the same colour children can play a blocks as they like with 43 pieces of bricks in total we do not figne out what blocks will they play but children's parents and brother or sister can help them to train their construction sense or ability.
> To childrens' Mathers
>   We explained briefly to you the way how to play these toys "Picture and Letter Match," but the first of all we wish to mention is that you must have children put toy to rights in the box as it ought to be by themselves right after they have played with it. Also we wish you would think over that a good toy will help them to secure "a good "Health," "a good brain," "a good ability" and "a good Sentiment."

It might be almost as easy to learn Japanese as to understand the "English" of these instructions. And even Chinese couldn't be much more incomprehensible than the following, which the *New Yorker* (January 10, 1948) reprinted from the *North China Daily News*:

The undersigned hereby announce to the public in representing Messrs. F.Y. Wong, F.C. Yee the representatives among twelve buyers of Metropolitan Motors, Ltd. Co. on account of ordering from the same twelve American "Studebaker Champion Deluxe" motor cars respectively which as notified by the same are already arrived in Shanghai. As the above mentioned company set an extremely high price on each one of the cars, even they asked the same to deliver the cars to them, yet the same refused to do so. The negotiations between two parties are just in proceeding now. Whoever wants to buy those cars ordered by them is kindly requested to take notice of the above mentioned affairs in order to avoid trouble.

C.Y. Tai
Barister-at-Law
Office: 190 Kiukiang Road
Floor 3

Incidentally, the clear difference between this garbled English and Pidgin English is one of the grosser reasons why pidginists reject the popular formation of "grammar of one language with lexicon of another."

It is easier to figure out the English spoken or written by someone whose native language is one of the Romance or Germanic group. Spanish, or Spanglish, is so familiar to many of us that we don't even notice it when we hear, "It makes two years that I am here." Although there are differences in the ways in which Spanish and English allot time relationships in the immediate present or immediate past (expecially where continuity in the past is concerned), the grammatical systems are even on the surface rather similar. In fact, a teacher's main problem is persuading his students that there are differences which must be taken into account.

The cumulative effect of "deep" Spanglish can, nevertheless, produce communicative problems. The *New Yorker* (January 8, 1949: 45) provided this example from *El Ferrocarril,* Lima, Peru:

A English Section

The want of to make arrived to know the exigence by to build more railways over our territory, us compel at we led all north Americans citizens divelling into Perus for to invite we assistance in the compaing by the railroads building.

. . .

A translation into Spanish

La necesidad de hacer llegar a conocer la exigencia de construir mas ferrocarriles sobre nuestro territoria nos compele a . . .

removes the mystery up to the last word of the third line. (Is this meant to be *let* or *lead*?) A re-translation then yields

The need to make known the urgency of constructing more railroads in our territory forces us to . . .

For me, the interpretation is impossible without the intermediate translation into Spanish, even for this much. Misspelling here adds, perhaps unusually, to the confusion: *divelling* is obviously *dwelling,* but is *compaing* meant for *company*?

Communication obviously can break down when a user of one language tries to write another in which he is less proficient. And a contrived example at least shows that the meaning can be clarified by one who is proficient in the two languages. Another such sentence (from further along in the same text)

One railroad magazine she cannot sustain self with the an scanty advertisements

can be rendered as

Una revista de ferrocarriles no puede sostenerse con la [una?] escasez de anuncios

which can easily be translated as

A railroad magazine cannot be sustained by a limited number of advertisements

Impressionistically, the second example (this paragraph) seems less difficult to understand without the intermediate translation than the first.

It does not require a wholehearted dedication to the contrastivist approach to second language learning to make one suspect that someone with a fluent command of Japanese could interpret the clause *if could is happend to lick it* with equal confidence. Guesswork will yield the probably correct *if a child happens to lick it,* but without the certainty of the Spanish example. That a Chinese-English bilingual could interpret *respectively which as notified by the same* from the *North China Daily News* is equally probable. Can it be that the study which most Americans with college degrees have made of at least one or two Romance languages is what makes it easier for us to communicate, in English, with a Frenchman or Spaniard than with a Chinese or a Japanese?

One thing seems very certain: World-wide use of English as a language of wider communication, coupled with the direct method of teaching (instruction only or primarily in English, with little or no translation into the native language) has bred a world-wide assurance that often amounts to overconfidence, even among academic organizations. The International Association for Research and Diffusion of Audio-Visual and Structuro-Global Methods circulated, in 1972, an English-language letter that began:

Dear Sir/Madam:
Either because we have heard of your pre-occupations or else because your name has been brought to our notice by a colleague . . .

The Brussels dateline for the letter is probably enough to warn most readers not to take *pre-occupations* in its literal English sense of 'absorption, or engrossment in one's own thoughts'. Most will probably determine that the meaning 'occupation' or 'previous occupation' is meant. Orally, a strong foreign accent can provide an equally useful warning. But just occasionally the kinds of ESL teachers who emphasized pronunciation and intonation almost to the exclusion of other factors produced a student who could mimic the sounds of English quite well without making much sense in the language.

It is possible to make extremely wrong interpretations of grammatical data even when understanding in the narrower sense does not suffer. One obvious case is that of a speaker of Ilocano, a Filipino language that does not have sex-gender contrast in the pronoun system, who while studying in the United States was called in for a conference by a psychology professor who interpreted the student's writings as evidence of homosexuality. Black children, who were so often accused of linguistic deprivation in the 1960s (C. Deutsch 1964), often do not have this masculine-feminine pronoun distinction in the early age grades; a group of five and six year olds in a child development program in Natchitoches, Louisiana, had some speakers (according to their teacher, who called me in to observe them) who did not make the distinction. One of them looked at a picture of a woman in bed and responded, as members of the class had often responded before apparently, "Him sleep. Weinstein (1962) saw rather male dominance in the creole use of *him* to mean 'she/her; he/him' in the Virgin Islands; he also adduced the general term of address *man*, for masculine and feminine addressees, for the same population. He apparently did not know that in Puerto Rico, and perhaps in other varieties of New World Spanish, *hombre* is frequently used in the same way.

Academic models, even including language textbooks, can be misleading insofar as second-language influence is concerned. Aspillera (1964), instructing English speakers in Tagalog, tells them how to say "Happy Greetings" and "Good afternoon, too" in the official language of the Philippines. At a meeting or a convention, one is encouraged to request to speak by saying, "May I lose my courtesy?" (That is, the English speaker is instructed to say "Mawalang — galang po," but the author apparently thinks that the English translation is idiomatic in that language.) In more homey domains, English speakers are taught how to produce Tagalog for "The dress and the pairs of shoes are clean" and "How many are their children?" Translation exercises, English into Tagalog, include *We are clean and good* and *Their pencil is long.*

There is probably no more than momentary difficulty in understanding the foreign-English writing of Goilu (1962), but he comes an occasional cropper in translations like

Mi falta dos florin 'I am short of two guilders'

The book also contains a rather large number of English examples, for translation into Papiamentu, like

I have no many friends because I have no money.

It is arguable that a textbook like Goilu's should not be "corrected," that it is more important for an English speaker in Curaçao (or Aruba, or Bonaire) to understand Papiamentu-tinged English than to learn Papiamentu itself. As in most parts of the Caribbean and indeed in many parts of the world, self-appointed interpreters abound. They are sometimes genuinely disappointed when they learn that "the American" does not need their translations. Linguistic sophistication, as distinct from multilingualism, may facilitate the interaction. A teacher in (for example) Burundi needs to be able to hear *The secretary is in labor* (for more idiomatic English *at work*) without breaking into laughter or even smiling. If he is lucky, his students will never see the humorous possibilities in the response of one of them.

Such examples are extremely commonplace to anyone who has been exposed to English abroad. It is hard to avoid the conclusion that, if native language syntax is not very important in the type of English spoken, native language lexicon and idiom are extremely important. Of course, idiom is precisely the area in which the most dedicated universalists may have to back down a little (Makkai 1975). Humorists have found ready-made examples in the speech of insistent users of non-native English, both here and abroad, but it has usually been considered unliberal to point out the obvious. Martin (1983: 201-2) is a relatively rare treatment of the humorous nature of such "mistakes" in a professional collection.

Even during the period when it was said in introductions to linguistics that one needed to learn only something like 20% of the vocabulary of a language, 85% of its grammar, and almost none of its inventory of idioms in order to communicate, there were relatively few learners who really mastered the sound system in ESL classes. There is a resultant ease in learning to identify the native language of the speaker by his characteristic sound substitutions (and perhaps by some clues from his general appearance.) Teaching methods based on contrastive analysis do not always work; an Arab student of mine was able to articulate his indifference to the /b/ ≠ /p/ contrast to the degree of saying, "It's not imbortant," and "It's no broblem." It probably isn't any great problem; we all knew, when he said he was late because "I couldn't find a barking place" that he hadn't really been howling like a dog.

Vocabulary differences, often involving what are called false cognates, are another thing. There's always the possibility that the German who offers one a "gift" may be proffering poison. But a Spanish speaker who talks of a company of "fabricators" probably just means 'manufacturers'. Americans in embassy communities (in this case, Yaoundé, Cameroun, in 1963-4) develop their own local glossaries, learning for example that even in English *chiffon* likely means 'dishrag' to a French-dominant speaker. Equivalent rules apply in the opposite direction: An American lady in the same community finally realized — and entertained us with the story of — how she had amused her drinking companions in a Paris bar each night by saying, "*Je vais m'accoucher*," not realizing she was saying "I am going to give birth" when she was trying to say "*Je vais me coucher*," with the less extreme meaning "I am going to bed."

The false cognates are hackneyed concerns insofar as linguists are concerned, which may be one reason why recent treatments (Burt and Kiparsky 1972) give so little attention to possibilities for confusion. There really isn't so much of a problem with the Frenchman, for example, who knows a little English because he may mean 'bacon' when he says *lard*, 'face' when he says *figure*, and 'wide' when he says *large*. The real difficulty comes when he anticipates your reinterpretation of what he says and becomes entangled in attempts to avoid the troublesome words altogether.

The fact that a word once had the meaning in English that its French or Spanish cognate has now is not at all relevant to the ability to understand the word. The fact that English *travail* once meant 'work' rather than 'pain' or 'suffering' is no help at all in understanding the Frenchman's word spelled the same way or his false-cognate use of the English word. The fact that English *assist* once meant 'be present' is equally useless in interpreting what a Frenchman or a Spaniard means when he says that he "assisted" a meeting. The OED lists two nineteenth-century uses of the word in the Romance sense in an obviously archaizing stylistic context along with two others that specifically evoke French *asistir* and a few others in which it seemingly had the earlier sense for the writer.

Probably the only insuperable barrier in a bilingual contact situation is overtranslation, the process that may turn *Río Piedras* into *Rock(s) River*, *(Isla) Mona* into *Monkey Island*, and *Culebra* into *Snake Island*. The real problem here may be an unwillingness to communicate rather than a purely linguistic one. Visitors to places which cater to tourists become accustomed to the native attitude that certain things are almost invisible to outsiders. After nearly five years in Puerto Rico. I was almost put off a *público* by a lady who thought I must be trying to get to Calle Loiza rather than to Loiza Aldea, the destination of the car, which she did not really believe existed for me.

On the other hand, a combination of interference and accommodation can produce problems almost as insurmountable. The Spanish-speaking student who says, "I cannot get the book at the library, because I have no money," can presumably be straightened out by the explanation, *"Librería* in Spanish is translated by *bookstore; library* means *'biblioteca'*." But one can get the answer — I have gotten at least the equivalent — "I know, mister, but I cannot get the book at the library because I have no money." Spanish-influenced English is by now so widely used that it may have claims to being a variety of its own, not subject to correction by monolinguals. In like manner, Camerounians, including some children of French ancestry who have grown up there, tended to say in the 1960s *l'aviacion* for *l'aerodrome*; they would brook no correction from a speaker of continental French — and certainly not from an American. Furthermore, I was never sure whether my partially English-speaking houseboy, who knew *rat* but not *mouse*, ever really believed my explanation that there is a difference in English.

The real beginner, in the full flush of interference, often causes less confusion than the intermediate speaker who has attained a certain amount of fluency. (ESL teachers recognize, of course, "plateau" and "retrogression" factors for some of their relatively successful students.) A Frenchman of the first description may say [taip] in such a way that we can figure out that he means 'guy'. But the one who has learned enough English to think that he can get slangy may on occasion believe that it is an acceptable abbreviation for *typewriter* and cause difficulty in communication. (Again, this has actually happened to me.)

For the many Americans who have gone abroad in the last few decades, particularly since World War II, there has been little or no instruction in this most vital phase of their communication problems. (One is tempted to say that, in this respect, they could prepare themselves better by reading certain stories by James Thurber than by taking a linguistics course.) Herman and Herman (1943) has some practical value, but their material on "Mexican Spanish dialect" contains a great deal that is questionable and inspires something less than confidence in their treatment of the English produced by speakers of more "exotic" languages. But, somehow, the American businessman and tourist have managed the difficult job of communication without instruction in how to understand strange brands of English. That there has not beer more difficulty may be to the credit of the unsung hero of English as a world language, the teacher of foreign languages in schools and colleges.

Is the astounding success, among occasional failures, of English on an ·almost global scale a sure proof of universalism? Do we find here ultimate proof that the lack of any "deep structure" differences between languages directly affects verbal interaction? The answer would probably have to be "not proved." But there are some observable processes at work, some of them educational in nature. We should not ignore even the latter, although the linguists' scorn for the language pedagogue is almost embarrassingly well known.

A great deal has been said about the American foreign language teacher, much of it concerned with his deficiencies. A teacher of French, Spanish, or German for the most part, the typical professor branched off into Russian, Norwegian, or Modern Greek very rarely, and into such exotic languages as Turkish, Mongolian, or Mandarin Chinese almost never. He had to combat the attitude that Latin and Greek were the only languages worth studying in a university setting, although that attitude was disappearing rapidly after World War II. Before and immediately after that war, the foreign language teacher might be less than really fluent in the language he taught, and there were some cases of teachers of a language who may never have really communicated with a native speaker in that language. From about 1940 onwards, almost everyone who wrote about language teaching spent a few pages denouncing him.

American foreign-language teaching was almost universally regarded as "bad" up to World War II at least, and there was a lot of chest-beating and shouting of *mea culpa* from language teachers. It was asserted – truthfully – that college and high school students were not learning to speak the languages they studied; and it was assumed – unthinkingly – that no other purpose could be served by such courses. There were a lot of conferences, paid for from funds aimed at the improvement of education and usually provided by the government or the well-known foundations, on how this regrettable situation could be improved.

Many books issued from such conferences; a fairly typical one is Roucek (1968). In that collection, Claudel's "The Changing Aspects of Teaching Spanish" dealt with lower-level college Spanish in these quite representative terms:

Elementary grammar was covered in one year, to be followed by a review grammar accompanied by literary or practical reading dealing with the culture of Spain or Spanish America. Although numerous texts might be labelled "conversational," in reality their contents and use in class in general paid only lip service to an oral method. While in many areas a reading knowledge of the language was the main objective, in some areas such as New Orleans, both a conversational and a cultural ability in Spanish were required and ultimately achieved. But this high level of achievement has declined today because of regimentation into the audiolingual method which demonstrates "unprecedented activity – although not unprecedented success."

Although Claudel and the other contributors – to this and other volumes – did not consider the possibility that such "inadequate" language teaching was useful for a student whose future language experience might be primarily in terms of the Spanish-influenced English of Spain or of Spanish America, they documented the fact that American language teaching was undergoing radical changes. Oliva (1968) attests that "modern trends" in foreign-language teaching were at an "all time low in the 1940s" but came into "national prominence in the 1960s." The government aided in the process with Title VI Language Institutes and Title III equipment for foreign-language departments in public schools. Prior to World War II, ability to read the foreign language had been the goal, but now a speaking knowledge was the aim. Oliva was very sanguine about the change to audio-lingual methodology, the use of such "advanced" methods as contrastive analysis, and the continued growth of enrollment in foreign-language classes.

The Northeast Conference on the Teaching of Foreign Languages would not have shared Oliva's enthusiasm. In 1972, only four years after the publication of Roucek, it was necessary to set up a task force on the problem of teaching another language as part of another culture (Dodge 1972). One reason why it was found advisable to take this step was a thorough disillusionment with the audiolingual method as a device for teaching a language. More than that, however, it was becoming clear that mere mastery of a foreign language, without familiarity with the culture of the speakers, was not really enough for communication – assuming that the acquisition of the language under such circumstances was likely. And there was a third, highly practical motivation for an organization whose membership was almost entirely foreign-language teachers: enrollment in foreign-language classes in high schools and even in colleges was declining rapidly. In these days of specialization in such matters as computer "languages," even an occasional professional linguist feels that he does not need any real fluency in a second "natural" language.

This was a strange development from the viewpoint of many who had reasoned about America's need for foreign language study. Oliva (1968: 329) asserted that "barring a great war or depression, Americans will continue to travel in unprecedented numbers," and he seemed to regard it as axiomatic that such travel would increase their awareness of the need to speak foreign languages. But perhaps he failed to take into account that such American travelers would be met by increasing numbers of students of English as a foreign language who would insist upon "traducing" for the Americans.

Among the post-World War II tourists and traveling American businessmen were no doubt many who had studied foreign languages in the "bad" old method – and most of them probably did as well in actual communication, since there were virtual taboos against the use of any language except English where Americans were present. Although few of them may have realized it, what they had been given in college may well have been just exactly what was needed for the kind of communication problem they faced as they traveled, for business or pleasure, about the world that spoke often fluent but frequently flawed English and was often grimly determined to use it. Even those populations that spoke non-Indo-European languages were frequently more fluent in a Romance language, especially French, than in English; the "interference" patterns of many such speakers were thus somewhat similar to the patterns of a native speaker of French or Spanish.

No one, so far as I know, has recently suggested going back to the old grammar-translation method of language teaching. It might, however, fill up a few more classes than the methods currently practiced, since a lot of students resent those weekly hours in the laboratory. Delattre (1968) did have a few good words to say about a text by Fraser and Squair, in its various editions, for grammar-translation-oriented teaching of French.

The use of English as a world language seems to be increasing rather than diminishing, even if England no longer has a dominant position in world affairs – despite whatever military prestige may have accrued from the Falkland Islands operation – and even the United States has occasionally seemed shaky in the past few years. Americans, who will probably continue to go abroad in great numbers in any forseeable future even though the number of Japanese tourists may occasionally exceed their number, will need a great deal of linguistic sophistication to understand this world use of "their" language. As foreign language class enrollment continues to decline, there needs to be a source of practical linguistic knowledge, especially of how to deal with "bizarre" forms. Study of variation patterns of American

English, particularly according to the new theories that take into account social differences and "inherent variability," may be just the replacement needed. The older studies of purely geographic variation, however, seemed to make no such contribution; it hardly helped to know about "Northern" and "Southern" dialect in a foreign country where a resident of Natchez, Mississippi, or Dallas, Texas, was called a "Yankee." Barring some drastic and largely unforeseen change, this generation will need some strategy for doing what earlier generations did, for understanding English with all kinds of foreign accents and patterns. It is, in fact, rather hard to see just what could fully replace the old fashioned study of foreign languages.

Within this context, it is of the utmost importance to English speakers that their language has entered a world phase. However fascinating it may be to speculate about hte home and habits of the Indo-Europeans, what we can learn about them is of doubtful value in understanding the language of many millions of people, especially when the ancestors of only a very small percentage of them were really Indo-European in any meaningful sense. One need only look at textbooks designed for History of the English Language classes, however, to realize how much emphasis is still placed on the reconstructive tradition and how little on the many worldwide varieties of English. American English itself still tends to be treated in connection with, or at least in the section following, the puristic tendencies of the eighteenth century.

This book has been predicated on the assumption that there are things more revealing about American English than the finding of a corner of rural England where a particular verb form or turn of phrase may have come from. In fact, it elucidates American English very little to place it within the conventions of the reconstructive tradition. Contrary to some recent assumptions, however, departing from the reconstructive tradition is not tantamount to abandoning all historical perspective.

It is conventional to moralize a bit about the usage patterns of the language at the end of a work on English language history. Many histories of English, specializing in or concentrating on Old and Middle English, have wound up with a super-modern admonition to school teachers and their ilk that users of the language – even Americans – are having their own way with English and that not much can be done about it. It was something of a triumph to establish the principle that American English is all right, that it isn't necessary for Americans to keep running back to London (or Oxford or Cambridge) every few years to replenish their language, to reestablish contact with the "real" English. The battle is perhaps not yet entirely won; in 1968, a student in Burundi informed me gravely that British teachers had taught them "standard" English and that I was teaching them "American" English, presumably a kind of nonstandard variety. Such statements are, however, at least a great deal less frequent now than they were in the past.

If we resist the back-to-England principle, we may find ourselves obligated to grant as much autonomy as we claim. International English is "British" or "American" only by the merest technicality. In the West Africa of Chinua Achebe and Amos Tutuola, a greatly different local flavor is hardly to be avoided – or deprecated. If Americans are now the main carriers of English about the globe, there is no law whatsoever that says speakers everywhere must try to talk like Americans. Most of them will not try, and of those few who do only a tiny percentage will have any noticeable success. "Foreigners" who find it useful to speak English – and in the current world situation it is hardly possible to predict how long they will continue to do so or to what extent – will make their own use of it. They will not come to any British or American dialect, not even to Network Standard, to have their English remedied. Furthermore, there is no more guarantee that an American or an Englishman can understand every variety of International English without special preparation than there was that an Italian could understand Old French or Old Spanish. It seems safe to predict that, the longer the language continues to be used by other populations, the more variety will come to be subsumed under what we call English.

Language study is thus an important part of the educational needs of at least some Americans. American English came to be in a highly multilingual context and many of us – perhaps increasing numbers in the next few decades – use it in almost equally multilingual circumstances. To understand its past, as well as to do what little we can to predict its future, we need to know how it relates to other languages. We need, also, to know as much as possible about other languages – if only to be able to understand what other populations are likely to believe is our own. There are many ways in which knowledge about other languages and about our own can be acquired. Even the old-fashioned method of sitting alone reading grammar books, although thoroughly out of fashion for a few decades, can have its uses.

Perhaps the greatest need, however, is the avoidance of dogmatism. "You can't learn the language unless you imitate the pronunciation of a native speaker" can be as deadly as the older, now probably no-more-repeated, "You don't really know any language unless you know Latin." For American English speakers, it may be most important to realize that one need not be praised for his mastery of a foreign language to have profited from its study.

Competitors for English as the world lingua franca have a way of fading. The recent decline of the economic power, based on petroleum, of Arabic-speaking countries makes it seem unlikely that that language will develop into a rival, although such a development seemed not unlikely a few years ago. Speakers of American English may have to go on for a long time trying to understand foreigners who have not imitated the native speaker very well.

References

A Language in Common.
1962   The Times Literary Supplement, London. No. 3,154 (Friday, August 10, 1962).
Aarons, Alfred C., Barbara Y. Gordon, and William A. Stewart, eds.
1969   *Linguistic-Cultural Differences and American Education.* Miami, 1969.
Abenethy, Francis Edward, ed.
1974   *The Folklore of Texas Cultures,* Austin, Texas, The Encino Press, 1974.
Abercrombie, David.
1955   *Problems and Principles: Studies in the Teaching of English as a Second Language.* London, 1955.
Abrahams, Roger D.
1964   *Deep Down in the Jungle . . .Negro Narrative Folklore from the Streets of Philadelphia,* Hatboro, Pa., Folklore Associates.
1976   *Talking Black,* Rowley, Mass., Newbury House.
Adair, James.
1930   *The History of the American Indians,* ed. Samuel Cole Williams, New York, Promontory Press, 1930.
Adams, Andy.
1931   *The Log of a Cowboy,* Boston & New York.
Adams, Charles C.
1971   *Boontling, An American Lingo,* Austin, Texas, The University of Texas Press.
Adams, Rev. James, S.R.E.S.
1799   *The Pronunciation of the English Language Vindicated from Imputed Anomaly and Caprice.* Edinburgh.
Adams, Ramon F.
1944, 1968   *Western Words, A Dictionary of the American West,* Norman, University of Oklahoma Press.
Alderson, William L.
1953   "Carnie Talk from the West Coast", *American Speech* 28:112-119.
Alegriá, Ricardo.
1954   *La Fiesta de Santiago Apostol en Loiza Aldea,* Madrid.
Alexander, Captain J.E.
1833   *Transatlantic Sketches,* London, Richard Bentley.
Algeo, John.
1960   "Korean Bamboo English", *American Speech* 35:117-23.
Allen, Harold B.
1973, 1975   *The Linguistic Atlas of the Upper Midwest,* University of Minnesota Press.
Allen, Harold B. and Gary Underwood.
1971   *Readings in American Dialectology,* (New York, Appleton Century-Crofts).
Allen, Harry E.
1959   *Bush and Backwoods,* East Lansing, Michigan State University Press.
Alleyne, Mervyn C.
1980   *Comparative Afro-American,* Ann Arbor, Karoma Press.
Alvarez-Nazario, Manuel
1974   *El Elemento Afronegröide en el Español de Puerto Rico,* San Juan de Puerto Ricó.
Anderson, Nels.
1923   *The Hobo; the Sociology of the Homeless Man,* Chicago, University of Chicago Press.
Andrews, Charles M.

1919   *The Fathers of New England, A Chronicle of the Puritan Commonwealth,* The Chronicles of America, Vol. 6
Armstrong, Virginia
1971   *I Have Spoken; American History through the Voices of Indians,* New York
Asbury, Herbert
1933   *The Barbary Coast,* New York.
1938   *Sucker's Progress,* reprinted 1966, Patterson Smith, Montclair, New Jersey.
Aspillera, Paraluman S.
1956   *Basic Tagalog for Foreigners and Non-Tagalogs,* Manila.
Atkins, John.
1737   *A Voyage to Guinea, Brasil, and the West Indies,* London.
Atwood, E. Bagby.
1953   *A Survey of the Verb Forms in the Eastern United States,* Ann Arbor, Michigan.
1962   *The Regional Vocabulary of Texas,* Texas University Press.
1963   (1971) "The Methods of American Dialectology", *Zeitschrift für Mundartforschung* (reprinted in Allen and Underwood, *Readings in American Dialectology,* pp. 5-35).
Babcock, C. Merton.
1949   "The Social Significance of the Language of the American Frontier," *American Speech* XXIV: 256-63.
Bach, Emmon and Robert T. Harms, eds.
1968   *Universals in Linguistic Theory,* New York.
Bailey, Beryl Loftman.
1965   "Towards a New Perspective in American Negro Dialectology", *American Speech* 40:171-77.
Bailey, Charles-James N.
1974   Review of Dillard, *Black English, Foundations of Language* 11:299-309.
1973   *Variation and Linguistic Theory,* Center for Applied Linguistics, Washington, D.C.
1982a   "Irish English and Caribbean Black English: Another Joinder," *American Speech,* 57: 237-239.
1982b   *On the Yin and Yang Nature of Language,* Ann Arbor, Karoma Press.
Bailey, Richard W. and Manfred Gorlach, eds.
1982   *English as a World Language,* Ann Arbor, University of Michigan Press.
Bailyn, Bernard.
1955   *The New England Merchants in the Seventeenth Century,* New York, Harper and Row.
Baker, Sydney J.
1966   *The Australian Language,* Sydney.
Banfield, Edmund James
1908   *The Confessions of a Beachcomber,* London, T.F. Unwin
Baratz, Joan C.
1969   "A Bidialectal Task for Determining Language Proficiency in Economically Disadvantaged Children", *Child Development* 40:889-901.
Baratz, Joan C., Roger W. Shuy, and Walter Wolfram.
1969   *Sociolinguistic Factors in Speech Identification,* Final Report, NIMH Grant No. 15048.
Barbot, John.
1732   *Description of the Coast of North and South Guinea; and of Ethiopia Inferior, Vulgarly Angola,* London.
Barnes, W.C.
1913   *Western Grazing Grounds and Forest Ranges,* Chicago.
Barrere, Albert and Charles G. Leland.
1889   *A Dictionary of Slang, Jargon, and Cant,* London.
Barry, Michael V.

1982   "Hiberno English", in Gorlach and Bailey, *Worldwide Varieties of English*, New Work.
Barsness, Larry.
    1962   *Gold Camp, Alder Gulch, and Virginia City, Montana*, Hastings House.
Bartelt, H. Guillermo.
    1980   "Semantic Overgeneralization in Apachian English Interlanguage", *Journal of English Linguistics* 15:10-20.
Bartlett, John Russell.
    1877   *Dictionary of Americanisms.*
Bascom, William R.
    1941   "Acculturation Among the Gullah Negroes", *American Anthropologist* 43:43-50.
Bateman, Rebecca.
    n.d.   "Attestations of Seminole Pidgin English from Florida", ms.
Baugh, Albert C. and Thomas Cable.
    1957,1978 *History of the English Language*, Third Edition, Englewood Cliffs, N.J., Prentice-Hall.
Baum, Paul.
    1976   "The Question of Decreolization in Papiamentu Phonology", *International Journal of the Sociology of Language* 7:83-93.
Baur, John E.
    1975   "Cowboys and Skypilots", in William M. Kramer, ed., *The American West and the Religious Experience*, Los Angeles, Western Study Series, pp. 41-70.
Beadle, John H.
    1873   *The Undeveloped West; or Five Years in the Territories*, Chicago, National Publishing Co.
    1878   *Western Wilds and the Men Who Redeem Them*, Philadelphia.
Beecher, Lyman and Joseph Harvey.
    1818   *Memoirs of Henry Obookiah, a Native of Owhyhee and a Member of the Foreign Mission School, Who Died at Cornwall, Conn., February 27, 1818, Aged 26 Years*, New Haven, Office of the Religious Intelligencer.
Bense, J.F.
    1939   *Dictionary of the Low Dutch Element in the English Vocabulary*, The Hague.
Bentley, Harold.
    1931   *A Dictionary of Spanish Terms in English, with Special Reference to the Southwest*, New York.
Berdan, Robert.
    1973   *Have/Got in the Speech of Anglo and Black Children*, Southwest Regional Laboratory Research and Development Paper 22.
Berger, Marshall.
    1980.   "New York City and the Antebellum South: The Maritime Connection", in Dillard, ed., *Perspectives on American English*, pp. 135-41.
Bernard, J.R.L.-B.
    1969   "On the Uniformity of Spoken Australian English", *Orbis* XVII: 63-73.
Berry, Jack.
    1961   "English Loanwords and Adaptations in Sierra Leone Krio", in R.B. LePage, ed., *Creole Language Studies* II, London.
Bettersworth, John K., ed.
    1961   *Mississippi in the Confederacy, As They Saw It*, Baton Rouge, LSU Press.
Beyer, Richard Lawrence.
    1932   "Robert Hunter, Royal Governor of New York: A Study in Colonial Administration", *Iowa University Studies in the Social Sciences*, X.
Bickerton, Derek.
    1972   Review of Dillard, ed., *Perspectives on Black English*, *Language* 53:466-69.
    1979   "The Status of *bin* in the Atlantic Creoles", in Hancock, ed., *Readings in Creole Studies.*
    1982   *Roots of Language*, Ann Arbor, Karoma Publishers.

Bickerton, Derek and Aquilas Escalante.
1970 "Palenquero: A Spanish-Based Creole of Northern Colombia", *Lingua* 24:254-67.
Bills, Garland D., ed.
1974 *Southwest Area Linguistics*, Institute for Cultural Pluralism, San Diego State University.
Billington, Ray Alden.
1956 *The Far Western Frontier*, New York, Harper and Brothers.
Birmingham, John.
1976 "Papiamentu: the Long-Lost Lingua Franca?", *The American Hispanist* 2:13.
1980 "Black English Near Its Roots: The Transplanted West African Creoles", in Dillard, ed., *Perspectives on American English*.
Bishop, Morris.
1971 "Four Indian Kings in London", *American Heritage*, December.
Blanc, Haim.
1954 *Communal Dialects of Baghdad Arabic*, Harvard Middle Eastern Monographs No. 10, Harvard University.
1968 "The Israeli Koiné as an Emergent National Standard", in Fishman, Ferguson, and das Gupta, eds., *Language Problems of Developing Nations*, New York.
Blanco, Tomas.
1955 *Anglicomodismos en el Vernáculo Puertorriqueño*, Havana, Sociedad Económica de Amigos del País I.
Blanton, Linda L.
1974 "The Verb System of Breathtitt County, Kentucky: A Sociolinguistic Analysis," Illinois Institute of Technology diss. (unpublished)
Blassingame, John W.
1972 *The Slave Community: Plantation Life in the Antebellum South*, New York, Oxford University Press.
1977 ed. *Slave Testimony: Two Centuries of Letters, Speeches, Interviews, and Autobiographies*, Baton Rouge, LSU Press.
Boatright, Mody C.
1949 *Folk Laughter on the American Froniter*, New York, The Macmillan Co.
Bolton, Herbert and Mary Ross.
1925 *The Debatable Land: A Sketch of the Anglo-Spanish Contest for the Georgia Country*, Berkeley, California.
Bossu, Jean-Bernard.
1925 (1962) *Travels in the Interior of America* (trans. Seymour Feiler), University of Oklahoma Press.
Botkin, B.A. and Alvin F. Harlow, eds.
1953 *A Treasury of Railroad Folklore*, New York, Crown Publishers.
Boucicault, Dion.
1861 *The Octoroon: or, Life in Louisiana*.
Bourke, John G.
1892 *On the Border with Crook*, New York.
Bowles, Samuel.
1869 *Our New West*, Hartford.
Bowman, Kent.
n.d. *Pidgin English Children's Stories*, Hula Records.
Bowman, Walter Parker and Robert Hamilton Ball.
1961 *Theatre Language*, New York, Theatre Arts Books.
Bradbury, John.
1817 *Travels in the Interior of America*, London.
Braddy, Haldeen.
1937 "Cowboy Lingo of the Texas Big Bend", *Dialect Notes* VI.
Bradford, William.

1896   *Bradford's History of Plymouth Plantation, From the Original Manuscript,* Boston, Wright and Potter Printing Company.
Branch, Douglas.
1961   *The Cowboy and His Interpreters,* New York, Cooper Square Publishers.
Brandt, Elizabeth A. and Christopher McCrate.
1979   "Multilingual Variation, or Contact Vernacular in the Southwest: Make Like Seem Heap Injin", American Ethnolingual Symposium, XLII International Congress of Americanists, Vancouver, Canada (abstract).
Brooks, Cleanth.
1935   *The Relation of the Alabama-Georgia Dialect to the Provincial Dialects of Great Britain,* Baton Rouge, LSU Press.
Brooks, Nelson.
1967   "Language Learning: The New Approach", *Florida FL Reporter.*
Browne, J. Ross.
1854   *Adventures in the Apache Country,* New York.
Bruce, Donald E. and John Walsh.
1983   "English in Guam and Micronesia", *English Around the World,* No. 28.
Brunwand, Jan.
1965   "Sailors' and Cowboys' Folklore in Two Popular Classics", *Southern Folklore Quarterly.*
Bryan, George.
1926   *Edison, The Man and His Work,* Garden City, N.Y., Doubleday.
Bryant, Margaret.
1962   *The English Language and Its History,* New York.
Bryden, James.
        An Acoustic and Social Dialect Analysis of Perceptual Variables in Listener Identification and Rating of Negro Speakers, U.S. Office of Education, Final Report Project No. 7-C-003.
Buckner, Mary Dale.
1933   "Ranch Diction of the Texas Panhandle", *American Speech* 8:25-32.
Burt, Marina K. and Carol Kiparsky.
1972   *The Gooficon, A Repair Manual for English,* Rowley, Mass., Newbury House.
Burton, Sir Richard.
1860   *The Look of the West,* London.
1863   *Wanderings in West Africa,* London.
Butters, Ronald R.
1983   "Can I Ax You about that Arruh," New York *Times* Magazine, 21 August, pp. 11-12.
Buxbaum, Katherine.
1929   "Some Iowa Locutions", *American Speech* 4:303.
Caballero, Ramon C.F.
1852   *La Juega de Gallos o El Negro Bozal, Comedia en dos actos y en prosa,* Ponce, Puerto Rico.
Cabrera, Lydia.
1951, 1971   *Anago, Vocabulario Lucumí del Yoruba Que Se Habla en Cuba,* Miami, Mnemosyne Publication Co.
1959   *La Sociedad Secreta Abakua, Narrada por Viejos Adeptos,* Havana.
1968   *El Monte, Igbo, Finda, Ewe, Orishi, Vititi, Nfinda,* Miami.
1969   "Ritual y símbolos de la Iniciación en la Sociedad Secreta Abakua", *Journal de la Societé des Américanistes* LVIII:139-71.
Cade, John Brother.
1935   "Out of the Mouths of Ex-Slaves", *Journal of Negro History* 20:294-337.
Campbell, Duncan.
1873   *Nova Scotia in Its Historical, Mercantile, and Industrial Relations,* Montreal.
Campbell, E.C.
1928   "Down Among the Red Men", *Kansas State Historical Society Review,* XVII.

Candler, Isaac
    1824   A Summary View of America, London.
Carawan, Candie and Guy Carawan.
    1967   *Ain't You Got a Right to the Tree of Life?*, New York.
Carey, Mathew.
    1787   "Account of a Buyer of Bargains", *The American Museum or Repository*.
Carr, J.W. and G.O. Chase.
    1910   "A Word List from Aroostook", *Dialect Notes* III:407-18.
Carr, J.W. and Rupert Taylor.
    1910   "A List of Words from Northwest Arkansas", *Dialect Notes* III:392-406.
Cassidy, Frederic G.
    1961   *Jamaica Talk: Three Hundred Years of the English Language in Jamaica*, London.
    1971   "Tracing the Pidgin Element in Jamaican Creole (with notes on method and the nature of pidgin vocabularies)", in Hymes, ed., *Pidginization and Creolization of Language*, Cambridge University Press.
    1977   "A Note on West-African Pidgin English", *Names* 25:182.
    1978   "Another Look at Buckaroo", *American Speech*, pp. 49-51.
Cassidy, Frederic G. and David DeCamp.
    1966   "Names for an Albino Among Jamaican Negroes", *Names* 14:129-33.
Cassidy, Frederic G. and Robert B. LePage.
    1967   *Dictionary of Jamaican English*, Cambridge University Press.
Catlin, George.
    1856   (1959, ed. Marvin C. Ross) *Illustrations of the Manners, Customs, and Conditions of the North American Indians*, London.
    1874   *Life Among the Indians*, London.
Cebollero, Pedro.
    1945   *A School Language Policy for Puerto Rico*, San Juan.
Chase, George Davis.
    1942   "Sea Terms Come Ashore", *The Maine Bulletin* 44(8).
Chomsky, A. Noam.
    1966   *Cartesian Linguistics*, New York.
Chomsky, A. Noam and Morris Halle.
    1968   *The Sound Pattern of English*, New York.
Christian, Donna,
    1978   "Aspects of Verb Usage in Appalachian Speech," Georgetown University diss. (unpublished).
Christophersen, Paul.
    1953   "Some Special West African English Words", *English Studies* 34:282-91.
    1959   "A Note on the Words *dash* and *ju-ju* in Western African English", *English Studies* 39:115-18.
Clark, Joseph G.
    1847   *Lights and Shadows in Sailor Life*, Boston.
Clark, Ross
    1983   "Social Contexts of Early South Pacific Pidgins", in Woolford and Washabaugh, eds., *The Social Context of Creolization*, pp. 10-27.
Clark, Virginia P., Paul A. Eschholz, and Alfred R. Rosa, eds.
    1972   *Language: Introductory Readings*, New York.
Clarkson, John.
    1792   Journal, August 6, 1791 through March 18, 1792, Howard University Library manuscript.
Clayton, Lawrence.
    1983   "Satiric Humor in Carter's *The Education of Little Tree*", in Nilsen and Nilsen, eds., *The Language of Humor and the Humor of Language*, Arizona State University.
Cleaver, Eldridge.
    1968   *Soul on Ice*, New York, McGraw Hill.

Cody, Iron Eyes.
   1970   *Indian Talk, Hand Signals of the American Indians*, Healdsburg, Cal.,
          Naturegraph Publishers.
Colcord, Joanna Carver.
   1945   *Sea Language Comes Ashore*, New York.
Coleman, William Macon.
   1881   *The History of the Primitive Yankees, or the Pilgrim Fathers in England and
          Holland*, Washington, D.C.
Coleridge, Henry N.
   1826   *Six Months in the West Indies in 1825*, London.
Coltharp, Lurline Hughes.
   1964   *The influence of English on the "language" of the tirilones*. University of
          Texas (Austin), unpublished Ph.D. diss.
Combs, Josiah H.
   1916   "Old, early, and Elizabethan English in the southern mountains," *Dialect
          Notes* 4: 283-97.
Cook James.
   1854   *Fifty Years of the Old Frontier*, Norman, University of Oklahoma Press.
Cook, Minnie.
   1976   *Apostle to the Pima Indians*, Tiburon, California, Omega Books.
Cornelius, Ed.
   1955   *How to Learn a Foreign Language*, New York.
Covington, Michael A.
   1981   "Computer Terminology: Words for New Meanings", *American Speech*
          64-71.
Craigie, William A. and James R. Hulbert, eds.
   1938-44 *A Dictionary of American English on Historical Principles*, University of
           Chicago Press.
Crane, Verner W.
   1929   *The Southern Frontier, 1670-1732*, Philadelphia.
Cremony, John C.
   1968   *Life Among the Apaches*, San Francisco.
Creswell, Nicholas
   1924   *The Journal of Nicholas Creswell, 1774-77*, London.
Crèvecoeur, Michel Guillaume Jean de.
   1782   *Letters from an American Farmer*, London.
Crofutt, George A.
   1871 *Transcontinental Tourist Guide*.
Crouch, Nathaniel.
   1704   *Two Journeys to Jerusalem*, London.
Crow, Hugh
   (1791), 1970 *Memoirs of the Late Hugh Crow of Liverpool*, Frank Cass and Co, Ltd.
Dalby, David.
   1969   *Black Through White: Patterns of Communication in Africa and the New
          World*, Hans Wolff Memorial Lecture, Bloomington, Indiana.
   1972   "The African Element in Black American English", in Thomas Kochman,
          ed., *Rappin' and Stylin' Out*, University of Illinois Press.
Dana, Richard Henry.
   1840   *Two Years Before the Mast*, New York.
Daniels, Harvey A.
   1983   *Famous Last Words, The American Language Crisis Reconsidered*, Carbon-
          dale, Southern Illinois University Press.
Danker, Donald F., ed.
   1959   *Mollie: The Journal of Mollie Dorsey Sanford in Nebraska and Colorado
          Territories, 1857-1866*, University of Nebraska Press.
Daughen, Joseph R. and Peter Binzen.
   1971   *The Wreck of the Penn Central*, Boston, Little, Brown.

Davis, John.
  1909   *Travels of Four Years and a Half in the United States of America During 1798, 1799, 1800, 1801, and 1802*, New York.
Davis, Lawrence M.
  1971   "A Study of Appalachian Speech in a Northern Urban Setting," US O. of E. Report OEG-5-70-0046 (509)
Davis, Ossie.
  1967   "The English Language Is My Enemy", *American Teacher* LV, 13, 18.
DeBose, Charles E.
  n.d.   *A Reanalysis of the Black English Verb System as Decreolization.* Manuscript.
DeCamp, David.
  1967   "African Day Names in Jamaica", *Language* 43:139-47.
  1971   "Introduction: The Study of Pidgin and Creole Languages", in Hymes, ed., *Pidginization and Creolization of Languages.*
D'Eloia, Sarah G.
  1973   "Issues in the Analysis of Nonstandard Negro English: A Review of J.L. Dillard's *Black English*", *Journal of English Linguistics* 7:87-106.
de Goeje, C.H.
  1908   *Verslag der Toemoekhoemakexpeditie*, Leiden.
de Granda, German.
  1972   *Transculturación e Interferencia Lingüística en el Puerto Rico Contemporaneo (1898-1968)*, Bogotá.
de Josselin deJong, Jan Petrus Benjamin.
  1924   "Het Negerhollandsch Van St. Thomas in St. Jan", *Mededelingen der Koninklijke Akademie. . .*, Deel 57, Serie A, no. 3, pp. 55-71.
Delattre, Genevieve
  1968   "The Changing Aspects of Teaching French," in Roucek (ed.) *The Study of Foreign Languages*, New York.
Delattre, Pierre
  1966   *Studies in French and Comparative Phonetics*, The Hague, Mouton
Deutsch, Cynthia.
  1964   "Auditory Discrimination and Learning: Social Factors", *Merrill-Palmer Quarterly*, 10:171-96.
Dewees, William B.
  1852   *Letters from an Early Settler of Texas Complied by Cara Cordelle* (pseudonym), Louisville, Kentucky, Morton and Griswold..
Diaz Soler, Luis M.
  1974   *Historia de la Esclavitud Negra en Puerto Rico*, Rió Piedras, Editorial Universitaria.
Dick, Everett N.
  1926-28 "The Long Drive", *Collections of the Kansas Historical Society*, XVII.
  1941   *Vanguards of the Frontier*, New York.
  1944   *The Sod House Frontier*, New York.
  1948   *The Dixie Frontier, A Social History of the Southern Frontier from the First Transmontane Beginnings to the Civil War*, New York.
Dickens, Charles.
  1842   *American Notes*, London.
  1844   *Martin Chuzzlewit*, London.
Dickinson, Johnathan.
  1944   *Jonathan Dickinson's Journal: or, God's Protecting Providence, Being the Narrative of a Journey from Port Royal in Jamaica to Philadelphia Between August 23, 1696, and April 1, 1697*, ed. Evangeline Walker Andrews and Charles McLean Andrews, New Haven, Yale University Press.
Dictionary of Canadianisms on Historical Principles.
  1967   Toronto.

Dike, K.O.
1956   *Trade and Politics in the Niger Delta*, Oxford.
Dillard, J.L.
1972a   *Black English, Its History and Usage in the United States*, New York: Random House.
1972b   "On the Beginnings of Black English in The New World", *Orbis* 21:523-536.
1972c   "The Neglected Side of Afro-American Communication", unpublished paper.
1973   "The History of Black English in Nova Scotia – A First Step", *African Language Review* (Also *Inter-American Review*).
1975   ed. *Perspectives on Black English*, The Hague, Mouton.
1976a   *American Talk, Where Our Words Came From*, New York, Random House.
1976b   *Black Names*, The Hague, Mouton.
1977   *A Lexicon of Black English, The Words the Slaves Made*, New York, Continuum Books.
1980   *Perspective on American English*, The Hague, Mouton.
1983   "Black English: Two Approaches", *Language Policy and Language Planning*, Vol. 7, No. 2:179-187.
Dodge, James W., ed.
1972   *Other Words, Other Worlds; Language-in-Culture*, Reports of the Working Committee, Northeast Conference on the Teaching of Foreign Languages, Montpelier, Vermont, Capital City Press.
Dodge, Lt. Richard Irving.
1876   *The Black Hills*, New York, James Miller.
Dollard, John.
1937   *Class and Caste in a Southern Town*, New Haven.
Drago, Harry Sinclair.
1965   *Red River Valley*, New York, Clarkson N. Potter.
Drechsel, Emanuel J.
1976   "'Ha! now me stomany that!' A Summary of Pidginization and Creolization of North American Indian Languages", *International Journal of the Sociology of Language* 7:63-81.
1979   *Mobilian Jargon: Linguistic, Sociocultural, and Historical Aspects of an American Indian Lingua Franca*, University of Wisconsin-Madison dissertation.
Drechsel, Emanuel J. and T. Haunani Makuakane.
1982   "Hawaiian Loanwords in Two Native American Pidgins", *International Journal of American Linguistics* 48, No. 4 (Oct.):460-66.
Dresel, Gustav.
1954   *Houston Journal: Adventures in North America and Texas 1837-1841*, translated from the German by Max Freund, Texas University Press.
Dubois, Betty Lou and Isabel M. Crouch.
1983   "He/She, S/He, He or She", in Nilsen and Nilsen, eds., *The Language of Humor, The Humor of Language*, pp. 208-210.
Dulay, Heidi C. and Marina K. Burt.
1974   "Natural Sequences in Child Second Language Acquisition", *Language Learning* 24:37-53.
Dulag, Heidi, Marina Burt, and Stephen Krashen
1982   *Language Two*, New York, Oxford University Press.
Dulles, Foster Rhea.
1930   *The Old China Trade*, Boston.
Dunn, Milton.
1920   "History of Natchitoches", *The Louisiana Historical Quarterly* III:26-56.
Durham, Philip L. and Everett L. Jones.
1965   *The Negro Cowboys*, New York.
Duval, John Crittenden.
1870   *The Adventures of Big-foot Wallace*, Philadelphia.
Eagleson, Robert D.

1982   "English in Australia and New Zealand", in Bailey and Gorlach, *English as a World Language*, pp. 415-38.

Eastman and Reese
1981
Eddis, William.
1770   (1969, ed. Aubrey C. Land) *Letters from America*, (Cambridge, Belknap Press of Harvard University Press.
1770   (1917) *A Narrative of a Tour Through Hawaii, or Owhyhee; with Remarks on the History, Traditions, Manners, Customs, and Language of the Inhabitants of the Sandwich Islands*, Honolulu, Hawaiian Gazette.

Esau, Helmut, Norman Bagnall, and Cheryl Ware.
1982   "Faulkner, Literary Criticism and Linguistics", *Journal of the Linguistic Association of the Southwest* IV:275-302.

Escabí, Pedro C., ed.
n.d.   *Morovis: Vista Parcial del Folklore de Puerto Rico*, Universidad de Puerto Rico, Centro de Investigaciones Sociales.

Escalante, Aquilas.
1954   "Notas sobre el Palenque de San Basilio, una Communidad Negro en Colómbia", *Divulgaciones Etnológicas* 3:207-359.

Eskew, Harry and Elizabeth Eskew.
1954   *Alexandria and Old Red River Country*, El Paso, Texas, Southwest Heritage Press.

Evarand, Wayne M.
1972   "Bourbon City, New Orleans", *Louisiana Studies* XI:240-51.

Faine, Jules.
1936   *Philologie Créole*, Port-au-Prince, Impr. de l'Etat.
1939   *Le Creole dans l'Univers*, Port-au-Prince, Impr. de l'Etat.

Fairclough, G. Thomas.
1960   " 'New light' on 'Old Zion' ", *Names*.

Falconbridge, Maria.
1794   *Two Voyages to Sierra Leone*, London.

Falconer, William.
1805   *The Mariner's Dictionary*.

Farmer, John Stephen and W.E. Henley.
1897   (1965) *Slang and Its Analogues*, New York.

Farrison, William Edward.
1936   *The Phonology of the Illiterate Negro Dialect of Guilford County, North Carolina*, Ohio State University dissertation.

Fasold, Ralph.
1969   "Tense and the form *be* in Black English", *Language* 45 (Dec.):763-76.
1975   Review of Dillard, *Black English*, in *Language in Society* 4:198-225.
1981   "The Relation Between Black and White Speech in the South", *American Speech* 56:163-89.

Fasold, Ralph and Roger W. Shuy, eds.
1970   *Teaching Standard English in the Inner City*, Washington, D.C.

Feagin, Crawford.
1979   *Variation and Change in Alabama English: A Sociolinguistic Study of the White Community*, Washington, D.C., Georgetown University Press.

Feinsilver, Lilian Mermin.
1970   *The Taste of Yiddish*, New York.

Ferguson, Charles.
1959   "Diglossia", *Word* 15:325-40.

Ferguson, Charles, Joshua Fishman, and J. das Gupta, eds.
1968   *Language Problems of Developing Nations*, New York.

Ferguson, Charles A. and John J. Gumperz
1960   Introduction to "Linguistic Diversity in South Asia" Indiana University Research Center in Anthropology, Folklore, and Linguistic, 13: 1-8.

Ferguson, Charles and Shirley Brice Heath, eds.
1981   *Language in the USA*, Cambridge, Cambridge University Press.
Ferguson, William.
1856   *America by River and Rail*, London.
Fernández, Roberto G.
1983   "English Loanwords in Miami Cuban Spanish", *American Speech* Spring pp. 13-21.
Ferraz, Luis
1976   "The Substratum of Annobonese Creole," *International Journal of the Sociology of Language* 7: 37-48
Fickett, Joan.
1970   *Aspects of morphemics, syntax, and semology of an inner-city dialect (Merican)*, West Rush, NY, Meadowood Publications.
Fisher, Miles Mark.
1953   *Negro Slave Songs in the United States*, New York, The Citadel Press.
Fisher, Ruth A.
1924   *Extracts from the Records of the African Companies*, Washington, D.C.
Fisher, Sydney G.
1919   *The Quaker Colonies: A Chronicle of the Proprietors of the Delaware.*
Fishman, Joshua A.
1964   "Language Maintenance and Language Shift as Fields of Inquiry", *Linguistics* 9:32-70.
1965   "Who Speaks What Language to Whom and When?" *La Linguistique* 2:67-88.
1966   *Language Loyalty in the United States*, The Hague.
1968   ed. *Readings in the Sociology of Language*, The Hague.
Fishman, Joshua A., R.L. Cooper, Roxana Ma, et al., eds.
1968   *Bilingualism in the Barrio*. Final Report to DHEW under contract no. OEC 1-7-061817-1297, New York.
Fiske, John.
1889   *The Beginnings of New England, or The Puritan Theocracy in Its Relation to Civil and Religious Liberty*, Boston & New York: Houghton, Mifflin & Co.
Flick, Alexander C., ed.
1938   *History of the State of New York*, Columbia University Press.
Folb, Edith A.
1980   *Runnin' Down Some Lines, The Language and Culture of Black Teenagers*, Harvard University Press
Foner, Philip S., ed.
1947   *Jack London, American Rebel*, New York, The Citadel Press.
Forbes, Jack D.
1962   *The Indian in America's Past*, Englewood Cliffs, New Jersey, Prentice-Hall.
1966   *Mexican-Americans, A Handbook for Educators.*
1967   *Nevada Indians Speak*, Reno, University of Nevada Press.
Foreman, Grant.
1926   "Notes from the Indian Advocate", *Chronicles of Oklahoma* 14:76-79.
Fortier, Alcee.
1891   "The Acadians of Louisiana and Their Dialect", *Publications of the Modern Language Association* VI:1-33.
Foster, Brian.
1968   *The Changing English Language*, New York.
Foster, Herbert Lawrence.
1974   *Ribbin', Jivin', and Playin' the Dozens: The Unrecognized Dilemma of Inner City Schools*, Cambridge, Mass., Ballinger Publishing Co.
Frake, Charles O.
1971   "Lexical Origins and Semantic Structures in Philippine Creole Spanish", in Hymes, ed., *Pidginization and Creolization of Languages*, Cambridge University Press.

Francis, W. Nelson
   1958   *The Structure of American English*, New York, Ronald Press
   1961   "Some Dialectal Verb Forms in England", *Orbis*.
Fraser, Colin
   1982   *Advances in the Social Psychology of Language*, Cambridge University Press
Frazier, E. Franklin.
   1957   *Black Bourgeoisie: The Rise of a New Middle Class*, New York.
   1963   *The Negro Church in America*, New York: Schocken Books.
Freeman, Edward.
   1883   *Some Impressions of the United States.*
Fries, Charles Carpenter
   1940   *American English Grammar*, New York, Appleton-Centuru-Crofts
Fyfe, Christopher.
   1962   *History of Sierra Leone*, Freetown.
Garrell, Julia Kathryn.
   1939   *Green Flag Over Texas*, Dallas.
Garvin, Paul.
   1959   "The Standard Language Problem: Concepts and Methods", *Anthropological Linguistics* 1:28-31.
Geipel, Jan.
   1971   *The Viking Legacy, The Scandinavian Influence on the English and Gaelic Languages*, Davis & Charles Newton Abbot.
Genovese, Eugene D.
   1974   *Roll, Jordan, Roll; The World the Slaves Made*, New York, Pantheon Books.
Giddings, Joshua R.
   1858   *The Exiles of Florida*, Columbus, Ohio.
Gilbert, Glenn G., ed.
   1970   *Texas Studies in Bilingualism*, Berlin, Walter de Gruyter.
Gilman, Charles.
   1979   "Cameroonian Pidgin English: A Neo-African Language", in Hancock, Polome, Goodman, and Heine, eds., *Readings in Creole Studies*.
Gipson, Lawrence Henry.
   1936   (1960) *The British Isles and the American Colonies, Vol. III, The Northern Plantations 1748-1754*, New York, Alfred A. Knopf.
Goddard, Yves.
   1977   "Some Early Examples of American Indian Pidgin English from New England", *international Journal of American Linguistics* 43:37-41.
   1978   "A Further Note on Pidgin English", *International Journal of American Linguistics* 44:73.
Goedel, Gustav.
   1902   *Der Deutsche Seemansprache*, Kiel.
Goilo, E.R.
   1962   *Papiamentu Textbook*, Aruba.
Gold, Robert S.
   1975   *Jazz Talk, A Dictionary of the Colorful Language That Emerges from America's Own Music*, Indianapolis, Bobbs-Merrill Co.
Gonzalez, Ambrose.
   1964   *The Black Border*, Columbia, South Carolina.
Goveia, Elsa V.
   1965   *Slave Society in the British Leeward Islands at the End of the Eighteenth Century*, Yale University Press.
Grade, P.
   1892   "Das Neger-Englisch an der Westkuste von Afrika", reprinted in Dillard, ed. *Perspectives on Black English* (1973) pp. 109:142.
Graham, Stephen.
   1914   "The American Language", in *With Poor Immigrants to America*, New York.

Granville, Stuart.
    1925   *Forty Years on the Frontier*, edited by Paul C. Phillips, Cleveland.
    1962   *A Dictionary of Sailors' Slang*, London.
Grant, William and David D. Munson, eds.
    1931-   *The Scottish National Dictionary*, Edinburgh, The Scottish National History
               Association
Greaves, Ida C.
    1930   *The Negro in Canada*, McGill Economic Studies.
Green, Archie.
    1972   *Only a Miner*, Urbana, University of Illinois Press.
Green, Lawrence G.
    1962   *Islands Time Forgot*, London.
Greene, Lorenzo J.
    1942a   "Slave Holding New England and Its Awakening", *Journal of Negro History*
               XII:495-533.
    1942b   *The Negro in Colonial New England 1620-1776*, Columbia University
               Studies in History, Economics and Public Law No. 494.
Greenway, John
    1950   "Australian cattle lingo," *American Speech* 33: 163-9
Gregg, Josiah
    1844   *Commerce of the Prairies*, Dallas
Gumperz, John
    1958a   "Dialect and Social Stratification in a North Indian Village," *American
               Anthropologist*, 60: 668-692;
    1958b   "Phonological Differences in Three Hindi Dialects." *Languages*, 34: 212-224.
Gutman, Herbert G.
    1975   *Slavery and the Number Game*, Urbana, University of Illinois Press.
Hackenberg, Robert
    1972   *Appalachian English, A Sociolinguistic Study*, Georgetown University
               dissertation
Hakluyt, Richard
    1850   *Divers Voyages*. London, The Hakluyt Society
Hall, Robert A., Jr.
    1983   Review of Ingueld Broch & Ernest Huban, *Russe-norsk: Pidginsprak in
               Norge*, in *Language* 59 No. 3: 668-75.
Hall, Susan
    1972   *Gentleman of Leisure*, New York, Rapoport Printing Corp.
Haman, James Blanding.
    1939   *The Growth of the use of Negro Dialect in American Verse and Short Story
               to 1900*, Duke University M.A. Thesis, unpublished.
Hamilton, Alexander.
    1907   *Hamilton's Itinerarium, Being a Narrative of a Journey from Annapolis
               Maryland. . .from May to September, 1744*, St. Louis, Mo.
Hamilton, Thomas.
    1833   *Men and Manners in America*, Philadelphia.
Hammarstrom, Goran.
    1980   *Australian English*, Helmut Buske Verlag, Hamburg.
Hancock, Ian F.
    1969   "A Provisional Comparison of the English-based Atlantic Creoles", *African
               Language Review* 7:7-72.
    1971   *A Study of the Sources and Development of the Lexicon of Sierra Leone
               Krio*, unpublished dissertation, School of Oriental and African Languages,
               University of London.
    1972   "A Domestic Origin for the English-derived Atlantic Creoles", *Florida FL
               Reporter* 10:9-11.

1975   "Lexical Expansion Within a Closed System", in Ben Blount and Mary Sanches, eds., *Sociocultural Dimensions of Language Change*, pp. 161-71, New York, Academic Press.
1976   "Nautical Sources of Krio Vocabulary", *International Journal of the Sociology of Language* 7:23-36.
1979   ed., with Edgar Polome, Morris Goodman, and Bemt Heine, *Readings in Creole Studies*, Ghent, E. Story-Scientia.
1980   "Texas Gullah: The Creole English of the Bracketville Afro-Seminoles", in J.L. Dillard, ed., *Perspectives on American English*, The Hague, Mouton, pp. 257-64.
Forthcoming "A Preliminary Classification of the Anglophone/Atlantic Creoles, with Syntactic Data from 23 Representative Dialects", in Glen Gilbert, ed., *Pidgin and Creole Languages: Essays in Honor of John E. Reineche*, Ann Arbor, Karoma.
Forthcoming "On the Anglophone Creole Item *Kekrebu*", *American Speech*.
n.d.   "Malacca Creole Portuguese", manuscript.
Handler, Jerome S. and Charlotte J. Frisbie.
1972   "Aspects of Slave Life in Barbados: Music and its Cultural Aspects", *Caribbean Studies* II:5-46.
Hansen, Marcus Lee
1940   *The Atlantic Migration 1607-1860: A History of the Continuing Settlement of the United States*, Cambridge, Harvard University Press.
1940   *The Immigrant in American History*, Cambridge, Harvard University Press.
n.d.   "The Problem of the Third Generation Immigrant", *Augustana Historical Society Publications*.
Harder, Kelsie B.
1976   *Illustrated Dictionary of Place Names, United States and Canada*, New York: Van Nostrand Reinhold Co.
Harrison, J.W.
1880   "Negro English", *Anglia*.
Harvey, Bartle T.
1913   "A Word List from the Northwest," *Dialect Notes* 4.
Harvey, Gina.
1974   "Dormitory English: Implications for the Teacher", in Bills, ed, *Southwest Area Linguistics*.
Haskins, Jim and Hugh F. Butts.
1973   *The Psychology of Black Language*, New York.
Haugen, Einar.
1956   *Bilingualism in the Americas: A Bibliography and Research Guide*, University, Alabama.
1958   "Language Contact", in *Proceedings of the Eighth International Congress of Linguists*, Oslo.
1969   *The Norwegian Language in America: A Study of Bilingual Behavior*, University of Pennsylvania Press.
Hayden, Marie Gladys.
1915   "Terms of Disparagement in American Dialect Speech", *Dialect Notes*, IV.
Hayward, Jane Screven.
1923   *Brown Jackets*, Columbia, South Carolina.
Hellman, John
1973   "I'm a Monkey; The Influence of the Black American Blues Argot on the Rolling Stones," *Journal of American Folklore* 86: 367-73
Hench, Atcheson.
1937   "Kentucky Pioneers", *American Speech* 12:75-6.
Herlein, J.D.
1718   *Beschryvinge van de Volksplantingne Zuriname*, Leeuwarden.
Herman, Lewis and Marguerite Shalett Lewis.
1943   *Foreign Dialects: A Manual for Actors, Directors and Writers*, New York.

1947 *American Dialects for Actors, Directors, and Writers*, New York.
Hernandez, William J. and Henry S. Johnson.
1971 *Educating the Mexican American*, Valley Forge, Pennsylvania.
Herndobler, Robin and Andrew Sledd.
1976 "Black English – Notes on the Auxiliary", *American Speech* 51:185-200.
Herskovits, Melville J.
1942 *The Myth of the Negro Past*, Boston.
Herskovits, Melville J. and Frances Herskovits.
1936 *Suriname Folk-Lore*, Columbia University Contributions to Anthropology 27.
Hesseling, Dirk Christian.
1905 "Het Negerholands der Deense Antillen. Bijdrage tot de geschiedris der Nederlandse taal in America", Leiden, A.W. Sijthoff.
Highfield, Arnold and Albert Valdman, eds.
1981 *Historicity and Variation in Creole Studies*, Ann Arbor, Karoma Press.
Hill, Archibald A.
1975 "Habituative Aspects of Verb in Black English, Irish English, and Standard English", *American Speech* 54:223-4.
1979 "*Buckaroo* Once More", *American Speech* 54:151-3.
Hills, E.C.
1928 "Linguistic Substrata of American English", *American Speech* 4:43-47.
Hirshberg, Jeffrey A.
1982a Review of Dillard, *Lexicon of Black English, American Speech* 57: 52-73
1982b "Towards a Dictionary of Black American English on Historical Principles," *American Speech* 57: 163-82
Hitchcock, Ethan Allen.
1833 (1930) *A Traveller in Indian Territory*, Cedar Springs, Iowa.
Hobart, Benjamin.
1866 *A History of the Town of Abingdon, Plymouth County, Massachusetts*, Boston.
Hockett, Charles.
1958 *A Course in Modern Linguistics*, New York.
Hoenigswald, Henry M.
1960 *Language Change and Linguistic Reconstruction*, University of Chicago Press.
Hoetink, Harmannus.
1962 "Americans in Samaná", *Caribbean Studies* II:3-22.
Holbrook, Stewart H.
1947 (1981) *The Story of American Railroads*, New York, American Legacy Press.
Hollinger, Robert E.
1948 "DeQuincy's Use of Americanisms", *American Speech* 23:204-209.
Holm, John A.
1980 "African Features in White Bahamian English", *English World-Wide*, I:45-65.
1983 ed. *Central American English*, Heidelberg, Julius Gros Verlag.
1983 "On the Relationship Between Gullah and Bahamian", *American Speech* 58:303-318.
Holm, John A. and Alison W. Shilling.
1982 *A Dictionary of Bahamian English*, Cold Spring, New York, Lexik House Publishers.
Horsmanden, Daniel P.
1744 *The New York Conspiracy, or a History of the Negro Plot, with the Journal of the Proceedings against the Conspirators at New York in the Years 1741-2*, New York.
Hotten J. C.
1877 *The Slang Dictionary*, London.
Hubbard, Claude.
1968 "The Language of Ruxton's Mountain Men", *American Speech*, pp. 216-21.

Hulbert, Archer B.
1929   *Frontiers, the Genius of American Nationality*, Boston.
Hull, Alexander.
1979   "On the Origin and Chronology of the French-based Creoles", in Hancock, ed., *Readings in Creole Studies*, Ghent, E. Story-Scientia.
Humphrey, David.
1815   *The Yankee in England: A Drama in Five Acts.*
Hymes, Dell, ed.
1971   *Pidginization and Creolization of Languages*, Cambridge University Press.
Inge, M. Thomas
1977   "The Appalachian backgrounds of Billy DeBeck's Snuffy Smith," *Appalachian Journal* 4: 120-32
Ingraham, Joseph Holt.
1835   *The Southwest by a Yankee*, New York.
Irving, Washington.
1885, 1895   *Astoria, Anecdotes of an Enterprise Beyond the Rocky Mountains*, New York. G.P. Putnam's Sons.
Isley, Bliss
1939   Blazing the Way West, London.
Jackson, Blyden.
1976   *The Waiting Years, Essays in American Negro Literature*, Baton Rouge, La., LSU Press.
James, G.L.
1892   *Shall I Try Australia?*, London.
Janson, Charles William.
1807   *Stranger in America*, London.
Jensen, Arthur R.
1981   *Straight Talk about Mental Tests*, New York, Free Press
Jenson, Kenneth Michael.
1980   *A Longitudinal Study of Certain Morphemes in the Interlanguage of Indonesian Learners of English as a Foreign Language*, University of Texas, Austin, dissertation.
Jespersen, Otto.
1964   *Mankind, National and Individual from a Linguistic Point of View*, Bloomington, Indiana.
John, Elizabeth A.H.
1983   "Portrait of a Wichita Village, 1808", *Chronicles of Oklahoma* LX. No. 4 (Winter):412-437.
Jones, C.
1972   *An Introduction to Middle English*, New York, Holt, Rinehart, and Winston, Inc.
Jones, E.C.
1962   "Mid-Nineteenth Century Evidences of a Sierra Leone Patois", *Sierra Leone Language Review* I:19-26.
Jones, LeRoi.
1963   *Blues People, Negro Music in White America*, New York, W. Morrow.
Jones, Morgan E.
1962   *A Phonological Study of English as Spoken by Puerto Ricans Contrasted with Puerto Rican Spanish and American English*, University of Michigan dissertation.
Jordan, Terry.
1966   *German Seed in Texas Soil*, Austin, University of Texas Press.
1972   "The Origin of *Mott* and *Island* in Texan Vegetation", *Southern Folklore Quarterly* 36:121-35.
1981   *Trails to Texas, Southern Roots of Western Cattle Ranching*, Lincoln, University of Nebraska Press.

Joyaux, Georges J.
   1965   "Foreign Languages and the Humanities", *The Modern Language Journal,* XLIX.
Joyce, P.W.
   1910   *English as We Speak It in Ireland,* London, Longman, Green & Co.
Julius, Jerry.
   1983   "Jewish Humor: Its History and Uniqueness", in Nilsen and Nilsen, eds., *The Language of Humor and the Humor of Language.*
Kahane, Henry and Renee Kahane.
   1976   "Lingua Franca: The Story of a Term", *Romance Philology* XXX:25-41.
Kahane, Henry, Renee Kahane, and A. Tietze.
   1958   *The Lingua Franca in the Levant, Turkish Nautical Terms of Italian and Greek Origin,* Urbana, Illinois, University of Illinois Press.
Katz, William Loren.
   1971   *The Black West,* Garden City, N.Y.
Kazasiz, Kostas.
   1970   "The Relative Importance of Parents and Peers in First Language Acquisition: The Case of Some Constaninoplian Families in Athens", *General Linguistics* 10, No. 2:111-20.
Kell, Katherine T.
   1966   "Folk Names for Tobacco", *Journal of American Folklore* 79:590-99.
Kelley, A. Tabouret.
   1968   "Sociological Factors of Language Maintenance and Shift", in Ferguson, Fishman, and das Gupta, eds., *Language Problems of Developing Nations,* New York.
Kendall, George Wilkins.
   1946   *Narrative of the Texas Santa Fe Expedition,* New York.
Kennedy, Stetson.
   1942   *Palmetto County,* New York, Duell, Sloan, and Pearce.
Kephart, Hurace
   1913   *Our Southern Highlanders,* New York, Outing.
Kime, Wayne R.
   1967   "Washington Irving and Frontier Speech", *American Speech* pp. 5-19.
Kittredge, George Lyman.
   1904   *The Old Farmer and His Almanac,* Boston, W. Ware and Co.
Kochman, Thomas, ed.
   1969   "Rapping in the Black Ghetto", *Trans-Action* 6:26-34.
   1970   "Toward an Ethnography of Black American Speech Behavior", in Whitten and Szwed, eds., *Afro-American Anthropology.*
   1972   *Rappin' and Stylin' Out: Communication in Urban Black American,* Urbana, Illinois, University of Illinois Press.
Krapp, George Phillip.
   1925   *The English Language in America,* New York.
   1969   ed. A. Marckwardt, *Modern English, Its Growth and Present Use,* New York, Charles Scribner's Sons.
Kurath, Hans.
   1928   "The Origin of Dialectal Differences in Spoken American English", *Modern Philology* XXV:385-95.
   1936   "The Linguistic Atlas of the United States and Canada", in D.B. Fry and Daniel Jones, eds., *Proceedings of the Second International Conference of Phonetic Sciences.*
   1964   (1971) "British Sources of Selected Features of American Pronunciation, Problems and Methods", in Fry et al., eds., *In Honor of Daniel Jones,* London, Longman, Green & Co., reprinted 1964 in Allen & Underwood 1971:265-72.
   1965   "Some Aspects of Atlantic Seaboard English Considered in Connection with British English", *Communications et Rapports, Troisieme Partie,* Louvain.

1968   "The Investigation of Urban Speech", *Publications of the American Dialect Society* 49:1-7.
1969   "English Sources of Some American Regional Words and Verb Forms", *American Speech* pp. 60-68.
1972   *Studies in Area Linguistics*, Bloomington and London, Indiana University Press.

Labov, William.
1963   "The Social Motivation of a Sound Change", *Word* 19:273-309.
1964   "Stages in the Acquisition of Standard English," in Shuy (ed.) *Social Dialects and Language Learning*, Champaign, Ill., NCTE.
1966   *The Social Stratification of English in New York City*, Washington, D.C., Center for Applied Linguistics.
1969   "Contraction, Deletion, and Inherent Variability in the English Copula", *Language* 45:715-62.
1972a *Language in the Inner City*, University of Pennsylvania Press.
1972b *Sociolinguistic Patterns*, University of Pennsylvania Press.
1972c "Academic Ignorance and Black Intelligence", *Atlantic Monthly* 229:59-67.
1972d "The Recent History of Some Dialect Markers on the Island of Martha's Vineyard", in L. Davis, ed., *Studies Presented to Raven* McDavid, University of Alabama Press.
1980   "Is There a Creole Speech Community?" in Valdman and Highfield, *Theoretical Orientations in Creole Studies*.

Labov, William, Paul Cohen, Clarence Robins, and John Lewis.
1968   *A Study of the Non-Standard English of Negro and Puerto Rican Speakers in New York City*, U.S. Office of Education Cooperative Research Project No. 3288, Final Report.

Laird, Charlton.
1970   *Language in America*, New York.

Lawson, Sarah
1983   *"Chauvinist," American Speech* 58: 92

Layton, C.W.T.
1955   *Dictionary of Nautical Words and Terms*, Glasgow.

Leckie, William H.
1967   *The Buffalo Soldiers*, University of Oklahoma Press.

Leechman, Douglas and Robert A. Hall, Jr.
1955   "American Indian Pidgin English: Attestations and Grammatical Peculiarities", *American Speech* 30:163-71.

Leland, John.
1900   *Pidgin English Sing-Song*, London.

Lentzner, Karl.
1892   *Wörterbuch der Englischen Volkssprache in Australien und einiger Englische Mischsprachen*, Halle-Leipzig.

Leonard, John William.
1910   *History of the City of New York*, New York.

Leopold, Werner F.
1959   "The Decline of German Dialects", *Word* 15:130-53.

LePage, Robert B., ed.
1961   *Proceedings of the Conference on Creole Language Studies*, Creole Language Studies II, London.

LePage, Robert B. and David DeCamp.
1960   *Jamaican Creole*, Creole Language Studies I, London.

"Letters of Rev. Jonathan Boucher".
1916   *Maryland Historical Magazine* X:15-36.

Levitt, John and Joan Levitt.

1959   *The Spell of Words,* London.
Life and Adventures of James P. Beckwourth.
1836   New York, Harper and Brothers.
Lifson, David S.
1969   *The Yiddish Press – An Americanizing Agency,* New York.
Lindquist, Gustavus E.
1923   *The Red Man in the United States,* New York.
Llorens, Washington.
1968   "Language of Germaniá en Puerto Rico", *El Habla Popular de Puerto Rico,* Cuaderno No. III.
Loflin, Marvin D.
1967   "A Note on the Deep Structure of Non-Standard English in Washington, D.C.", *Glossa* I:26-32.
1969   "Negro Non-Standard and Standard English: Same or Different Deep Structure?" *Orbis* XVIII:74-91.
Loflin, Marvin D. Nicholas Sobin, and J.L. Dillard.
1969   "Auxiliary Structures and Time Adverbs in Black American English", *American Speech* 48:22-36.
Lohrli, Anne.
1962   "Dickens's *Household Works* in American English", *American Speech* 1962: 83-94.
Lomax, Alan.
1959   *The Rainbow Sign,* New York.
1960   *The Folk Songs of America,* Garden City, New York, Doubleday & Co.
Lomax, John A. and Alan, eds.
1934   *American Ballads and Folk Songs,* New York, The Macmillan Co.
Lopes, David.
1936   *A Extensão do Portugues na Oriente,* Lisbon.
Luellsdorff, Phillip A.
1970   *A Segmental Phonology of Black English,* Georgetown University dissertation.
Mackay, Alex.
1850   *The Western World, or Travels in the United States in 1846-47,* London.
Major, Clarence.
1970   *Dictionary of Afro-American Slang,* New York, International Publishers.
Makkai, Adam, ed.
1975   *A Dictionary of American Idioms,* Woodbury, N.Y., Barron's Educational Series.
Maldonado-Denis, Manuel.
1972   *Puerto Rico: A Socio-Historic Interpretation,* New York, Random House.
Marckwardt, Albert.
1958   (1980) *American English,* revised by J.L. Dillard, Oxford University Press.
Marckwardt, Albert H. and Fred G. Walcott.
1938   *Facts About Current English Usage,* New York, Appleton Century-Crofts, Inc.
Marcy, Colonel R.B.
1866   *Thirty Years of Army Life on the Border,* New York.
Markey, T.L.
1983   "Focus on Creolists (7); Dirk Christian Hesseling", *The Carrier Pidgin,* Vol. 10, No. 2 (June) 1-2.
Markman, Alan M. and Erwin R. Steinberg.
1970   *English Then and Now: Readings and Exercises,* New York.
Marley; or the Life of a Planter in Jamaica.
1828   Glasgow.
Marryat, Captain Frederick.
1960   *Diary in America,* ed. Jules Zanger, Bloomington, Indiana University Press.
Martin, Charles B.
1983   "Unintentional Humor in the Written and Spoken Language of International

Students", in Nilsen and Nilsen, eds:, *The Language of Humor and the Humor of Language.*

Mason, Julian.
1960   "The Etymology of *Buckaroo*", *American Speech* XXV:51-5.

Masterson, Vincent Victor.
1952   *The Katy Railroad and the Last Frontier*, Norman, University of Oklahoma Press.

Mather, Cotton.
1721   *The Angel of Bethesda.*

Mathews, Mitford M.
1931   *The Beginnings of American English*, University of Chicago Press.
1948   *Some Sources of Southernisms*, University of Alabama Press.
1951   *A Dictionary of Americanisms on Historical Principles*, University of Chicago Press.

Matsell, George W.
1859   *Vocabularium, or the Rogue's Lexicon*, New York.

Matthews, W.
1935   "Sailors' Pronunciation in the Second Half of the Seventeenth Century", *Anglia.*
1937   "Sailors' Pronunciation, 1770-1783", *Anglia.*

Maurer, David W.
1930-1   "Carnival Cant: A Glossary of Circus and Carnival Slang", *American Speech* 6:327-37.
1976   "Language and the Sex Revolution: World War I through World War II", *American Speech* 51:5-24.

McBeth, Leon.
1983   "Highlights of Baptist Heritage", *Baptist Messenger*, March 24, p. 11.

McCulloch, Walter P.
1958   *Woods Words: A Comprehensive Dictionary of Logging Terms*, The Oregon Historical Society and the Champoeg Press.

McDavid, Raven I., Jr.
1955   "The Position of the Charleston Dialect", *Publications of the American Dialect Society.*
1967   "Historical, Regional, and Social Variation", *Journal of English Linguistics* 1:24-40.
1971   "Addendum" to McDavid and McDavid 1951, in Walter Wolfram and Nona R. Clarke, eds., *Black-White Speech Relationships*, Washington D.C.
1980   "The Folk Vocabulary of Eastern Kentucky", in *Varieties of American English*, Stanford University Press.

McDavid, Raven I., Jr. and Virginia Glenn McDavid.
1951   "The Relationships of the Speech of American Negroes to the Speech of Whites", *American Speech* 26:3-17.

McDavid, Raven I., Jr. and Raymond K. O'Cain.
1973   "Sociolinguistics and Linguistic Geography", *Kansas Journal of Sociology* 9:137-56.

McLaughlin, John C.
1970   *Aspects of the History of English*, New York.

McLeod, Alexander.
1948   *Pigtails and Gold Dust*, Caldwell, Idaho, The Caxton Printers, Ltd.

McReynolds, Edwin C.
1957   *The Seminoles*, Norman, Oklahoma.

Mead, Margaret.
1966   *New Lives for Old: Cultural Transformation – Manus 1928-1953*, New York.

Melville, Herman.
1846   (1892) *Typee*, New York, Russell and Russell.

Mencken, Henry Louis.

1919   *The American Language*, First Edition.
1921   *The American Language*, Second Edition.
1923   *The American Language*, Third Edition.
1936   *The American Language*, Fourth Edition.
1945   *The American Language*, Supplement One.
1948   *The American Language*, Supplement Two.
1963   *The American Language*, ed., abridged and annotated by R.F. McDavid, Jr. and David W. Maurer, New York: Alfred A. Knopf.

Meredith, Mamie.
1919   "Tall Talk in America Sixty Years Ago", *American Speech* 4:(April) 593.
1929   "Longfellow's Excelsior Done Into Pidgin English", *American Speech* IV: 148-51.
1931   "Negro Patois and Its Humor," *American Speech*, 6: 317-321.
1932   "*Squaw* Words in Nebraska", *American Speech* VIII: 420

Miller, Mary Rita.
1967   "Attestations of American Indian Pidgin English in Fiction and Non-Fiction", *American Speech*, pp. 142-47.

Milner, Christian and Richard Milner.
1972   *Black Players, The Secret Life of Black Pimps*, Boston, Little, Brown and Co.

Mitchell, A.G.
1946   *The Pronunciation of English in Australia*, Sydney.

Mitchell, Henry M.
1970   *Black Preaching*, Philadelphia, J.B. Lippincott.

Mitchell-Kernan, C.
1969   *Language Behavior in a Black Urban Community*, Berkeley, California.

Molloy, Robert.
n.d.   *Charleston: A Gracious Heritage.*

Moore, Archie and Leonard H. Pearl
1971   *Any Boy Can: The Archie Moore Story*, Englewood Cliffs, N.J., Prentice-Hall

Morgan, Murray.
1960   *Skid Road: An Informal Portrait of Seattle*, New York, Viking.

Morgan, Raleigh, Jr.
1959   "Structural Sketch of St. Martin Creole", *Anthropological Linguistics* 1:20-24.
1960   "The Lexicon of Saint Martin Creole", *Anthropological Linguistics*, 2:7-29.

Morris, Marshall
1981   *Saying and Meaning in Puerto Rico*, New York, Pergamon Press

Morrison, Samuel Eliot.
1961   *The Maritime History of Massachusetts*, Boston.

Mufwene, Salikoko S.
1983   "Some Observations on the Verb in Black English Vernacular", University of Texas, Austin, African and Afro-American Studies and Research Center Papers: Series 2.

Mühlhäusler, Peter.
1982   In Woolford and Washabaugh, eds., *The Social Context of Creolization*, Ann Arbor: Karoma Press, pp. 28-76.

Murray, Henry Anthony.
1857   *Lands of the Slave and the Free; or, Cuba, The United States, and Canada*, London, G. Routledge and Co.

Muysken, Pieter, ed.
1980   *Generative Studies on Creole Languages*, Dodrecht, Foris Publications.

Narita, Kyoko
1983   "Humorous Aspects of Mistakes by Japanese Speaking English" in Nilsen and Nilsen (eds.), *The Language of Humor*.

Naro, Anthony J.
  1978   "A Study of the Origins of Pidginization," *Language* 54: 314-47
Nash, Rose.
  1973   *Readings in Spanish and English Contrastive Linguistics,* Hato Rey, Puerto Rico.
  1971   "The Emergence of a New Variety of English in Puerto Rico", *American Speech.*
Nathan, Hans.
  1962   *Dan Emmett and the Rise of Early Negro Minstrelsy,* University of Oklahoma Press.
Navarro Tomas, Tomas.
  1948   *El Español en Puerto Rico,* Rio Piedras, Puerto Rico.
  1951   "Observaciones sobre el Papiamentu", *Nueva Revista de la Fiología Española,* VII.
Nee, Victor G. and DeBary Nee.
  1972   *Longtime Californ': A Documentary Study of an American Chinatown,* New York.
Needler, Geoffrey D.
  1967   "Linguistic Evidence from Alexander Hamilton's Intinerarium", *American Speech.*
Neihardt, John Gneisenau.
  1932   *Black Elk Speaks,* Lincoln, University of Nebraska Press.
Nelson, Lawrence Emerson.
  1945   *Our Roving Bible; tracking its influence through English and American Life,* Nashville, Abington-Cokesburg Press.
Newman, Edwin.
  1974   *Strictly Speaking: Will America Be the Death of English?,* Indianapolis, Bobbs-Merrill Co.
  1966   *A Civil Tongue,* Indianapolis, Bobbs-Merrill Co.
Nichols, Patricia.
  1981   "Creoles of the USA", in Ferguson and Heath, eds., *Language in the USA,* pp. 69-91.
  1983   "Black and White Speaking in the Rural South: Difference in the Pronomial System", *American Speech* 58, No. 3 (Fall):201-15.
Nida, Eugene and Harold Fehdereau.
  1971   "Indigenous Pidgins and Koinés", *International Journal of American Linguistics,* 37.
Nilsen, Don L.F. and Aileen Pace Nilsen, eds.
  1983   *The Language of Humor and the Humor of Language,* Proceedings of the 1982 W(estern) H(umor) and I(rony) M(embership) Conference, Tucson, Arizona.
Noreen, Robert S.
  1965   "Ghetto Worship: A Study of the Names of Chicago Storefront Churches", *Names* XIII:19-38.
Norman, Arthur M.Z.
  1955   "Bamboo English, the Japanese Influence Upon American Speech in Japan", *American Speech* 30:44-48.
Norton, A. Banting.
  1862   *History of Knox County, Ohio,* Columbus.
Norton, Thomas.
  1632   *New England Canaan.*
O'Brien, Esse F.
  1961   *The First Bulldogger,* San Antonio, Texas, The Naylor Company.
O'Hara, John.
  1958   *From the Terrace,* New York.
Oliva, Peter F.

1968 "Modern Trends in Foreign Languages", in Roucek, ed., *The Study of Foreign Languages*, New York.

O'Neill, Wayne.
1972 "The Politics of Bidialectism", *College English* XXXIII:433-38.

Orbeck, Anders.
1927 *Early New England Pronunciation*, Ann Arbor, Michigan.

Ornstein, Jacob.
1983 "Dem Kibitzers Maven: Yiddish Language Contact and Affective Borrowing", in Nilsen and Nilsen, eds., *The Language of Humor, The Humor of Language*.

Otheguy, Ricardo.
1973 "Linguistic Arguments in the Determination of Creole Typology. The Case of 'Habla Bozal Antillana'", in Bailey and Shuy, eds., *New Ways of Analyzing Variability in English*, Georgetown University Press.

Ottley, C.R.
1965 *Trinidadianese, How to Old Talk in Trinidad*, Port of Spain, Diego Martin.

Ottley, Roy and William J. Weatherby.
1967 *The Negro in New York, An Informal Social History*, New York.

Owen, W.F.W.
1833 *Voyages to Explore the Shores of Africa, Arabia, and Madagascar*, New York.

Owens, Bess Alice
1931 "Folk Speech of the Cumberlands," *American Speech*, 7: 89-95.

Packard, Vance.
1957 *The Hidden Persuaders*, New York, David McKay.

Paddock, Harold.
1966 "The Study of the Speech of Canberra, Newfoundland", M.A. Thesis, Memorial University of Newfoundland.

Paine, Ralph.
1919 *The Old Merchant Marine, A Chronicle of American Ships and Sailors*, New Haven, Yale University Press. (Chronicles of America Series, Vol. 38)

Pardoe, T. Earl.
1937 *A Historical and Phonetic Study of Negro Dialect*, LSU dissertation, Baton Rouge.

Parkhurst, James W.
1938 "The Role of the Black Mammy in the Plantation Household", *Journal of Negro History*, XXIII.

Parkman, Francis.
1964 *The Oregon Trail*, New York, Airmont Publishing Co.

Parrinder, Geoffrey.
1953 *Religion in an African City*, Oxford University Press.

Partridge, Eric.
1967 *A Dictionary of Slang and Unconventional English*, New York.

Partridge, Eric and John W. Clark.
1951 *British and American English Since 1900*, London.

Pattie, James Ohio.
1830 *Pattie's Personal Narrative of a Voyage to the Pacific and in Mexico, June 20, 1824-August 30, 1830*, Cleveland, Ohio, A.H. Clark Co.

Paullin, Charles and John K. Wright.
1932 *Atlas of the Historical Geography of the United States*, Washington, D.C.

Paulston

Payzant, Henry Young.
1935 *People: A Story of the People of Novia Scotia*, Bridgewater, Novia Scotia.

Pedersen, Lee, Raven I. McDavid, Jr., William Foster, and Charles E. Billard eds.
1972 *A Manual for Dialect Research in the Southern States*, Atlanta.

Perez Moris, Jose and D. Luis Cueto y Gonzalez.
1872   *Historia de la Insurrectión de Lares*, Barcelona.
Perez Sala, Paulino.
1973   *Interferencia Lingüistica del Inglés en el Español Hablado en Puerto Rico*, San Juan.
Perry, Bliss.
1918   *The American Spirit in Education, A Chronicle of Great Interpreters*, Chronicles of America Series, Vol. 34.
Peters, Robert A.
1968   *A Linguistic History of English*, Boston.
Phares, Ross.
1964   *Bible in Pocket, Gun in Hand*, New York, Doubleday.
Pickford, Glenna Ruth.
1956   "American Linguistic Geography: A Sociological Appraisal", *Word* 12:211-29.
Pike, Zebulon.
1966   *The Letters of Zebulon Pike, with Letters and Related Documents*, ed. Donald Jackson, Norman, University of Oklahoma Press, I & II.
Pilch, Herbert.
1982   Review of Dillard, *Perspectives on American English*, *Anglia* Band 100:482-4.
Pipes, William H.
1970   *Say Amen, Brother! Old-Time Negro Preaching*, Westport, Connecticut, Negro Universities Press.
Plooij, D.D.D.
1952   *The Pilgrim Fathers from a Dutch Point of View*, New York.
Pop, Sever.
1950   *La Dialectologie, Aperçu Historique et Methods de Enquetes Linguistiques*, Louvain.
Porter, Kenneth Wiggins.
1970   *The Negro on the American Frontier*, New York, Arno Press.
Powell, Adam Clayton.
1967   *Keep the Faith, Baby*, Jubilee JMG 2062.
Power, Tyrone, Esq.
1836   *Impressions of America During the Years 1833, 1834, and 1835*, London.
Price, Richard.
1973a   "Avenging Spirits and the Structure of Saramaka Lineages", in *Bijdragen tot de Tal-, Land-, en Volkenkunde*.
1973b   *Maroon Societies: Rebel Slave Communities in the United States*, Garden City, New York.
Prince, J. Dyneley.
1910   "Jersey Dutch", *Dialect Notes* III:459-60.
1912   "An Ancient New Jersey Indian Jargon", *American Anthropologist* 14: 508-24.
Pringle, Henry Fowkes.
1931   *Theodore Roosevelt*, Harcourt.
Puckett, Newbell Niles.
9126   *Folk Beliefs of the Southern Negro*, Chapel Hill, N.C.
Putnam, George N. and Edna O'Hern.
1955   "The Status Significance of an Isolated Urban *Dialect*", *Language* 34 (Language Dissertation No. 53).
Pyles, Thomas.
1952   *Words and Ways in American English*, New York.
1964   *The Origins and Development of the English Language*, New York.
Ramsey, Carolyn.
1957   *Cajuns on the Bayous*, New York, Hasting House.
Ramson, W.S.

1966   *Australian English, An Historical Study of the Vocabulary, 1788-1898,* Canberra, The National University Press.

Rawick, George P., ed.

1972   *The American Slave: A Composite Autobiography,* Contributions in Afro-American Studies, 19 Vols.

Ray, Punya Sloka.

1963   *Language Standardization,* The Hague.

Read, Allen Walker.

1933   "British Recognition of American Speech in the Eighteenth Century", *Dialect* Notes 6:313-34.

1938   "Assimilation of the Speech of British Immigrants in Colonial America, *Journal of English and Germanic Philology* 37:70-79.

1941   "English of Indians, 1705-1745", *American Speech* 16:72-74.

Read, Kenneth E.

1965   *The High Valley,* New York.

Read, William A.

1963   *Louisiana French,* Louisiana State University Press.

Reed, Carroll E.

1967   *Dialects of American English,* Cleveland.

Reinecke, John.

1969   *Language and Dialect in Hawaii,* University of Hawaii Press.

Reinhardt, Richard.

1970   *Working on the Railroad; Reminiscences from the Age of Steam,* American West.

Reinstein, S. and J. Hoffman.

1972   "Dialect Interaction Between Black and Puerto Rican Children in New York City: Implications for Language Arts", *Elementary English* 49:190-96.

Reisner, Robert.

1971   *Graffiti: Two Thousand Years of Wall Writing,* Chicago, Henry Regency Co.

Rens, L.L.E.

1953   *The Historical and Social Background of Surinam Negro-English,* Amsterdam.

Richardson, A.D.

1865   *Beyond the Mississippi: From the Great River to the Great Ocean, Life and Adventure in the Prairies, Mountains, and Pacific Coast,* Hartford.

Rickford, John.

1975   "Carrying the New Wave into Syntax – the Case of B.E. BIN", in Bailey and Shuy, eds., *New Ways of Analyzing Variation,* Washington, D.C., Georgetown University Press.

Robertson, Stuart F. and Frederic G. Cassidy.

1954   *The Development of Modern English,* Second Edition, Englewood Cliffs, New Jersey.

Rollins, Philip A.

1936   *The Cowboy: an Unconventional History of Civilization on the Old-Time Cattle Range,* New York, Charles Scribners' Sons.

Ross, A. and A. Moverley.

1964   *The Pitcairnese Language,* London.

Rosten, Leo.

1968   *The Joys of Yiddish,* New York.

Roucek, Joseph S.

1968   *The Study of Foreign Languages,* New York.

Rowe, J.R.

1959   "Archaeological Dating and Cultural Process", *Southwestern Journal of Anthropology* 15:317-24.

Rowse, A.L.

1959   *The Elizabethans and America,* New York and Evanston, Harper and Row.

Roy, John *et al.*

1974   *A Brief History, Description, and Dictionary of the Everyday Language of Virgin Islands Children*, Charlotte Amalie, St. Thomas, mimeo draft.

Rusling, Brigadier General James F.
1875   *Across America; or, the Great West and the Pacific Coast*, New York.

Russ, Charles V.J.
1982   "The Geographical and Social Variation of English in Scotland and Wales", in Bailey and Gorlach, eds., *English as a World Language*, pp. 56-83.

Russell. I. Willis.
1955   "Among the New Words", *American Speech*, 30:283.

Ruxton, George Frederick.
1848   (1951) *Life in the Far West*, ed. Le Roy R. Hafen, Norman, University of Oklahoma Press.

Safire, William.
1983   "Not Knowing from Beans", *New York Times Magazine*, August 7:6-8.

Salmor, Julian.
1966   *La Raza: Forgotten Americans*, South Bend.

Samarin, William.
1980   "Standardization of Creole Language", in Valdman and Highfield 1980:231-36.

Samuels, M.L.
1963   "Some Applications of Middle English Dialectology", *English Studies* 44:81-94.

Sandahl, Bertol.
1951   *Middle English Sea Terms*, Essays and Studies on English Language and Literature, ed. S.B. Liljegren, VIII.

Sawyer, Janet B.
1959   "Aloofness from Spanish Influence in Texas English", *Word* 15:270-8.

Sayer, Edgar Sheappard.
1939   *Pidgin English; A Textbook, History, and Vocabulary of Pidgin English for Writers, Travellers, and Students of the English Language and Philologists*, Toronto, the author.

Scargill, M.H.
1977   *A Short History of Canadian English*, Victoria, B.C.

Schach, Paul.
1954   "Comments on Some Pennsylvania-German Words in *The Dictionary of Americanisms*", *American Speech* 29:45-54.

Schneider, Edgar W.
1983   "The Diachronic Development of the Black English Perfective Auxiliary Phrase", *Journal of English Linguistics* 16:55-64.

Schneider, Gilbert.
1963   *First Steps in Wes-Kos*, Hartford.
1964   *Dey Don Klin; Rida Nomba Fo,* Hartford, mimeo.
1965   *Wes-Kos Proverbs, Idioms, Names*, Hartford, mimeo.
1966   *West African Pidgin English*, Hartford Seminary Foundation dissertation.
1967   "West African Pidgin English: An Historical Overview", Ohio University Papers in International Studies No. 8.

Schuchardt, Hugo.
1909   "Die Lingua Franca", *Zeitschrift für Romanische Philologie* XXXIII:441-61.
1914   *Die Sprache der Saramakkaneger in Surinam*, Amsterdam.

Schumann, John H.
1975   *Second Language Acquistion: The Pidginization Process*, Harvard University dissertation.

Schur, Norman.
1973   *British Self-Taught, with Comments in American*, New York.

Scott, Charles T. and J.L. Erickson.
1968   *Readings for the History of the English Language*, Boston.

Searight, Sarah.
1973   *New Orleans*, Stein and Day.
Sellers, J.T.
1972   "English Not Dialect", New York Times, June 9, p. 37.
Sey, K.A.
1973   *Ghanaian English, An Explanatory Survey*, London, Macmillian.
Şen, Ann Louise Frisinger
1974   "Dialect Variation in Early American English," *Journal of English Linguistics*, 8: 41-47.
Sheard, J.A.
1966   *The Words of English*, New York.
Sheldon, E.S.
1892   "What is a Dialect?" *Dialect Notes* I:293.
Sheldon, George.
1895-6 *A History of Deerfield, Massachusetts*, Deerfield.
Shuy, Roger W.
1962   *The Northern-Midland Dialect Boundary in Illinois*, Publications of the American Dialect Society 38.
1967   *Discovering American Dialects*, National Council of Teachers of English.
Shuy, Roger W., Walter A. Wolfram, and William K. Riley.
1967   *Linguistic Correlates of Social Stratification in Detroit Speech*, U.S. Office of Education, Project No. 6-1347, Final Report.
Silverman, Stuart H.
1971   *The Effects of Peer Group Membership on Puerto Rican English*, Ferkauf Graduate School of Yeshiva University Dissertation.
Silverstein, Michael.
1972   "Chinook Jargon: Language Contact and the Problem of Multi-Level Generative Systems", *Language* 48:378-406, 596-625.
Simon, John Ivan.
1980   *Paradigms Lost: Essays on Literacy and Its Decline*, Potter.
Skinner, Constance.
1920   *Adventures of Oregon: A Chronicle of the Fur Trade*, Yale University Press.
Slater.
1956
Sledd, James.
1980   Review of Dillard, *Perspectives on American English*, *English World-Wide*.
1983   Review of Ferguson and Heath 1981, *American Speech*, Spring 1983:42-46.
Slosson, Edwin F.
1918   *The American Spirit in Education*, Chronicles of America Series, Vol. 33.
Smith, Bradford.
1953   *Captain John Smith, His Life and Legend*, Cornwall, New York, Cornwall Press.
Smith, David and Roger W. Shuy, eds.
1972   *Sociolinguistics in a Cross-Cultural Analysis*, Washington, D.C.
Smith William.
1744   *A New Voyage to Guinea*, London.
Smitherman, Geneva.
1981   *Talkin' and Testifyin': The Language of Black America*, New York, Houghton Mifflin.
Smyth, J.F.D.
1784   *A Tour of the United States of America*, London.
Snader, Howard.
1965   *The English-Pennsylvania Dutch Dictionary*, Reading, Pennsylvania, Culinary Arts Press.
Sommerfelt, Alf.

1954   "The Origin of Language: Theses and Hypotheses", *Journal of World History* 1:885-902.
Sothern, James M.
1970   *Cajun Dictionary: A Collection of Some Commonly Used Words and Phrases by the People of South Louisiana,* Houma, La., Cheri Publications.
Sowell, Thomas.
1981   *Ethnic America, A History,* New York, Basic Books.
Spears, Richard A.
1981   *Slang and Euphemism,* New York, Jonathan David.
Spencer, J.
The English Language in West Africa, London.
Spicer, Edward H.
1962   *Cycles of Conquest; the Impact of Spain, Mexico, and the United States on Indians of the Southwest,* University of Arizona Press.
Springer, Otto.
1943   "The Study of Pennsylvania German Dialect", *Journal of English and Germanic Philology* XLII:1-39.
Stanton, Elizabeth Cady, Susan B., Anthony and Matilda Joslyn Gage
1889   *History of Woman Suffrage,* Rochester, New York.
Stearns, Marshall.
1956   *The Story of Jazz,* New York.
Stearns, Marshall and Jean Stearns.
1968   *Jazz Dance: A History of Dancing to Jazz, from its African Origins to the Present,* New York.
Stefánsson, Vilhjalmur (*Alias* A.).
1909   "The Eskimo Trade Jargon of Herschel Island", *American Anthropologist* 11:217-232.
Steinmetz, Sol.
1981   "Jewish English in the United States", *American Speech* 56, No. 11:3-16.
Stern, Henry R.
1979   "The Changing Language of American Catholicism", *American Speech* 54:83-89.
Stevick, Robert D.
1968   *English and Its History, The Evolution of a Language,* Boston.
Stewart, William A.
1962a   "Creole Languages in the Caribbean", in F.A. Rice, ed., *Study of the Role of Second Languages in Asia, Africa, and Latin America,* Washington, D.C., Center for Applied Linguistics.
1962b   "An Outline of Linguistic Typology for Describing Multilingualism", in F.A. Rice, *Study of the Role of Second Languages in Asia, Africa, and Latin America,* Washington, D.C., Center for Applied Linguistics.
1962c   "The Functional Distribution of French and Creole in Haiti", Georgetown University Monography Series on Languages and Linguistics No. 15.
1964   "Foreign Language Teaching Methods in Quasi-Foreign Language Situations", in Stewart, ed., *Nonstandard Speech and the Teaching of English,* Washington, D.C.
1965   "Urban Negro Speech: Sociolinguistic Factors Affecting English Teaching", in Shuy, ed., *Social Dialects and Language Learning,* NCTE.
1967   "Sociolinguistic Factors in the History of American Negro Dialects", *Florida FL Reporter* 5:1-7.
1968a   "Continuity and Change in American Negro Dialects", *Florida FL Reporter* 6:3-14.
1968b   "A Sociolinguistic Typology for Describing National Multilingualism", in Joshua A. Fishman, ed., *Readings in the Sociology of Language,* The Hague.
1969   "On the Use of Negro Dialect in the Teaching of Reading", in Baratz and Shuy, eds., *Teaching Black Children to Red,* Washington D.C., Center for

Applied Linguistics.
1970 "Sociopolitical Issues in the Linguistic Treatment of the American Negro", in Alatis, ed., Report of the 20th Round Table, Georgetown University.
1972 "Acculturative Processes and the Language of the American Negro", in William Gage, ed., *Language in Its Social Setting.*
Stokes, I.N. Phelps.
1915-28 *The Iconography of Manhattan Island,* 6 Vols., New York.
Stowe, Harriet Beecher.
1863 "Sojourner Truth: The Libyan Sibyl", *Atlantic Monthly,* pp. 473-81.
Strecker, John K.
1926 "Reptiles of the South and Southwest in Folklore", *Publications of the Texas Folk-Lore Society.*
Struble, George C.
1935 "The English of the Pennsylvania Germans", *American Speech* X:163-72.
Stuart, Granville.
1865 *Montana As It Is,* New York.
Sturtevant, Edgar.
1917 *Linguistic Change,* University of Chicago Press.
Sullivan, James Patrick.
1974 *Interference, Integration, and Shift: The Genesis of Anglo-Irish,* Ferkauf Graduate School, Yeshiva University, dissertation.
Sumption, Jonathan.
1975 *Pilgrimage, An Image of Medieval Religion,* London, Faber and Faber.
Szasz, Ferenc M.
1967 "The New York Slave Revolt of 1741: A Re-Examination", *New York History,* XLXIII.
Tate, Charles Montgomery.
1889 *Chinook as Spoken by the Indians of Washington Territory, British Columbia, and Alaska,* Victoria.
Taylor, Allan R.
1981 "Indian Lingua Francas", in Ferguson and Heath, eds., *Language in the USA.*
Taylor, Douglas McRae.
1956 "Language Contacts in the West Indies", *Word* 12:399-414.
1957 Review of Whinnom, *Spanish Contact Vernaculars in the Philippine Islands, Word* 13:489-99.
1960 "Language Shift or Changing Relationship?" *International Journal of American Linguistics* 26:155-61.
1961 "New Languages for Old in the West Indies", *Comparative Studies in Society and History* 3:155-61.
1963a "The Origin of West Indian Creole Languages: Evidence from Grammatical Categories", *American Anthropologist* 65:800-14.
1963b Review of LePage and DeCamp, *Jamaican Creole, Language* 39:316-22.
The Religious Intelligencer.
1821 New Haven, Connecticut.
Thomas, Charles K.
1927 "Recent Discussion of Standardization in American Pronunciation", *Quarterly Journal of Speech* XII:442-57.
Thomason, Sarah Grey.
1983 "Chinook jargon in a real and historical context", *Language* 59, 4:820-870.
Thompson, Henry F.
1907 "Maryland at the End of the Seventeenth Century", *Maryland Historical Magazine* II.
Thompson, Robert.
n.d. "An Aesthetic of the Cool", Xerox.
Thompson, Robert W.
1961 "A Note on Some Affinities Between the Creole Dialects of the Old World and the New", in LePage, ed., *Creole Studies II.*

Thornborough, Emma Lou.
1957   *The Negro in Indiana*, Indiana Historical Bureau.
Thorpe, Thomas Bangs.
1854   *The Hive of the "Beehunter"*, New York.
Throm, Edward L., ed.
1952   *Popular Mechanics Picture History of American Transportation*, New York, Simon and Schuster.
Thurber, James and E.B. White.
1929   *Is Sex Necessary?* New York and London, Harper and Brothers.
Thurman, Sue Bailey.
1952   *Pioneers of Negro Origin in California*, San Francisco.
Tinker, Edward Larocque.
1932   "Louisiana Gumbo", *The Yale Review*, New Series XXI:566-79.
1936   *Gombo: The Creole Dialect of Louisiana. Together with a Bibliography*, Worcester, Massachusetts.
1957   "Creole Comes to Philadelphia", *American Antiquarian Society Proceedings* 67:50-76.
Tocqueville, Alexis de.
1835   *Democracy in America*.
Todd, Loretto.
1974   *Pidgins and Creoles*, London and Boston, Routledge and Kegan Paul.
Torrans, Anne and Barbara R. Zimmerman.
1981   "Implications from a Study of the Vernacular of North Louisiana Black Children", ms. World Congress on Black Communication, Nairobi, Kenya.
Traugott, Elizabeth Closs.
1972a   "Principles in the History of American English, a Reply", *Florida FL Reporter X, 5-6, 56*.
1972b   *A History of English Syntax*, New York.
1973   "Pidginization, Creolization, and the 'Naturalness' Hypothesis", Papers of the IXth International Congress of the Anthropological and Ethnological Sciences.
Trelease, Allen W.
1960   *Indian Affairs in Colonial New York*, Cornell University Press.
Trittschuh, Travis.
1956   "Words and Phrases in American Politics: 'Boom'", *American Speech* 31:172-79.
Trollope, Mrs. Frances.
1832   (1949) *Domestic Manners of the Americans*, ed. Donald Smalley, New York, Vintage Books.
Truman, Harry S.
1955   *Memoirs*, Garden City, New York, Doubleday.
Tsuzaki, Stanley M.
1971   "Problems in the Study of Hawaiian English", in Hymes, ed., *Pidginization and Creolization of Language*.
Tucker, G. Richard and Wallace A. Lambert.
1969   "White and Negro Listeners' Reactions to Various American-English Dialects", *Social Forces* 47:463-68.
Tucker, Gilbert M.
1921   *American English*, New York.
Turner, Frederick Jackson.
1906   *Rise of the New West in the American Nation: A History*, New York.
Turner, G.W.
1966   *The English Language in Australia and New Zealand*, London.
Turner, Lorenzo Dow.
1949   *Africanisms in the Gullah Dialect*, University of Chicago Press.
Umiker-Sebeok, D. Jean and Thomas A. Sebeok, eds.
1978   *Aboriginal Sign Languages of the Americas and Australia*, Vol. I & II, New

York and London, Plenum Press.

Underwood, Gary N.
1968 "Vocabulary Change in the Upper Midwest", *Publications of the American Dialect Society* 49:8-28.
1974 "American English Dialectology: Alternatives for the Southwest", *International Journal of the Sociology of Language VI.*

Valdman, Albert and Arnold Highfield, eds.
1980 *Theoretical Orientations in Creole Studies,* New York, Academic Press.

Valkhoff, Marius.
1931 *Les Mots Francais d'Origine Neerlandaise,* Librairie E.D.
1960 "Contributions to the Study of Creole", *African Studies* 19:77-87.
1966 *Studies in Portuguese and Creole,* Witwatersrand University Press.

Vanderbilt, Gertrude Lott.
1881 *The Social History of Flatbush, and Manners and Customs of the Dutch Settlers in Kings County,* New York.

Van Loon, L.G.
1938 *Crumbs from an Old Dutch Closet,* The Hague.

Van Wijk, H.A.
1958 "Origenes y Evolución del Papiamentu", *Neophilologus,* XLII.

Vass, Winifred Kellersberger.
1979 *The Bantu Speaking Heritage of the United States,* Afro-American Culture and Society, AAS Monograph Series, Vol. II.

Veltman, Peter.
1940 "Dutch Survivals in Holland, Michigan", *American Speech* 15:80-83.

Vendrys, J.
1923 *Le Language,* Paris.

Viereck, Wolfgang.
1973 "The Growth of Dialectology", *Journal of English Linguistics* 7:69-86.

Visser, F. Th.
1963-73 *An Historical Syntax of the English Language,* Leiden, Brill.

Vogel, Virgil L.
1970 *American Indian Medicine,* University of Oklahoma Press.

Voorhoeve, Jan.
1973 "Historical and Linguistic Evidence in Favour of the Relexification Theory in the Formation of Creoles", *Language in Society* II:133-46.
1980 "Multifunctionality as a Derivational Problem", in Pieter Muysken, ed., *Generative Studies on Creole Languages,* Dodrecht, Faris Publications.

Voorhoeve, Jan and Ursy M. Lichtveld.
1975 *Creole Drum, An Anthology of Creole Literature in Surinam,* New Haven and London, Yale University Press.

Wade, Richard C.
1959 *The Urban Frontier,* University of Chicago Press.

Wagner, Max Leopold.
1949 *Lingue e Dialette del'America Spagnole,* Florence.

"War Bow — Poet, Philosopher and Farmer".
1930 *Chronicles of Oklahoma* XIV:224.

Warburton, Austen D.
1966 *Indian Lore of the North California Coast,* Santa Clara, California: Pacifc Pueblo Press.

Ward, Christopher.
1952 *The War of the Revolution,* New York, Macmillan.

Warner, Anthony.
1982 *Complementation in Middle English and the Methodology of Historical Syntax,* Pennsylvania State University Press.

Warner, Maureen.
1971 "Trinidad Yoruba — Notes on Survivals", *Caribbean Quarterly* 17:40-49.

Warner, W. Lloyd, Marchia Meeker, and Kenneth Ealls.
1960   *Social Class in America*, New York.
Waterman, John D.
1970   *Perspectives in Linguistics*, University of Chicago Press.
Watts, Peter C.
1977   *A Dictionary of the Old West*, New York, Knopf.
Weinreich, Uriel.
1953   *Languages in Contact: Findings and Problems*, New York.
1954   "Is a Structural Dialectology Possible?", *Word* 10:388-400.
1962   "Multilingual Dialectology and the New Yiddish Atlas", *Anthropological Linguistics* 4:6-22.
Weinreich, Uriel, W. Labov, and M. Herzog.
1968   "Empirical Foundations for a Theory of Language Change", in W.P. Lehmann and Y. Malkiel, eds., *Directions for Historical Linguistics*, University of Texas Press.
Weinstein, Edwin A.
1962   *Cultural Aspects of Delusion*, New York, The Free Press of Glenwe.
Weller, Jack En.
1965   *Yesterday's People: Life in Contemporary Appalachia*, University of Kentucky Press.
Welmers, William and Warren d' Azevedo.
1970   *Some Terms from Liberian Speech*, Second Edition. Monrovia, U.S. Peace Corps in Liberia.
Wentworth, Harold.
1942   "The neo-pseudo-suffix'-eroo'", *American Speech* XVII:10-15.
1946   *American Dialect Dictionary*, New York, Thomas Y. Crowell.
Wentworth, Harold and Stuart B. Flexner.
1960   *Dictionary of American Slang*, New York, Crowell.
Weseen, Maurice Harley.
1934   *A Dictionary of American Slang*, New York, Thomas Y. Crowell.
Western Electric.
n.d.   *The Dialect of the Black Americans*, 33-1/3 rpm LP.
Whinnom, Keith.
1956   *Spanish Contact Vernaculars in the Philippine Islands*, Hong Kong University Press.
1965   "The Origin of the European-Based Pidgins and Creoles", *Orbis* 14:590-627.
1971   "Linguistic Hybridization and the 'Special Case' of Pidgins and Creoles", in Hymes, ed., *Pidginization and Creolization of Languages*, Cambridge University Press.
Whitney, Annie Weston.
1901   "Negro American Dialects", *Independent* 53:1979-81, 2039-2042 (22 and 29 August 1901).
Whitten, Norman E.
1962   "Contemporary Patterns of Malign Occultism Among Negroes in North Carolina", *Journal of American Folklore* 75:311-25.
Whitten, Norman E. and John Szwed, eds.
1970   *Afro-American Anthropology: Contemporary Perspectives*, New York.
Williams, Ethel T. and Brown, Cliffin F.
1977   *The Harvard University Bibliography of African and Afro-American Religious Studies*, Wilmington, Del.
Williams, Frederick, ed.
1970   *Language and Poverty, Perspectives on a Theme*, Chicago.
Williams, Gomer.
1897   *The Liverpool Privateers and the Liverpool Slave Trade*, London.
Williamson, Juanita V.
1961   *A Phonological and Morphological Study of the Speech of the Negro of Memphis, Tennessee*, Publications of the American Dialect Society 50.

1968   *The Speech of Negro High School Students in Memphis, Tennessee,* U.S. Office of Education OEC-6-10-207 Final Report.
Williamson, Juanita and Virginia Burke, eds.
1971   *A Various Language, Perspectives on American Dialects,* New York.
Willson, Minnie Moore.
1910   *The Seminoles of Florida,* Kissimee, Florida.
Winks, Robin.
1971   *The Blacks in Canada,* Montreal.
Winslow, Ola Elizabeth.
1968   *John Eliot, "Apostle to the Indians",* Boston, Houghton Mifflin Co.
Wise, Claude M.
1933   "Negro Dialect", *Quarterly Journal of Speech* 19:522-28.
1935   "Specimen of Louisiana French-English: or Cajun Dialect in Phonetic Transcription", *American Speech* 8:63-64.
1957   *Applied Phonetics,* Englewood Cliffs, New Jersey.
Wissler, Clark.
1922   *The American Indian,* Oxford University Press.
Wister, Owen.
1958   *Owen Wister Out West: His Journals and Letters,* ed. Fanny Kemble Wister, University of Chicago Press.
Witherspoon, John.
1781   "The Druid", Numbers V, VI, and VII, *Pennsylvania Journal and the Weekly Advertiser.*
Wolck, Wolfgang.
1972   "A Sociolinguistic Survey of Bilingualism in Buffalo", Preliminary Draft of a Report Delivered at the Third International Congress of Applied Linguistics in Copenhagen.
Wolfram, Walter.
1973   Review of Dillard, *Black English, Language XLIX,* 670-679.
1974   "The Relationship of White Southern Speech to Vernacular Black English", *Language* 50:498-527.
1977a   "Language Assessment in Appalachia: A Sociolinguistic Perspective," *Appalachian Journal* 5: 224-34.
1977b   "On the Linguistic Study of Appalachian Speech." *Appalachian Journal* 5:92-102.
1982   "Language Knowledge and Other Dialects", *American Speech* 57:3-18.
Wolfram, Walter and Donna Christian
1976   *Appalachian Speech,* Arlington, Va., California..
Wolfram, Walter and Nona H. Clarke, eds.
1971   *Black-White Speech Relationships,* Washington, D.C.
Wolfram, Walter and Ralph Fasold
1974   *The Study of Social Dialects in American English,* Englewood Cliffs, New Jersey, Prentice Hall.
Wolfram, Walter, Marie Shiels, and Ralph Fasold.
1971   *Overlapping Influence in the English of Second Generation Puerto Rican Tennagers in Harlem,* Final Report, U.S. Office of Education Grant No. 3-70-033(508).
Wood, Peter H.
1974   *Black Majority: Negroes in Colonial Carolina Through the Stono Rebellion,* New York.
Wood, Ralph, ed.
1942   *The Pennsylvania Germans.*
Wood, Richard.
1972a   "New Light on the Origins of Papiamentu: An Eighteenth Century Letter", *Neophilologus,* LVI.
1972b   "The Hispanization of a Creole Language", *Hispania,* 55.

Woodson, Carter G.
1928   *The Negro in Our History*, 5th Edition, Washington, D.C.
Woodward, Thomas Simpson.
1859   *Reminiscences of the Muscogee Indians*, Montgomery, Alabama.
Woolford, Ellen and William Washabaugh, eds.
1983   *The Social Context of Creolization*, Ann Arbor, Michigan, Karoma Publishers.
Work, John Wesley.
1940   *American Negro Folk Songs*, New York.
Wright, Joseph.
1898-1905   *English Dialect Dictionary*, Oxford University Press.
1905   *English Dialect Grammar*, Oxford University Press.
Wright, Richard R.
1969   "Negro Companions of the Spanish Explorers", in August Meier and Elliott M. Rudwick, eds., *The Making of Black America*.
Wright, Thomas
1857   *Dictionary of Obsolete and Provincial English*, London.
Wright, William (Pseudonym Dan DeQuille).
1879   *History of the Big Bonanza*, Hartford.
Wullschlagel, H.R.
1856   *Deutsch-Negerenglische Wörterbuch, Nebst einem Anhang, Negerenglisch Sprüchworter enthaltend*, Lobau, T.U. Duroldt.
Wyld, Henry C.
1920   *A History of Modern Colloquial English*, Oxford.
1927   *A Short History of English*, Third Edition, New York.
Yule, Henry and A.C. Burnell.
1903   *Hobson-Jobson, A Glossary of Colloquial Anglo-Indian Words and Phrases, and of Kindred Terms, Etymological, Historical, Geographical, and Discursive*, London.
Zentella, Ana Celia.
1981   "Language Variety Among Puerto Ricans", in Ferguson and Heath, eds., *Language in the USA*.
Zettersten, Arne.
1969   *The English of Tristan da Cunha*, Lund.

Index

Contributions to the Sociology of Language

J. L. Dillard (ed.)
Perspectives on American English
1980. 14.8 x 22.8 cm. XIII, 468 pages.
Cloth. Approx. $ 36.75; DM 110,- (CSL 29)
ISBN 90 279 3367 7

Nessa Wolfson and Joan Manes (ed.)
Language of Inequality
1985. 14.8 x 22.8 cm. XV. 411 pages.
Hardback. Approx. $ 40.00; approx. DM 120,- (CSL 36)
ISBN 0-89925-052-1
ISBN 3 11 009946 2

Isabelle T. Kreindler (ed.)
Soviet National Languages
Sociolinguistic Perspectives on Their Past,
Present and Future

1985. 14.8 x 22.8 cm. Approx. 392 pages.
Hardback. Approx. $ 41.30; approx. DM 124,- (CSL 40)
ISBN 0-89925-055-6
ISBN 3 11 010211 0

Prices are subject to change without notice

mouton
Mouton Publishers · Berlin · New York · Amsterdam

Contributions to the Sociology of Language

Joshua A. Fishman
The Rise and Fall of the Ethnic Revival

1985. 14.8 x 22.8 cm. XVI, 531 pages.
Hardback. Approx. $ 53.30; approx. DM 160,– (CSL 37)
ISBN 0-89925-048-3
ISBN 3 11 010604 3

Lucia Elias-Olivarez, Elizabeth A. Leone
René Cisneros, and John Gutiérrez (ed.)
Spanish Language Use and Public Life in the USA

1985. 14.8 x 22.8 cm. VIII, 238 pages.
Hardback. Approx. $ 32.70; DM 98,– (CSL 35)
ISBN 0-89925-054-8
ISBN 3 11 009628 5

Raja Ram Mehrotra
Sociolinguistics in Hindi Contexts

1985. 14.8 x 22.8 cm. Approx. 172 pages.
Hardback. Approx. $ 21.70; DM 65,– (CSL 38)
ISBN 0-89925-056-4
ISBN 3 11 009942 X

Prices are subject to change without notice

mouton
Mouton Publishers · Berlin · New York · Amsterdam

International Journal of the Sociology of Language

General Editor: *Joshua A. Fishman*

IJSL is dedicated to the development of the sociology of language in its broadest sense, as a truly international and interdisciplinary field in which various approaches, theoretical and empirical, supplement and complement each other, contributing thereby to the growth of language related knowledge, applications, values and sensitivities. To better achieve its purpose most issues of IJSL will be devoted to specific topics (although occasional issues of separate and unrelated papers may also be published).

In 1985 IJSL will publish six issues (nos. 51–56) devoted to the following themes:

Issue Editor	
Hywel Coleman	Language and Work II: The Health Professions
Thomas F. Magner	Yugoslavia in Sociolinguistic Perspective
Adalberto Aguirre	Language in the Chicano Speech Community
Andrée Tabouret-Keller	Sociolinguistics in France: Current Research in Urban Settings
Raja Ram Mehrotra	Sociolinguistic Surveys in South Asia
Robert L. Cooper	'Singles' Issue

A selection of back issues available from the Publishers:

Issue Editor	
Betty Lou Dubois	American Minority Woman in Sociolinguistic Perspective (no. 17, 1978)
Haver C. Currie	Sociolinguistic Theory (no. 31, 1981)
I. Kreindler	The Changing Status of Russian in the USSR (no. 33, 1982)
Joshua A. Fishman	The Decade Past, the Decade to Come (Special) 10th Anniversary Issue (no. 45, 1984)
Hywel Coleman	Language and Work I: Law, Industry, Education (no. 49, 1984)

Subscription information 1985

Institutions	DM 205,–; approx. US $ 82,–
Individuals	DM 77,–; approx. US $ 30.95

DM prices are definitive; equivalents in other currencies are subject to exchange rates.

Orders may be placed through your local bookseller or directly with Mouton Publishers, Division of Walter de Gruyter, at the following addresses:

For USA and Canada
Mouton Publishers
Division of
Walter de Gruyter, Inc.
200 Saw Mill River Road
Hawthorne, NY 10532

For all other countries
Mouton Publishers
Division of
Walter de Gruyter & Co.
Postfach 110240
D-1000 Berlin 11, FRG

mouton

Mouton Publishers · Berlin · New York · Amsterdam

PE 2809 .D544 1985

Dillard, J. L. 1924-

Toward a social histo
of American English   ry